《瑷珲海关历史档案辑要》编委会

主　编：石巍巍

副主编：魏　巍

编　辑：杜　晔　张　念　张丽娜　陈　顿

瑷珲海关
历史档案辑要

组织机构
（第一卷）

黑龙江省档案馆　编译

社会科学文献出版社
SOCIAL SCIENCES ACADEMIC PRESS (CHINA)

图书在版编目（CIP）数据

瑷珲海关历史档案辑要：全七卷／黑龙江省档案馆
编译. --北京：社会科学文献出版社，2022.6（2023.8重印）
　　ISBN 978-7-5201-7139-7

　　Ⅰ.①瑷… Ⅱ.①黑… Ⅲ.①海关-史料-黑河-
1908-1933　Ⅳ.①F752.59

　　中国版本图书馆 CIP 数据核字（2020）第 264049 号

瑷珲海关历史档案辑要（全七卷）

编　　译／黑龙江省档案馆

出 版 人／冀祥德
责任编辑／李建廷
责任印制／王京美

出　　版／社会科学文献出版社
　　　　　地址：北京市北三环中路甲 29 号院华龙大厦　邮编：100029
　　　　　网址：www.ssap.com.cn
发　　行／社会科学文献出版社（010）59367028
印　　装／上海世纪嘉晋数字信息技术有限公司

规　　格／开 本：889mm×1194mm　1/16
　　　　　印 张：192.75　字 数：1568 千字　幅 数：1860 幅
版　　次／2022 年 6 月第 1 版　2023 年 8 月第 3 次印刷
书　　号／ISBN 978-7-5201-7139-7
定　　价／3680.00 元（全七卷）

读者服务电话：4008918866

前　言

　　自1854年至1950年，中国近代海关经历了96年的外籍税务司制度，建立了包罗万象、庞杂无比的行政机构，它有着极其严格的人事制度和财物制度，所辖业务也非常广泛，除了监管进出口货物，征税、查缉走私等海关基本职能外，海关还兼办沿海及内河航务、港务、邮政、外交事务等。外籍税务司制度下的中国近代海关涉足中国内外事务之广之深，对中国政局及社会影响之大，为世人震惊。

　　中国近代海关系统在其历史发展过程中产生了大量的档案及资料，也称"旧海关档案"。它是了解近代中国，特别是中国沿海、沿边区域变化的重要文献，通过对文献的梳理也可以看到区域政治、经济与社会变迁的历史脉络。黑龙江省档案馆现存二十世纪上半叶的哈尔滨海关、瑷珲海关、绥芬河海关档案数百卷。本套书甄选了瑷珲海关自1909年至1932年具有重要历史价值与现实意义的档案500余件，按其内容编译为组织机构卷、章程协议卷、监管征税卷、海务港务卷及地方见闻卷。书中所节选的档案均为档案原件的影印件，受开本和篇幅限制，档案幅面有不同程度的调整。汉译在形式、程式以及文字上尽量靠近历史。本套书为黑龙江省档案馆首套海关档案编译出版物，其中汇集的大量珍贵海关档案也为首次对外公开。

　　瑷珲海关地处黑龙江中游右岸，与俄远东城市布拉戈维申斯克市隔江相望，曾是东北地区边境水路对外贸易的重要海关之一，是中俄边境贸易的重要节点。1908年（光绪三十四年），随着满洲里、绥芬河两个陆路边境关的设立，加之中俄边境贸易的恢复发展，水路设关问题被提上日程。同时，由于日本在大连设关征税，而北满水路尚未设关，中俄进出口货物仍实行免税自由贸易，日本以南北贸易不平衡为由，向清政府提出在北满江上设关的要求。1909年8月18日，经清政府批准设立瑷珲关，由哈尔滨海关管辖。1921年9月瑷珲关从哈尔滨关下属分关改设为独立关。为了征收出入边境百华里之外的货税，在距大黑河屯（海关驻地）百华里的梁家屯设立分卡，因取消百华里内免税专条，于1924年正式撤销梁家屯分卡。后为防止客商偷运过界，又分别设立了卧牛河分卡、小黑河分卡。1933年1月，随着日军入侵黑河，日伪强行接收了位于大黑河屯的瑷珲海关。至此，瑷珲海关业务随之终止。

瑷珲海关的主要职能集中在监管进出口贸易、征收关税、查缉走私及编制进出口统计。这些贸易统计资料记载了中俄边境贸易的兴衰。据档案记载，1913 至 1922 年间，中俄进出口贸易出现了兴盛局面。进出口贸易货价总值十年间平均每年在 550 万两关平银以上，其中出口远远超过进口，对俄出口，包括本地自产商品与外地转运出口商品。1923 年至 1931 年，中俄边境贸易因俄实行增加税率、封锁边界、限制贸易的政策以及卢布价跌、自然灾害、中东路事件等受到很大影响，进入贸易衰落期。随着开埠通商，俄、日等国大肆运输原料，倾销商品，进行掠夺式贸易。然而随着世界市场的建立，现代化的交通工具、生产工具和生产技术，都输入进来，也促进了黑龙江沿岸农业、工业、商业、交通运输、城市建设等方面的发展。特别是进入民国时期以后，由于边境贸易的开展，俄岸对我岸农副产品的大量需求，促进了农业商品生产的形成和发展，耕种面积不断扩大，农作物产量大幅提高，农业生产技术有了一定的进步。在瑷珲口岸附近，俄岸一些先进的农业生产工具被引入我岸，从瑷珲出口到俄岸的农副产品也有 20 种之多。1922 年我岸出口俄岸小麦 2079 石，占瑷珲县年产小麦的 15%，到 1931 年，瑷珲县内有打场机、割地机、播种机、拖拉机等，这些农业机械都是由布拉格维申斯克的孔士洋行、秋林公司、俄满洋行购进。这些商号在黑河设有分号，经营农业机械的出口和农机零件的销售。中俄边境贸易也带动了民族工商业的发展。黑龙江各地不仅兴起了粱米加工、酿酒、木材加工、电力、采金等工业，还兴起了煤炭、制革、食品、印刷等行业。至 1923 年，黑龙江沿岸地区经济飞速发展，定居人口大幅增加，耕地面积亦在逐年增长，富农家几乎家家有耕犁、除草机、收割机。大黑河附近 70 到 100 俄里范围内已发现数个金矿，聚集矿工 6000 余名，有超过 30 家金矿公司进行勘探并开采黄金，一度成为本地区重要产业。数家磨坊生意红火，酿酒厂大量收购农产品，大黑河、瑷珲、呼玛河、漠河等地区均设有邮政局和电报局，对沿岸贸易有极大助益。

瑷珲海关承办的另一主要业务为黑龙江航务、港口事务。黑龙江及其支流可供航行之水道共计一万余俄里，俄国政府自大革命爆发伊始，又值货币危机，用于航路标志维护工作的资金不足以维持运转，遂萌生出与中国共同管理黑龙江边界河道的想法。1922 年中俄双方首次就共同维护黑龙江边界河道航路标志一事成立中俄航路标志联合委员会，并签署了《临时地方工程协议》，决议通过黑龙江边界河道航路标志的维护费用从双方所征江捐中支出。中俄航路标志联合委员会成立后，开展了引水、灯塔、航标等各项海事业务，建立水位观测站、在水位低的浅滩设立水深信号站、在狭窄水路设立通行信号站，沿浅滩设置灯桩、灯塔，清理河道礁石、修缮码头、维修冬季停泊处，编制河段航图并制订了航务条例等。每年自航运季开始中方及俄方委员会各派代表,巡查黑龙江上下游,检查航路标志维护情况,沿途有测量师进行检测,检查航道标桩是否准确,并确定各项支出预算,并在随后数年开展航标维修工作。据档案记载,1924 年整个边界河道(计 1703 俄里)共有 1285 座江式信标和 171 座海式信标。1927 年中俄双方共支出 33 万金卢布用于黑龙江、额尔古纳河、乌苏里江的航路标志工程以及黑龙江上游疏浚、额尔古纳河石块清理。随着中俄边境贸易的开展,黑龙江流域的航运业也应运而生。1922 年大黑河口岸共有民船 60 余只,载重从 400 普特到 5000 普特不等,为当地居民提供各种物资。1925 年,戊通航运公司改组为东北航务局,并拥有数艘大型轮船,在黑龙江、乌苏里江、及松花江沿岸提供运输服务。

瑷珲海关档案中也包含了一些社会情报及外交活动的史料。中国近代海关是受帝国主义操纵的外籍税务司控制下的一个畸形机构,一方面要始终维护帝国主义的利益,另一方面又要维护中国统治阶级的利益。海关通过半官方性信函等搜集当地的政治、军事、经济情况以及重大事件等一切社会情况,只要中国社会发生某一重大事件,各地税务司即加紧活动,及时不断地向总税务司密报情况。在任命税务司的时候,总税务司都会有这样的要求:"您需要每两周'半官方性'地向我致函,补充说明您呈文中的未尽事宜,随时告知我您所辖港口或其邻近之所发生的趣闻或要事,这些内容需要我了解但不宜列入官方通信之中。"从瑷珲海关历任税务司写给海关总税务司的半官函中可以看到海关视角下的历史事件及社会要闻等,不仅让读者全方位了解黑龙江近代政治、经济、社会情况以及对外关系,也有助于深入了解中国近代海关运作规则。

编译出版此套书,重现中俄边境在贸易监管、征收赋税、查禁走私、航路港口建设、外交往来及文化传播等方面的历史,全面梳理中俄边境海关及边境贸易发展进程,为学术研究提供档案支撑,为服务"一带一路"建设发挥档案的资政参考作用。

目 录

第一部分 机构及分卡

第二部分　人事管理

第一部分

机构及分卡

专题一

设立瑷珲分关

1. 为于瑷珲、齐齐哈尔及松花江和黑龙江交汇处设立海关税卡事

Copy

No.110
Harbin.
No. 23,020

保存

Inspectorate General of Customs,

Peking, 15th April, 1908.

Sir,

1. Enclosed I send you a despatch from the Shui-wu Chu in which is embodied one from the Wai-wu Pu: detailing a despatch which it has received from the Japanese Minister Baron Hayashi complaining that Japanese trade in Southern Manchuria is not on an equal footing regarding levy of taxation as Russian trade in Northern Manchuria so long as there are no taxing stations at certain frontier points. Aigun, Tsitsihar and the junction of the Sungari and Amoor Rivers, the name of any town, if there is one at that place, not being specified:

2. The despatch winds up by directing me to instruct the Harbin Commissioner to

Monsieur N. A. Konovaloff,
Commissioner of Customs,
Harbin.

speedily devise plans for establishing collecting stations at the Trade marts of Aigun and Tsitsihar and to fix an early date when they will commence work. Inquiry is also to be made as to whether it is necessary in the interests of the revenue and to prevent leakage to establish a Custom House on the Sungari river, probably at or near its junction with the Amoor.

3. The tenour of the despatch makes it clear that a distinction is made between the status of the two first named and the last places, the former being assumed to be places at which international trade is permitted and the latter a place where smuggling is done, possibly because trade is not specially permitted there.

4. You are to go into this whole question and suggest what should be done. I need scarcely say that I foresee that this despatch will add several new and difficult questions to those which already confront us in your district.

1) We have the question of the 50 verst free zone laid down in the Regulations for trade by land. Is this to be taken as meaning that the whole Northern frontier formed by the Amoor River a Water

Water frontier and Trade route is, for Customs purposes, 50 verst inland from the River on both sides. In that case how can the Custom House at Aigun on the River work? What duties will it levy and so on? What duties would be leviable at Tsitsihar? Does any foreign trade pass through and become properly taxable there? If not, how does its position give any special advantage to it which places away from the railway and frontier in Southern Manchuria have not got?

2) Sungari - Amoor Junction is not a specified place of Trade but is it a place, seeing that presumably up till now some Manchurian - Siberian trade has been done there, which can be looked upon as a place at which, not being a Treaty port or mart, trade can be prohibited? The same question practically applies to the whole long Northern frontier which we cannot possibly guard. Is there any taxing station of any sort there now? Does it appertain to the Kirin or Heilungkiang province, for it seems

seems the Sungari river is a dividing line between the two?

5. Let me know promptly what men you will require for this work, which of course implies that you will begin by asking as few as possible. How many Chinese? How many foreigners? How many must know some Russian?

As Mr. Grone is not much occupied at Kirin it may be possible that he should accept some part of this burden. I expect him here in a few days and will discuss the matter with him.

I want you to write me something, accompanied by a Chinese version, which I can send to the Chu promptly on the subject of these places. Of course full arrangements cannot be made for some time nor can they be fairly expected but a beginning will have to be made mien wei jih jen chieh kou as the despatch says.

I am,
Sir,
Your obedient Servant
(Signed) R. E. Bredon
Deputy Inspector General.
Officiating as Inspector General

True copy:
2nd Assistant, A.

Copy
No. 142   Commr.   Inspectorate General of Customs,
Harbin   No. 24,101   Peking, 23rd July, 1908.

Sir,

1.   Having reference to and in continuance of previous correspondence:
            regarding the establishment of Customs Stations in North Manchuria:
I have now to send you, herein enclosed, copy of a despatch received yesterday evening from the Shui-wu Chu in answer to one of mine on the subject of which a copy was sent you semi-officially a few days ago.

2.   You will observe the following points in the despatch — I have to-day sent you the substance of them by telegram.

    1°   A Customs Station is to be established at an early date at Aigun which is to be looked upon as a substation of the Harbin Custom and to be under the control of the Customs at that post.

    2°   The manner in which the trade of the Sungari river is to be controlled, and the points at which stations collecting and/or inspecting are to be placed, are to be considered by the territorial authorities, presumably in consultation with the Customs Commissioners.

    3°   Harbin is to be made a duty collecting Station — the Board seems to think it

N. Konovaloff Esquire,
Commissioner of Customs,
Harbin.

it should have been such before. (In the matter of rail carried goods it has hardly been absolutely necessary seeing that its substations Manchouli and Suifenho did its work.) We may assume from the despatch that it is to collect duty on goods carried on the Sungari river whether

    (a)   between Harbin and Sansing.
    (b)   Harbin, Sansing and Russia — viâ Lahasusu; or
    (c)   Harbin and other native places. In the first two instances trade may be assumed to be conducted according to the International tariff as an interport or intercoast trade: the last case would imply a procedure something analogous to Native Customs and Inland Water trade.

3.   The first point to consider is — What are we called upon to do?; and it is upon you on the spot, and in touch with those interested, on whose shoulders the doing of the preliminary work must be placed.

4.   Arrangements have to be made for the placing of an examining and collecting staff at Aigun and the providing them with whatever they may require in the way of supplies, etc.: this work must be begun at once so that everything may be ready to commence on a fixed date — say 1st October, or earlier

/.

if possible. You will have to find out what the local people are doing to meet the Board's instructions that Offices and Quarters are to be provided by them. You will have to arrange how and what duties are to be collected, and who is to receive and hold the funds. It will probably be necessary to provide for adequate military or police protection. A proper courier service to keep up communication via Tsitsihar will be wanted. These are preliminary points which occur to me: more will occur locally.

What staff will be required to begin with? and in asking for it you must think of our difficulties in supplying it — of which you have some knowledge. Mr. Lawson-Grove, now temporarily in charge at Anlung, should be available if required some time towards the end of August. Mr. Von Seckendorff, who speaks Russian, could be sent on short notice, and Messrs Bernadsky and Gregorieff are available for such work as so inexperienced men can be put to. Chinese clerks will have to be found, and there are some Russian speaking Chinese from the Canton School. A senior man will have to go to start the place, and a foreigner may have to be in charge for some time, but in the end I think we must

try to work with a Chinese Assistant-in-charge appointed from our Clerks list. You may have to transfer Mr. Malichenko. Waiters, Shupans, Weighers and servants presumably can be found locally through the local officials.

6. Regarding the preparations to be made for the Sungari Trade, I feel I can say little until I know more. You will have to work with the Taotai and others and see what is wanted and what is suitable and workable.

7. As to duty collecting at Harbin, I have been led to believe that an arrangement for that purpose would be rather welcomed than objected to; but in this matter also I must expect initiation from your end. We must aim at fixing a date as soon — and notifying it as far in advance — as possible. So much is sufficient for the time being. Such further instructions as may be necessary in this connection will follow.

I am,
Sir,
Your obedient Servant,
(signed) R.E.Bredon,
Acting Inspector General.

True copy,

2nd Assistant, A.

Copy.

No.247. Commre.   INSPECTORATE GENERAL OF CUSTOMS,

Harbin. No.26,215.   Peking, 26th January, 1909

Sir,

1.   I have received your despatches Nos. 132,

150, and 164:

           regarding opening of trade in Northern

           Manchuria, and more especially as to

           the steps to be taken at Aigun, on

           the Sungari River, and at Lahasusu;

and I have generally to approve of the suggestions

you make and to sanction your acting as proposed.

2.   I have, before proceeding to give more

detailed instructions, to express my satisfaction

with the work done by Mr. Schmidt on his journey

to Aigun and back. I am sorry it had to be done

under the very trying conditions he had to encounter

and to which he seems to have so cheerfully

submitted.

3.   I may now say that, in a general way,

you are to proceed promptly, on the lines you

propose, with such arrangements as may be necessary

for commencing work at the places mentioned on the

re-opening of trade in the Spring, say about 1st

May, by which date you must arrange to have the

several staffs necessary on the spot.

4.   The first thing to be done is to draft

the Customs Regulations which are to be observed at

Harbin, Aigun, Sansing and on the Sungari generally, and

at Lahasusu. These you are to take in hand at once, in

consultation with the Harbin Taotai. When ready, they are

to be sent here in English and Chinese, and, when approved

by the Shui-wu Ch'u, they will be returned to be

                                              immediately

N. A. Konovaloff, Esquire,

     Commissioner of Customs,

          Harbin.

---

immediately published in English, Chinese and Russian,

and given effect to from date of commencing trade.

Whatever regulations are drawn up must be considered

provisional and liable to change, or modification, as

may be found necessary.

5.   Although it may be a debatable point as to

whether or not the 50 verst duty free zone,

specified by the Regulations of 1881 for the Land

Trade as existing on each side of the frontier, has

to be recognised on a riverine frontier on which a

water-borne trade is done, it will be as well to

frame the regulations with the idea that it does

exist, though no reference that can be avoided need

be made to its existence. The Land Regulations are

liable to revision every ten years, and the free

zone provision will no doubt have to be reconsidered

in 1911, when the next opportunity for revision will

come.

6.   The right to levy Tonnage Dues at Chinese

ports on the Amur should in my opinion be claimed.

At the same time it may be well to specify that

collection will be waived till the end of 1911, by

which time revision of the Regulations should have

taken place, and we shall have seen what Navigation

Aids will be required.

7.   Arrangements will have to be made for the

issue of transit certificates for goods from the

interior to be exported, and I see no reason why

certificates to cover live cattle, which seem to

be one of the articles of trade commonly met

with in those parts, should not be issued. On

this point it will be well to come to an

understanding with the Taotai, and to point out

to him the desirability of issue. Such certificates

will be useful, as well for other purposes, as

                                              to

to afford means of identifying exports from
outside the free zone.

8. It may be as well to continue to call
the offices on the Amur "Aigun", as such is the
name by which it seems best known to the general
public.

9. I understand that sub-stations of Aigun
will be required at Tsheiho and Tokoutsu: for the
rules and procedure at these places, provision will
also have to be made in the Aigun regulations.

10. The arrangements for the Sungari River
trade had better be made much on the lines you
propose in your No. 161.

11. It seems that a Custom House more
especially for the Riverine trade must be established
at Harbin: the Board orders such to be done. It
would apparently be best that we have a shore
station, presumably in the Pristan district of
Harbin, if we can get a site with adequate water
frontage, and our independence as a Chinese
establishment can be secured in the locality. If
any question arises, or any Russian or Railway
objection is made, we must establish ourselves,
even if inconvenient, in a locality where we shall
be free of possible interference: or we may find
working in a pontoon off the Pristan district
sufficient for the time being. You will have to
settle this matter locally, but in principle we
must have a Customs station: the Chinese Government
will surely and properly not be satisfied with
anything less.

12. I am in favour of treating all vessels
trading on the Sungari as nearly as possible on the
principles

principles of the Inland Water Rules, it being
understood that the duties payable on goods passing
the marts of Harbin and Sansing shall be the Import,
Export and Coast Trade duties as per Import Tariff
of 1902 and general tariff of 1858.

13. In case a Sungari steamer should pass
into the Amur for Habarovsk or any Amur port, she
should surrender her Inland Water (Sungari) pass at
Lahasusu, taking it back on her return. As to
fees to be paid, that can be settled locally.
Vessels doing such trade should hand in inward and
outward manifests at Lahasusu, and some arrangement
should be made that duty, if not paid at Lahasusu,
should be guaranteed for payment at the proper
place elsewhere.

14. I don't think we can extend Tonnage Dues
for the period steamers are laid up during winter:
that is contrary to principles elsewhere. In
practice Sungari vessels need only pay twice a
year: for example, a vessel pays 1st April and is
protected till 1st August. The certificate renewed
after 1st August will carry on for the remainder
of the season and the next certificate will be
issued on clearance from her laying up berth in
the following spring.

15. As on the Amur, I think we must claim
Tonnage Dues on the Sungari, but it may be well
to suspend their enforcement until we see what the
trade requires in the way of Navigation Aids, say
for two years.

16. Your proposals for duty payment in
paragraph 6 - as to the tariff to be applied in
paragraph 7 - of your No. 164. will do to begin
with: arrangements for the issue of special exemption
certificates

certificates on deposit of Bonds will have to be made, that however had best be done locally.

17.   Regarding notifications, you will be authorised to issue what may be necessary later, when the general regulations referred to above have been approved. It will be better to begin with only such regulations as are absolutely necessary, as simple and as brief as possible. It can be stated at the end of the Customs (first-issue) Regulations that further ones on such and such subjects will follow later.

18.   Aids to Navigation on Sungari. If possible, Captain Eldridge will be sent up to Harbin early in April to study Navigation matters on the Sungari: if he cannot be made available, some one else will be sent. Until the officer despatched has reported, it will be better to hold our hand in this connection.

You had better, however, take over the beacons the Railway now holds, and place them as they were last year, using the Roubles 3,000 you have in hand as far as it will go, or may be needed, for that purpose.

Regarding blasting near Sansing, it is better to wait till we see what is wanted, what the whole "Aids to Navigation scheme" will cost, and how it can be financed; however, anything that seems really needed and which can be done at small cost, had better be done, as it will be well to make an appearance of doing something as soon as possible.

19.   You will do well to open with the Roubles 3,000 received from the former Sungari River Committee, a Local Moneys Account, subsidiary to your Account D, to be styled "Aids to Navigation" Account

Account, and to pass through it, for the present, all moneys used in River improvement or marking work. An Account C should be opened with the first Tonnage Dues collected.

20.   Arrangements must be made, in concert with the Manchurian Postal Commissioner, for the establishment of Post Offices at whatever points Customs stations are located, and also for the conveyance of mails by steamer or courier as may by necessary.

I am,

Sir,

Your obedient Servant,

(signed) Robert E. Bredon

Acting Inspector General.

True Copy:

2nd Assistant, A.

Copy

No. 208. Commrs.   INSPECTORATE GENERAL OF CUSTOMS.

Harbin. No. 27,527.
                                    Peking, 13th May, 1909.

        Sir,

                As regards the status of the offices

        about to be opened at Harbin River, Sansing,

        Lahasusu and Aigun, I have to send you, enclosed,

        for your information and guidance, copy of a

        despatch which is being sent to the Statistical

        Secretary in this connection.

                        I am,

                            Sir,

                        Your obedient Servant,

                        (signed) R. E. Bredon

                            Acting Inspector General.

N. Konovaloff, Esquire,

        Commissioner of Customs,

            Harbin.

                        The Inspector General to the Statistical Secretary.

No. 777.   Staff.

Stat.Sec. No.2,956.   Peking, 14th May, 1909.

        Sir,

    1.   In view of the impending opening of Customs

        Houses at Sansing and Aigun, I have to inform you

        that, while these offices are to be subordinate to

        the Harbin Commissioner, they are to be treated, and

        to function, as separate ports for purposes of trade

        returns and statistics, periodical reports and returns

        to the Inspector General, etc., and are to **have** their

        own seals. They will have no direct correspondence

        with the Inspectorate, and their returns, etc., are

        to be transmitted and initialled by the Harbin

        Commissioner.

    2.   The collection figures, statistics, periodical

        returns, etc., etc., of the Customs barrier about

        to be established at Lahasusu are to be included

        in those of the Sansing Custom House (its Head

        Office), but collection and chief articles of trade

        may be shown as well, on special tables appended

        to those of the Sansing Office.

                                                        3.

3.   The Office to be opened on the river at Harbin is a part of the Harbin Customs and is to be treated similarly to but separate from Manchouli and Suifenho.

4.   After the opening of the above-mentioned new offices, the order of ports in the quarterly and annual Revenue tables is to be the following:

     1. Aigun.

     2. Sansing.

     3. Harbin district

        Manchouli.

        Harbin.

        Suifenho.

     4. Antung.

     5. Tatungkow.

     6. Dairen.

     7. Newchwang.

     X X X X

The "Total Collection" and other collection figures are to be given in the respective columns concerned for Suifenho, Harbin, and Manchouli, each separately, and no figures are to appear on the line " 3. Harbin District", but, in the "Total Collection"

                  column

column opposite to it, is to be a mark referring to the following note - to be added to the tables:

    Total Collection of Harbin District, i.e.,

       including Manchouli, Harbin and Suifenho Hk.Tls....

    I prefer the Revenue Tables not to have an appearance of being cramped, and authorise you therefore to carry them over into four pages, if necessary. Notes referring to items on the first two pages will then appear on them and those to items on the last two, similarly. The type of the notes is rather small. None of the notes hitherto shown on the tables should be done away with, not even that referring to the Kowloon and Lappa collections on the annual table.

        I am, etc.,

        (signed) Robert E. Bredon,

           Acting Inspector General.

True Copies:

  2nd Assistant, A.

致哈尔滨关第 <u>110/23029</u> 号令 ^①　　　　　总税务司署（北京）1908 年 4 月 15 日

尊敬的哈尔滨关税务司：

1. 兹附税务处令文（内附外务部令文）：

"日本公使林权助（Hayashi）先生来函称，中俄边境沿线各地、中俄陆路贸易所经之瑷珲及齐齐哈尔两地，乃至松花江与黑龙江交汇处各地，均未闻有设置海关税卡之举，与俄国于北满洲之贸易相比，中国海关对日本于南满洲之贸易征收关税，实有不公之处。"

2. 根据税务处指令，请哈尔滨关税务司尽快就于瑷珲及齐齐哈尔两地设关征税一事制定方案，确定该两处税卡可最快投入使用之日期；另请调查，若欲避免征税遗漏，确保税收利益，是否有必要于松花江与黑龙江交汇处附近设置海关税卡。

3. 税务处令文强调，瑷珲及齐齐哈尔两地与松花江和黑龙江交汇处各地之状况截然不同，前者乃为国际通商之处，而后者则或许会因禁止贸易而成为走私之所在。

4. 请于调查后提出可行建议。本署深知，哈尔滨关区目前处境艰难，问题颇多，但以下各项还须予以解答。

（1）关于于瑷珲及齐齐哈尔设立分关事：《陆路通商章程》中有 50 俄里免税区之规定，不知该项规定可否理解为中俄两国自黑龙江这条界河贸易路线至内陆 50 俄里之间的区域均为海关免征关税之地？若如此，海关于黑龙江沿线的瑷珲设立分关后，又将如何开展征税工作？又能征收何种关税？如于齐齐哈尔设立分关，又将征收何种关税？齐齐哈尔有无对外贸易往来？海关能否向其征税？齐齐哈尔若无对外贸易往来，与那些远离南满边境及铁路之地相比，又有何种优势？

（2）关于于松花江与黑龙江交界处设立分关事：松花江与黑龙江交界之处虽非指定贸易地点，但如今满洲与西伯利亚之间的贸易已有于此开展者，然而此地区既非通商口岸，亦非贸易市场，不知管控能否实现？绵长的北部边境地区亦是如此，海关很有可能难以防卫。另外，该地区是否已设有税卡？如有，鉴于松花江为吉林与黑龙江两省之分界线，不知此税卡隶属哪省？

5. 请尽快告知此番调查工作所需之华洋关员及通晓俄语关员之数目，初期还望尽量精简人手。

---

① 参照旧中国海关总税务署通令选编一书，本文的文号致哈尔滨关第 110/23029 号令可译为关字第 110 号，司字第 23029 号。

此外，克勒纳（H. Dawson-Grone）先生目前于吉林之公务并不繁忙，或许可以分担部分工作。其不日将至北京，本署届时将与之商谈此事。

汇报时请随附相应中文版本，本署将直接发送至税务处，借以说明上述各地之情况。当然，短时之内无法完成全面的部署安排，亦不会有此等要求，唯望尽快着手，以求"免为日人借口"（如税务处令文所述）。

您忠诚的仆人

裴式楷（R. E. Bredon）

副总税务司

代行总税务司职务

该抄件内容真实有效，特此证明。

录事：周骊（C. H. B. Joly）二等帮办前班

致哈尔滨关第 142/24101 号令　　　　总税务司署（北京）1908 年 7 月 23 日

尊敬的哈尔滨关税务司：

1. 根据此前信函：

"为于北满洲设立税关事。"

现附上昨晚所收税务处令文之抄件一份，内容为对本署相关呈文（抄件日前已通过半官函发给贵署）之回复。

2. 令文要点如下（另见本署今日致哈尔滨关电报）：

（1）尽早于瑷珲设立一关作为哈尔滨关分关，由哈尔滨关管辖；

（2）松花江上的贸易管理办法及须设征税或稽查关卡之地均由地方政府斟酌裁定，但税务司或须参与商议；

（3）哈尔滨关应开始行使其征税职能。

关于哈尔滨关征税一事，税务处似乎认为早应如此，但对于铁路运输之货物，哈尔滨关既已有满洲里和绥芬河两处分关执行征税事宜，便应无再征收之必要，因此税务处该项指示可以理解为应向松花江水运货物征税，可征货物包括：

① 松花江上自哈尔滨至三姓河段往来者；

② 松花江上自哈尔滨和三姓经由拉哈苏苏入俄境者；

③ 松花江上自哈尔滨至沿线内陆各地者。

前两类货物往来可作为转口贸易照国际税则办理，最后一类可作为内港贸易照常关征税办法办理。

3. 贵署须负责具体事宜的落实，并与前期准备工作所涉各方取得联系，但首先还须将应办各事理清列明。

4. 关于瑷珲分关设立一事，应即刻派遣可负责查验及征税工作的关员前往瑷珲，并为之提供一切所需，以便瑷珲分关可顺利于 10 月 1 日或更早的时间开始征税工作；应与当地政府确定是否可照税务处指示为海关提供办公场所和宿舍；应对征税办法、征税类别及税收接管方等事做出安排。此外，可能还需请当地军警出面保护，需有能够与齐齐哈尔方面保持通信的途径。然以上各项仅为本署所能想到的初步准备工作，日后还会有更多事宜需要解决。

5. 人员配置方面，应将可能遇到的困难考虑在内，对此贵署应当已有所了解。克勒纳（H. Dawson-Grone）先生暂时负责管理安东关，如有需要，可于 8 月末到任；司根德（O. V.

Seckendorff）先生可随时到任；裴纳玑（E. Bernadsky）先生和葛绎真（M. T. Grigorieff）先生可从事不要求经验的工作。此外，还需挑选华籍同文供事，挑选会讲俄语的华籍关员，可能还需调任马珍诰（A. M. Maltchenko）先生。瑷珲分关的设立工作应由一名高级关员负责，最初的管理工作可由洋籍关员负责一段时日，但最后可能还须从供事中任命一名华籍代理税务司负责管理。至于文案、书办、司秤和仆人应当可于当地通过地方政府雇用。

6. 关于松花江贸易相关事宜的筹备工作，本署暂时还无法给定意见，待有消息后，再进一步说明。但贵署须配合道台等所涉各方，查明海关需做可做之事。

7. 关于哈尔滨关征税一事，相信赞成者居多，但还望贵署可掌握主动权，尽快确定起征日期，提前予以公布。以上各项事宜，暂照此办理，如有必要，再做进一步指示。

您忠诚的仆人

裴式楷（R. E. Bredon）

副总税务司

代行总税务司职务

该抄件内容真实有效，特此证明。

录事：周骊（C. H. B. Joly）二等帮办前班

致哈尔滨关第 <u>247/26215</u> 号令　　　　　　　总税务司署（北京）1909 年 1 月 28 日

尊敬的哈尔滨关税务司：

1. 哈尔滨关第 132 号、150 号及 164 号呈收悉：

"汇报北满洲贸易开放事；呈报计划于瑷珲、松花江及拉哈苏苏采取之措施。"

基本赞同呈中各项提议，可以批准执行。

2. 在下达具体指示之前，首先要对式美第（A. Schmidt）先生在往返瑷珲途中所做的工作予以肯定，对在如此艰难的条件下开展工作表示同情。令人欣慰的是，他似乎一直颇为乐观。

3. 总体而言，贵署应立即按照提议着手于上述各地做出相应安排，以便为春季重开贸易（预计 5 月 1 日）做好必要准备，同时确保各地所需人员能够及时到位。

4. 首先需要完成的是为哈尔滨关、瑷珲分关、三姓分关、哈尔滨江关及拉哈苏苏分关草拟海关章程。此事须即刻着手办理，同时还须与滨江道道台商议。章程草拟完毕，须向总税务司署呈交汉英两版，税务处批准后会将之发回。随后贵署便可颁布汉、英、俄三版海关章程，并自开放贸易之日起施行。章程之草拟，无论类别，均须视为临时办法，如有必要，应可随时更改或调整。

5. 尽管对于 1881 年《陆路通商章程》中关于中俄边境 50 俄里免税区之规定是否应同样适用于水路边境还存有争议，但在草拟章程的过程中，还是应将此考虑在内，不过文内不必提及。《陆路通商章程》通常每十年修订一次，下一次修订应在 1911 年，届时免税区之规定势必会重新商议。

6. 至于在黑龙江华岸各口岸征收船钞一事，兹认为海关确有此权利。但鉴于《陆路通商章程》或将于 1911 年底完成修订，届时航路标志方面会有何新的需求亦将清晰明了，因此最好说明在 1911 年底之前暂不征收。

7. 另须安排为自内地出口之货物签发运照。生牛亦为当地常见货品之一，为之发放运照应属合理，不过此事还须与道台达成共识。请向其说明发放此类运照之益处，比如可帮助鉴别从免税区以外各地运来的出口货物。

8. 鉴于 "Aigun" 一名已为大众所熟知，故赞成延用。

9. 据了解，瑷珲分关将需于大黑河和陡沟子下设两处分卡，因此关于该两处分卡之规定亦须列入瑷珲海关章程。

10. 至于松花江上的贸易，最好依照哈尔滨关第 164 号呈所提建议做出安排。

11. 为管理松花江沿岸的水运贸易，似须于哈尔滨设立一处江关，且税务处亦有此命令。如能于江岸设卡,当然最为适宜,比如在哈尔滨布里斯坦(Pristan)①区的岸边一带,但前提是海关可于河岸上寻得足够空间,且能够于设立后保证自己作为中国机关的独立性。一旦出现任何问题,或者俄方或铁路公司提出任何异议,海关须另择一地设卡,以免受到干扰,即使因此会遇有不便;或者也可以于布里斯坦区暂设一处浮码头以处理相应海关工作。此事将须由贵署于地方上解决,但原则是必须设立一处海关分卡,此亦为中国政府的最低要求。

12. 对于要求所有于松花江上贸易的船只都尽量遵循内港行轮章程办事之提议,本署表示赞成,但根据1902年进口税则及1858年税则之规定,哈尔滨及三姓江关对往来货物应征之关税应包括进口税、出口税及复出口半税。

13. 松花江上的轮船如欲驶入黑龙江前往哈巴罗夫斯克(Habarovsk)或其他沿线口岸,则应于经由拉哈苏苏分卡时上交(松花江)内港专照,并于返程时取回。至于应缴纳之费用,则可由地方决定。参与此类贸易的船只还应于拉哈苏苏分卡上交进出口舱单;至于关税,船只如不能于此分卡支付,则应设法令于其他关卡缴纳。

14. 船只冬季停泊期间,海关不应收取船钞执照展期费用,因为此举与其他口岸之惯例不符。实际上,松花江上的船只一年仅需支付两次船钞执照费用,例如4月1日支付一次后,执照有效期将会延至8月,8月1日再次支付后,执照有效期便可延至航运季结束。而当轮船于次年春季离开泊地出港时,海关为之签发新的船钞执照。

15. 至于船钞的征收问题,兹认为,松花江应与黑龙江一样,海关均有权对其往来贸易征收船钞。但于目前而言,此事还不宜落实,应待两年之后确定贸易对航路标志有何需求,再行决定。

16. 哈尔滨关第164号呈第6段关于征收关税之提议及第7段关于适用税则之提议可以从特别免重征执照的签发着手安排,应当制定凭保单签发之办法,当然此事最好还是由地方决定。

17. 至于海关公告,待上述通用章程获批后,再予批准颁布。初期应优先颁布绝对必要之规章,内容亦应尽量简明。另可于海关章程(优先颁布)文末说明后续将颁布其他相关公告。

18. 对于松花江上的航路标志工作,如果情况允许,将于四月初派遣额得志(G. T. B. J. Eldridge)上校前往哈尔滨研究松花江上的航运事宜,但如果其无法前往,将另派他人;派

---

① 经查为今哈尔滨道里区,因当时此处被开辟为码头,故被称"埠头","布里斯坦"为其俄文名称的音译。

遣人员到任之前,不宜有任何行动。

此外,最好将铁路公司现有的航行标志接管过来,按照去年的办法存放。至于已接管的 3000 卢布,应做到物尽其用,但要用于航路标志的相关工作。

对于三姓附近的爆破工程,当下还是静观其变,待了解整体"航路标志方案"的费用预算及资金来源后,再行决定。不过,为尽快有所作为,如遇到切实需要且成本较低之工程,当予完成。

19. 对于从前松花江河道委员会(River Committee)接管的 3000 卢布,应于哈尔滨关 D 账户项下设一暂记账,命名为"航路标志"账户,目前凡用于河道改善及航路标志工作之款项均记入此账户。待起征船钞后,再开立 C 账户。

20. 须与满洲邮政司协力解决于海关关卡所在地设立邮政公署及安排轮船或信使运送邮件等事。

您忠诚的仆人

(签字)裴式楷(R. E. Bredon)

署总税务司

该抄件内容真实有效,特此证明。

录事:周骊(C. H. B. Joly)二等帮办前班

致哈尔滨关第 <u>308/27527</u> 号令　　　　　总税务司署（北京）1909 年 5 月 13 日

尊敬的哈尔滨关税务司：

关于开设哈尔滨江关、三姓分关、拉哈苏苏分关及瑷珲分关一事，兹附上致造册处税务司的令文抄件，以供参考。

您忠诚的仆人

（签字）裴式楷（R. E. Bredon）

署总税务司

附件

致造册处税务司第 <u>777/2956</u> 号令　　　　总税务司署（北京）1909 年 5 月 14 日

尊敬的造册处税务司：

　　1. 关于将于三姓及瑷珲两地开设之分关，须知，该两处分关虽由哈尔滨关税务司管理，但凡涉及向总税务司署呈交之贸易统计表和定期报告及报表等资料，均应由其单独编制；在此等事情上，两处分关可作为独立口岸行使职权，且拥有各自印章。但两处分关编制报表后须呈送至哈尔滨关，再由哈尔滨关税务司转呈总税务司署。

　　2. 关于将于拉哈苏苏开设之分卡，须知，该分卡之税收数据、统计数据及定期统计表将编入三姓分关（拉哈苏苏分卡的总关）相应资料内；主要贸易货品及应征税项应专门列表并随附于三姓分关相应表单后。

　　3. 关于将于哈尔滨开设之江关，须知，该江关隶属于哈尔滨关，与满洲里及绥芬河两处分关享有同等待遇，但仍需加以区分。

　　4. 上述分关开设后，应按以下顺序列入季度及年度税收报表：

（1）瑷珲

（2）三姓

（3）哈尔滨关区

　　满洲里

　　哈尔滨

　　绥芬河

（4）安东

（5）大东沟

（6）大连

（7）牛庄

　　其中"（3）哈尔滨关区项下之绥芬河、哈尔滨及满洲里三处分关"的"征收总数"及其他税收数据均应单独列入相应栏中；哈尔滨关区一栏中不必填入数据，唯须于"征收总数"对应之位置备注：

"哈尔滨关区（包括满洲里、哈尔滨及绥芬河）征收总数为海关两①……（两）。"

税收报表不宜显得过分拥挤，如有必要，可以使用四页表单。每页表单各项所需注释均应于当页列明，注释字体应尽量调小。表单上的所有注释均不得删除，年度报表中九龙关和拱北关征收数据的相关注释亦不例外。

您忠诚的仆人

（签字）裴式楷（R. E. Bredon）

署总税务司

该抄件内容真实有效，特此证明。

录事：周骊（C. H. B. Joly）二等帮办前班

---

① 海关两为近代海关的记账单位，本卷中一律标为"海关两 XX 两"。自第二卷始，标为"XX 海关两"。

2. 为瑷珲分关工作于 1909 年 8 月 17 日开始及工作安排事

No. 61.

I. G.

Harbin, 8th May, 1909.

Sir,

1. In continuation of my preceding despatch No. 60:

Reporting on the question of Customs of the
Sungari River Trade:

I have now the honour to report on the question of the establishment
of Customs stations at Aihun and Tsitsihar, as instructed in your
despatch No. 110.

2. Tsitsihar ( ) - Mergen ( ) - Aihun ( )
trade route is availed of to an extent during the winter, when the
roads are frozen hard. Apart from a little local movement of
merchandise from, and to, the few small places en route the goods
traffic is chiefly northwards and consists of foreign and native
goods intended for Blagovestchensk ( ) which depends
for most of it requires upon the outside world. Blagovestchensk
produces nothing for exportation. Prior to the establishment of
the Manchuria and Suifenho Customs foreign goods destined for
transmission to Blagovestchensk via Mergen and Aihun used to pay
to the Tsitsihar authorities a tax of 5% ad valorem and this exempted them from further levies en route. The Customs Commission
at Harbin was discussing this trade and the Russians delegates
advocated its being recognised as a trade in transit, and, as such,
exempted from taxation. The Chinese members of the Commission
quoted article 12 of the 1881 Land Trade Regulations which provides
for levy of import duty on analogous traffic of foreign goods from
Tientsin to Kiachta via Kalgan and Ourga, but in view of the question having been a subject of negotiations between the governor of
Tsitsihar and the Russian Consul, the matter was omitted from
further discussion and the question remains still unsettled.
Since the beginning of collection goods from Russia paid an import
duty at Manchuria and claimed immunity from the provincial 5% levy
at Tsitsihar. The merchants interested were even willing to pay
transit dues to secure free passage as far as Aihun and on a couple

of

The Inspector General of Customs.

KING.

of occasions a sort of Transit Certificate was issued at the
Manchuria office. This shows that Russian or other foreign, goods
going via Aihun to Blagovestchensk could not be made to pay anything more, having, in fact, paid on some occasions everything
prescribed by the treaties plus Inland levies. On the other hand,
such foreign re-exports are by treaties entitled at Aihun to a
refund of import duties originally paid, and for this category of
goods the functions of a Customs establishment at Aihun would be
to refund, rather than to levy, duties if Russian goods and merchants are to enjoy the usual Treaty privileges they are entitled to.

3. Any Native goods that may be going that way are presumably
subject to the same 5% tax at Tsitsihar and other levies perhaps
besides. A Custom House, if established, at Tsitsihar, should
not, it would seem, levy more than that, and goods might claim the
Manchurian Exemption Certificates to protect them as far as Aihun.
Aihun would thus neither collect anything on Native produce.

4. There is practically no movement of Russian imports from
Blagovestchensk into Manchuria and nothing could be levied by the
Aihun and Tsitsihar Customs.

5. The Tsitsihar - Mergen - Aihun route is too bad, too long
and too costly during the summer and is not used. And why should
it be followed if goods can be sent by the quicker and cheaper way
of the Sungari and Amour by steamers ?

6. I beg therefore to draw a conclusion that Customs establishments at Tsitsihar and Aihun are unnecessary from the fiscal point
of view - there is no revenue at stake, and any movement of goods
through these places is in no way more favourably circumstanced as
compared with other part of Manchuria. On the contrary, a Customs
Office at Aihun would only enable Russian merchants to pay less than
they do now during the winter season and the Russian authorities
would surely claim the same treatment for this trade as is enjoyed
by others on the strength of treaties. Pending the final settlement of this question, it was my intention to request permission to
adopt the practice of issuing Exemption Certificates for duty paid
foreign and native goods (Circular No. 1472) which merchants might

wish

wish to send from Manchuria, Harbin or Suifenho to Aihun and
thence to Blagovestchensk.

7.   Aihun is a trade mart on the Amour, and it may be asked why
a Customs Office at Aihun should not control the shipping and river
trade ?   Amour is however an "International River".   Special
conventions exist in the case of other similar water ways (e.g.
Danube) and an understanding between China and Russia, it would
seem, should precede any initial Customs developments.   A Russo-
Chinese Commission will shortly take up the subject of the Amour
navigation rules for the prevention of collisions, etc..   Whether
its object is to arrive at a sort of "regime conventionel des
fleuves internationaux" or not, I do not exactly know.   It would
therefore be better perhaps to await the result of the discussion or
still better, let this subject be included to some extent in the
scope of the negotiations.   Last but not least, Aihun is situated
in the centre of the 50 versts Frontier Zone and the free trade
clause of the 1881 Treaty supplies another reason for not starting
immediately any Customs work at Aihun, a mere village of no importance at present.

8.   In case, however, there should be strong political reasons
to open a Customs station at Aihun, this could be easily done.   A
Chinese Assistant, or Clerk, may be sent there and I should select
a Tidewaiter with a knowledge of Chinese and Russian to accompany
and assist him and then his reports could be awaited before further
steps are planned.   The Aihun authorities should be instructed
before hand to prepare temporary house accommodation for quarters
and offices of employés sent if it be decided to send any.

9.   The Tsitsihar - Mergen - Aihun - Blagovestchensk winter
trade apart, Tsitsihar is in the same position as Hailar, Kirin,
Kwangchengtze, Liaoyang, Moukden, etc., and requires a Customs
Office just as little as these other trade marts and certainly much
less than for instance Hailar where a Customs Office would be welcomed by some Russian firms buying, and preparing for exportation,
wool hides and other Mongolian produce.   I beg therefore to suggest
that the opening of a Puk'uei Kuan (   ) at Tsitsihar be under
these circumstances temporarily deferred unless, again, the presence
of a

of a Customs representative be considered necessary at this provincial capital.

10.   A Chinese version of this despatch, in duplicate, is
enclosed herewith.

                  I have the honour to be,

                         Sir,

                  Your obedient Servant,

                  (signed) N. A. Konovaloff,

                      Commissioner.

True copy:

      C. B. Foli

      2nd Assistant, A.

Note: No Chinese characters in the original.

AIHUN: Establishment of Sub-station at;
Mr A. Schmidt, Actg. Dep. Commissioner,
detailed for duty in connection with.

No. 101.

I. G.

Harbin,   20th August, 1909.

Sir,

1.　　　　Having reference to your despatch No. 142:
Conveying instructions from Shui-wu Ch'u
regarding speedy establishment of a Sub-
office of the Harbin Customs at Aihun
（爱珲设立一间作为哈滨设分间）；
and in continuation of my semi-official letters on
the subject, I have the honour to report that the
Superintendent has wired at my request to the Aihun
Fututung enquiring whether accommodation had been secured
for Offices and Quarters. A telegram in reply was
communicated to me on the 11th instant to the effect
that a lease of three chien for office use had been
ordered. Under the circumstances I have deputed Mr A.
Schmidt, Acting Deputy Commissioner, to proceed by
steamer to Aihun to make a preliminary study of the
place. He will stop at Lahasusu en route to look
into the Customs question there. Mr Schmidt will return
from Aihun by the overland route via Mergen （墨尔根）
to Tsitsihar and thus get an insight into the trade
conditions of the hinterland as well.

2.　　　　Mr Schmidt left this morning accompanied by
Mr W. I. Bluhm, Probationary Tidewaiter, and one Tingch'
ai, the only two units I can spare at present. From
the point of view of real revenue work the arrival
of the party at Aihun may be considered as the
opening of a Customs Office there. If necessary or
advisable

Robert E. Bredon, K. C. M. G.,
　Acting Inspector General of Customs,
　　P E K I N G.

advisable Mr Bluhm will be left at Aihun.

3.　　　　My instructions to Mr Schmidt are embodied in
Harbin despatch No. 1 to Aihun of which I beg to
enclose herewith a copy.

I have the honour to be,

Sir,

Your obedient Servant,

(signed) N. A. Konovaloff,

Commissioner.

True copy:

2nd Assistant, A.

No. 126.

Aigun: Opening of Customs Station at; arrangement arrived at by Kuangcheng officials authorised career using duty treatment of good and duty free zone reporting; copy despatch in forwarding

I. G.

Harbin, 27th September, 1908.

Sir,

With reference to my despatch No. 101:
Reporting Mr Schmidt's departure for Aigun in connection with the question of opening a Customs Office at that part and enclosing copy of my despatch No. 1 to Aigun:

and in compliance with the Chinese Secretary's Memorandum No. 274 of 3rd September, I have the honour to enclose herewith copy of a despatch received from the Superintendent in June last communicating a despatch from their Excellencies the Viceroy and the Governor of Heilungchiang in which the arrangement arrived at last year regarding the treatment of merchandise to, and from, Blagovestchensk and the exemption from duty of the 100-li frontier zone trade is put on record.

The original despatch having been taken by Mr Schmidt to Aigun, I regret I was not able to have it copied before his return.

I have the honour to be,

Sir,

Your obedient Servant,

(signed) N. A. Konovaloff,

Commissioner.

True copy:

2nd Assistant, A.

Sir Robert E. Bredon, K.C.M.G.,
Acting Inspector General of Customs.
PEKING.

No. 132.

Aigun: Opening of Customs Station at; general report in forwarding; Dept. Comm Schmidt's report, submitted; instructions re applicability of duty free zone to Amur frontier. Soliciting; levy of tonnage dues; inadvisable of reporting; exemption from duty of Chinese goods moved at Manchouli & reported to Blagg, under hand Special I.C. proposing

I. G.

Harbin, 11th November, 1908.
28th

Sir,

1. With reference to your despatch No. 142:
substation to be established at Aigun:

and in continuation of my despatch No. 101:
reporting departure of Mr Schmidt, Acting Deputy Commissioner, for Aigun in connection with the question:

I have the honour to submit herewith a copy of Mr Schmidt's account of his journey by a Sungari steamer to Lahasusu, thence by Amour steamers to Aigun and Blagovestchensk, and overland from Aigun via Mergen and Tsitsihar to Harbin, supplemented by separate reports on Hsintien (新甸), Lahasusu (拉哈蘇蘇), Aigun (愛琿), and Blagovestchensk (布拉郭威厄斯克), on the Sungari shipping and the present Aids to Navigation, and some remarks on the question of the I. P. C. extension to Aigun. A Chinese map of Manchuria (reprint from a Russian map with some additions and transliterations to illustrate the reports is sent herewith.

2. The principal object of Mr Schmidt's trip being to study Customs requirements at Aigun, I propose dealing with this question separatively, leaving out for the present matters connected with the Sungari control.

3. Mr Schmidt's report confirms the main features of my despatch No. 61:
reporting on the question of the establishment of Customs Stations at Aigun and Tsitsihar:
to

Sir Robert E. Bredon, K.C.M.G.,
Acting Inspector General of Customs.
PEKING.

to the effect that, from the fiscal point of view, Aigun does not promise a large Customs revenue and that, on the other hand, for whatever trade there is a system of taxation is already in existence.

4. With the information at our disposal now there is no difficulty in completing the arrangements towards the actual beginning of Customs work at Aigun. Adequate accommodation has been secured for Offices and Quarters; the most essentials have already been procured; a Tide-waiter has been left at Aigun to look after the premises and Office property, to study the locality and its conditions and to assist generally such other members of the staff as may be appointed to Aigun. For all the work we are likely to handle at Aigun, I think, I am able to provide with my present Staff and the persons selected can receive adequate instructions at Harbin for their preliminary guidance as well as all the necessary information about the place from Mr Schmidt's report and such verbal elucidations as may be called for.

5. Before attempting to draft a Set of Regulations I beg to submit for your consideration some questions of principle arising out of the geographical situation of Aigun and the treaty clauses connected with it.

6. The Russo-Chinese Land Trade Regulations of 1881 (Art. 1) exempt the trade within 50 versts (100-li) on each side of the frontier from taxation. The Regulations at the first glance, deal specially with the Mongolian trade and a question suggests itself as to whether they apply to the Amour River frontier and whether the trans-river trade could be styled "land trade". An authoritative decision is for Peking to pronounce and its nature must naturally lay down the principles on which the Customs rules must be based. Art. 1 of the Supplementary Treaty of Peking of 1860, in elucidating

and corroborating Art. 1 of the Aigun Treaty of 1858, reads

"Desormais la frontiere orientale entre les deux empires, a commencer du confluent des rivieres Chilka et Argoun, descendra le cours de la riviere Amour jusqu'au confluent de la riviere Oussouri avec cette derniere. Les terres situees sur la rive gauche (au nord) de la riviere Amour appartiennent a l'empire de Russie, et les terres situees sur la rive droite (au sud) appartiennent a l'empire de Chine .. .. .."

Art. IV of the same treaty of 1860 says

"Sur toute la ligne frontiere etablie par l' article I du present traite, un commerce d'echange libre et franc de droits est autorise entre les sujets des deux Etats.. .. .."

Art. 1 of the Land Trade Regulations of 1862, 1869 and 1881 repeat the duty free frontier zone trade stipulation, from which it may be deduced that the Aigun - Blagovestchensk trade might be considered as covered by this treaty clause. If this should meet with your and the Board's views the Aigun Customs taxation system might be elaborated on the lines given below.

7. The Aigun Office work may roughly be divided into two, or rather threes, categories, viz:

1. Steamer borne trade, and (1)
  trans-river trade with the Russian (2)
  places on the left bank of the Amour ; and
2. Land trade with the hinterland. (3)
and I will attempt to treat each class separately.

8. Steamer borne trade and trans-river trade.

a) The present Aigun offers few attractions to passing steamers and those going down river hardly ever stop there. The Amour is open by treaty only to the Chinese

Chinese and Russian shipping and up to now the Chinese flag is not yet represented. A Russo-Chinese Commission had been appointed last year to draw up a set of regulations to be observed by steamers of the two countries. The Commission has not yet met and it is difficult at this stage to foresee what matters it is likely to take in hand. The Amour is lighted by the Russian Government which levies nothing from the shipping for this service. In my opinion, it would be advisable to follow Russian example and exempt any steamers that might call at Aigun from payment of Tonnage Dues. This would encourage them to call oftener, whereas it demand for Tonnage Dues will certainly keep them away alto-gether. In any case, the receipts would be very trifling and quite inadequate for any river work usually paid for from this collection. Should future experience make it advisable, a sort of light Port Dues might be instituted later on. The Customs control of steamers would thus be limited to a verification of cargo landed and shipped by them and preventive measures against traffic in contraband goods.

b) Imports from Blagovestchensk and other Russian places on the Amour to be exempted from Import Duty if intended for Aigun and places within 100-li from the river frontier in accordance with Art. 1 of the 1881 Land Trade Regulations.

c) Imports from Blagovestchensk and other Russian places on the Amour, if intended for conveyance to places outside the 100-li zone, to pay the ordinary Tariff Import Duty and to receive

 A) a Duty Receipt if the place of destination is not stated;

 b) the Special Exemption Certificate (Circulars Nos.1441,

1472

1472, 1499 and 1544) if intended for conveyance to one of the Manchurian Trade Marts.

d) Aigun Import duty paid Foreign Imports sent inland will either

 a) pay inland taxes at the barriers met with en route; or

 b) on payment of ordinary Transit Dues, receive Transit Certificates and be exempt from inland taxation en route to the place of destination.

e) Imports, Foreign, from Chinese places on the Amour or Sungari; to be dealt with in the same way as the Imports from Blagovestchensk, i.e. even if they are not accompanied by Exemption Certificates or the Special Exemption Certificates.

 a) to be admitted in duty-free if for use within the zone;

 b) to pay however, as above, if intended to go beyond the zone limits.

f) Imports, Native, from Chinese places on the Amour or Sungari:

 a) if accompanied by Special Exemption Certificate from one of the Customs Offices, to be admitted duty-free.

 b) if accompanied by Duty Paid Certificates from one of the Chinese Customs Offices, to pay Coast Trade Duty;

 c) if not so accompanied, to pay Import Duty.

 d) Coast Trade duty-paid Native goods to receive a drawback for this duty if eventually re-exported abroad.

N.B. Foreign merchants may however claim exemption in accordance with Art. 1 of the 1881 Regulations and it may be politic to waive our claim to Import and Coast Trade Duties on native goods to be used within the limits of the zone so as to give the native

goods

goods the same treatment as is enjoyed by foreign goods; otherwise there would be an inducement to carry them via Blagovestchensk - an unnecessary burden on trade.

g) Exports of local produce to Blagovestchensk and other Russian places to be passed duty-free in accordance with the free zone privilege.

h) Exports of native produce to Chinese places on the Amour and Sungari to pay Export duty and to receive a Duty Paid Certificate.

N.B. Remarks regarding the advisability of exemption under f) would also apply to this category.

9.   Land Trade with the hinterland.

The inward movement of Imports has already been dealt with. As regards the outward movement of Native produce, Aigun itself being a small market, this movement is primarily of a transit character via Aigun to Blagovestchensk, a large consumer of Chinese products. Cattle is the principal item of this trade and as such difficult to control. It may however be hoped that the lightness of our taxation would bring the cattle dealers to us for Transit Certificates if such could be issued for live stock. At Toukoutsu (头沟子), or at a point outside the frontier zone, the "last barrier" could be established and the usual practice of depositing three times the duty would secure to the Customs Transit dues plus Export duty on quantities sent on to the Russian side of the Amour without conflicting with the free zone clause as being a trans-zone taxation. Another checking station at Taheiho would control the actual exportations across the river. Cattle arriving at Toukoutsu from the South without Transit Certificates would be held liable to a full Import duty then and there or, by a special arrangement, on reaching Aigun. When exported to Blagovestchensk it would have to be passed duty-free under the free zone clause but this would not constitute a discriminative treatment since

it will have been exposed, in the absence of a Transit Certificate, to inland taxation before reaching Toukoutsu or Aigun. The Sundries carried similarly do not amount to much and would probably be covered by the above procedure.

10.   Another kind of trade will be one of the features of Aigun for the next few years and that is the movement of imports from Manchuria and Saifenho (and Harbin eventually via Taitsihar and Mergen with the ultimate destination for Blagovestchensk. This traffic only takes place during the winter when Blagovestchensk is not accessible by river steamers and will cease with the construction of the Amour railway. Such goods will be supplied by the other North Manchurian Custom Offices with the Special Exemption Certificates to be stamped at Aigun in proof of arrival. Whenever these goods are declared for re-exportation to Blagovestchensk the Taheiho Controlling Office would verify the quantities sent across the river and issue certificates to that effect which would entitle owner of the goods to drawbacks for the original Import duty at the port of first entry.

11.   The above is an outline of a possible provisional and experimental procedure for Aigun based upon the recognition of Art: 1 of the 1881 Land Trade Regulations and the corresponding adaptation of the ordinary trade regulations applicable at treaty ports and trade marts generally. The procedure would have to be modified if the free trade zone clause be interpreted differently, but the modification would be in the direction of the ordinary treaty port practice of levying import duties on Imports, Export duties on Exports, Coast Trade duties on Native re-imports, Transit dues for inland transit privileges, issue of the usual documents, etc., matters which need not be gone into in detail now. The suggestion to abstain from the levy of Tonnage dues (8, a) would however still hold good for the same reasons.

12.   The closing of the porto franco regime in the Russian Amour Province may favourably affect the conditions at Aigun but its future growth can hardly be gauged at

Present

present.   As will be seen from Mr Schmidt's report,
Aigun is still in an embryonic stage and there is no
certainty as to whether the Official Aigun re-established
on the old ante-1900 site with the already marked out
trade settlement, Shang fu (商埠), will be able to hold
its own in view of the activity displayed by the private
enterprise at Tahaiho, just opposite of Blagoveatchensk with
which the Aigun district is so intimately connected in
trade matters.

13.   For this reason I should be in favour of a
mobile Customs organisation at the start and until we
have gained more experience and studied the trend of
developments.   The accommodation secured by the Fututung
would serve as a suitable Head Office.   We ought to
have besides points d'appui at Tahaiho, the real terminus
of trade with Blagovestchensk, at Toukoutzu or another
suitable spot to control the trade to, and from, the 100-
li zone, and, perhaps, at one of the city gates.   As
the establishment of the Aigun Customs is a political
necessity it may be hoped that suitable directions could
be issued to the Heilungchiang Authorities to let the
Customs share the existing accommodation at such of the
above mentioned places as may be found necessary.

14.   Another matter that has been touched in your
despatch No.142, namely the establishment of a postal
communication, has been looked into by Mr Schmidt and his
remarks will form the subject of special despatches to the
Postal Secretary and the Postal Commissioner for Manchruia.

15.   Your final instructions regarding the taxation
principles must now be awaited before further staff arrangements are made, supplies and forms procured, etc..

16.   "AIGUN" is the old established designation of the
locality and hitherto more frequently used in Inspectorate
Despatches and Circulars than the ordinary romanization of
the Chinese Characters (璦琿) - "Aihun".   In ordering
                                            the

the Commissioner's seals for the new Office I propose
adhering to the first version; the Chinese would be
(璦琿分關稅務司印) and, as in the case of the Harbin,
Manchruia and Suifenho seals, the Russian equivalent would
be inserted to make the seal intelligible to Russian
merchants who would have the most dealings with that Offic

17.   In conclusion I beg to suggest again that the
proposed establishment of a Customs Office at Aigun be
notified to the Russian Legation in order to avoid questions
in connection with contracts entered into in the supposi-
tion that no such measures are contemplated, such as we
have experienced as a result of the sudden beginning of
Collection at Manchuria and Suifenho.

                    I have the honour to be,
                              Sir,
                    Your obedient Servant,

                    (signed) N. A. Konovaloff,
                         Commissioner of Customs.

True copy:

                    2nd Assistant, A.

COPY:

Aigun Customs Regulations + opening of Station

No. 503. *published reporting. Mr Sch.* CUSTOM HOUSE.

Comm. Schmidt sent to Aigun.

I.G. *and custom work commenced* Harbin, 19th October, 1910.

on 17th August 1909 reporting.

Mr Schmidt's report on arrangements made.

forwarding.

Sir,

1.   With reference to your despatch No. 325:

                Forwarding Aigun Customs Provisional Regulations together with instructions as to their enforcement from 1st August, 1909;

and my semi-official letters on the subject, I have the honour to place here on record that the Regulations were published as instructed and I beg to enclose herewith 10 copies of the printed Regulations in the English, Chinese and Russian languages.

2.   Simultaneously Mr A. Schmidt, (the then Acting) Deputy Commissioner, was supplied with a Memorandum of Instructions (copy enclosed) and directed to proceed to Aigun to initiate the work.   The Customs work was actually started at Aigun on the 17th August, 1909, and the arrangements made are fully described in Mr Schmidt's report, a copy of which I beg to enclose herewith.

3.   It will be seen from the report that the Barrier for controlling the trade between the 100-li Zone and the hinterland was established at Liangchiat'un (梁家屯), 40 li from Aigun, instead of Toukoutsu (陡沟子) as originally proposed in my despatch No.132, owing to the fact that no suitable accommodation was procurable at the latter place.

           A rough sketch showing the relative position of Aigun, Taheiho, Liangchiat'un, Blagovestchensk, etc., accompanies this despatch.

True copy:

2nd Assistant, A.

F. A. Aglen, Esquire,

Officiating Inspector General of Customs ad interim.

P E K I N G .

           I have the honour to be,

               Sir,

           Your obedient Servant,

           (signed) N. A. Konovaloff,

               Commissioner.

Enclosure to Harbin No. 503.

Sir,

    In accordance with your instructions I left Harbin on the 31st July for Aigun to inaugurate Customs work at that Trade Mart.

    On the 3rd August reached Sansing, visited the Customs, and found everything in fair working order.

    On the 4th August arrived at Lahasusu, where we stopped only one hour. Landed Mr Vylegjanin, and left instructions for Mr Semliansky to return to Harbin.

    At midnight on Monday, the 9th August, arrived at Aigun. On Tuesday morning visited Taotai, who returned my call the same afternoon. Was informed that on receipt of a telegram from the Harbin Taotai, a proclamation, regarding the opening of the Aigun Customs on 1st August, had been issued.

    On Wednesday at 3 a.m. started for Toukoutsu, accompanied by Messrs Grigorieff, Strehlneck, and Angleitner, on ponies kindly lent to us by the Taotai, to go once more over the ground and decide on a place for our Inland Barrier, returned the same evening at 11 p.m.

    Toukoutsu is 70 li from Aigun, in the middle of a forest which during the summer is simply alive with hsiameng and mosquitoes. The solitary mud house in existence here is occupied by 24 soldiers, leaving no accommodation for our staff. The nearest village being 30 li distant there is also great difficulty in obtaining provisions of any kind. For this and various other reasons shown hereafter I decided to establish our Inland Barrier at Liangchiat'un ( ), a village 40 li from Aigun, just at the foot of the steep mountain Pass, with the main road running right through the village.

    On Friday, the 13th August, proceeded to Taheiho to complete arrangements for starting work.   Work was commenced and the first duty collected on Tuesday, the 17th August.

TRADE: Aigun has practically no trade, and apparently foreigners are not wanted. The trade settlement being assigned a position where no vessel can get near it for want of deep water.

    With the exception of Live stock and grain, the trade of Taheiho consists practically of nothing but in articles eventually intended to be smuggled into Russia, such as Spirits, Tobacco, Russian Sugar,

Japanese

Japanese Piece Goods, etc., coming by steamer or overland from Harbin. Very little is consumed locally.

Up to the time of the opening of our office, the local Authorities charged duty at the rate of 7.2% ad valorem on nearly everything, except live stock on which the duty was 3.6%, from outside the 100 li Zone, even if covered by Harbin Customs documents showing the goods to have already paid 1½ duties, i.e. Native goods: Export and Coast Trade duties, foreign goods: Import duty and Transit Dues. On it being pointed out to the Taotai that such levy is now against the Regulations, it has been stopped on goods covered by Customs documents with the exception of Spirits and Tobacco on which the former duty is now collected as "Lo Ti Shui". An iron keg of Spirits having to pay Rbles 10.

In view of the above there appears to be no reason why the Coast Trade duty on goods from Sungari Trade Marts should not be collected (vide Aigun Reg. Art.7, Note), especially as this kind of trade is scarcely one to officially encouraged and could well bear this taxation which is not likely to be objected to.

Live Stock and Frozen Meat is almost entirely for consumption on the Russian side of the Amour - only a few sheep being consumed in the Aigun district - and must cross the river at Taheiho, so that but little can escape duty even if they pass our Inland Barrier by a round-about way.

Spirits: brought overland in large iron kegs, must be watched for at the Inland Barrier, as not all of it reaches Taheiho, there being other storing places- Sanchiatzu, etc.- on the road, where the spirits are filled into smaller receptacles for smuggling across to Russian. As these kegs are very heavy and unhandy, and the by-roads in bad condition very little is to be likely to be conveyed by any but the main road.

Foreign Goods coming overland have no reason to avoid our Barriers, having already paid duty elsewhere.

Grain, Eggs, Tobacco, etc., from the interior, though mostly going to Blagovestchensk

Blagovestchensk, must be carefully watched for. They are usually carried in light carts - Ta Ku Lu Erh Ch'e ◊ ◊ - which can pass almost anywhere, and once past the Barrier, it will be difficult to prove their origin, the same class of goods being also produced locally.

ROUTES: The main route from Tsitsihar to Heiho leads from Erh Chan, which is outside the 100 li Zone being 110 li from Aigun, across the mountain plateau via Toukoutzu to Liangchiat'un, from here across a swampy valley via Yehchiat'un to T'ou Chan, or Hai Kangtzu, and thence over an undulated plain via Sanchiatzu, Erhtaokou, Santaokou, Ssutaokou, SsuChiaTzu to Heiho. This main road is in fair condition and the shortest route.

Between Erh Chan and Toukoutzu, a road branches off eastward at Erhlung, via Naerhlung, Telomu, to Tou Chan.

Between Toukoutzu and Liangchiat'un, a road branches of westward to Haikoup'u, a village about 12 li westward of Liangchiat'un, right at the end of the swampy valley, which is closed in all around, except towards Aigun, by abruptly rising mountains.

During the summer these two last mentioned roads cannot be used, the ground near the foot of the hills being too swampy to be crossed, except by the main road; even on this, after heavy rain, it is often impossible for carts or live stock to cross the river at its shallowest ford at T'ou Chan.

During the winter, carts and live stock might possibly follow these diverging roads, in order to avoid our Barrier at Liangchiat'un, but the road is longer, in worse condition than the main road, villages demand a toll for the use of thier roads, and the local Authorities have their spies all over the country to catch anything, which might have escaped us, for payment of local taxation. Even if this local levy does not always reach the office entitled to it, the merchant is no better off, he is mulcted by someone and still runs the risk of being caught by our officers at Taheiho, so that they prefer following the main road and pay our comparatively light duty. Goods, except spirits and Tobacco, covered by our documents are exempt from local taxation.

At Taheiho the main road leads right down to the Ferry for Blagovestchensk

Blagovestchensk, passing the Chiao She Chü in which our office is situated, so that the traffic across the river can easily be controlle

    The only safe means of crossing the river is by the Ferry in the summer, and at the same place on the ice during the winter, crossing at other places is prohibited by the Russian Customs.

STAFF   With the exception of the Assistant, and one Officer at Taheiho for convenience in dealing with Russian merchants and vessels, there is no necessity for Russian speaking officers. Chinese speaking would be of more advantage, and in fact the Non-Russian Officers are treated with more respect.

    Aigun being the Trade Mart and therefore the Head Office, the Assistant in Charge and the Chinese Clerk must be stationed here. A foreign Out-door Officer should also be stationed here to attend to shipping and not to leave office without some foreign during the absence of the Assistant.

Liangchiat'un: One foreign officer and a Native Watcher, together with 4 soldiers, provided by the Taotai, are stationed here. The foreign Officer must be an intelligent man, if possible with some knowledge of Chinese, and value of goods, having to assess and collect duty.

Taheiho: At this the most important of the Aigun stations, the Senior Out-door Officer, Mr Examiner Strahlneck, and one foreign Tidewaiter, Mr Bluhm are stationed. Also one Native Watcher, who has sufficient knowledge of written characters to fill in Chinese documents when necessary, and one Tingch'ai.

    As both the river and the Inland routes have to be watched in summer and winter, another foreign Officer is required, to make the control effective.

    The Officer at Liangchiat'un should be relieved every few months, as it will be too heavy a strain for one man to be at such a place for too long a time.

    Two mounted Couriers, providing their own mounts, have been engaged at Rbles 18. per month, to maintain communication between the three offices, bring provisions, etc., there being at present no other means, the little steamer which used to run between Taheiho and Aigun being laid up.

WORK

WORK.   Liangchiat'un: Goods going inland will have to produce Duty Proof before being allowed to proceed.

    Dutiable Goods and Live stock from the interior are to be examined and experimentally dealt with as follows:

    Duty amounting to Tls.0.50 or less on any one consignment is for the present not to be collected.

    Live Stock: A Memo., giving particulars as to number, value, etc. is to be handed in closed cover to owner or his representative who must be told to present this Memo at the Aigun or Taheiho Office for payment of duty, and warned that failure to comply with this order will entail severe punishment and fine.

    Copy of the Memo should be forwarded to Aigun by first courier.

    Other Goods: If the duty does not exceed Tls.10., to be paid at Liangchiat'un; but if the duty exceeds Tls.10., or the owner cannot raise sufficient funds to pay, he is to be escorted to Aigun for payment of duty, unless he can find some satisfactory local guarantee, in which case the goods may be dealt with in the same manner as Live Stock.

    The above is temporary and experimental practice, in order to hamper the merchants as little as possible, and at the same time to avoid accumulation of large Revenue funds at Liangchiat'un which might only invite robbery.

Taheiho: Goods arriving from Inland or by water must be carefully checked and recorded. Unless proof can be produced that the duties due according to the Regulations have already been paid, this office will collect such duties before the goods are allowed to enter or cross the river.

    Goods going Inland, beyond the 100 li Zone, must pay their respective duties, the Receipt must be production at Liangchiat'un Barrier.

    Goods arriving from the Russian side of the Amour, not originating from the 100 li Zone, are liable to Import duty, even if for local consumption, such as Tinplates. Corks, etc., used in making receptacles for spirits.

    Passengers carrying small quantities should not be worried. There are practically no Exports by water, except what goes across the river by Ferry and a few Native boats carrying market produce.

Spirits

Spirits, Tobacco, etc., for up-river places, should pay Export duty, unless proof can be produced that duty has already been paid.

AIGUN: All correspondence with outside offices should be carried on from here. All Reports, Returns, Accounts, Records, etc, should be compiled at the Aigun Office, there being little else to do. The Assistant should make frequent visits to the Barriers to see that work is carried on properly, each such visit should be entered in the Occurrence Book.

ACCOMMODATION: AIGUN: The house hitherto occupied by Mr Bluth will suffice for office, and quarters for one or even two officers. In the same compound there are two other houses. One brick built, but Chinese type, with Kang, would do for the Chinese Clerk, Servants, etc.. The other, also brick built, can be made suitable for the Assistant and his family. The compound is excellently situated, near the river and the proposed landing stage, not far from the Taotai's Yamen. The rent at first demanded was Roubles 4500. for two years, but Aigun is not a rising place, rather the contrary, many houses, only built last year, are now standing empty and closed. An agreement was eventually arrived at, to lease the whole compound for a term of two years at Rbls 2500. in total; the owner bearing all expense of fitting up the place to suit our requirements.

LIANGCHIAT'UN: A Chinese house and compound have been rented for one year at Roubles 300+10 for doing up the place. The house has hitherto been used as an Inn, faces south and appears to be warm - a very important point in these cold regions. There are three rooms. One a large one, fitted with Kang on three sides, suitable for Native Watcher, Soldiers, etc.; one a smaller one, also fitted with Kang, suitable for the foreign officer; and the Kitchen in the middle separating the two other rooms.

The main road leads right past the front of the compound, so that control is comparatively easy.

TAHEIHO: Two rooms in the Chiao She Chü have been placed at our disposal. One living room and an office, but it is doubtful how long we may keep these, when the newly appointed Chih fu, Wu Wen-t'ai, arrives.

Under present conditions it is advisable that the Staff live at Taheiho, but without proper quarters it is difficult to have foreign food

food prepared. Houses are to be had, but rents demanded are exorbitant. The houses are mostly built for shops and would have to be altered internally to suit the requirements of foreigners. Until suitable and reasonable accommodation can be secured Rent Allowances will have to be issued. In fact, in my opinion, Rent Allowances would be more satisfactory to the Officers and less trouble to the Service.

There are two suitable houses to let; one brick-built house, not yet quite finished, in two parts; one blockhouse, in three parts.

The brick-built house is excellently situated, at the corner of the main road from inland to the ferry and the main street running next and parallel to the river, but is rather small for our requirements, i.e. Office and Quarters for the whole staff.

The blockhouse is a few hundred yards further up the main street, about the middle of the town as it stands at present, and would give ample room for all our requirements.

The position is likely to be a good one in the future, as the river is silting up below the town and the shipping will gradually have to go further up, about abreast of this house.

These houses were built for shops, simply 4 walls, windows, doors, and 1 stove for each part, but could easily be made suitable by partition walls. The rent asked for them as they now stand is: Brickhouse Rbls110. Blockhouse Rbls.135. per month; if internal fittings according to plan are made at owner's expense, Rbls. 1800 per annum is asked for the blockhouse provided a lease of two years is taken, and six months rent paid in advance.

GROUND SECURED: AIGUN: Two pieces of ground of which we can have the choice, have been reserved for our requirements. Each piece measures about 200 feet square. They are situated close to the river, one on each side of the main street running from the East City gate to the proposed Landing stage. There are at present no houses on the adjoining lots nor likely to be as Aigun is declining fast. The lot reserved on the north side of the street would be the most suitable, as the building could face south, towards the street, an important matter on account of the extreme winter cold.

TAHEIHO: Two small lots, but sufficient for our requirements as far as can be judged at present, have been reserved. They are alongside the River bank

bank to the right and left of the Chiao She Chü, which they adjoin.
An excellent position, whence the whole river can be overlooked, and
the main road from Inland also leads past it.

LIANGCHIAT'UN: There is no necessity of securing ground here, especially
in view of the possibility of the closing of the free zone, when this
station will be no longer needed.

BANK ARRANGEMENTS: All Revenue moneys will be paid into the Russo-Chinese Bank
as soon as possible, no sum exceeding Roubles 100 should be allowed to
accummulate at any of the stations. Once paid in no money can be
drawn from the Revenue Account, unless by authority of the Commissioner
of Customs, Harbin; whose signature should be forwarded as soon as
possible.

The Bank has agreed to pay 4% per annum on the daily Balance of
the Revenue Account; charges for Government Document Stamps on Receipts
for money paid in will be deducted from interest at the end of the year.

Having concluded all official business and everything working
smoothly, I left Taheiho, via Habarovsk and Pogranichnaya, on the 1st
September reaching Harbin on the 8th.

(signed) A. Schmidt,

Actg. Dep. Commissioner.

Custom House.
Harbin, 10th September, 1909.

True copy:

2nd Assistant, A.

No. 518.

AIGUN CUSTOMS: alleged irregularities
in the working of and inconvenience of
Barrier at, reporting.

I. G.

Sir,

Having reference to my despatch No. 503:
reporting arrangements made for starting
Customs work at Aigun:

I have the honour to say that shortly after the
Customs work began at Aigun, I received through the
Harbin Taotai copy of a complaint from the Aigun Taotai concerning an alleged irregualrities in levying
duty on some pigs brought from Tsitsihar. It was
my intention to look into the case during my intended
visit to Aigun in October 1909 which, however, had
to be given up owing to the threatening closing of
the river. The Aigun Office was therefore eventually
communicated with in writing, and from the enclosed
copy of Aigun despatch No. 23 it will be seen that
the Customs action was quite in order.

Another question arose later concerning the
functions of the Liangchiat'un Barrier. On the strength
of petitions received from the Aigun Ting (瑷珲廳)
and some local merchants, the Aigun Taotai requested
the Governor of Tsitsihar to issue instructions regarding the closing of the Barrier in order to remove
certain alleged inconveniences to merchants. I
enclose herewith copy of the Superintendent's despatch
on the subject. At my request the Superintendent
wired to the Governor to the effect that as the
existence of the Barrier is provided for by the Aigun
Customs Provisional Regulations, its removal required a
careful

F. A. Aglen, Esquire,
Officiating Inspector General ad interim.
PEKING.

careful consideration.   Mr Grigorieff, the Assistant
in Charge at Aigun, explained in his despatch No. 27
(copy enclosed) that the complaints made by the
merchants were baseless.   The Aigun Taotai Yao Fu-sheng
(姚梅卅) has shown himself from the very beginning
as friendly disposed to us and was apparently acting
on these occasions under the influence of one of the
local officials.   I have directed therefore Mr Grigorieff
to explain to him privately that any agitation for the
removal of the Barrier is unwise as likely to upset
the Aigun Customs arrangements generally and lead to
complications in the South.

    I took advantage of Mr Schmidt's visit to
Aigun in August last to have the two above questions
discussed with, and explained to, the Aigun Taotai who
eventually agreed to withdraw his former accusations
officially through the same channels and I have in due
course received a despatch from the Superintendent to
that effect: it will be seen from the enclosed copy
of it that the two questions may be considered as
closed.

        I have the honour to be,
           Sir,
           Your obedient Servant,
           (signed) N. A. Konovaloff,
               Commissioner.

True copy:

2nd Assistant, A.

ENCLOSURES;   copy of Aigun Despatch No. 23 of 23rd October,
           and copy of Aigun Despatch No. 27 of 29th
           November, 1909 to Harbin not forwarded.

Copy
  868
  I. G.

Revenue: Collection and Remittance of at Aigun: Special
"Aigun Customs Duties A/C" opened at Harbin, reporting
Interest accrued for 1911, query to disposal of.

          2nd November, 1912.

Sir,

1.   Having reference to your Despatch
No. 905/42,809 (in reply to Harbin Despatch No. 842
to I. G.):
      Revenue: Collection and Remittance of at
Aigun. Present system may be continued
if Aigun Revenue Moneys are kept in
separate Bank account,

I have the honour to report that I have to day
opened a special "Aigun Customs Duties Account"
with the Russo-Asiatic Bank here into which
I have paid the sum of Roubles 87,468.45.
Of this amount Roubles 84,356.73 represent
Revenue collected, while the remaining
Roubles 3,111.72 is interest for 1911 on the
Aigun Revenue Account lodged with
the Russo-Asiatic Bank at Blagoveschensk.
The Aigun Revenue Account now stands as
follows:-
  In Bank at Blagoveschensk: Rbls. 164,672.04
  In Bank at Harbin   : Rbls 87,468.45
  Total Collection at Aigun
  from opening of Office up} Rbls. 252,140.49
  to 30th September, 1912 }

2.   In regard to the question of
Roubles 3,111.72 being interest for 1911 accruing
on Revenue held by the Bank at Blagoveschensk,
               Your

The Inspector General of Customs.
Peking.

your Despatch No.817 authorises interest accruing on moneys held by the Harbin Branch of the Russo-Asiatic Bank, and due to the date of I.G. Assumption of control of Revenue, to be handed over to the Superintendent. Am I to apply this authority to interest accruing at the Blagovestchensk Bank on Aigun moneys?

I have the honour to be,
Sir,
Your obedient Servant,
(Signed) W.C.H. Watson
Commissioner.

True copy:

2nd Assistant, A.

COMMISSIONER'S TOUR OF INSPECTION to Sansing,
Lahasusu and Aigun; Report on ; forwarding.

1333.

I.G.

Rec. Reg. A. Cu.
15 JUN 1923

Harbin, 29th June, 1915.

Sir,

I have the honour to submit the following report on my tour of inspection of the Customs establishments on the Sungari and Amur rivers.

On the morning of the 6th June I left Harbin in the Customs motor-launch "Heilung" accompanied by Mr. Harbour Master Steinacher, who took charge of the launch, and Mr. Assistant Myers, who came with me in the capacity of Russian Secretary as Mr. Ohrnberger had to stay in Harbin to attend to the Russian correspondence. We anchored at night from 9 p.m. to 3 a.m. and on the
morning

The Inspector General of Customs,

PEKING.

morning of the 7th visited the quarters of
the Aids Officers who during the winter
superintend the work of removing stones and
rocks which endanger the navigation in the
channels over the shallows. These quarters,
which consist of log cabins, were built at
the recommendation of the late Commissioner,
Mr. Watson, and afford comfortable accommodation.

Sansing was reached on the 7th June
at 1.45 p.m.. I inspected the Customs station
which now under the charge of Mr. Assistant
Mansfield, and as far as the work is
concerned I found everything in a satisfactory
condition. I also visited the Customs barrier
which controls the native craft on the
Mutanchiang (牡 丹 江). The work there - a
responsible one - is carried out from a Barge,
placed yearly in position at the opening of
the river by Mr. Tidewaiter Sidortchook, who
struck me as a very intelligent Officer well
acquainted with the duties he has to perform.
The quarters at Sansing were in bad need of

repairs.

repairs. I went carefully over them with the
Assistant in charge and the Tidesurveyor, and
drew up an estimate of repairs which was
submitted to you in my Despatch No. 1326.

Most of the Sansing Revenue is
collected on Beans and Grain which are
exported to the Primorsk District and thence
to Europe. Our collection there steadily
increases and we are faced with the difficulty
of transferring to the Head Office comparatively
large amounts, e.g., the Assistant had more
than Roubles 10,000 in his safe at the time
I passed through. Means of remitting to
Harbin either by Bank or by Post do not
exist, and I have devised means to have the
collection sent to Harbin in small instalments -
Roubles 1,000 to 2,000 - through River-steamer
Captains who are well known to the Customs.
This solution, though not entirely satisfactory,
is still infinitely better than to allow the
present state of affairs to go on. On the
day following my arrival I called upon the

Taoyin

Taoyin who is a territorial official and has consequently very little to do with Customs matters. The Prefect was absent so that I was unable to see him. Both these officials are, I am glad to say, on the best possible terms with Mr. Mansfield. The third day was spent in inspecting the Sansing Shallows, and I left Sansing on the 10th June to arrive at

Lahasusu on the afternoon of the 11th. I found everything in order at this station, which is under the charge of Mr. Assistant Baranoffsky, and the work being carried out satisfactorily. The quarters are in tolerably good repair, and while on the spot I sanctioned a few alterations which will add to the comfort of the Staff. Here as at Sansing the Revenue is mostly derived from Beans and grain and the collection to date shows a considerable increase over the previous years. Revenue moneys were accumulating in the safe - with no means whatever of transferring

them

them to the Head Office - and I authorized the Assistant in charge, whenever necessary, to remit them to Harbin through the Russian Post Office at Mihailo-Semenovsk, which is situated on the Amur 30 versts from Lahasusu. The journey to Mihailo-Semenovsk is done by steamer and occupies 2 hours on the way down and 3 on the way back. Of course the Assistant will have to carry the money himself but there is no way out of it and I consider this arrangement the best that could be made under existing conditions.

Besides the main branch of the Sungari there is, a few versts above Lahasusu, a channel of the river also communicating with the Amur, which the native junks not infrequently use as a short cut, thus avoiding our Customs station. To obviate this two Customs boatmen are stationed during the summer months at the entrance of the channel to control the junk traffic. This, however, does not seem to give satisfactory results and Mr. Baranoffsky

suggested

suggested having one Tidewaiter stationed there
who, with the assistance of the two boatmen,
would exercise a more efficient control. This
suggestion is one which deserves consideration
and your sanction may subsequently be solicited
but in the present circumstances, i.e., with the
difficulty of procuring Outdoor Staff Officers
and the possibility of some of our Russian
employés being called to the colours, it is
preferable, in my opinion, not to make any
change just now.   There being no
possibility to take the Customs launch into
the Amur, I had booked at Harbin berths for
Blagovestchensk on one of the Sungari steamers
which was scheduled to arrive at Lahasusu on
the evening of the 12th. The steamer, however,
was delayed as I heard on my arrival at
Lahasusu, and, having had the Russian Customs
motor-launch gracefully placed at my disposal,
I decided to proceed to Mihailo-Semenovsk in
order to catch there one of the Russian
mail-steamers which ply between Habarovsk and
                              Blagovestchensk.

Blagovestchensk. I therefore left Lahasusu on
the morning of the 12th June.
Taheiho (Aigun). I arrived there on the
morning of the 16th. My intention was to
stay in Blagovestchensk, and from Lahasusu I
had wired to Mr. Barentzen, the Assistant in
charge, to that effect. On my arrival, however,
I found that this arrangement would cause a
great deal of inconvenience and waste of time
as the ferry communications between
Blagovestchensk and Taheiho are very uncertain
during the day and completely non-existent
after 6 p.m.. I therefore put up with Mr.
Barentzen who had prepared rooms for that
purpose. The first day was employed in
inspecting the Custom House where I found
everything in order, the work, as far as I
could see, being carried on smoothly and
satisfactorily. The staff, with the exception
of the Senior Outdoor Officer, all live in
rented quarters, and the Custom House is
similarly in rented premises pending erection
of the new buildings sanctioned in your
                              Despatch

Despatch No.1194/S1,774 of 17th April, 1914.

Before we begin, however, we shall have to wait for more opportune times. Materials, since the estimate was submitted to you, have considerably increased in value, and it is very doubtful whether a contractor could be found who would undertake to do the job within the limits of our estimate. I convinced myself that the offices at present in use were adequate and the Outdoor Staff sufficiently well housed and there is, therefore, no special objection to postponing the construction of the new buildings say for another year or even later as the course of events may demand. The Assistant in charge also can wait. he now occupies a flat for which the Service pays a yearly rent of Rbls.1,200. It is roomy, well situated and at 5 minutes walk from the Custom House, and with some additional furniture, for the purchase of which I eventually propose to request your sanction. he will be housed in very comfortable quarters.

The

The whole of my second day was spent in visiting Aigun and Liangchiat'un （梁家屯） barrier. This inspection - periodically done by the Assistant in charge - generally takes two days. I did it in a motor car in one day. Of Aigun there is nothing to say, all its trade has gone to Taheiho and whatever work there is is done by a Tidewaiter who lives in an old ramshackle building - styled the Custom House - for which we pay a yearly rent of Rbls.800.00. The building scheme provides for the construction of a Custom House at a cost of Rbls.4,500. Though I cannot yet express a definite opinion, I am rather inclined, from what I have seen, to think that such an outlay is hardly warranted, but this question is out of place in this report and will be laid before you in due course. Liangchiat'un offers much more interest than Aigun. It is the Customs barrier which controls all the land trade between Hailar-Tsitsihar and Blagoveshchensk and the

Primorsk

Primorsk District. This route is chiefly used
during the winter months when the navigation
is closed and large herds of cattle come this
way from the Hailar region. The country round
Liangchiat'un is hilly and picturesque, but the
Tidewaiter stationed there has to lead a very
isolated life under particularly severe
conditions. The house accommodation is very
poor and primitive to the extreme and all
comforts of life utterly missing. I fail,
however, to see how these present conditions
can be improved, and we have to jog along as
best as we can.   My third day at
Tahoiho was employed in making official visits
in Blagovestchensk - the Taoyin was away on
business - and I successively called upon the
Chief of the Russian Customs, the Russian
Frontier Commissioner, and the General in
command of Blagovestchensk, who is also the
Attaman of the Cossacks. Everywhere I was most
cordially received and - and this is more to
the point - I had the impression that the

                                Chinese

Chinese Maritime Customs bore a very good
name among the Russian Officials, and that
their representative, the Assistant in charge,
was, on the best terms with all of them.
It was my intention to return via Habarovsk-
Nikolsk-Ussurisk and Suifenho, but there being
no berths available for several days on the
Amur steamer, I decided to return by the
Sungari. I left Blagovestchensk on the
afternoon of the 18th June arriving at Harbin
at 8.45 p.m. on the 23rd - a very quick journey.
Hsin Tien (新 甸) and Chiamussu Barriers:
The object of these barriers - as reported in
my predecessor's Despatch No.1152 of June,
1914 - is to supervise the shipping of cargo,
chiefly grain - destined to the Amur District
and Nikolaevsk, and to issue documents
addressed to the Assistant at Sansing or
Lahasusu, as the case might be, where export
duty is levied. The two barriers were to be
opened in 1914, but their establishment was
postponed to the spring of 1915 (I.G. No.1854/

                                53,472

33,472 of 25th August, 1914). During my trip I did not fail to visit these localities and I fully realized their importance from a Customs standpoint. In view, however, of prevailing conditions and the possibility of having, at any time, part of our staff called out to join the colours, I consider that the opening of these barriers is, at least for the present, altogether out of question and must be postponed sine die.

Aids to Navigation on the Sungari:

Accompanied by Mr. Steinacker I visited the Sansing Shallows and found the Aids all in regular position and well maintained by Mr. Eglit who is in charge of that section. The river being then very high the conditions were naturally more favourable to the navigation and the work not so arduous and responsible as is the case at low water when channels are varying and beacons have to be continually shifted. Nevertheless I could convince myself that the Aids were a great help to Navigation even

even at high water when river banks and various islands are submerged. Generally speaking the Aids Department is in a good state of efficiency, and it is only to be regretted that its budget, which is met by the River Dues, does not allow of more development in the lighting of the river.

Plague Prevention Service:

In my capacity of Lay Director of that Service, I visited the Sansing, Lahasusu and Taheiho hospitals and found all the buildings in good condition and well kept but, with the exception of Taheiho, the services of the Doctors attached to them are hardly ever availed of by the natives who prefer to consult the practitioners of the old school.

General Remarks:

After what I have seen during my trip and without attempting to prophecy, I am inclined to think that Sansing and Lahasusu, as revenue collecting centres, will show considerable development in the near future, situated as they

they are in a District where grain and beans
are produced in ever increasing quantities.
The same cannot be said of Taheiho which, in
my opinion, has attained its zenith and owes
its mushroom-like growth to the salt and
spirit smugglers who, owing to its proximity
to Blagovestchensk, have chosen this locality
as their head quaters. The town is full of
gambling saloons and houses of evil repute,
it reeks of vice and there is very little
evidence of legitimate trade.

          I have the honour to be,

              Sir,

          Your obedient Servant,

          (Signed) P. Grevelon.

             Commissioner.

True Copy:

Chief Asst. Sp. List.

呈总税务司署 61 号文 　　　　　　　　哈尔滨关 1908 年 5 月 8 日

尊敬的海关总税务司（北京）：

1. 续哈尔滨关致总税务司署第 60 号呈：

"汇报为松花江沿岸贸易设立海关事。"

谨照总税务司署第 110 号令指示汇报于瑷珲及齐齐哈尔两地设立分关事。

2. 冬季道路结冰后，齐齐哈尔—墨尔根—瑷珲贸易路线仍有货物运输往来；其中，除有少量货物运至沿途小镇外，大部分货物（包括洋货和土货）均运往北方的布拉戈维申斯克（Blagovestchensk）①。当地对外部货物的依赖极大，但可以出口之货物却寥寥无几。在满洲里分关和绥芬河分关设立之前，凡洋货经由墨尔根及瑷珲运往布拉戈维申斯克者，均须按值百抽五之税率向齐齐哈尔政府缴税，此后沿途则免税通行。哈尔滨关华俄代表已就此等货物的征税问题进行了讨论，俄代表认为应将之视为转运货物免税放行，而华代表则指出《1881 年陆路通商章程》第十二条曾规定，"凡洋货自天津经由张家口（Kalgan）及乌兰巴托（Ourga）②运往恰克图（Kiachta）者，均须缴税"。据此海关便有理由向经由墨尔根及瑷珲运往布拉戈维申斯克的洋货征税。然因该问题乃为黑龙江巡抚与俄国领事协商之事，哈尔滨关便就此作罢，不再继续讨论。

满洲里分关开始征税后，自俄国而来之货物便可于此完纳进口税，无须再按值百抽五之税率向齐齐哈尔政府缴税，而商人为免税通行至瑷珲亦愿于此缴纳子口半税，满洲里分关通常会为之发放运照以作凭证。由此可见，俄货或其他洋货经由瑷珲运往布拉戈维申斯克者，如已照条约规定完纳税款（包括内陆税），则无须再次缴税。另外，按照条约规定，洋货经由瑷珲复出口时，有权要求退还已纳进口税，因此对于此类洋货，只要货主按照条约规定提出退税请求，于瑷珲所设分关的职能便只有退税，并无征税。

3. 凡土货经由齐齐哈尔—墨尔根—瑷珲路线运输者，亦须按照值百抽五的税率向齐齐哈尔政府缴纳税款，沿途可能还需缴税。海关如于齐齐哈尔设立税关，似乎最多亦只能按照值百抽五之税率进行征税，而完税货物亦有权索要满洲免重征执照前往瑷珲，因此，对于此类土货，于瑷珲所设分关亦无法征税。

---

① Blagovestchensk 现在一般翻译为布拉戈维申斯克，原件中中文写作"布拉郭威臣斯克"，还有另一个非常有名的中文名"海兰泡"。为便于读者理解，本书翻译中此地名译为布拉戈维申斯克。

② 乌兰巴托始建于清朝崇德四年（1639 年），时称"敖尔告"（Ourga 之俄语拼写），据原文所述，Ourga 为天津至恰克图贸易途经之地，而乌兰巴托恰于该路线之上，地理位置与读音均相符，故有此译。

4. 而且,实际上几乎没有俄货自布拉戈维申斯克进口至满洲,因此于瑷珲和齐齐哈尔设立分关后,亦可能无税可征。

5. 夏季,齐齐哈尔—墨尔根—瑷珲路线的路况极差,漫长难行,货物运输成本过高,相比之下,货物经由松花江和黑龙江以轮船运输的时间更短,成本更低,如此一来,商人又怎会选择陆路运输呢?

6. 综上,兹认为,就税收而言,实无于齐齐哈尔和瑷珲两地设立分关之必要,而且在货物运输方面,该两地与满洲其他地区相比并无任何优势。此外,海关于瑷珲设立分关后,俄商冬季应缴纳之税款将比现在更少,俄国政府亦会要求俄货经由此处时与其他洋货一样享有条约规定之待遇。在此事有所定论之前,兹建议,凡洋货或土货自满洲里分关、哈尔滨江关或绥芬河分关完税经由瑷珲运往布拉戈维申斯克者,均照总税务司署第 1472 号通令由完税海关发给免重征执照。

7. 当然,贵署或有疑问,瑷珲既为黑龙江沿线的通商之地,为何于此设立的海关不可监管江上的往来贸易及船运?诚然,黑龙江乃为"国际河流",与其他相似河流〔如多瑙河(Danube)〕一样须遵循特有之惯例,海关若要于此地有所行动,中俄双方必须率先达成共识。另一方面,华俄委员会不日将着手拟订黑龙江行船章程,以防止出现轮船碰撞等事故的发生,但是否会达到"传统国际河流制度"的标准,尚不确定。目前,静待协商结果或许是最佳选择。另鉴于 1881 年《陆路通商章程》[①]中有 50 俄里边境免税区之规定,而瑷珲恰位于免税区之中心,且目前亦只是无关紧要的小村庄,因此海关不宜立即于此设立分关。

8. 但如由于政治方面的原因,须于瑷珲设立分关,亦非难事。可先派遣一名华籍帮办或供事前往瑷珲考察,另择一名通晓汉文与俄文的钤子手与之同行,待其汇报考察结果后,再做打算。若决定派遣海关关员前往瑷珲,则需事先请瑷珲当局为关员准备临时办公场所及宿舍。

9. 至于齐齐哈尔,除在齐齐哈尔—墨尔根—瑷珲—布拉戈维申斯克这一冬季贸易路线的作用外,其地位与海拉尔、吉林、宽城子、辽阳、奉天等地一般,只需设立一个较小的分关即可,但与如海拉尔此等因羊毛皮及其他蒙古产品而吸引大批俄商前来采买出口的分关相比,其规模甚至应该更小。因此,建议暂缓于齐齐哈尔设立卜奎关(Pukuei Kuan)[②]一事,

---

① 即 1881 年 2 月 24 日签订的中俄《改订陆路通商章程》。见王铁崖编:《中外旧约章汇编》第一册。
② 卜奎为达斡尔语"勇士"之音译,本为达斡尔族头领名字,后成为地名,之后又改称齐齐哈尔。

日后查有必要时,再行商议。

    10. 随呈附上此呈汉文版本,一式两份。

您忠诚的仆人

（签名）葛诺发（N. A. Konovaloff）

哈尔滨关税务司

该抄件内容真实有效,特此证明。

录事：周骊（C. H. B. Joly）二等帮办前班

呈总税务司署 101 号文   哈尔滨关 1908 年 8 月 20 日

尊敬的海关署总税务司（北京）：

1. 总税务司署致哈尔滨关第 142 号令收悉：

"传达税务处指令，在瑷珲设立一关作为哈尔滨关分关。"

兹汇报，海关监督已应本署请求向瑷珲副都统发送电报，询问是否可为海关提供办公室及宿舍。瑷珲副都统于本月 11 日电报回复本署，称已命令属下租赁三间房作为海关办公之用。因此本署已命署副税务司式美第（Schmidt）先生乘轮船前往瑷珲，对当地情况进行初步考察。途中式美第先生将在拉哈苏苏分关停靠并视察该分关工作。待考察设立瑷珲分关情况完毕后，式美第先生将由陆路返回哈尔滨，沿途经过墨尔根和齐齐哈尔，了解当地贸易情况。

2. 今晨，式美第先生与试用铃子手布卢穆（W.I.Bluhm）先生及一名听差一同出发（此二人是本署目前唯一可指派的关员）。三人抵达瑷珲后，便可开始筹备征税工作，瑷珲分关亦可算基本落成。若有必要，布卢穆先生可留在瑷珲分关任职。

3. 兹附哈尔滨关致瑷珲分关第 1 号令抄件，从中可见本署向式美第先生所下达之指示。

您忠诚的仆人

（签名）葛诺发（N. A. Konovaloff）

哈尔滨关税务司

该抄件内容真实有效，特此证明。

录事：周骊（C.H.B.Joly）二等帮办前班

呈总税务司署 <u>126</u> 号文　　　　　　　哈尔滨关 1908 年 9 月 27 日

尊敬的海关署总税务司（北京）：

根据哈尔滨关致总税务司署第 101 号呈：

"汇报式美第（Schmidt）先生前往瑷珲考察于当地开设分关一事；随呈附上哈尔滨关致瑷珲分关第 1 号令。"

兹汇报，本署于 6 月收到海关监督函件，函中随附黑龙江巡抚和东三省总督关于布拉戈维申斯克（Blagovestchensk）往来货物的征税办法及 100 里免税区相关事宜之公文。现遵照 9 月 3 日管理汉文文案税务司第 274 号通函指示，附上海关监督函件抄件。然因黑龙江巡抚和东三省总督之公文原件已由式美第先生携带前往瑷珲，故唯有待其返回后方可将该公文抄录。

您忠诚的仆人

（签名）葛诺发（N. A. Konovaloff）

哈尔滨关税务司

该抄件内容真实有效，特此证明。

录事：周骊（C.H.B.Joly）二等帮办前班

呈总税务司署 <u>132</u> 号文　　　　　　　　哈尔滨关 1908 年 11 月 11 日

尊敬的海关署总税务司（北京）：

1. 根据总税务司署第 142 号令：

"为于瑷珲设立海关分关事。"

及哈尔滨关第 101 号呈：

"汇报署副税务司式美第（A. Schmidt）先生前往瑷珲筹备设立瑷珲分关事。"

兹呈交式美第先生关于沿松花江前往拉哈苏苏、沿黑龙江前往瑷珲和布拉戈维申斯克（Blagovestchensk）及沿墨尔根和齐齐哈尔陆路路线返回哈尔滨的巡查报告抄件,关于新甸、拉哈苏苏、瑷珲及布拉戈维申斯克等地以及松花江航运及现有航路标志的考察报告抄件,以及关于邮政局于瑷珲拓展业务事的意见报告抄件。兹附汉文版满洲地图一份,该地图改自俄文版,为阐明报告,地名等均采用音译,内容亦有所增补。

2. 鉴于式美第先生此行的主要目的是考察瑷珲地区是否有必要设立分关,故此提议,此次仅处理于瑷珲设立分关一事,至于松花江航运管理事宜,稍后再议。

3. 哈尔滨关第 61 号呈（为于瑷珲及齐齐哈尔设立海关分关事）中曾指出瑷珲地区可征之税寥寥,且当地往来贸易已有相应征税办法,这与式美第先生此次考察结果一致。

4. 以目前情况来看,于瑷珲开展海关工作应非难事：当地已有可满足海关办公及关员住宿之需的房屋；基本办公设施业已置办妥当；一名钤子手已留在瑷珲负责照看关产、考察当地实际情况等事,还可协助今后委派至瑷珲的关员开展工作。兹认为,本署及本关关员可为瑷珲分关日后可能会遇到的问题做好充分准备,凡将要派至瑷珲分关的关员均可提前于哈尔滨关接受充分的指导,以便对瑷珲地区有一些初步的了解,也可从式美第先生的报告中了解与瑷珲有关的必要信息,必要时还可由式美第先生亲自讲解。

5. 然在着手起草瑷珲分关相关章程之前,对于瑷珲的地理位置及相关条约条款,本署还有一些问题需提请贵署斟酌考虑。

6. 虽然 1881 年《陆路通商章程》（第 1 条）关于中俄边境 50 俄里（100 里）免税区之规定起初只是针对中国与蒙古之间的贸易,但不知黑龙江流域边境贸易是否适用此条款,跨江贸易是否可等同于"陆路贸易"。此事还需由北京方面裁决,如此海关起草章程时方有据可依。

1860 年《中俄北京（续增）条约》第一条对 1858 年《瑷珲条约》第一条加以确认说明：

"此后两国东界定为由石勒喀河、额尔古纳河两河交汇处,即顺黑龙江下游至该江与乌苏里江交汇处。黑龙江北边地属俄罗斯国，南边地属中国……"

1860 年《中俄北京（续增）条约》第四条规定：

"此约第一条所定交界各处，准许两国所属之人随便交易，并不纳税……"

1862 年、1869 年和 1881 年的《陆路通商章程》第 1 条都重申了边境免税区之规定，以此推断，瑷珲与布拉戈维申斯克（Blagovestchensk）之间的贸易亦应适用于该规定。如果总税务司及税务处对此表示认同，那么瑷珲分关或可采用下述征税办法。

7. 瑷珲分关的征税对象大致可分为两至三类，即：

（1）轮船货物贸易（1）及跨江对俄贸易（2）；

（2）与内陆地区的陆路贸易（3）。

各项贸易具体征税办法如下。

8. 轮船货物贸易及跨江贸易

（1）如今瑷珲口岸过往轮船数量甚少，前往黑龙江下游的轮船几乎不会在此停留。依照条约规定，黑龙江只对中俄两国轮船开放航运，但迄今为止尚未有华籍轮船在江上航行。去年中俄两国已成立中俄委员会，准备起草一套供两国轮船遵守的章程，然该委员会双方至今仍未会面，章程所涉事项亦难以预测。俄国政府已于黑龙江俄岸沿线安设灯桩等照明设施，但并未因此而对往来船只征收费用。兹建议，瑷珲分关照俄国现行办法对经由瑷珲分关的轮船免征船钞。若征收船钞，轮船必会绕过瑷珲行驶，免征可鼓舞轮船频繁往来此地。而且，目前黑龙江上往来的华籍船只数量较少，无论怎样，海关可征的船钞数额均不会太大，无法满足航路维护的费用所需。兹建议，待往来船只数量增加后再考虑对其征收税率较低的船钞。如此一来，海关对轮船的管控便仅限于核查上下货物和防止运输违禁物品。

（2）据 1881 年《陆路通商章程》第 1 条规定，凡货物自布拉戈维申斯克及黑龙江俄岸其他各地进口至瑷珲或黑龙江华岸 100 里免税区以内各地者，免征进口正税。

（3）凡货物自布拉戈维申斯克及黑龙江俄岸其他各地进口至黑龙江华岸 100 里免税区以外各地者，缴纳进口正税，并由海关发给：

① 完税收据（未申明运输终点者）；

② 特别免重征执照（参阅总税务司署第 1441 号、1472 号、1499 号及 1544 号通令）（申明前往任一满洲贸易市场者）。

（4）凡洋货在瑷珲分关完纳进口税者，运往内地时：

① 或于沿途关卡缴纳内陆税；

② 或于瑷珲分关缴纳子口半税,并由瑷珲分关发给运照;持此运照可在内陆地区的运输途中免缴内陆税款。

（5）凡洋货自黑龙江华岸或松花江沿岸各地进口者,均照自布拉戈维申斯克进口之洋货的征税办法办理,即,即使未持有免重征执照或特别免重征执照:

① 若运至 100 里免税区内,则免征税;

② 若运至 100 里免税区外,则须缴税。

（6）凡土货自黑龙江华岸或松花江沿岸各地进口者:

① 若持有任一中国海关签发的特别免重征执照,则免征税;

② 若持有任一中国海关签发的收税单,则须缴纳土货复进口半税;

③ 若无上述文件,则须缴纳进口正税;

④ 若最终复出口国外且已完纳土货复进口半税,则予以退税。

注: 鉴于洋商可能会依据 1881 年《陆路通商章程》第 1 条之规定,要求允许其货物免税过关,因此瑷珲分关最好平等对待土货和洋货,放弃对运往 100 里免税区以内各地之土货征收进口正税或土货复进口半税,以免土货货主会因受到不公平对待而选择通过布拉戈维申斯克运输,对贸易造成不必要的负担。

（7）依照免税区之规定,凡土货自瑷珲地区出口至布拉戈维申斯克及俄国其他地区者,免征税。

（8）凡土货出口至黑龙江华岸或松花江沿岸各地者,均须缴纳出口正税,并由瑷珲分关发给收税单。

注:（6）项所注对土货免税之规定也适用于（8）项所列货物。

9. 与内陆地区的陆路贸易

瑷珲地区货物进口相关事宜已基本汇报完毕,本段主要涉及瑷珲当地土货出口相关事宜。瑷珲本身贸易市场很小,所以瑷珲分关需要管控的出口事务将主要为经瑷珲转运至布拉戈维申斯克的大量土货。其中,生牛出口量最大,亦较难管控。但瑷珲分关所征税率并不高,若可为家畜签发运照,牛商应会愿意自瑷珲分关出口。另可于陡沟子或免税区外某处设立"最后一道分卡",并照惯例对出口至黑龙江俄岸各地的土货收取三倍应纳税款作为押金,以确保瑷珲分关可如数征收子口半税及出口正税,且因该项收费属于跨区域征税,故与免税区相关条款不发生冲突。最后,实际过江出口之货物还须通过大黑河分卡的查验。凡生牛自南部运至陡沟子且未持有运照者,均须于陡沟子或经特殊安排至瑷珲分关缴纳进口正税;虽然根据免税区条款规定,生牛出口至布拉戈维申斯克时,须免征税,但因凡生牛未持有运照者,均已于运抵陡沟子或瑷珲之前缴纳内陆税,故该项免税不会有任何不公之处。其他运输途径相似的货物数量不多,均可照上述办法征税。

10. 另外,自满洲里分关或绥芬河分关进口（最终运至哈尔滨关）,再经齐齐哈尔和墨尔根运至布拉戈维申斯克的货物亦将成为瑷珲分关未来数年间的主要管控对象。但商人仅会于冬季轮船无法通行至布拉戈维申斯克时选择该运输路线,且待阿穆尔铁路（Amour Railway）建成后,此路线亦将废止。经此路线运输的货物,将由北满洲其他海关发给特别免重征执照,瑷珲分关仅于执照上盖章确认。凡货物申报复出口至布拉戈维申斯克者,大黑河分卡均会核实数目并发给执照,货主可凭此执照申请退还此前于始运口岸所纳进口正税。

11. 上述各项乃据1881年《陆路通商章程》（第1条）及通商口岸和贸易市场通用贸易章程为瑷珲分关所拟之临时试用征税办法。若免税区条款出现变动,该征税办法亦将做出相应调整,但届时应以普通通商口岸的征税办法为准绳,即对进口货物征收进口正税,对出口货物征收出口正税,对复进口土货征收土货复进口半税,对内陆过境特权货物征收子口半税,签发执照等,然具体细节暂无探究之必要。同时,建议免征船钞。

12. 俄阿穆尔州关闭免税港之举目前对瑷珲可能比较有利,但未来之影响实难预测。式美第先生在报告中指出,瑷珲虽早于20世纪之前便是有贸易往来的商埠之地,且与布拉戈维申斯克有密切的贸易往来,但如今与布拉戈维申斯克隔江相望的大黑河私人商铺贸易活跃,不知瑷珲是否会因此而受到影响。

13. 有鉴于此,建议在海关获取更多经验,对贸易发展趋势有更多了解之前,暂于瑷珲设立流动分关,将瑷珲副都统所提供之房屋作为瑷珲分关办公楼,另于大黑河（真正与布拉戈维申斯克开展贸易之地）、陡沟子或其他便于管控100里免税区往来贸易之地,或者某城门处设立分卡。此外,鉴于瑷珲分关乃是出于政治需要而设,如有必要,或可请黑龙江衙署于上述地区为海关提供住宿及办公场所。

14. 关于总税务司署第142号令中所提建立邮政通信事,式美第先生已完成相关调查,并将其对此事之意见呈给满洲邮政局总办及满洲邮政司。

15. 待贵署下达瑷珲分关征税办法的最终指示后,本署将对人员及供给等事做出进一步安排。

16. "AIGUN"为瑷珲的旧有名称,与汉字"瑷珲"罗马化后的单词"Aihun"相比,在海关总税务司令文和通令中使用得更加频繁,因此建议瑷珲分关税务司印章上的英文采用"AIGUN"字样,汉文采用"瑷珲分关税务司印"字样,并与哈尔滨关、满洲里分关及绥芬河

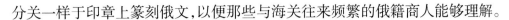

分关一样于印章上篆刻俄文，以便那些与海关往来频繁的俄籍商人能够理解。

17. 最后建议将于瑷珲设立海关分关一事告知俄国公使，以避免与俄方签订的条约发生冲突，避免出现设立满洲里分关和绥芬河分关时所遇到的问题。

您忠诚的仆人

葛诺发（N. A. Konovaloff）

哈尔滨关税务司

该抄件内容真实有效，特此证明。

录事：周骊（C. H. B. Joly）二等帮办前班

呈总税务司署 <u>503</u> 号文　　　　　　　　　　**哈尔滨关 1910 年 10 月 19 日**

尊敬的海关代理总税务司（北京）：

1. 根据总税务司署第 325 号令：

"发送《瑷珲分关临时章程》；请于 1909 年 8 月 1 日起实施；附相关指令。"

及哈尔滨关相关半官函：

特此汇报，已照指令颁布《瑷珲分关临时章程》，现附上 10 份英文、汉文及俄文版《瑷珲分关临时章程》抄件。

2. 已命哈尔滨关署副税务司式美第（A. Schmidt）先生前往瑷珲开展海关工作。瑷珲分关的工作实际上自 1909 年 8 月 17 日起便已启动，相关工作安排已在式美第先生的报告中详细阐明，报告抄件已随呈附上。

3. 本署曾建议于陡沟子设立一处内陆分卡以管控 100 里免税区内往来的货物运输（参阅哈尔滨关第 132 号呈），但因此地并无合适的办公及住宿场所，故而将分卡设在了距离瑷珲分关 40 里处的梁家屯（参阅式美第先生的报告）。

现随呈附上标明瑷珲分关、大黑河、梁家屯分卡及布拉戈维申斯克等地的位置草图。

您忠诚的仆人

葛诺发（N. A. Konovaloff）

哈尔滨关税务司

该抄件内容真实有效，特此证明。

录事：周骊（C. H. B. Joly）二等帮办前班

哈尔滨关致总税务司署第 503 号呈附件

尊敬的哈尔滨关税务司：

此前奉税务司命于 7 月 31 日启程前往瑷珲开展分关建设工作；途中于 8 月 3 日抵达三姓，查该处分关运转良好；又于 8 月 4 日抵达拉哈苏苏，但仅停留一个小时，并将瓦立仁（I. Y. Vylegjanin）先生留于该分卡任职，另命岑良吉（A. Zemliansky）先生返回哈尔滨关；最终于 8 月 9 日（星期一）抵达瑷珲，并于次日上午拜访瑷珲道台。当日下午，瑷珲道台前来告知，滨江道道台已发来电报说明瑷珲分关于 8 月 1 日开始工作之事已正式获批。8 月 11 日（星期三）凌晨 3 时又与葛绎真（M. T. Grigorieff）先生、史德匦（E. A. Strehllneek）先生和安来那（J. Angleitner）先生一同骑马（由道台借给）前往陡沟子，视察此地是否适合设立内地关卡，并于当日夜里 11 时返回瑷珲。

陡沟子距瑷珲 70 里，位于森林之中，夏季蚊虫较多。当地仅有一处独立泥房，且已有 24 名士兵居住，并无可供分卡关员居住之地。距离陡沟子最近的村庄亦有 30 里远，若于此设卡，定会很难获取任何补给。综上，陡沟子的环境并不利于海关开展工作，因此已决定将内地分卡设在梁家屯。梁家屯距瑷珲 40 里，位于陡峭高山的山脚下，村中还有一条主干路穿过。

8 月 13 日（星期五）前往大黑河对初期工作进行部署安排，最终于 8 月 17 日（星期二）启动分关工作，开始征税。

贸易：

瑷珲当地几无贸易往来，洋籍商人显然亦不会来此，而且贸易交接地的水位很浅，船只根本无法靠近。

至于大黑河，除牲畜和谷物外，基本也没有什么贸易往来，其他经陆路或水路自哈尔滨运来的酒类、烟草、俄国糖品及日本按件货物等均将通过走私途径运入俄境，仅有极少数会于当地销售。

瑷珲分关设立之前，当地政府一直对 100 里免税区以外各地运来之货物征税，除牲畜的税率为 3.6% 外，其他货物均为 7.2%，即使持有哈尔滨关签发的 1.5 倍完税凭证，即土货的完纳出口税及复出口半税凭证，洋货的完纳进口税及子口半税凭证，亦不例外。与瑷珲道台说明此等征税与海关章程有冲突后，当地政府已停止对持有海关凭证的货物征税，但酒类及烟草仍须缴税，只不过现征税之名目已改为

"落地税"。一小桶酒须缴纳 10 卢布。

有鉴于此，对于自松花江沿岸贸易市场运来之货物，征收土货复出口半税（参阅瑷珲分关章程第 7 条）似乎亦属合理，尤其对于那些官方并不鼓励的贸易，加征此税应不会遭到反对。

牲畜及冷冻肉几乎皆销往黑龙江俄岸各地，仅有部分绵羊销售瑷珲关区。此类货物均须于大黑河过江出口，因此即使有绕路经过内路分卡者，逃税之机会亦是微乎其微。

酒类：多装于大铁桶中经陆路运至瑷珲关区，但沿途有三家子等可以存酒之地，商人会于此等地方将烈酒装入更小的容器中以便于走私至俄境，所以并非所有酒类都会运入大黑河。如此一来，便须由内陆分卡实现稽查管控。大铁桶十分笨重不易运输，小路又难行，因此大多都会选择通过主路运输。

洋货：经陆路运来之洋货已于其他关卡完纳关税，并无绕过分卡之必要。

谷物、蛋类、烟草等：经陆路运来，主要运往黑龙江俄岸的布拉戈维申斯克，须严查。此等货物通常由不受道路限制的轻型运货车（大轱辘车）运输，经过分卡后，便难以辨别始运地，因为大黑河当地亦有生产。

运输路线：

齐齐哈尔至大黑河的主要运输路线以百里免税区外的二站（距瑷珲 110 里）为起点，经陡沟子通过高山地带至梁家屯，后经叶家屯通过沼泽地带至头站或西岗子，再经三家子、二道沟、三道沟、四道沟、四家子通过起伏的平原地带至黑河。此路线路况良好，乃最为便捷之途径。

在二站与陡沟子之间，道路在二龙向东分出一条岔道，经那二龙（Naerhlung）及德勒姆（Telomu）至头站（Tou Chan）。

在陡沟子与梁家屯之间，道路在梁家屯以西约 12 里的西沟堡向西分出一条岔道，但此处即为沼泽地带的末端，除瑷珲方向外，皆被叠嶂山峦阻断。

夏季期间，上述两条岔道根本无法通行，山脚附近的地面太过泥泞，行人车辆只能选择主路往来；然而即便是主路，如遇大雨，车辆牲畜亦往往无法通过头站的浅水处。

冬季期间，车辆及牲畜或许可以经上述岔道绕过梁家屯分卡，但与主路相比，岔道路程更长，路况更差，而且沿途村落亦会索要过路费，地方政府的密探也是遍布各处，即使有逃脱海关征税者，亦会被要求缴纳地方税。再退一步讲，即使有权征收地方税的机关未能实现此项征税，商人亦会被处以罚金，同时还有被大黑河海关关员稽查的风险。因此商人都更愿意选择主路运输货物，并至海关缴纳相对较低的关税，毕竟除酒类及烟草外，凡持有海关凭证的货物,均可免纳地方税。

在大黑河,此条主路直接通向开往布拉戈维申斯克的渡船处,中途须经过交涉局,即海关关卡设立之地,由此,过江运输便难逃海关之管控。

夏季唯一安全的过江方式便为乘坐渡船,冬季于冰面上过江亦须经由渡船处,如从他处过江,俄国海关将禁止入境。

人事:

语言方面,除帮办须通晓俄文外,大黑河亦需有一名会讲俄语的关员以便应对俄籍商人及船只。于瑷珲关区而言,通晓汉文更具优势,实际上非俄籍关员更受尊重。

瑷珲既为商埠,总关自然设于此地,帮办及华籍同文供事亦须常驻于此,此外还需要1名洋籍外班关员处理船运相关事宜。帮办不在期间,如无其他洋籍关员当值,该名洋籍关员不得离岗。

梁家屯:须有1名洋籍关员,1名华籍巡役及4名卫兵(由瑷珲道台派遣)驻守。洋籍关员须负责计税及征税工作,如有可能,最好通晓汉文,对货物估值方面亦应有所了解,最为重要的是需有较强的领悟能力和学习能力。

大黑河:此处为瑷珲分关最为重要的关卡,现由担任超等外班关员的二等验货史德匿(E. A. Strehllneek)先生和洋籍钤子手布卢穆(W. I. Bluhm)先生驻守。此外还有1名擅长书写的华籍巡役,以便于必要时处理汉文单据的填具工作,及1名听差。

此外,鉴于冬夏两季水陆两条路线均须管控,为增强工作的有效性,还需1名洋籍关员。

梁家屯分卡的关员应每隔数月换岗一次,因为长期驻守于此等地方于关员而言负担过重。

另已雇用2名陆路马差,每月18卢布,由其自备马匹,以负责三处关卡之间的通信及运送供给等工作。除此之外,暂无他法,因为大黑河与瑷珲之间的小船已停止使用。

海关工作:

梁家屯:对于运往内陆之货物,须凭已完正税凭单放行。

对于自内地运来之应税货物及牲畜,须查验并按照以下试用办法处理:

单批货物税费为海关两0.05两或以下者,暂不征税。

牲畜:将相关数量、价值等信息详细开具备忘录一份,密封后交与货主或其代理人,告知须至瑷珲或大黑河海关出示此备忘录以缴纳关税,并警告如未能照此办理将受到严惩并处以罚金。

此备忘录之抄件应由陆路马差送至瑷珲。

其他货物：税费为海关两 10.00 两及以下者，由梁家屯分卡征收；税费超过海关两 10.00 两或货主因钱银不足无法缴税者，由关员护送至瑷珲缴纳税款，然若货主可于当地寻得可靠担保，亦可采用针对牲畜的处理办法。

上述皆为临时试用办法，一来可尽量免使商人受阻，二来可避免梁家屯分卡留存大量税金，引起不法之徒的注意。

大黑河：无论是自内陆或是由水路运来之货物，均须严格查验并记录。凡海关章程中规定之应税货物，如无完税凭证，大黑河分关均须于征收税款后再放行过江。

对于运往百里免税区以外内陆各地的货物，须征收相应税款，并告知须至梁家屯分卡出示完税凭证。

对于自黑龙江俄岸百里免税区以外各地运来之货物，须征收进口正税，销售本埠者亦不例外，如镀锡铁皮、软木塞等用于制作盛酒容器之物。

携带少量行李的旅客无须征税。

出口方面，除渡船及一些载运当地物产的民船外，几无通过水运出口者。

运往黑龙江上游各地的酒类、烟草等，如无完税凭证，须征收出口正税。

瑷珲：

凡与其他海关的往来函文，均由此关承接传达；凡报告、报表、账簿、记录等海关文件，均由此关编制。除此之外，应无其他要事。帮办应时常至各分卡视察，确保各项工作能够正常运行。此等视察应按次载于出勤簿上。

住宿：

瑷珲：布卢穆（W. I. Bluhm）先生此前一直使用的房屋足供分关办公及一名甚至两名关员居住。在此大院内还有两处砖房：一为中式房屋，内置大炕，可供华籍同文供事及仆人等居住；另一处可供帮办及其家人居住。此院落地理位置极佳，靠近江岸及拟建的浮码头，与瑷珲道台衙门的距离亦不很远。房屋租金最初要求为两年 4500 卢布，但瑷珲的发展前景并不乐观，很多去年新建的房屋现已无人居住，闭门紧锁。因此经协商，整个大院的租金最终降至两年 2500 卢布，为满足海关需求的改善费用亦全由房主承担。

梁家屯：已租用一处带院落的中式房屋，租金及修缮费用为一年 300+10 卢布。此房屋之前一直用作旅馆，南向，应该会很温暖。在此寒冷之地，房屋温暖十分重要。房屋内共有三个房间：一间较大，三面有炕，可供华籍巡役及卫兵居住；一间较小，亦有一面炕，可供洋籍关员居住；厨房位于中间，将另外两个房间分隔开来。

院落门前便是梁家屯的主干路，十分便于分卡管控往来货运。

大黑河：交涉局（Chiao She Chü）的两个房间现已交由海关使用，一间为客厅，一间为办公室。但不知新任知府吴文泰到任后，海关是否还可以继续使用。

于当前情况而言，职员最好可于大黑河居住，但如果没有合适的宿舍，洋籍关员的餐食将难以烹制。此地虽有房屋可租，但是租金都过于昂贵，而且此处房屋多为商铺而建，室内需要重新布局方能满足洋籍关员的生活所需。因此在租到价钱合理且适宜居住的房屋之前，应当为关员发放房租津贴。实际上兹认为，发放房租津贴既可令关员更为满意，亦可为海关减少麻烦。

现有两处房屋适宜租用，一为砖房，只是尚未建完，共有两部分；一为木房，共有三部分。

砖房地理位置极佳，坐落于通往内陆的主路及与江岸平行相邻的主街道的交口处，只是面积偏小，难以满足分关办公及全体关员的居住需求。

木房建于主街道向上数百码的位置，现处于大黑河镇的中间，面积足够，可满足分关各项需求。

此位置日后会更为有利，因为镇子下面的河道已开始出现淤塞，船运亦会渐渐向上游转移，到达与此房屋并排之处。

两处房屋最初皆为商铺而建，因此仅有四面墙及相应的门窗，但各部分均有暖炉，且于室内修建隔断墙即可满足使用需求。现要求的房屋租金为：砖房每月110卢布，木房每月135卢布；如由房主按海关要求对屋内结构进行改建，木房租金为每年1800卢布，租约为两年，需预付六个月租金。

预留地块：

瑷珲：已预留两个地块，以便日后可根据实际需要来选择。每个地块均有约200平方英尺，靠近江岸，分别坐落于东城门至拟建之浮码头的主街道两侧。目前两地块上均未建房屋，日后亦不太有修建之可能，毕竟瑷珲城已日渐萧条。街道北侧的地块位置最佳，因为所建房屋可为南向，面朝街道，在严冬季节将会更加温暖，这一点颇为重要。

大黑河：已预留两个地块，面积虽小，但依照当前情况判断，应可满足需要。两地块均濒临江岸，分别坐落于交涉局的左右两侧，位置极佳，整条江面都在视线范围内，通向内陆的主路亦经由此处。

梁家屯：此处并无预留地块之必要，尤其日后百里免税区很有可能会关闭，届时此分卡将再无需要。

银行安排：

所有税收资金都将尽快存入华俄道胜银行，各关卡允许留存的资金均不得超过100卢布。税金一经存入税收账户，如无哈尔滨关税务司的批准，概不允许支领；哈尔滨关税务司的签字样本应尽快发送。

银行方面已经同意税收账户每日存款的年利息为4%；存款收据的官票印花税费用将于年底从利息中扣除。

待处理好所有官方业务，看到分关各项工作正常运转后，本署便于9月1日启程离开大黑河，经哈巴罗夫斯克（Habarovsk）和波格兰尼奇内（Pogranichnaya）返回，最终于9月8日抵达哈尔滨。

（签字）式美第（A. Schmidt）

署副税务司

1909年9月10日，哈尔滨关

该抄件内容真实有效，特此证明。

录事：周骊（C. H. B. Joly）二等帮办前班

呈总税务司署 518 号文   哈尔滨关 1910 年 ①

尊敬的海关代理总税务司（北京）：

根据哈尔滨关致总税务司署第 503 号呈：

"为汇报瑷珲分关初期工作安排事。"

特此汇报，瑷珲分关开展工作后不久，滨江道道台便转来瑷珲道台关于控诉此分关在对自齐齐哈尔运来的生猪征税时存在违规行为。本署原计划于 1909 年 10 月至瑷珲分关视察时调查此事，但由于当时航运即将关闭未能实现，最终只得通过书面形式与瑷珲分关沟通此事。从随附之瑷珲分关致哈尔滨关第 23 号呈抄件中可知，分关工作并无差错。

随后梁家屯分卡的职能又遭受质疑。瑷珲道台在收到瑷珲厅及当地商人的请愿书后向黑龙江巡抚致函请求下达指令关闭梁家屯分卡，以消除商人关于不便的控诉。随呈附上海关监督关于此事之函文抄件。嗣后应本署要求，海关监督电函黑龙江巡抚说明梁家屯分卡乃依据《瑷珲分关临时章程》而设立，关闭之事须谨慎考虑。瑷珲分关主管帮办葛绎真（M. T. Grigorieff）先生已于瑷珲分关致哈尔滨关第 27 号呈（随附抄件）中说明商人之控诉毫无根据。瑷珲道台姚福升先生对海关的态度一向友好，此两次控诉显然是受到某位地方官员的影响。故随后已命葛绎真先生私下向瑷珲道台说明任何煽动撤销梁家屯分卡的举动均非明智之举，因为裁撤后，受到影响的将不仅仅是瑷珲分关的整体工作安排，南满的情况亦会因此变得更加复杂。

另已借式美第（A. Schmidt）先生去年 8 月至瑷珲处理分关事务之机，命其与瑷珲道台商议上述两项事宜。瑷珲道台最终同意通过相同的渠道正式撤回此前对瑷珲分关的控诉，海关监督随后亦来函（随附抄件）说明此两项控诉均已解决。

您忠诚的仆人

（签名）葛诺发（N. A. Konovaloff）

哈尔滨关税务司

该抄件内容真实有效，特此证明。

录事：周骊（C. H. B. Joly）二等帮办前班

———————————

① 原文未标注文件的月日。

呈总税务司署 868 号文　　　　　　　　哈尔滨关 1912 年 11 月 2 日

尊敬的海关总税务司（北京）：

1. 总税务司署第 905/42809 号令（回复哈尔滨关第 842 号呈）收悉：

"为瑷珲分关税款征收及汇解事：若可为瑷珲分关于哈尔滨开立单独的银行账户存放税款，则可继续照现行办法办理。"

兹汇报，今日已于道胜银行哈尔滨分行开立专门的"瑷珲海关税收账户"，并存入 87468.45 卢布。其中 84356.73 卢布为瑷珲分关所征之税款，余下 3111.72 卢布为华俄道胜银行布拉戈维申斯克（Blagovestchensk）分行账户于 1911 年产生之利息。

瑷珲分关税收账户当前明细如下：

	卢布
道胜银行： （布拉戈维申斯克分行）	164672.04
道胜银行： （哈尔滨分行）	87468.45
瑷珲分关税收总计： （自开设之日起至 1912 年 9 月 30 日止）	252140.49

2. 另外，总税务司署第 817 号令曾指示，道胜银行哈尔滨分行所存税款在由总税务司署接管之前产生之利息需移交给海关监督。故请指示，瑷珲分关于道胜银行布拉戈维申斯克分行所设账户产生之 3111.72 卢布利息，是否也需如此办理？

您忠诚的仆人

（签名）花荪（W. C. H. Watson）

哈尔滨关税务司

该抄件内容真实有效，特此证明。

录事：周骊（C. H. B. Joly）二等帮办前班

呈总税务司署 <u>1333</u> 号文　　　　　　　　哈尔滨关 1915 年 6 月 29 日

尊敬的海关总税务司（北京）：

兹呈交本署前往松花江和黑龙江视察海关建设情况之报告。

除本署外，理船厅戴纳格（Steinacher）先生（负责开船）和帮办梅维亮（Myers）先生［充当随行俄文秘书，因安伯克（Ohrnberger）先生需留在哈尔滨关处理往来的俄文信件］也一同外出视察。6 月 6 日早，本署一行乘坐"黑龙号"摩托艇离开哈尔滨，当日晚上 9 时至次日早 3 时停靠岸边，于 6 月 7 日抵达航务关员宿舍。航务关员的职责为监督河工于冬季移除河道浅滩中可能会危及航运的石头。这几处航务关员宿舍（全部为小木屋）于哈尔滨关前任税务司花荪（Watson）先生任期内建造，可为航务关员提供舒适的居住环境。

本署一行于 6 月 7 日下午 1 时 45 分抵达三姓，随即本署视察了由帮办满士斐（Mansfield）先生负责管理的三姓分关。本署对三姓分关视察结束后，对该分关之工作十分满意。随后本署还视察了牡丹江上管控中国船只的海关分卡。钤子手西多处（Sidortchock）先生了解海关工作，提出将海关分卡设在驳船之上。他每年都将一艘驳船停靠在江口之处，以便在此设立海关分卡。本署仔细了解了三姓分关帮办及钤子手之宿舍，认为关员宿舍急需修整。房屋修整的初步预算已在哈尔滨关致总税务司署第 1326 号呈中呈交。

三姓分关大部分税收来源于出口至普里莫尔斯克地区（Primorsk District），随即运往欧洲的大豆和谷物。近来三姓分关税收持续增涨，但现今面临着如何将相对大额的分关税收汇入哈尔滨关账户的问题。例如，本署抵达三姓分关时得知三姓分关帮办在其保险箱中存有税收 10000 卢布。此地通过银行或者邮局汇款至哈尔滨均不可行，本署只好令三姓分关帮办小额分期汇款（每次 1000 卢布至 2000 卢布），由海关熟识的船长经松花江带至哈尔滨关。尽管此种做法并不完全符合海关规定，但是也比让税款继续存于三姓分关帮办的保险箱中更安全。虽然当地道尹与海关工作并无太多联系，但本署还是于抵达三姓的第二日便前去拜访，由于道尹外出故而无法会面。值得高兴的是满士斐先生与当地地方官员建立了良好的私人关系。

第三天本署一行前往三姓屯浅水滩视察，随后于 6 月 10 日下午离开三姓分关，并于 6 月 11 日下午抵达拉哈苏苏分关。在帮办巴拉诺斯（Baranoffsky）先生的管理下，拉哈苏苏分关各项工作均进行得井井有条，所有工作之进展均令本署满意。拉哈苏苏分关之关员宿舍修缮尚可，本署批准修缮部分房屋内部陈设以令关员居住更加舒适。与三姓分关一样,拉哈苏苏分关的税收主要来自大豆和谷物,且比照前几年有较大幅度增长。因无法向哈尔滨关汇款,拉哈苏苏分关之税收均存于保险箱中。鉴于拉哈苏苏前往黑龙江俄岸地区的米开罗—塞米诺瓦斯科(Michailo-Semenovsk)(距拉哈苏苏30俄里)航路已通(乘轮船前往该地需2小时,返回拉哈苏苏需3小时),故而本署已指示拉哈苏苏分关帮办,必要时可经米开罗—塞米诺瓦斯科的俄国邮局将税收汇至哈尔滨关(但拉哈苏苏分关帮办需亲自汇款,以确保税款安全无虞)。此汇款方法虽不符海关规定,但也是根据实际情形做出的最佳方案。除松花江之主要支流外,在拉哈苏苏上游数俄里处还有一条河道可通往黑龙江。中国平底船常从此河道行驶,以此躲避海关征税。为避免有人借此逃税,拉哈苏苏分关帮办在夏季派遣两名海关水手前往河道交汇处管控往来之平底船。虽有海关水手驻守于此,但效果并不理想,故而巴拉诺斯(Baranoffsky)先生建议再派遣一名铃子手前往该河道,在两名水手之协助下可更有效地管控对往来之平底船。本署认为巴拉诺斯先生的建议值得考虑,贵署也有可能批准其建议。但现今海关很难雇用到外班关员,且部分俄籍关员可能受到俄国内革命影响而返回俄国,如此一来海关关员人手更加紧缺。故而本署建议现在最好不要做出任何人事上的任命。因海关汽艇不可驶入黑龙江,故而本署于哈尔滨订购三张自拉哈苏苏前往布拉戈维申斯克的卧铺船票。该轮船原定于6月12日晚抵达拉哈苏苏,但当本署抵达拉哈苏苏后得知轮船延误,故而在本署的请求下,俄国海关同意派遣摩托艇接送本署一行前往米开罗—塞米诺瓦斯科,以便搭乘往来于哈巴罗夫斯克和布拉戈维申斯克的邮轮前往布拉戈维申斯克。本署遂于6月12日早乘俄国摩托艇离开拉哈苏苏。

大黑河口岸(瑷珲分关):本署于6月16日早抵达大黑河。本署原意在视察大黑河口岸期间可于布拉戈维申斯克居住,因此在拉哈苏苏分关视察期间便已将此安排电告瑷珲分关帮办巴闰森(Barentzen)先生。而抵达布拉戈维申斯克后本署发觉先前之安排多有不便且耗费时间:白日里往来于布拉戈维申斯克和大黑河之轮渡发船时间并不固定,且晚6时后所有轮渡均停运。本署一行人只能住进巴闰森先生事先安排之房间。抵达大黑河的第一日本署视察了海关办公楼,现今海关工作进展有序,令人满意。除超等外班关员外,所有关员均居住于租赁宿舍。贵署虽已批准修建新海关办公楼(参阅1914年4月17日总税务司署致哈尔滨关第1194/51774号令),但因目前时局不利,需待出现最佳时机之时方可开展修建工程,因此现今仍需在大黑河租赁房屋充当海关办公楼。自本署呈交修建预算后,建材价格便大幅提升,现在没有承包商愿意在海关预算较少的限制下承包修建海关办公楼工程。本署只能自我安慰称目前海关办公楼足以支持大黑河口岸办公,外班关员之居住条件也尚可接受。所幸大黑河口岸关员对于明年或更久之后再修建海关办公楼一事并无异议。瑷珲分关帮办也在耐心等待开展修建工程的恰当时机,其现居住的房屋租金为每年1200卢布(由海关支付),房屋宽敞,地点极佳(距离海关办公楼仅有5分钟路程),并配备由贵署批准购置的家具,其宿舍极其舒适。

本署于6月17日在瑷珲分关及梁家屯分卡视察。通常瑷珲分关帮办视察上述两地需两天,但本署乘坐汽车往来仅需一天。瑷珲分关之海关工作无须赘述,因瑷珲所有贸易均转移至大黑河,仅需一名铃子手便可处理瑷珲分关工作。该名铃子手现居住在一处破旧房屋(亦是其办公之地)之中,海关每年需支付租金800.00卢布。在瑷珲修建海关办公楼之预算为4500卢布。本署现在尚未做出最后判断,但是就视察情形而言本署认为此地并无修建海关办公楼之必要。鉴于此事并非视察报告之内容,故而本署待适当之时再行汇报。管控所有海拉尔—齐齐哈尔与布拉戈维申斯克及普里莫尔斯克地区陆路贸易的梁家屯分卡之情形较瑷珲分关更复杂。此贸易线路仅在冬季航运季关闭后使用,牛商们从海拉尔地区将大批的牛赶运至梁家屯分卡。梁家屯所处的山陵地带虽然风景宜人,但在此任职的铃子手却在极度严峻的生活条件下过着与世隔绝的生活:他们所居住的房屋极其破旧和原始,并无任何舒适可言。因时间关系,本署需尽快赶回大黑河,因此并未能鉴证此地居住环境应如何改善。

本署原计划于6月18日拜访黑河道尹,但道尹因公外出未能成行,于是临时改变行程,前往布拉戈维申斯克拜访俄国地方官员。本署拜访的官员包括俄国海关长官(Chief of the Russian Customs),俄国边境长官(Russian Frontier Commissioner),布拉戈维申斯克司令[General in Command of Blagovestchensk,同时也是哥萨克司令(Attaman of the Cossacks)],所到之处均受到热烈欢迎。更重要的是本署发觉俄国官员对中国海关给予的评价极高,其中俄国海关署税务司便是俄国官员最好的代表。

本署本欲经哈巴罗夫斯克(Habarovsk)—尼科利斯克(Nikolsk)—乌苏里斯克(Ussurisk)和绥芬河返回哈尔滨,但是由于近几日黑龙江轮船并无适当卧铺船票,只能经松花江返回哈尔滨。本署于6月19日下午离开布拉戈维申斯克,并于6月23日晚8时45分抵达哈尔滨。

新甸分卡及佳木斯分卡:据哈尔滨关致总税务司署第1152号呈(哈尔滨关前任税务司在1914年6月呈交),设立新甸分卡和佳木斯分卡是为监管运往黑龙江流域和尼古拉耶夫斯克(Nikolaevsk)的货运(主要为谷物),并签发出口正税已征收的文件发送给三姓分关或拉哈苏苏分关的帮办。新甸分卡和佳木斯分卡本应于1914年开设,但实际延期至1915

年春季才开设（参阅 1914 年 8 月 25 日海关总税司公署致哈尔滨关第 1254/53472 号令）。本署视察期间也前往新甸和佳木斯视察，完全理解其对海关工作的重要性。但鉴于现实情形及部分关员可能会回到俄国参加革命，本署认为开设新甸分卡和佳木斯分卡一事应无限延期。

松花江上的航务工作：

本署在戴纳格（Steinacher）先生的陪同下前往三姓浅滩视察，该地的航务关员艾格力（Eglit）先生将航路标志均摆放在规定位置并且保存完好。现今松花江水位很高，自然条件更有利于航行，因此维护航路标志工作并不艰难；但当松花江水位下降，河道情况出现变化后，艾格力先生便需时常调整江上的浮标。不过本署认为即使松花江水位高涨至淹没江岸和江上小岛，其自然条件有利于航行时，航路标志对航运的帮助依旧极大。总体而言航务部门工作效率较高，唯一的不足是航务部门预算由江捐支付，不足以支付在江上设置照明设施的费用。

防疫办事处：

本署以防疫办事处会办（Lay Director）的身份前往三姓分关、拉哈苏苏分关及大黑河口岸的医院视察，三姓和拉哈苏苏两个分关的医院干净卫生且保存完好。而大黑河口岸的华籍关员习惯于寻找老中医看病而非前往医院问诊。

总结：

视察完毕后兹汇报：因哈尔滨关区内谷物和豆类的产量持续增长，作为本关区税收中心的三姓分关和拉哈苏苏分关将于近期得到更大发展；但因大黑河邻近布拉戈维申斯克，便于商人走私，故而盐和酒的走私贩子全部汇集于此，将大黑河作为走私的大本营。城镇里到处是赌场和糜烂场所，完全没有合法贸易。有鉴于此，大黑河口岸已达到其发展的顶峰，日后极有可能走向衰落。

您忠诚的仆人

柯必达（P.J. Grevedon）

哈尔滨关税务司

该抄件内容真实有效，特此证明。

录事：司丹博（J. Steinberg）超等帮办特班

专题二

瑷珲关独立管理运作

1. 为保证瑷珲关独立后正常运作的财务问题事

CUSTOM HOUSE,

Aigun/Taheiho , 7th December, 1921.

Sir,

I have the honour to acknowledge the receipt of your Despatch No. 9/86,799 :

dealing with the financial arrangements necessary to enable the Aigun Office to function as a separate establishment ;

and to say that your instructions have been duly noted.

1.　　　　No heavy expenditure is foreseen in Account D, but the receipts will be almost nil during the Winter months; I have therefore to apply for a supplementary grant in aid of Account D of Haikwan Taels five hundred (Hk.Tls. 500.00) for the 246th (March) Quarter, 1922.

2.　　　　At the end of the year there will be a

certain

Inspector General of Customs,

　　　PEKING.

certain amount of duties collected on deposit, which cannot obviously be transferred at once to Harbin ; I am of opinion that, if and when they are carried to account, it will be unnecessary to remit them to Harbin, as the trouble would be in excess of the amounts involved, which will be reduced to a minimum. I shall be obliged however to receive your instructions on this point.

3.　　　　A certain amount of seizures will be un-settled at the end of the Quarter : shall the outstanding cases be transferred from Harbin to Aigun, and appear henceforth in the Aigun Confisca-tion Report , or shall this Office remit to Harbin the proceeds, when theyn are realised ?

4.　　　　Your authority is solicited for opening, through the good offices of the Harbin Commissioner, a Service Account in dollars in Harbin, with a Foreign Bank to be designated by the Harbin Com-missioner, preferably the Hongkong and Shanghai Bank. For years past the Aigun Office has been paying the North Manchurian Plague Prevention Hospital at Taheiho whatever sums the Hospital needed (an

average

average of $ 500 a month) treating the payments as remittances to Harbin; I think the same procedure may be followed after the financial separation from Harbin, and the moneys refundable by Harbin could be used in feeding the Aigun Customs Dollar Account in Harbin whenever necessary. - The account would be very useful for making payments due in Harbin, such as rental of the Acting Commissioner's quarters to the owner who resides in Harbin ($ 1,200 a year), purchase of stores, payment of part of the salaries whenever desired. The principal scope of the account however would consist in the possibility of transferring Service Moneys there in case of failure or temporary difficulties of the Chinese Banks here. There are no Foreign Banks in this District, and the course suggested seems the most suitable in case of financial panic: it would be possible to transfer moneys to the Service Account in Shanghai, but it would be more expensive, and a change of currencies, from dollars to Shanghai Taels, would complicate matters.

5.   I also have to request your sanction of the

following

following payments, which have been authorised for the Harbin District :

Mess Allowances on tours of Inspection (I. G. despatch No. 31,442):

1. Commissioner or Dep. Commr. per diem $ 4.50
2. Assistants and Harbour Master (to whom the Senior Officer should be assimilated) $ 3.50

Mess Allowances on transfer : (I. G. No. 80,977)
1. Members of the Foreign Indoor Staff per diem $ 2.50
2. Members of the Foreign Outdoor " per diem $ 3.50
3. Chinese Clerks and Writers per diem $ 2.00
4. All other Chinese Employes per diem $ 1.00

2/3rs cost of forewood consumed by the Staff in Winter. (I. G. No. 34, 908)

Medical attendance on Staff. (I. G. No. 38,841)

Rent of Commissioner's House (I.G.No. 69,304), of Clerks' Quarters (No. 78,369), of Taheiho Custom House (No. unknown) and Aigun C. H. (No. 69,669).

and of the following receipts :

Rent of Examination shed Site (No. 72,154) and of Winter Road Site (No. 86,818 in reply to Harbin No. 2551).

      Copy of this despatch is forwarded to the Harbin Commissioner.

            I have the honour to be, Sir,

                  Your obedient Servant.

                  Acting Commissioner.

呈总税务司署 <u>15</u> 号文　　　　　　　　瑷珲关 / 大黑河 1921 年 12 月 7 日

尊敬的海关总税务司（北京）：

根据总税务司署第 9/86799 号令：

"为保证瑷珲关独立后可正常运作，请汇报须解决的财政问题。"

兹回复如下：

1. 虽然预计账户 D 暂无大额支出，但因本年第四季度亦无进项，故申请一笔海关两 500.00 两的补发款以协济账户 D，计入瑷珲关 1922 年第一季度（第 245 结）款项。

2. 年末将会有一笔税款入账，但显然无法立即转至哈尔滨关。兹认为，若届时将该笔税款汇至哈尔滨关，则势必会因汇兑损失等问题而减少最终所收之金额，因此本署建议，待该笔税款入账时，不必汇至哈尔滨关。请贵署指示。

3. 鉴于截至本季度末，仍会有部分罚没款项无法结算，兹请示本季未结新旧各案之处理办法：是将其从哈尔滨关转至瑷珲关，并计入瑷珲关罚没款清算，还是待结算后，将收益汇至哈尔滨关。

4. 兹请批准由哈尔滨关税务司协助于哈尔滨一家洋籍银行（由哈尔滨关税务司选定，但最好为汇丰银行）为瑷珲关开立海关银圆账户。多年来，瑷珲关为大黑河北满洲防疫医院发放所需资金（平均每月 500 银圆），并将其记作汇至哈尔滨关的款项；兹认为，待瑷珲关之财政从哈尔滨关独立出来后，可继续使用该记账方式，如此一来，哈尔滨关归还的款项便可于必要时计入瑷珲关于哈尔滨开立的银圆账户中。该账户对于支付哈尔滨当地的应付账款十分有益，比如向瑷珲关署理税务司房屋的房主（定居哈尔滨）支付房租（每年 1200.00 银圆），购买商铺，必要时亦可用于发放薪俸。此外，若大黑河的华籍银行面临倒闭或者暂遇危机，还可以由该账户划拨发放海关经费。鉴于大黑河地区尚无外国银行，该办法似乎是应对金融危机的最佳选择；当然亦可将海关经费转至上海的海关账户，但将货币从银圆兑换成上海规银不但过程较为复杂，费用亦更大。

5. 请示批准以下支出（哈尔滨关已获批准）：

巡查途中的膳食津贴（总税务司署第 31442 号令）：

（1）税务司或者副税务司，每日 4.50 银圆

（2）帮办和理船厅（应与超等关员一致），每日 3.50 银圆

调任途中的膳食津贴（总税务司署第 80977 号令）：

（1）洋籍内班职员，每日 3.50 银圆

（2）洋籍外班职员，每日 2.50 银圆

（3）华籍供事及文案，每日 2.00 银圆

（4）其他华籍职员，每日 1.00 银圆

职员冬季薪柴费的 2/3（总税务司署第 24908 号令）：

职员医疗护理费（总税务司署第 38241 号令）

税务司房屋租金（总税务司署第 69304 号令）

供事宿舍租金（总税务司署第 78369 号令）

大黑河口岸海关办公楼租金（未知文件）

瑷珲口岸海关办公楼租金（总税务司署第 69869 号令）。

请示批准将以下收入入账：

验货厂关址租金（总税务司署第 72154 号令）

冬令过江检查处租金（总税务司署第 86818 号令回复哈尔滨关第 2531 号呈）。

此抄件发送至哈尔滨关税务司。

您忠诚的仆人

包安济（G. Boezi）

瑷珲关署理税务司

2.为向瑗珲关职员发放满洲特殊津贴事

Aigun / Taheiho 24th December, 1921.

Sir,

1.   I am informed by the Harbin Commissioner that, in accordance with the instructions of your Despatch No. 2514 / 85,369 to Harbin (copy of which is not in the Aigun Archives yet), I must report on the advisability of continuing the issue of the Special Manchurian Allowance to the Aigun Staff.

2.   The result of a diligent enquiry on the prices of the principal commodities is embodied in the enclosed List, which shows the actual market prices now ruling in Taheiho, as compared with prices ruling in Harbin in July 1920. You will see that, while Taheiho is cheaper with regard to certain articles especially meat, other commodities, and particularly those imported from China or abroad, are considerably dearer. The general tendency is unmistakably towards the increase : raw materials,

manufactures

Inspector General of Customs,
    PEKING.

manufactures, labour, are all more expensive now than even one year ago.

3.   I would also like to mention the fact that in a small and pretentious place like this, most of our Employees are generally considered as officials of a fairly high rank, and they have to keep up to expectations : this is beneficial to the prestige of the Customs but expensive for the Employees even if they keep expenses within the limits of the strictest economy compatible with dignity. There is hardly here an official even of not high rank, who doesn't keep a carriage with a fine Russian Horse, or a Motor Car, or both ; dinners, feasts, charities, are daily events - and it is difficult, sometimes impossible, and often inadvisable, to stand apart.

4.   I have therefore the honour to recommend that the issue of the allowance be continued, in the same amount originally sanctioned by you.

I have the honour to be,

Sir,

Your obedient Servant,

J. Bock

Acting Comissioner.

Enclosure to Aigun Despatch No. 17 to I.G.

LIST OF PRICES.

Description	Classifier	In July, 1920. Harbin.	In December, 1921, Taheiho.	Remarks.
		Dollars.	Dollars.	
Beef, Soup	Pound	0.22	0.15-0.20	
Beef Stock	"	0.67	0.20	$0.25 in summer.
Beef Roast	"	0.45	0.20	
Mutton	"	0.33	0.22	$0.30 in summer.
Pork	"	0.33	0.25	
Veal	"	0.67	none	
Dust	"	..	0.25	
Fish	"	0.22	0.10-0.60	
Eggs	Ten	0.20	0.50	Price varies from 0.25 to 1.50 per 10.
Chicken	Each	0.85-1.35	1.00-1.10	
Geese	"	..	2.50-3.50	
Duck	"	..	1.50	
Pigeons	"	..	..	
Turkey	"	..	..	
Pheasant	Pair	..	1.10-1.80	In season.
Partridges	"	..	0.90-1.00	
Beetroot	Pound	0.17	0.10	In summer.
Cabbage, Native	"	..	0.15	In summer, from 0.01 in winter to 0.30.
Cabbage, foreign	Each	0.44	0.40	
Carrots	Pound	0.33	0.05	
String Beans	"	0.28	0.25	
Green Peas	"	0.17	0.18	In season.
Onions	"	0.17	0.20	
Potatoes	"	0.05	0.05	$0.01 to 0.08 according to season.
Leeks	"	..	0.01-0.80	According to season.
Mushrooms, Dried	"	..	2.30-2.50	

Spinach

Description	Classifier	In July, 1920. Harbin.	In December, 1921, Taheiho.	Remarks.
		Dollars.	Dollars.	
Spinach	Pound	0.06	0.09	$0.04 - 0.12 according to season.
Tomatoes	-	..	..	
Lemons	Each	..	0.30	
Apples	Pound	..	0.40	
Banana		..	..	Seldom on market.
Grapes		..	0.50	
Pears		..	0.30	
Oranges		..	..	
Chestnuts		..	0.20	
Walnuts		..	0.20	
Sugar, white	"	0.28	0.20	$0.30 in winter.
Sugar, Brown		0.22	0.18	$0.25 " "
Flour	Pood	2.15	3.00	Harbin II qual.
"		..	2.40	Local II "
"		..	2.20	" III "
Rice	Pound	0.15	0.15	Japanese, I qual.
"		..	0.14	Native, II qual.
"		..	0.13	.. III "
Bread		0.25	0.15	
Milk	Pint	0.10	0.20	
Cream		0.60	..	
Salt	Pound	0.11	0.10	
Tea	"	G.Y.2.00	1.40-2.20	
Soy		..	0.20	
Coffee	"	0.67	0.80	
Sardines, French	Tin	3.00	3.30	
.. American	"	1.45	1.50	
Tinned Fruits		0.95	0.80-2.00	

Tinned Vegetables

Description	Classifier	In July,1920 Harbin. Dollars.	In December 1921, Tsitsihar. Dollars.	Remarks.
Mixed Vege-tables	Tin	0.93	1.00	
Soup, hand, etc.	"	..	2.00	
Asparagus	"	1.85	2.00	
Jam	Glass	0.93	} 0.70-1.00	
Jam	Tin	0.30		
Milk	"	0.74	0.45-0.60	
Currants	Pound	0.41	0.60	
Cheese	"	1.48	..	
Butter	"	1.48	1.40	
Ham	"	..	0.75	
Dried Cabbage	"	..	0.40-0.90	
Kerosene	Tin	3.00	7.00	Heavy discount for large amounts.
Gasolene	10 Gal-lons	18. - 20.	80.00	
Electric Light	Kilowatt	0.45 (Min.Charge - G.T.0.675 per lamp per month	..	No meters; $2.00 per lamp of 25 c.p. per month (25 c.p. is a minimum, the light being very poor). $4.20 in winter.
Peiho Brandy	Bottle	..	3.50	
Gin	"	5.00	7.00	
Vermouth	"	4.44	7.00	
Whisky	"	4.44	10.00	
Beer, Peking	"	..	0.75	
.. Japanese	"	..	0.30	
Samshu,Shaohsing	Pound	..	0.60	
.. Local	"	..	0.10-0.12	
Soap, Laundry	Piece	..	0.10-0.15	
.. Toilet	"	..	0.50	
Candles	Package of 14 oz. (4 pcs.)	..	0.35	Poorest quality.
Coal	Ton	32.00	35.00	In summer, from $11.00; in winter, to $32.00
Wood	Cube	48.00	21.00	

Description	Classifier	In July,1920 Harbin. Dollars.	In December 1921,Tsitsihar. Dollars.	Remarks.
Laundry	100 pcs.	10.00	10.00	
Boys, cheapest	Month	20.00	20.00	
Cooks, ..	"	25.00	25.00	
Coolies, ..	"	11.00	11.00	
Maid-servant,Ch.	"	..	12.00-20.00	With food
.. Russian	"	..	18.00-25.00	" "
Governess, For.	"	80. - 150.	60. - 100.	
Chauffeur,Ch.	"	40. - 50.	50. - 80.	
.. For.	"	50. - 120.	80. - 120.	
Amah or	Day	2. - 3.	2.00	
Tailor, Chin-ese clothing	"	..	1.50	
.. For.	"	..	3.00	
Clothing, For., by Russian Tailor	Suit	80. - 110.	80. - 100.	
by Chinese Tailor	"	45. - 55.	40. - 70.	
Underwear,Cotton	"	..	4.00	
Shoes, Adults	Pair	25.00	12. - 20.	
.. Children	"	12. - 15.	7. - 10.	
Native Shoes, foreign style	"	..	7. - 15.	
Furcoats, For.	each	..	150. - 400.	
Furcoats,Native, foreign style	"	..	60. - 200.	
Furcoats,Camel lined	"	..	60. - 100.	
Furcoats,Sheep-skin lined	"	..	20. - 50.	
Fur Caps, For.	"	..	15. - 50.	
.. .. Native	"	..	2.50-40.00	
Fur Boots & Socks	Pair	..	17. - 25.	
Felt Boots	"	..	5. - 7.	Cotton padded suit,Ch.

Description	Classi-fier	In July, 1920 Harbin.	In December, 1921, Taheiho.	Remarks.
		Dollars.	Dollars.	
Cotton Wadded Suit, Chinese	Each	..	9. - 12.	
Silk Wadded Suit, Chinese	"	..	25. - 35.	
Silk Light Suit, Chinese	"	..	20. - 30.	
Chinese News-paper	Year		12.00	
Medicines, Foreign	..	2 to 4 times as expensive as China	3 to 5 times as expensive as China	
Medicines, Chinese	..	..	3 to 5 times as expensive as China	
Doctor's Fee	A Visit	5. - 10.	3. - 20.	
Veterinary	"	5. - 7.	..	
Cigarettes, I & II qual.	Hundred	..	0.80 - 1.92	
Freight on Chinese East-ern Railway	Food	..	..	
Freight by Steamer (Har-bin to Hasei)	"	..	0.30 - 1.00	(According to season.
Freight by Cart, in winter	"	..	1.00 - 1.80	

Acting Commissioner.

呈总税务司署 <u>17</u> 号文 　　　　　　　瑷珲关/大黑河 1921 年 12 月 24 日

尊敬的海关总税务司(北京):

　　1.哈尔滨关税务司告知,根据总税务司署至哈尔滨关第 2514/83369 号令之指示(此令抄件尚未存至瑷珲关档案),本署须对继续为瑷珲关职员发放满洲特殊津贴之合理性做出汇报。

　　2.兹附主要商品物价表,该物价表将目前大黑河商品的实际市场价格与 1920 年 7 月哈尔滨商品的实际市场价格以对比之形式呈现出来。据此物价表可知,大黑河的部分商品,如肉类的价格相对便宜;而其他商品,尤其是从中国其他地区或国外输入的商品价格却相当昂贵。同时,整体物价呈上升趋势:与上一年相比,原料、产品和劳动力等方面之物价均有大幅上涨。

　　3.事实上,大黑河口岸虽小却格外注重表象之事,海关大多职员皆被当地人视为高级关员,因此为维护海关之威望,职员们只能尽量以有限之薪俸满足民众之期望,即便如此,这些费用于海关职员而言亦过于高昂。然而,大黑河口岸并无高职级关员,无人配备马车和上等俄罗斯马匹,或者汽车;而且每日皆有晚餐、宴会或者慈善活动——实难甚至有时无法置身事外,且若不参加此类活动亦十分不妥。

　　4.因此,本署特此建议,按照总税务司署最初批准之津贴额度继续为瑷珲关职员发放满洲特殊津贴。

您忠诚的仆人

包安济(G. Boezi)

瑷珲关署理税务司

瑷珲关致总税务司署第 17 号呈附表

物价表

表1

商品名称	单位	1920 年 7 月 哈尔滨	1921 年 12 月 大黑河	备注
		银圆	银圆	
牛肉汤	磅	0.22	0.15－0.20	夏季 0.25 银圆
牛排	磅	0.67	0.20	夏季 0.25 银圆
烤牛肉	磅	0.43	0.20	夏季 0.25 银圆
羊肉	磅	0.33	0.22	夏季 0.30 银圆
猪肉	磅	0.33	0.25	夏季 0.30 银圆
小牛肉	磅	0.67	无	
板油	磅	..	0.25	
鱼	磅	0.22	0.10－0.60	
鸡蛋	十个	0.20	0.50	每十个鸡蛋价格在 0.25 到 1.50 银圆间
鸡	只	0.85－1.25	1.00－1.10	
鹅	只	..	2.50－3.50	
鸭	只	..	1.50	
鸽子	只	..	..	
火鸡	只	..	..	
野鸡	对	..	1.10－1.80	时令
鹧鸪	对	..	0.50－1.00	时令
甜菜根	磅	0.17	1.10	夏季
本地卷心菜	磅	..	0.15	夏季最低 0.01 银圆 冬季最高 0.30 银圆
洋白菜	棵	0.44	0.40	
胡萝卜	磅	0.33	0.05	

表2

商品名称	单位	1920年7月哈尔滨	1921年12月大黑河	备注
		银圆	银圆	
四季豆	磅	0.28	0.25	
青豌豆	磅	0.17	0.18	时令
洋葱	磅	0.17	0.20	
马铃薯	磅	0.03	0.05	根据时令0.01银圆至0.08银圆不等
洋葱	磅	..	0.01-0.80	根据时令变化
干蘑菇	磅	..	2.20-2.50	
菠菜	磅	0.06	0.09	根据时令0.04银圆至0.12银圆不等
西红柿	磅	..	..	根据时令0.04银圆至0.12银圆不等
柠檬	个	0.06	0.30	市场稀缺
苹果	磅	..	0.40	市场稀缺
香蕉	磅	..	..	市场稀缺
葡萄	磅	..	0.50	市场稀缺
梨子	磅	..	0.30	市场稀缺
橘子	磅	..	..	市场稀缺
栗子	磅	..	0.20	
核桃	磅	..	0.20	
白糖	磅	0.28	0.20	冬季0.30银圆
红糖	磅	0.22	0.18	冬季0.28银圆
面粉	普特	2.15	3.00	哈尔滨二等面粉
面粉	普特	..	2.40	大黑河二等面粉
面粉	普特	..	2.20	大黑河三等面粉
大米	磅	0.15	0.16	日本一等大米
大米	磅	..	0.14	土产二等大米

表3

商品名称	单位	1920 年 7 月 哈尔滨	1921 年 12 月 大黑河	备注
		银圆	银圆	
大米	磅	..	0.13	土产三等大米
面包	磅	0.25	0.15	
牛奶	品脱	0.10	0.20	
奶油	品脱	0.60	..	
盐	磅	0.11	0.10	
茶	磅	2.00 日金	1.40-2.20	
酱油	磅	..	0.10	
咖啡	磅	0.67	0.80	
法国沙丁鱼	罐	3.00	3.30	
美国沙丁鱼	罐	1.48	1.50	
罐装水果	罐	0.93	0.80-2.00	
罐装蔬菜	罐	0.93	1.00	
谷物豌豆等	罐	..	..	
芦笋	罐	1.65	2.00	
果酱	一玻璃杯	0.93	0.70-1.00	
果酱	罐	0.50	0.70-1.00	
牛奶	罐	0.74	0.45-0.60	
葡萄干	磅	0.41	0.60	
乳酪	磅	1.48	..	
黄油	磅	1.48	1.40	
火腿	磅	..	0.75	
干卷心菜	磅	..	0.40-0.90	
煤油	罐	5.00	7.00	数量越多折扣越大
汽油	十加仑	18-20	20.00	

表4

商品名称	单位	1920年7月 哈尔滨	1921年12月 大黑河	备注
		银圆	银圆	
电灯	千瓦	0.45 每只灯每月最低消耗 0.675 日金	..	无仪表；每月每只发光强度为25的灯泡消耗 2.00 银圆（发光强度 25 是最低值，灯光非常微弱）
白兰地	瓶	..	3.80	冬季 4.20 银圆
杜松子酒	瓶	5.00	7.00	
苦艾酒	瓶	4.44	7.00	
威士忌	瓶	4.44	10.00	
北京啤酒	瓶	..	0.75	
日本啤酒	瓶	..	0.80	
绍兴黄酒	磅	..	0.60	
本地黄酒	磅	..	0.10-0.12	
洗衣皂	块	..	0.10-0.13	
舆洗室肥皂	块	..	0.50	
蜡烛	14 盎司一包（4 根）	..	0.35	最差质量
煤	吨	32.00	35.00	
木料	立方	48.00	21.00	夏季最低 11.00 银圆 冬季最高 30.00 银圆
洗衣店	100 件	10.00	10.00	
最廉价男佣	一个月	20.00	20.00	
最廉价厨师	一个月	25.00	25.00	
最廉价苦力	一个月	11.00	11.00	
华籍女佣	一个月	..	12.00-20.00	提供餐食
俄籍女佣	一个月	..	15.00-25.00	提供餐食

表5

商品名称	单位	1920年7月 哈尔滨	1921年12月 大黑河	备注
		银圆	银圆	
洋籍家庭教师	一个月	80-150	60-100	
华籍汽车司机	一个月	40-60	50-80	
洋籍汽车司机	一个月	60-120	80-120	
木匠	天	2-3	2.00	
华服裁缝	天	..	1.50	
洋装裁缝	天	..	3.00	
俄籍裁缝制作的服装	套	80-110	80-100	
华籍裁缝制作的服装	套	45-65	40-70	
棉质内衣	套	..	4.00	
成人鞋	双	20.00	12-20	
儿童鞋	双	12-15	7-10	
洋式土产鞋	双	..	7-13	
洋式皮毛大衣	件	..	150-400	
洋式土产皮毛大衣	件	..	60-200	
驼绒内衬皮毛大衣	件	..	60-100	
羊皮内衬皮毛大衣	件	..	20-50	
洋式毛皮帽子	顶	..	12-60	
土产毛皮帽子	顶	..	2.50-40.00	
皮毛靴子和袜子	双	..	17-25	
毡制靴子	双	..	5-7	
中式棉质套装	套	..	9-12	
中式丝绸套装	套	..	25-35	
中式丝绸薄套装	套	..	20-30	
中文报纸	年	..	12.00	
进口药材	年	比中国其他地区高2-4倍	比中国其他地区高3-5倍	

表6

商品名称	单位	1920年7月 哈尔滨	1921年12月 大黑河	备注
		银圆	银圆	
中国药材	Tear	比中国其他地区高2-4倍	比中国其他地区高2-3倍	
就医费	次	5-10	3-20	
兽医	次	5-7	..	
一等/二等香烟	一百根	..	0.80-1.92	
中东铁路运费	普特	..	..	
轮船运费（哈尔滨至大黑河）	普特	..	0.30-1.00	根据时令变化
冬季二轮手推车运费	普特	..	1.00-1.80	

包安济（G. Boezi）

瑷珲关署理税务司

3. 为呈报瑷珲关图书馆藏书清单事

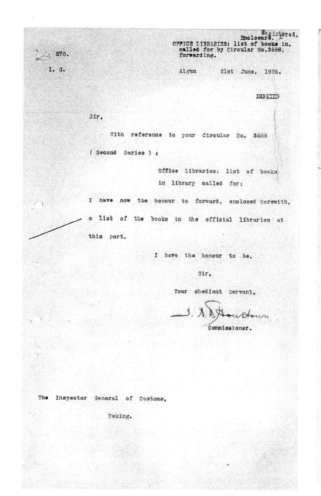

2.

III. Miscellaneous Series:

		Vol.
No.6.	List of Chinese Lighthouses, etc.: 1911, 1912, 1913, 1914, 1915, 1918, 1920, 1921, 1922.	9
.. 7.	List of Chinese Lighthouses,etc.(Chin.Version): 1912, 1914, 1920, 1922, 1924.	5
.. 10.	Names of Places on the China Coast and Yangtse River.	1
.. 12.	Rules regarding Notarial Acts.	1
.. 15.	English-Chinese Glossary of Technical Expressions (Lights, etc.).	1
.. 16.	List of Publications (3rd Issue) 1923.	1
.. 25.	Regulations, General, Local, etc.(2nd Issue) 2 volumes.	2
.. 30.	Treaties, Conventions, etc.between China and Foreign States (2nd Edition) 2 vols.	2
.. 31.	Table of Predicted Tides for Side-saddle in the Approach to the Yangtse River: 1922, 1923, 1924, 1925, 1926.	5

IV. Service Series:

		Vol.
No.1.	Service List. (Current volume)	1
	The Inspector General's Circulars:(1st & 2nd Series): Vols. 1 - 5 and vols.7 - 17. (bound). Also current Index and current volume.	16
	Factory Products Circulars.(3rd series): Vols.1 - 2. (bound). Also current Index and current volume.	2
No.6.	Instructions for keeping and rendering Customs Accounts.(5th Issue).	1
.. 8.	Instructions for keeping Returns of Trade and Revenue, etc.	1
.. 10.	The Working of the Shanghai Office	1
.. 11.	Alphabetical Arrangement of Tariff and Practice Questions Settled.(1881-1886).	1
.. 16.	Instructions for Revenue Steamers.(2nd Issue).	1
.. 18.	China and Foreign Powers.	1
.. 19.	Statistical Secretary's Printed Notes(2nd Issue). Also current volume.	1
.. 22.	Practice Questions Settled.(1881-1899).	1
.. 23.	Tariff	1
.. 26.	Instructions for measuring Vessels for Tonnage (1905)	1
.. 29.	Compendium of I.G.Circular Instructions(2nd Issue): Part 1: Service Organisation. Part 2: Office Practice.	1
	Compendium of I.G.Cir.Instructions(3rd Issue).	1
.. 34.	Instructions regarding Service Launches.	1
.. 37.	Service Atlas.	1
.. 38.	Handbook for Chinese Examinations.	1
.. 40.	Instructions for the Customs River Police,Shai.	1
.. 42.	Memorandum Concerning the Choice of Steam and Motor Launches for the Customs Service.	1
.. 43.	Tidewaiter Duties: Newchwang.	1
.. 46.	Williams' Canton Examiners' Reference Book(1923)	1

3.

IV. Service Series (continued):

		Vol.
No.48.	Outdoor Staff Duties: Shanghai: 2nd Issue.	1
	3rd Issue.	1
.. 51.	List of Customs Publications with Alph.Index.	1
.. 52.	Dangerous Cargo.	1
.. 54.	Instructions for Measuring Oil Tanks and Calculating Gauge Tables.	1

V. Office Series:

		Vol.
No.12.	Haikwan Banking System: Commissioner's Reports.	1
.. 17.	Joint Investigation Cases.	1
.. 19.	Customs Service: Officers in charge(1859-1880).	1
.. 30.	Foreign Legations in China: List of Members (1517-1889).	1
.. 38.	Memorandum on Transit Outwards at Chinkiang.	1
.. 44.	Customs Service: Officers in charge(1859-1898).	1
.. 46.	Memorandum on the Prospects of Trade at Shai.	1
.. 47.	Sycee: Weight, Value, Touch.	1
.. 51.	Inward Transit Passes: Shanghai Practice(1896).	1
.. 54.	Fiscal Treatment Inland and at Shanghai of goods going to,and coming from,the Interior;and a Memorandum on the Present Inland Taxation of Silk and Cocoons.	1
.. 57.	Outward Transit Trade. Reports on Port Practice.	1
.. 60.	Chinese Shan States.	1
.. 61.	Suggestions for Increasing Export Trade.	1
.. 64.	Two Trips in the Chinese Shan States.	1
.. 65.	Trip to Meng-Lien and Other Shan States.	1
.. 66.	Further Suggestions for Increasing Export Trade	1
.. 73.	Native Customs. (In 6 Parts).	6
.. 84.	Currency, Weights and Measures in China.	1
.. 97.	Memorandum Concerning the Journey to Hunchun.	1
.. 98.	,, ,, ,, from Ichang to Chungking	1
.. 99.	Report of the Marine Department, 1909 & 1910.	1
.. 100.	,, ,, ,, ,, 1911.	1
.. 101.	The Revolution in Hankow, 1911.	1
.. 102.	Currency: No. 2.	1
.. 103.	Report Concerning Steam Launch Traffic on the Grand Canal.	1
.. 104.	Report of the Marine Department, 1912.	1
.. 105.	,, ,, ,, ,, 1913.	1
.. 106.	,, ,, ,, ,, 1914.	1
.. 107.	Wuhu Native Customs.	1
.. 108.	Report of the Marine Department, 1915.	1
.. 109.	Report on System of Native Taxation in Fengtien Province.	1
.. 110.	Report of the Marine Department, 1916.	1
.. 112.	Timber Rafts on Lower Yangtse.	1
.. 113.	Report of the Marine Department, 1917.	1
.. 114.	Tengyueh: Notes on Journey to Niu Ch'Uan Ho.	1
.. 115.	Report of the Marine Department, 1918.	1
.. 117.	The Transfer Teel System.	1
.. 118.	Report of the Marine Department, 1919.	1

4.

LIST OF BOOKS : COMMISSIONER'S OFFICIAL LIBRARY.

(Continued)

V. Office Series (Continued): vols

		vols
No.119.	Report of the Marine Department, 1920.	1
,, 120.	,, ,, ,, ,, ,, , 1921.	1
,, 121.	,, ,, ,, ,, ,, , 1922.	1
,, 122.	Record of a Journey to Menglish and Iwn.	1
,, 123.	Report of the Marine Department, 1923.	1
,, 124.	,, ,, ,, ,, ,, , 1924.	1.

VI. Inspectorate Series:

No. 5.	Memorandum on the Establishment of the Imperial Maritime Customs in 1854: George Lanning.	1
,, 6.	The Collection and Disposal of the Maritime and Native Customs Revenue since the Revolution of 1911: S.F.Wright.	1

Sundry Customs Publications:

Movements in the Service:	
Gazettes Nos.154 - 351.	
Speakman,H.: Notes on Piece Goods.	1
Rules for the Use of Laodahs in charge of Customs Launches.	1
Regulations for Preventing Collisions at Sea.	1
Instructions for the Outdoor Staff.	1
Instructions for the Service Card Index System.	1
Handbook on Etiquette in Chinese Official Intercourse.	1
Tariff Revision, 1867-1869: Reports of Commissioners.	1
Williams,C.A.S.: A Manual of Chinese Metaphor.	1
Illustrated Catalogue of the Standard Furniture for the Chinese Customs Service.	1
Returns of Native Charges as far as they can be Ascertained levied on the Principal Imports and Exports at and near the different Treaty Ports in China, etc.	1
Memorandum : Journey to Ssemao.	1
Blanco,A.E.: Piece Goods Duty Index.	1
Export Tariff: 6th Issue.	1
Revised Import Tariff: 1922.	1
War : 1914 - 1918.	1

Miscellaneous Books and Pamphlets:

Harbour Regulations for the Port of Taheiho.	1
MacGowan,J.: Imperial History of China.	1
Edkins,J.: The Revenue Taxation of the Chinese Empire.	1
,, ,, : Chinese Currency.	1
,, ,, : Banking and Prices in China.	1
Aigun Customs Provisional Regulations.	1
Provisional Customs Regulations, etc., on the Sungari.	1

5.

LIST OF BOOKS : COMMISSIONER'S OFFICIAL LIBRARY.

(Continued)

Miscellaneous Books and Pamphlets:(Continued): vols

	vols
Morse,H.B.: The Trade and Administration of the Chinese Empire.	1
English-Russian Dictionary.	1
Russian-English Dictionary.	1
Storms in September, 1910.	1
Foreign Import Duties, 1910.	1
Stent,G.C.: English-Chinese Dictionary.	1
MacGillivary,D.: Mandarin Romanised Dictionary of Chinese.	1
Richard's Comprehensive Geography of the Chinese Empire.	1
Giles,A.: Chinese-English Dictionary(2 vols.).	2
Hirth,F.: Textbook of Modern Documentary Chinese	1
Arnold,J.: Commercial Handbook of China (2 vols.).	2
Hemeling,K.: English-Chinese Dictionary.	1
La Pluie en Chine (1900-1910).	
The Typhoon of July 28th 1915 (The Chinhai Typhoon) and its Effects at Shanghai.	1
Résumé Du Catalogue Des Tremblements De Terre Signalés En Chine.	1
Les Cartes Du Temps De Zi-ka-wei et Les Moyennes Mensuelles.	
Bulletin des Observations: 1906 - 1911.	6
Imprimerie de L'orphelinat de Tou-se-we, 1913.	1
Calendrier Annuaire: current volume.	1
North China Desk Hong List: current volume.	1
Postal Service List: current volume.	1
Reports on the working of the Chinese Post Office: 1909-1924.	16
Reports on the Chinese Post Office Savings Bank: 1919, 1921, 1922, 1923, 1924.	5
Shanghai Regulations: Customs, Harbour, Settlement,etc.	1
Handbook of Customs Procedure at Shanghai(& Addenda).	1
Ferguson,T.T.H.: Fragments of Confucian Lore.	1
Webster's Collegiate Dictionary with Chinese Translation.	1
Plant Memorial Monument.	1
Yangtze River Commission: 1st Annual Report,1923.	1
,, ,, ,, 2nd ,, ,, ,1924.	1
Palmer,F.: The Yangtze River Commission Report,Nov.1923.	1
British Municipal Council, Tientsin, 1920 Report.	1
North Manchurian Plague Prevention Service:Report 1914-17.	1
,, ,, ,, ,, :Regulations.	1
Levine,C.C.: The Water Buffalo for Dairy purposes.	1
Underwood Standard Typewriter: Instructions for Use of.	1
Bank of China: Annual Report, 1920.	1
List of Post Offices: current volume.	1
Postal Guide: current volume.	1
University of Nanking: Daily Meteorological Records; Nos.1-6.	6
University of Nanking: Summary of University Meteorological Records: 1895-1923.	1
The Chronicles of the East India Company trading to China. 1635-1834. Vols.I, II, III, & IV.	4
Otte,F.: Scientific Elements of Bank Accounting.	1
The Shanghai Market Prices Report: quarterly:	
1923: Jan.-Mar., Apr.-June, July-Sept., Oct.-Dec.	4
1924: July-Sept., Oct.-Dec.	2
1925: Jan.-Mar., Apr.-June, July-Sept.	3
Свод Законов Россійской Имперіи	

6.

LIST OF BOOKS : COMMISSIONER'S OFFICIAL LIBRARY.

(Continued)

Chinese Books and Pamphlets:

大黑河中外俱樂部組織大綱紀錄	1
黑河恒雅電話局裝修電話規則	1
中華民國黑龍江黑河糧服聯合會提議要求條件附款	1
黑龍江黑河糧服會蹉商阿穆爾國有兵工表協會答覆要求條件及電擇案附錄	1
大中華民國黑龍江省黑河糧服會宣言書	1
改訂俄的調查綱目表 附俄的異同表	1
海關常關地址道里表	1
稅務處第二次一覽統計表民國高年分	1
稅務處第三次一覽統計表民國壹年分	1

7.

LIST OF BOOKS: EXAMINERS' REFERENCE LIBRARY.

Customs Publications: II. -Special Series:

No.		
No. 3.	Shaw,N.: Silk : Manchurian Tussore Silk.	1
" 8.	Braun,R.: List of Medicines,Hankow(3rd issue).	1
" 16.	Henry,A.: Chinese Jute.	1
" 31.	Shaw,N.: The Soya Bean of Manchuria.	1
" 36.	Ho Chee Fai: Notes on Sericulture in Chekiang.	1
" 37.	Finlayson,M.: Contents of a Portable Sample Case.1	
" 38.	Watson,E.: Principal Articles of Chinese Commerce.1	

Customs Publications: III. -Miscellaneous Series:

No.		
No.17.	List of Chinese Medicines.	1
" 32.	List of Chinese Steam and Motor Vessels of 100 tons Gross and Over: 1920, 1921, 1922, 1923, 1924, 1925.	6

Customs Publications: IV. -Service Series :

No.		
No. 2.	Provisional Instructions for the Guidance of the Outdoor Staff (Second issue).	1
" 16.	Instructions for Commanders and Officers of Revenue Steamers(3rd issue).	1
" 30.	Braun,R.: Weighing.	1
" 32.	Steam-launches and Motor-launches: their Comparative Utility for Service Purposes.	1
" 34.	Instructions regarding Service Launches.	1
" 43.	Tidewaiters' Duties; Newchwang.	1
" 26.	Instructions for Measuring Vessels for Tonnage (1916).	1
" 42.	Memorandum Concerning the Choice of Steam and Motor Launches for the Customs Service.	1
" 45.	Memo. Economy of Stores, Care of Materials(1921).1	
" 46.	Williams, Canton Examiners' Reference Book.	1
" 48.	Outdoor Staff Duties: Shanghai(2nd issue).	1
"	" " " (3rd issue).	2*
" 51.	List of Customs Publications with Alph. Index.	1
" 52.	Dangerous Cargo: Its Nature and Treatment and the Usual Mode of packing.	1
" 54.	Instructions for Measuring Oil Tanks and Calculating Gauge Tables.	1

Customs Publications: V. -Office Series:

No.		
No. 40.	Samples	1
" 111.	Brumfield,F.J.: Memorandum on Chinese Ginseng.	1
" 112.	Wright,S.F.: Timber Rafts on the Lower Yangtze.	1

* In duplicate.

8.

LIST OF BOOKS : EXAMINERS' REFERENCE LIBRARY.

(Continued)

Customs Sundry Publications: Vols.

Blanco,A.E.: Piece Goods Manual.   1
Blanco,A.E.: Piece Goods Duty Index.   2*
Instructions for the Outdoor Staff.   2*
Regulations for Preventing Collisions at Sea.   1
Rules for the Use of Laodahs in Charge of Customs Launches. 1
Speakman,H.: Notes on Piece Goods.   1
Ricks,A.F.C.: Gauging.   1
Instructions to Clerks of Works on Painting,
  Distempering, etc.   1

Miscellaneous Publications:

Mitchell,C.A.: Oils.   1
Keable,B.B.: Coffee.   1
Stevens,H.P.: and Beadle, C.: Rubber.   1
Ibbetson,A.: Tea.   1
Tanner,L.E.: Tobacco.   1
Hooper,L.: Silk.   1
Peake,R.J.: Cotton.   1
Hood,C.: Iron.   1
Martineau,G.: Sugar.   1
Hunter,I.A.: Wool.   1
Rutley,F.: Elements of Mineralogy.   1
Bowman,F.H.: The Structure of the Wool Fibre.   1
Peet,G.H.: Weights and Measurements of Cargo Exported
  from Shanghai and North China. April,1925.   1
Stuart,C.A.: Chinese Materia Medica.   1
Poland,H.: Fur bearing Animals.   1
Slater, J.A.: Dictionary of World's Commercial Products.   1
Arnold,J.: Commercial Handbook of China (2 volumes).   2

                         Commissioner.

CUSTOM HOUSE.
Aigun/Taheiho, 21st June, 1926.

        * In duplicate.

呈总税务司署 <u>270</u> 号文   瑷珲关 1926 年 6 月 21 日

尊敬的海关总税务司（北京）：

    根据总税务司署第 3688 号通令（第二辑）：

    "海关图书馆：请呈送海关图书馆藏书清单。"

    兹附瑷珲关图书馆藏书清单。

您忠诚的仆人

瑚斯敦（J. H. W. Houstoun）

瑷珲关税务司

瑷珲关致总税务司署第 270 号呈附件

瑷珲关图书馆清单

——税务司官方图书馆

表 1

一、统计丛书：	卷数
第 2 号:《关册》——贸易季报：	
第 133-136 号：罚款及充公货物变价（1902 年）	1
第 165-171 号；第 173-204 号（1910-1919 年）	39
第 2-5 号：贸易季报：	
1920 年：1-3 月、4-6 月、7-9 月贸易报告	3
10-12 月贸易报告、年度贸易报告（2 卷）	2
1921 年：1-3 月、4-6 月、7-9 月贸易报告	3
10-12 月贸易报告、年度贸易报告（2 卷）	2
1922 年：1-3 月、4-6 月、7-9 月贸易报告	3
10-12 月贸易报告、年度贸易报告（2 卷）	2
1923 年：1-3 月、4-6 月、7-9 月、10-12 月贸易报告	4
第 3-5 号：年度贸易报告及报表：	
1923 年（1 卷）	1
第 2 号：贸易季报：	
1924 年：1-3 月、4-6 月、7-9 月、10-12 月贸易报告	4
第 3-5 号：年度贸易报告及报表：	
1924 年（1 卷）	1
第 2 号：贸易季报：	
1925 年：1-3 月、4-6 月、7-9 月、10-12 月贸易报告	4
第 3-4 号：贸易报告及报表：	
1909-1915 年（每年 2 卷）	14
第 3-5 号：贸易报告及报表：	
1916-1919 年（每年 2 卷）	8

表2

第2-5号：中国外贸：	
1920-1922年	3
第3-5号：中国外贸：	
1923-1924年	2
第6号：《各口海关十年报告》：	
1892-1901年第2期（2卷）	2
1902-1911年第3期	1
1912-1921年第4期	1
二、特种丛书：	卷数
第2号：医学报告：第68-80期	1
第3号：《丝绸》(1917年版)	1
第5号：航船布告：1910年、1911年、1912年、1913年、1914年	5
第6号：《中国音乐》	1
第8号：《药物清单》(1909年版)	1
第18号：中国救生艇等	1
第22号：铁路及内陆税捐	1
第23号：广东出口转运过境章程(临时章程)	1
第29号：《黄河摘记》	1
第32号：《云南西部贸易路线注释》	1
第33号：《左江》	1
第34号：《长江宜昌—重庆段船长指导手册》	1
第35号：《1920年10月江苏东北部游记》	1
第37号：《便捷式货样箱装运物品》(Contents of a Portable Sample Case)：芬雷森(Finlayson, M.)著	1
第38号：《中国主要商品》(Principal Articles of Chinese Commerce)：沃森(Watson, E.)著	1
第39号：龙州地区等	1
三、杂项丛书：	卷数
第6号：中国灯塔管理处列表等：	

表3

1911年、1912年、1913年、1914年、1915年、1918年、1920年、1921年、1922年	9
第7号：中国灯塔管理处列表等（中文版）：	
1912年、1914年、1920年、1922年、1924年	5
第10号：中国沿海地区及长江地区地名	1
第12号：公证手续细则	1
第15号：专业术语英汉汇编（灯桩等）	1
第16号：1923年刊物表（第3期）	1
第25号：通则及地方规章等（第2期），2卷	2
第30号：中外条约、公约等（第2版），2卷	2
第31号：长江潮汐预测统计表：	
1922年、1923年、1924年、1925年、1926年	5
四、关务丛书：	卷数
第1号：《海关题名录》（通用卷）	1
海关总税务司通令（第1-2辑）：	
1-5卷（装订成册）、7-17卷（装订成册）、通用索引及通用卷	16
工厂产品通令（第3辑）：	
1-2卷（装订成册）、通用索引及通用卷	2
第6号：关于编写及呈交海关账目之指示（第5期）	1
第8号：关于编写贸易及税收等报告之指示	1
第10号：总税务司署上海办事处工作	1
第11号：《税则及惯例问题解答》（按字母顺序排列）（1881-1886年）	1
第16号：《大巡船指南》（第2期）	1
第18号：《中外权力》	1
第19号：造册处税务司通启（第2期）及通用卷	1
第22号：《惯例问题解答》（1881-1899年）	1
第23号：《税则问题解答》（1881-1899年）	1
第26号：《测量船只吨位指南》（1905年）	1

表4

第 29 号：总税务司署通令指示概要（第 2 期）：	
第 1 部分：海关组织	1
第 2 部分：海关惯例	1
总税务司署通令指示概要（第 3 期）	1
第 34 号：海关汽艇相关指示	1
第 37 号：《海关地图集》	1
第 38 号：《中国海关验货手册》	1
第 40 号：沙市关内河水上警察厅须知	1
第 42 号：海关汽艇及摩托艇选择通函	1
第 43 号：铃子手职务：牛庄关	1
第 46 号：《广东验货员参考书目》（1923 年）：威廉（Williams）著	1
第 48 号：外班职员职务：江海关	1
第 2 期	1
第 3 期	1
第 51 号：《海关出版物清单索引》（按字母顺序排列）	1
第 52 号：《危险货物》	1
第 54 号：《油箱及计量表测量指南》	1
五、官署丛书：	卷数
第 12 号：海关银行系统：税务司报告	1
第 17 号：会讯案件	1
第 19 号：海关：负责关员（1859-1880 年）	1
第 30 号：外国驻华公使：职员表（1517-1889 年）	1
第 38 号：镇江出口转运通函	1
第 44 号：海关：负责关员（1859-1898 年）	1
第 46 号：沙市关贸易前景报告	1
第 47 号：银锭：重量、价值、特征	1
第 51 号：进口过境单：江海关惯例（1896 年）	1
第 54 号：内地及上海关于货物往来内地的财政政策；内地关于丝绸与茧的税收办法通函	1

表5

第 57 号：出口过境单：口岸惯例报告	1
第 60 号：中国傣族地区（Chinese Shan States）	1
第 61 号：关于增加出口贸易之建议	1
第 64 号：两次走访中国傣族地区（Chinese Shan States）	1
第 65 号：走访蒙里（Menglieh）及其他掸族地区（Shan States）	1
第 66 号：关于增加出口贸易之建议	1
第 73 号：常关（分为六部分）	1
第 84 号：中国货币、重量及单位	1
第 97 号：关于前往珲春关的通函	1
第 98 号：关于自宜昌至重庆的通函	1
第 99 号：1909-1910 年船钞部报告	1
第 100 号：1911 年船钞部报告	1
第 101 号：1911 年汉口革命	1
第 102 号：货币：第 2 号	1
第 103 号：大运河上的汽艇运输报告	1
第 104 号：1912 年海政局报告	1
第 105 号：1913 年海政局报告	1
第 106 号：1914 年海政局报告	1
第 107 号：芜湖常关	1
第 108 号：1915 年海政局报告	1
第 109 号：奉天省境内税收系统报告	1
第 110 号：1916 年海政局报告	1
第 112 号：《长江下游的木筏（Timber Rafts on the Lower Yangtze）》：魏尔特（S. F. Wright）著	1
第 113 号：1917 年海政局报告	1
第 114 号：腾越关：牛圈河游记	1
第 115 号：1918 年海政局报告	1
第 117 号：海关两转账系统	1
第 118 号：1919 年海政局报告	1

表6

内容	数量
第 119 号：1920 年海政局报告	1
第 120 号：1921 年海政局报告	1
第 121 号：1922 年海政局报告	1
第 122 号：勐烈与易武旅行报告	1
第 123 号：1923 年海政局报告	1
第 124 号：1924 年海政局报告	1
六、总署丛书：	卷数
第 5 号：《1854 年帝国海关成立的通函》： 乔治·兰尼（George Lanning）著	1
第 6 号：《辛亥革命后海关及常关税收的征收及处置办法》： 魏尔特（S. F. Wright）著	1
各类海关出版物：	
海关活动：	
《关册》第 154—351 号	
《按件货物注释》：斯皮克曼（Speakmen, H.）著	1
《海关汽艇负责人使用章程》	1
《航海避碰章程》	1
《外班职员须知》	1
《海关信息编录系统指南》	1
《中国关员交往礼节手册》	1
《税则修订》（1867—1869 年）：税务司报告	1
《中国隐喻手册》（A Manual of Chinese Metaphor）： 文林士（Williams, C. A. S.）著	1
《中国海关标准家具插图目录》	1
《国内收费统计表——明确由中国各通商口岸及其附近地区征收的主要进出口税》	1
关于前往思茅的通函	1
《按件产品税收编录》（Piece Goods Duty Index）： 布兰克（Blanco, A. E.）著	1
《出口税则》：第 6 期	1

表7

《进口税则修订》：1922 年	1
《战争》：1914-1918 年	1
杂书杂册：	卷数
大黑河口岸《理船章程》	1
《中华帝国史》：麦嘉温（MacGowan, J.）著	1
《中华帝国的财政和税制》（The Revenue and Taxation of the Chinese Empire）：艾约瑟（Edkins, J.）著	1
《中国的货币》（Chinese Currency）：艾约瑟（Edkins, J.）著	1
《中国的金融与物价》（Banking and Prices in China）：艾约瑟（Edkins, J.）著	1
瑷珲关《临时章程》	1
松花江上施行的海关《临时章程》等	1
《中华帝国的贸易与行政》：马士（Morse, H. B.）著	1
《英俄字典》	1
《俄英字典》	1
1910 年 9 月东三省水灾	1
1910 年洋货进口税则	1
《英汉字典》：司登得（Stent, G. C.）著	1
《国官话拉丁化字典》（A Mandarin Romanised Dictionary of Chinese）：季理斐（MacGillivary, D.）著	1
《中国坤舆详志》（Comprehensive Geography of the Chinese Empire）：夏之时（Richard, Louis）著	1
《华英词典》（2 卷）：翟理思（Giles, A.）著	2
《中国近代文集》（Textbook of Modern Documentary Chinese）：夏德（Hirth, F.）著	1
《中国商务指南》（2 卷）：安立得（Arnold, J.）著	2
《英汉字典》：赫美玲（Hemeling, K.）著	1
《中国大雨灾》（La pluie en Chine）（1900-1910 年）	1
《1915 年 7 月 28 日台风镇海台风（Chinhai Typhoon）及其对上海的影响》	1

表8

《中国地震标志简要记录》(Resume Du Catalogue Des Tremblements De Terre Signales En Chine)	1
徐家汇每月平均时间表	1
《观察公报》(1906-1911 年)(Bulletin des Observations)	6
《土山湾孤儿院印刷厂》(1913 年)	1
年度日历：通用卷	1
《字林西报行名录》(North China Desk Hong List)：通用卷	1
《邮政题名录》(交通部)：通用卷	1
中国邮局工作报告（ 1909-1924 年 ）	16
中国邮政储蓄银行报告 1919 年、1921 年、1922 年、1923 年、1924 年	5
江海关《海关章程》：海务、港务、清算等	1
江海关《海关程序手册》（及附录）	1
《儒家学说节选》(Fragments of Confucian Lore)：弗格森（ Ferguson, T.T.H. ）著	1
《韦氏大学生用辞典》（附汉译）	1
工厂纪念馆	1
长江委员会：1923 年年度报告（第 1 期） 1924 年年度报告（第 2 期）	1
1923 年 11 月长江委员会报告：帕尔默（ Palmer, F. ）著	1
1920 年天津英国市政议会报告	1
北满洲防疫事务处报告（ 1914-1917 年 ）	1
北满洲防疫事务处章程	1
《用以生产乳制品的水牛》(The Water Buffalo for Dairy Purposes)：列文（ Levine, C.O. ）著	1
［安德伍德］牌标准打字机使用说明	1
中国银行 1920 年年度报告	1
邮局清单：通用卷	1
邮政指南：通用卷	1
南京大学：每日气象报告：1-6 号	6

表9

南京大学：大学气象记录梗概：1895-1923 年	1
《东印度公司对华贸易编年史》(1635-1834 年)(第一、二、三、四卷)	4
《银行账户的科学要素》：奥特(Otte, F.)著	1
上海市场价格季度报告：	
1923 年：1-3 月、4-6 月、7-9 月、10-12 月	4
1924 年：7-9 月、10-12 月	2
1925 年：1-3 月、4-6 月、7-9 月	3
俄文书册：	卷数
汉文书册：(注：以下为中文原文)	卷数
大黑河中外俱乐部组织大纲记录	1
黑河恒曤电话局装修电话规则	1
中华民国黑龙江黑河粮服联合会提议要求／俄国大纲条件附呈文	1
黑龙江黑河粮服会经俄阿穆尔省兵工农协会答复要求条件文电摘要附录	1
大中华民国黑龙江省黑河粮服会宣言书	1
改订俄约调查纲目表附条约认同表	1
海关常关地址道里表	1
税务处第二次一览统计表(民国二、三、四年)	1
税务处第三次一览统计表(民国五、六、七年)	1

瑷珲关图书馆清单
——验货员参考书图书馆

表1

海关出版物：二、特种丛书：	卷数
第3号:《丝绸：满洲蚕丝丝绸》(Silk: Manchurian Tussore Silk)：肖(Shaw, N.)著	1
第8号:《药物清单》(汉口)(第3期)：布劳恩(Braun, R.)著	1
第16号:《中国黄麻纤维》：亨利(Henry, A.)著	1
第31号:《满洲的大豆》：肖(Shaw, N.)著	1
第36号:《浙江蚕丝业摘录》：何慈辉(Ho Chee Fai)著	1
第37号:《便捷式货样箱装运物品》：芬雷森著	1
第38号:《中国主要商品》：沃森(Watson. E)著	1
海关出版物：三、杂项丛书：	卷数
第17号：中药清单	1
第32号：总重≥100吨的中国汽船及摩托艇清单：1920年、1921年、1922年、1923年、1924年、1925年	6
海关出版物：四、关务丛书：	卷数
第2号：外班职员指南临时指示(第2期)	1
第16号:《大巡船船长及驾驶员指南》(第3期)	1
第30号:《称重》：布劳恩(Braun, R.)著	1
第32号：汽艇及摩托艇：海关使用途径比照	1
第34号：海关汽艇相关指示	1
第43号：铃子手职务：牛庄关	1
第26号:《测量船只吨位指南》(1916年)	1
第42号：海关汽艇及摩托艇选择通函	1
第45号：通函：商铺经济、材料处理(1921年)	1
第46号:《广东验货员参考书目》(1923年)：威廉(Williams)著	1
第48号：外班职员职务：江海关(第2期)	1
外班职员职务：江海关(第3期)	

表 2

第 51 号：《海关出版物清单（按字母顺序排列）索引》	2*
第 52 号：危险货物：性质、处理方式及通常包装形式	1
第 54 号：《油箱及计量表测量指南》	1
海关出版物：五、官署丛书：	卷数
第 40 号：样品	1
第 111 号：《中国人参摘记》（Memorandum on Chinese Ginseng）：布罗姆菲尔德（Brumfield, F.J.）著	1
第 112 号：《长江下游的木筏》：魏尔特著	1
各类海关出版物：	卷数
《按件货物手册》：布兰克（Blanco, A. E.）著	1
《按件产品税收编录》：布兰克（Blanco, A. E.）著	2*
《外班职员须知》	2*
《航海避碰章程》	1
《海关汽艇负责人使用章程》	1
《按件货物注释》：斯皮克曼著	1
《规格》：希克斯（Hicks, A. P. C.）著	1
《涂漆工师须知》	1
各类出版物：	卷数
《油》：米契尔（Mitchell, C. A.）著	1
《咖啡》：基布尔（Keable, B. B.）著	1
《橡胶》：史蒂文斯（Stevens, H. P.）与比德尔（Beadle, C.）著	1
《茶》：艾伯特逊（Ibbetson, A.）著	1
《烟草》：达涅尔（Tanner, A. E.）著	1
《丝绸》：胡珀（Hooper, L.）著	1
《棉花》：佩克（Peake, R. J.）著	1
《铁》：胡德（Hood, C.）著	1
《糖》：马蒂诺（Martineau, G.）著	1
《羊毛》：汉特（Hunter, I. A.）著	1

表3

《矿物元素》：鲁特利（Rutley, F.）著	1
《羊毛纤维结构》：鲍温（Bowman, P. H.）著	1
《上海及中国北方出口货物重量及测量法》（1925年4月）：皮特（Peet, G. E.）著	1
《中药》：斯图亚特（Stuart, G. A.）著	1
《毛皮动物》：柏兰德（Poland, H.）著	1
《世界商业产品大辞典》：斯莱特（Slater, J. A.）著	1
《中国商务指南》（2卷）：安立得（Arnold, J.）著	1

注：＊为一式两份

瑚斯敦（J. H. W. Houstoun）

瑷珲关税务司

1926年6月21日，瑷珲关／大黑河

4. 为汇报黑龙江边界沿线各税卡之情形事

543

I.G.

542
I.G.

A I G U N   2nd March 1931.

Sir,

1.   I have the honour to acknowledge receipt of your telegram of the 20th December, 1930:

"The Government has decided that all likin
"stations and barriers extra 50-li N. C. and
"inland Native Customs are to be abolished
"on 1st January 1931: but considers that it
"may be necessary as a consequence of such
"abolition to establish Customs stations at
"places on the frontier for checking import
"and export duties paid at ports.   You are
"therefore in collaboration with your
"colleague at Harbin to make immediate
"investigation of all extra 50-li N. C. and
"likin establishments on the Siberia frontier
"and to submit report dealing with staff
"revenue tariff and trade as soon as possible
"with Chinese version in triplicate.   If
"necessary detach an experienced member of
"your Chinese staff to make requisite
"investigation":

and to report that I duly consulted with the Harbin Commissioner as instructed by you.   I now beg to supply below the result of my investigations, with remarks on present conditions along the Amur frontier, and

The Inspector General of Customs,

S H A N G H A I.

and with recommendations in regard to Customs' requirements and control.   It should be explained that the severe cold and the lack of communications have precluded personal investigation by a member of my staff of each tax office along, and of conditions prevailing at the principal points of, this frontier. The information now submitted has had to be obtained from local sources, and I avail myself of this opportunity to express my gratitude to the former Mayor/Superintendent, Mr. Chang Shou-tsêng (張壽增), for his valuable assistance.   In his former capacity as Heiho Taoyin (黑河道道尹), he controlled the district from the mouth of the Argun River to the mouth of the Sungari River and each tax office in this section supplied him with reports on staff, revenue, and other fiscal matters.

2.   The first necessity in the preparation of this report has been to delimit the boundaries of the districts to be controlled from Harbin and from Aigun, respectively.   With the concurrence of the Harbin Commissioner, it has been considered advisable to limit the Aigun district, for the purpose of this report, to the frontier along the Amur from its source to its confluence with the Sungari River as the orographic configuration of this region is such that the river frontier is enclosed by an almost unbroken chain of mountains.   The Argun River district lies behind the Hingan Mountains (興安嶺) and is inaccessible from places along the Amur for seven or eight months in the year.   It depends for its existence on Hailar (海拉尔), within whose jurisdiction it falls, and, moreover, would appear to afford a natural extension for Customs' control based on Manchouli (满洲里) or

Hailar.

Hailar. Control of the Amur frontier from the
Sungari River to the Ussuri River by the Harbin
Customs would be a natural corollary to control by
that Office of these two rivers. The only section
of the Aigun district which would extend beyond the
Hingan Mountains would be that lying between Lopeihsien
(嵩 北 縣) and the Sungari River, but as this river,
with Harbin's sub-port of Lahasusu (拉 古 蘇 蘇), forms
the ideal point of junction of the two districts, it
would be impractical to confine the Aigun Customs too
rigidly to the Trans-Hingan region.

3.　　　　A list of the Tax Offices functioning along
the frontier, from Lokuho (洛 古 河), at the mouth
of the Argun River, to the Sungari River, with
particulars of staff, revenue, and trade, is forwarded,
appended hereto.

4.　　　　A copy of the Tariff promulgated by the
Heilungkiang Government in the year 1929 and in force
at all Tax Offices throughout the province is
forwarded, enclosed herewith. The portions of the
Tariff relevant to the present report are :-

Part V: Consolidated Tax Regulations.
　　Section I: Article 2: Tariff for Collection
　　　　　　　　　　　of Taxes on Local
　　　　　　　　　　　Produce.
　　　　　Article 3: Distribution Tax.
　　　　　Article 4: Miscellaneous Taxes and
　　　　　　　　　　　Dues: Items 1, 2, 3, 5
　　　　　　　　　　　and 17.
　　Section II: Method of Collection.
　　　　　Articles 5 to 9.
　　Section III: Tax Receipts.
　　　　　Articles 10 and 11.
　　　　　　　　　　　　　　Section

Section IV: Fines.
　　　　Article 12.
Section V: Remarks.
　　　　Articles 13, 14, and 15.
Part VI: Tariff for Provisional Military Surtaxes
　　　　on all taxes and dues of the Province
　　　　of Heilungkiang.
Section III: Local Produce Tax.
Section IV: Distribution Tax.
Section V: Miscellaneous Taxes and Dues.
　　　　Articles 1, 2, 3 and Remarks at
　　　　　　　　end of Section V.

The levy mentioned under Part V, Section I, Article 4,
Item No. 17, and in Part VI, Section V, Article 3,
has, I am informed, been changed to "Business Tax
(營 業 稅)" since the 1st July, 1930. It is
collected once a month from all shops and dealers on
sales made during the month. In addition to the
taxes and dues mentioned in the Tariff, there is a
"Local Authorities' Tax (地 方 捐)", varying in amount
in each district but fixed at 5% ad valorem at
Taheiho and Aigun, which is leviable whenever the
Tariff Taxes or Dues are paid. The proceeds of this
tax are used for education and for volunteer equipment.
To illustrate the working of the Tariff, I give
hereunder, examples of taxation imposed on goods moved
within the province, and on goods to and from other
provinces:

I.- Local Produce moved within the Heilungkiang
　　Province:
　A.- At time of export:
　1. Local Produce Tax (Part V, Section I, Article 2).
　2. Distribution Tax if Grain or Firecrackers (Part
　　　V, Section I, Article 3).

　　　　　　　　　　　　　　　　　3.

3. Military Surtax (Part VI, Sections III and IV).

4. Local Authorities' Tax, varying according to district.

5. Business Tax (Part V, Section I, Article 4, Item 17).

6. Military Surtax on Business Tax (Part VI, Section V, Article 3).

Note: Nos. 5 and 6 are collected once a month from all shops and dealers on sales made during the month.

7. Miscellaneous Tax (Part V, Section I, Article 4).

8. Military Surtax on Miscellaneous Tax (Part VI, Section V).

Note: Nos. 7 and 8 are collected on Livestock every time they change hands (Part V, Section II, Article 6, and Part VI, Section V, Article 1 and Remarks at end of Section V).

B.- On arrival at destination:

If covered by Tax Receipts:

1. Business Tax at end of each month calculated on actual sales (Part V, Section I, Article 4, Item 17).

2. Military Surtax on above (Part VI, Section V, Article 3).

3. Miscellaneous Tax, if Livestock (Part V, Section I, Article 4).

4. Military Surtax on above (Part VI, Section V, Article 1 and Remarks at end of Section V).

5. Document Inspection Tax (Part V, Section III, Article 11). This tax is levied at each Tax Office passed.

If not covered by Tax Receipts:

As under I: A. Also Business Tax and Surtax

as under B.

II.- Local Produce moved to other Provinces:

As under I: Local Produce moved within Heilungkiang: A.- At time of Export.

III.-Produce from other Provinces:

If covered by Tax Receipts for taxes enumerated in Heilungkiang Province Tariff:

As under I: B, but "Canton" Firecrackers and Grain and Timber pay in addition :

1. Distribution Tax (Part V, Section I, Article 3, Item 4) in the case of the first;

2. Distribution Tax (Part V, Section I, Article 3, Item 2) and Military Surtax (Part VI, Section IV, Article 2) in the case of the second;

3. Miscellaneous Tax (Part V, Section I, Article 4, Item 5) and Military Surtax (Part VI, Section V, Article 2) in the case of the third.

If not covered by Tax Receipts:

As under I: A. Also Business Tax and Surtax as under I: B.

From what I have been told, there is a good deal of leakage in the application of the Tariff. The Tax Office staffs receive such insignificant salaries that they are compelled to resort to dishonest methods to obtain the wherewithal to exist; furthermore, the values accepted for ad valorem articles are far below actual market prices.

5. Conditions along the frontier have been abnormal since the summer of 1923, when the Sino-Soviet frontier was closed and all private trading prohibited. The Chinese authorities retaliated by forbidding all trade across the river unless covered by special permission from the Heilungkiang Government. To enforce its policy, the Soviet lined its frontier from Pokrovka, at

at the mouth of the Argun River, to Habarovsk with military patrols and it is reported that it has at present two batallions of Frontier Guards, assisted by about two thousand G. P. U. (Secret Police) agents, directly or indirectly engaged in preventive work. With the Russian frontier closed and carefully guarded, it may be claimed that the Soviet is actually doing our preventive work for us and, from all accounts, doing it very successfully. Smuggling, which once provided a lucrative occupation for a large number of persons on both sides of the river, is now too hazardous and unprofitable to be attractive. Would-be smugglers must also reckon with the innumerable spies of the G. P. U., and the danger incurred can well be understood when it is realised that every man, woman and child in the Soviet Union is a potential informer as dire penalties are the reward of those who fail in this respect. Definite proof of the decrease in smuggling is afforded by the disappearance of the numerous small shops along the Chinese bank, above and below Taheiho, which formerly thrived on illicit trade with Siberia. Other deterrents to smuggling are : (1) the very low value of the Russian rouble in China; (2) the utter impoverishment and destitution of the entire population of Siberia: (3) the undeveloped state of the Chinese bank along the whole length of the Amur; and (4) the difficulties and expense of transportation through the encircling mountains. As long as the Soviet pursues its present economic policy, - and no change which would not fundamentally alter the constitution of the communist state can be foreseen, the danger to the revenue will not be from individual attempts to cross the frontier, but from organised smuggling by the Soviet Far Eastern Trading Bureau

(Dalgostorg),

(Dalgostorg), the department entrusted with the transaction of trade with this part of Manchuria. This organisation has unlimited scope for importing goods from Russia, and for exporting Chinese produce to Siberia, with little fear of detection. Natural conditions render the first unlikely as the Amur region, lacking in roads and railways, is not suitable as a distributing centre for the more prosperous and populous districts behind the Hingan Mountains, but it is possible, though improbable, that with the present high Tariff the cost of transportation by cart would be less than the import duties evaded. The principal danger is not the facility for the evasion of duties, but the unrestricted field offered for the illicit distribution of arms and ammunition and other contraband and prohibited articles. As regards the unauthorised exportation of Chinese produce, if the Trading Bureau took advantage of the unprotected state of the frontier, it is to be feared that neither the low value of the rouble in China, nor the lack of markets in Russia, would discourage its operations. The activities of this organisation will have to be very carefully watched. It has been authorised to open an agency at Taheiho for the importation and exportation of restricted quantities of goods under special permission from the Heilungkiang Government transmitted through the local Mayor, who, in turn, supplies the Customs with full particulars. Smuggling by individuals has not altogether ceased, but it is so little as to be negligible from a fiscal point of view. Horses and cattle are smuggled across the ice in winter by farmers and refugees, and furs and skins are exchanged by Chinese for gold on the Russian side, but an extensive preventive service would probably be unable to put a

stop

stop to these isolated cases, which occur notwithstanding
the intricate system of guards maintained by the Soviet.
The traffic in horses and cattle should steadily
decrease with the elimination of independent farms in
Russia, and the sale of Chinese skins and furs on the
Russian side should not attain large proportions unless
fostered by the Soviet authorities. The smuggling of
Russian skins and furs to China, a lucrative trade in
the past, has completely ceased as hunters and trappers
in Siberia are unable to obtain the stores and
ammunition necessary to enable them to follow their
former occupations.

6.   It will be seen from the foregoing that the
question of establishing Customs' stations is complicated
by the abnormal conditions which have prevailed for the
past eight years; the introduction of an extensive and
expensive preventive service does not seem justified,
but, on the other hand, this vast frontier should not
be left unprotected as there are several elements which
call for careful and constant investigation. I beg to
submit that the first step in an extension of Customs'
control should be the opening of stations at the
principal points along the river, especially where there
is communication with fertile districts and with places
behind the Hingan Mountains, to observe, investigate,
report, and recommend. Points of vantage at which
Customs' stations could be established are:-

UPPER AMUR:

Moho (漠河): about 520 miles above Taheiho.

Lienyin (连荫): about 450 miles above Taheiho.

Wohsimên (倭西们): about 280 miles above Taheiho.

Hsmaho (叶场河): about 170 miles above Taheiho.

Santaoka (三道卡): about 50 miles above Taheiho.

LOWER AMUR:

Chik'ot'e (寺克坤): about 85 miles below Taheiho,

with

with road communication with Mergen (墨尔根或嫩江)
and Lungmên (龙门), and in the midst of a
fertile district.

Wuyunhsien (乌云县): about 180 miles below Taheiho.
The centre of an agricultural district.

Chaoyangchên (朝阳镇): about 260 miles below
Taheiho.

Lopeihsien (萝北县): about 350 miles below Taheiho.

Chaohsingchên (兆兴镇): about 385 miles below
Taheiho.

Chunghsingchên (中兴镇): about 430 miles below
Taheiho.

The Aigun Customs already have two barriers, one at
Moniuho (外卡河) five miles above, and another at
Hsiocheiho (小黑河) five miles below, Taheiho, but
they have both been temporarily closed since 1927, in
accordance with the instructions of I. G. despatch No.
111,337, as it was found that owing to the severe
restrictive measures adopted by the Soviet authorities
smuggling across the frontier had ceased. I cannot
advocate the re-opening of the Liangchiat'un Barrier as,
in my opinion, all the arguments advanced in 1924, in
Aigun despatch No. 187/I. G., against the retention of
this inland post still hold good. An alternative to
the establishment of Customs' stations along the frontier
would be to follow the example of the Soviet and
restrict trade to certain specified areas, but this
would necessitate the close co-operation of the military
and the Customs, a development which is, perhaps, not
practical at present. There are two sections of the
frontier to which special attention should be given,
the first being that between Taheiho and Wuyunhsien,
and the second lying between Lopeihsien and the Sungari
River. Chik'ot'e and Wuyunhsien are in the midst of
a fertile district with roads leading to Mergen,

Moho

Noho (讷河) and Lungmen. The frontier between Lopeihsien and the Sungari River provides easy access to the wealthy city of Fuchin (富錦), and smuggled imports could be distributed to Harbin and other large centres. If, later, both frontiers are opened to private and unrestricted trading, it would be necessary to provide an efficient preventive service, with both land and water patrols, but such a possibility is not likely for a long time and, even if a change did occur in the Soviet's policy, recuperation in Siberia would probably be long and tedious as the country has been denuded of all resources. Development on the Chinese side will no doubt proceed independently of Russia and greater vigilance will be required when railways and good roads have been extended to various places on the Amur River, but all these contingencies appear too remote just now to warrant serious consideration. A nucleus, around which an extensive preventive service could be built later, is all that seems necessary at the beginning. I would add here that Chinese goods moved on the Chinese side of the frontier are not liable to Customs' duties until they are declared for places on the Sungari River.

7.　　　To facilitate the study of local conditions, and to supply information in a compact form regarding local peculiarities, I beg to forward, under separate cover, two maps:-

  One, on a scale of 100 versts to the inch, of
   North Manchuria and its frontier; and
  One, on a scale of 40 versts to the inch, of
   the Amur River with detailed particulars of
   the Chinese and Russian frontiers.

I regret that, in entering the names of Chinese places, my instructions that Giles's romanisation be used have not been closely followed.

8.

8.　　　A Chinese version of this report, in triplicate, is forwarded enclosed herewith.

   I have the honour to be,
    Sir,
   Your obedient Servant,

   (Signed) C. B. Joly
    (C. H. B. Joly)
   Acting Commissioner.

Appendix.

APPENDIX

TAX OFFICES ALONG THE CHINESE AMUR RIVER FRONTIER FROM LOKUHO, AT THE MOUTH OF THE ARGUN RIVER, TO THE MOUTH OF THE SUNGARI RIVER, WITH PARTICULARS OF STAFF, REVENUE, AND TRADE:

Name of Tax Office	Staff				Trade	Yearly Revenue: (Based on 1929 figures) Harbin $
	Director or officer in charge	Watchmen	Clerks	Inspector		
I.- UPPER AMUR						
MOHO DISTRICT (漠河区):						
Head Office						
Moho 漠河	1*	3	1	1	Local produce, such as rafts, timber, firewood, fungus, skins, deer horns, & mushrooms sent to other places on the Chinese bank, & provisions and stores from Taheiho & Sungari ports.	6,000.00$
Sub-offices						
Lokuho 洛古河	1*	1	.	.	Local produce, such as rafts, firewood, fungus, mushrooms, timber, skins, deer horns, medicine & birch tar sent to other places on the Chinese bank, and provisions and stores from Taheiho & Sungari ports.	300.00
额木尔河湾 Nachinhsta	1*	1	.	.		700.00
Wusuli 乌苏里	1*	1	.	.		200.00
巴尔喀? Paerhkali	1*	1	.	.		150.00
Lienyin 连荫	1*	2	1	.		1,000.00
阿穆尔? Amuerhshan	1*	1	.	.		250.00
卡库? Kaiku'ang	1*	1	.	.		400.00
OPU OR WOHSIMEN DISTRICT (鸥浦或漠西门区):						
Head Office						
漠西门 Wohsimen	1*	2	1	1	Local produce, such as grain, rafts, firewood, fungus, timber, etc., sent to other places on the Chinese side, provisions & stores from Taheiho and Sungari ports, & a few horses smuggled across the frontier by refugees.	3,000.00$
Sub-offices						
Anloka 安罗卡	1*	1	.	.	- do -	400.00
依西门 Ihsik'en	1*	1	.	.	- do -	1,600.00
HUMAHO						
HUMAHO DISTRICT (呼玛河区):						
Head Office						
Kuchan 古站	1*	2	2	1	Local produce, such as birch tar, rafts, timber, firewood, deer horns, skins & medicines sent to other places on the Chinese side, & provisions and stores from Taheiho & Sungari ports.	4,000.00$
Sub-offices						
Ankanka 安干卡 西克楞奇	1*	1	.	.	Local produce, such as rafts, timber, fungus, birch tar, bilberries, medicines, deer horns & skins sent to other places on the Chinese side, and provisions & stores from Taheiho and Sungari ports.	200.00
Haierhkenghi 黑尔奇	1*	1	.	.		300.00
Chaheyen 洛湛河	1*	1	.	.		1,000.00
Hutungho	1*	1	.	.		500.00
Humaho 呼玛河	1	2	1	.	Same as Kuchan	2,000.00$
II.- MIDDLE AMUR						
AIGUN DISTRICT (爱珲区):						
Head Office						
Taheiho 大黑河	1	6	5	4	Local produce from Upper Amur, exports to Amur & Sungari ports, & provisions & stores from Harbin & Sungari ports. Restricted quantities of wines and tobacco from Blagoveshchensk, & beans exported to Siberia under special permission.	23,000.00$
Sub-offices						
Manchowt'un 满洲屯	1	2	1	1	Local produce, such as rafts, firewood, skins, grain and fungus to Amur and Sungari ports, and provisions & stores from Taheiho and Sungari ports.	500.00
Woniuho 卧牛河	1	1	.	.	Hay, fodder & skins transported from places on the Chinese bank by sledges during the winter months.	150.00
Aigun						

Name of Tax Office	Staff				Trade	Yearly Revenue: (Based on 1929 figures) Harbin $
	Director or Officer in charge	Watchers	Clerks	Inspectors		
Aigun 瑷珲	1	2	1	1	Local produce from Upper Amur, exports to Amur & Sungari ports, & provisions & stores from Harbin & Sungari ports	12,000.00$
Tawuchiatze	1	1	.	1	Local produce, such as grain deer horns, & fungus to Amur & Sungari ports, & a few horses smuggled across the frontier by refugees	
Sunch't'un	1	1	1	.		2,000.00

Note: (1) The Woniuho Station is open from middle of October to middle of April. There is a Customs barrier here, but it has been temporarily closed since 1927 (vide §6 of despatch).
(2) There are also two inland barriers at Shanshanfu (山神府) and at Sanchiatza(三家子). The former is open from middle of October to middle of April to collect taxes on hay, fodder and skins, and the latter is open whilst the flour mill is operating to collect taxes on grain and wheat supplied to the mill. The total taxes collected by these two offices is about $350.00 a year.

III.- LOWER AMUR:

CHIK'OT'E DISTRICT (奇克特区):

Head Office

Chik'ot'e 奇克特	1+	3	1	1	Local produce, such as grain, fungus, skins, deer horns to Amur & Sungari ports, provisions & stores from Harbin & Sungari ports, & a few horses smuggled across the frontier by refugees. Some beans to Siberia under special permission	4,000.00$
Sub-offices						
Kapaliangtze 喀巴梁子	1	2	.	.	Local produce, such as grain, fungus, skins, deer horns to Amur & Sungari ports, provisions & stores from Harbin & Sungari ports, & a few horses smuggled across the frontier by refugees.	1,500.00$
Chelo 车仡	1	1	.	.	- do -	500.00$
Shangtaokan 上道杆	1	1	.	.	- do -	200.00$

WUYUN

Name of Tax Office	Staff				Trade	Yearly Revenue: (Based on 1929 figures) Harbin $
	Director or Officer in charge	Watchers	Clerks	Inspectors		
WUYUN DISTRICT (乌云区):						
Head Office						
Wuyun 乌云	1+	2	1	1	Local produce, such as grain, fungus, skins, deer horns to Amur & Sungari ports, provisions & stores from Harbin & Sungari ports, & a few horses smuggled across the frontier by refugees. Some beans to Siberia under special permission	5,000.00$
Sub-office						
Ch'angchiat'un 长家屯	1	2	.	.	Local produce, such as grain, fungus, skins, deer horns to Amur & Sungari ports, provisions & stores from Harbin & Sungari ports, & a few horses smuggled across the frontier by refugees	2,000.00$
FOSHAN DISTRICT (佛山区):						
Head Office						
Chaoyangchen 朝阳镇	1+	2	1	1	- do -	3,500.00$
LOPEI DISTRICT (萝北区):						
Head Office						
Lopei 萝北	1	4	1	1	Local produce, such as grain, fungus, skins & medicines to Amur & Sungari ports, provisions & stores from Harbin & Sungari ports.	9,000.00$
Sub-offices						
Taipingkou 太平沟	1	3	1	.	- do -	3,000.00$
Chaochingchen 肇兴镇	1*	1	.	.	- do -	600.00
Chunghsinchen 中兴镇	1	2	.	.	- do -	400.00

+ The District Magistrate is conjointly Director of the Tax Office. All taxes collected by offices under his control are remitted to the Heilungkiang Finance Commissioner.
* The Officer in charge of the Military Post is also in charge of the Tax Office. All taxes collected are remitted to the Head Office.
§ This figure includes various taxes and dues with which the present report is not concerned. Attempts to obtain separate figures for each heading have failed

呈总税务司署 <u>542</u> 号文　　　　　　　　　　瑷珲关 1931 年 3 月 2 日

尊敬的海关总税务司（上海）：

1. 1930 年 12 月 20 日总税务司署电令收悉：

"现经政府规定，1931 年 1 月 1 日起裁撤厘金税卡、五十里外常关及内地常关，惟自裁撤厘金税卡之后，沿边各地或须设立海关分关，以便稽查各口已完进出口税货之运输。遂请贵署会同滨江关税务司调查西伯利亚边界一带五十里外常关及厘金税卡之状况；关于雇员、税收税率及贸易各情形，请尽快据实呈报，并将该报告译成汉文一并呈交，一式三份。如须实地调查，可派遣贵关华员中有经验者一人前往。"

兹报告，本署已照贵署指示与滨江关税务司协商调查之事。兹谨将奉令调查所得及沿黑龙江边陲情况，以及关于海关所需要并管理之意见详细分析具陈仰祈。

因现属封冻时期，气候异常寒冷，交通尤为阻梗，故未能派员往赴各处厘金税卡进行实地调查，而各处情形今略得梗概，一切详情系由本口各方面来访所得。前黑河市政筹备处处长兼瑷珲关海关监督张寿增先生，曾任黑河道尹，管理自上游额尔古纳河口至下游松花江口所有各卡，对于员司税收及一切财政各状况，素具经验。关于此项调查各情形，承其协助，获益良多，特此敬表谢意。

2. 具此报告，首须划清本关与滨江关管辖之界限。嗣经滨江关税务司同意，瑷珲关暂拟订范围由黑龙江之溯源起至松黑两江合流之点为止。此中所包括者，不只黑龙江边界之一段，乃根据天然地势，此一段区域为兴安岭绵延数千里之山脉所环绕，与他处隔断。此区域之外，额尔古纳河流域在兴安岭之南，每年中有七八月之久与黑龙江流域各地方交通完全阻断。该处居民一切需要，均由海拉尔供给，但其地方不归海拉尔管理，倘海关以满洲里或海拉尔为根据地而管理此区域，其措置必较为顺畅。黑龙江下游自松黑两江合流处起至下游乌苏里江口止一带区域，其海关管辖权仍应依此前一般划入滨江关范围之内。至于黑龙江下游自萝北县起至松黑两江合流处止一带区域，虽在兴安岭山脉环绕以外，但因松花江口有滨江关设立之拉哈苏苏分关，正宜依松花江为界将此段之区域仍归瑷珲关管理，此段难以根据天然山脉之形势划分。

3. 兹谨按此拟定之界限，即由额尔古纳河口洛古河起至松黑两江合流处止，将黑龙江沿江各处税卡用员、税收及贸易各情形详列一表。

4. 并附黑龙江政府 1929 年所规定颁布全省现行征收章程及税则抄件一份，现各税收机关仍依据此章办理。兹将该税则内有关此报告各节摘录如下：

第五篇　黑龙江省征收统税章程

　　第一章　第二条　出产税

　　　　　　第三条　销场税

　　　　　　第四条　各种杂税捐课

　　　　　　　　第一、二、三、五、十七等项

　　第二章　征收手续　第五条至第九条

　　第三章　税票　第十及十一条

　　第四章　罚则　第十二条

　　第五章　附则　第十三、十四及十五等条

第六篇　黑龙江省赋税捐课各项临时军费附加捐捐率

　　第三章　出产税

　　第四章　销场税

　　第五章　各种杂税捐课

　　　　　第一、二、三等条及该章末尾之附注

　　查该章程内第五篇第一章第四条内之第十七项及第六篇第五章内之第三条，据调查所得，自1930年7月1日起已奉令改为营业税，于每月间就各商号按照所售物品多寡而征税。此税则中未及列入者，则有地方捐，其捐率因地而异。瑷珲及大黑河则为值百抽五捐与税同时征收，该捐款系作本地教育金及其他项地方自治之经费。兹谨列举数条，以便解释此税则对于省内及往来各省贸易运输货物之征收办法：

甲　土货在黑龙江省内运输者：

出口之时须征：

一、出产税（参阅第五篇第一章第二条）

二、若系粮食或鞭炮，则有销场税（参阅第五篇第一章第三条）

三、军费附加捐（参阅第六篇第三、四章）

四、地方捐，捐率因地而异

五、营业税（参阅第五篇第一章第四条第十七项）

六、营业税之军费附加捐（参阅第六篇第四章第三条）

附注：第五、第六两种系每月就各商号按其月中所售物品之多寡而征其税。

七、各种杂税捐课（参阅第五篇第一章第四条）

八、杂税捐课之军费附加捐（参阅第六篇第五章）

附注：第七、第八两种对于牲畜，则每经一次买卖即征收一次（参阅第五篇第二章第六条及第六篇第五章第一条及第五章末尾之附注）。

在到达地：

有完税税证者须征：

一、营业税，系每月就各商号按其月中所售物品之多寡而征其税（参阅第五篇第一章第四条第十七项）

二、营业税之军费附加捐（参阅第六篇第五章第三条）

三、若系牲畜，则有各种杂税捐课（参阅第五篇第一章第四条）

四、杂税捐课之军费附加捐（参阅第六篇第五章第一条及第五章末尾之附注）

五、税票验讫费（参阅第五篇第三章第十一条）；各征收局卡查验税票，每张均收验讫费。

无完税税证者须征：

上述出口之时所须征收各税，及到达地有完税税证者所须征收之营业税及军费附加捐。

乙　土货运往他省者：

须征上述土货在黑龙江省内运输，出口之时所须征收各税。

丙　货物之来自他省者：

有已完与黑龙江省征收税则内同等税项之税证者须征：

上述土货在黑龙江省内运输，在到达地有完税税证者所须征收各税，唯广东鞭炮、粮食及木料此外须另行加征：

一、若系鞭炮，则有销场税（参阅第五篇第一章第三条第四项）

二、若系粮食，则有销场税（参阅第五篇第一章第三条第二项）及军费附加捐（参阅第六篇第四章第二条）

三、若系木料，则有各种杂税捐课（参阅第五篇第一章第四条第五项）及军费附加捐（参阅第六篇第五章第二条）

无已完与黑龙江省征收税则内同等税项之税证者须征：

上述土货在黑龙江省内运输，出口之时所须征收各税，及到达地有完税税证者所须征收之营业税及军费附加捐。

据调查所得，各税卡征收捐税漏卮殊巨。税卡员司薪水微薄，实难枵腹从公，只能诉诸不正当之手段借以糊口，且征收从价税时，所估之价远低于市场价格。

5.查自1923年夏季以来,黑龙江沿江一带景况大异。苏俄于该年施行封锁边境政策,私人贸易皆遭禁止;华方亦取对抗之手段,令人民非经黑龙江省政府许可不得与俄方贸易。俄方为实行该政策起见,由额尔古纳河口之洛古河波克罗夫卡(Pokrovka)起至哈巴罗夫斯克(Habarovsk)止,所有沿边均置有戍守巡防军队。据报告所称,现在俄界防军约有两营人,另有秘密警探两千人相辅而行,均以直接或间接之方式参与边防事务。

俄国边防如此严重缜密,实已为南岸之华方国防代劳,所有以前曾为两岸人民私贩生财之途径,今则危险至极,且不能获利,非复如前之景象。现私贩之徒既见秘探之多,加以明悉苏俄之法律有无论妇孺敢对于此项情事知而不报犯罪连坐一条,其中危险不待言矣。

观现今大黑河上下游沿江之商号,以前全靠私贩一途为生者(与西伯利亚进行非法贸易),现均歇业,由此可知走私之衰败。更有数端足令走私艰难者:(1)俄纸币(卢布)在华方价格低落;(2)西伯利亚人民一贫如洗,毫无购买能力;(3)华方沿江一带亦未发达;(4)华岸多为崇山所环绕,各项货物运输困难且费用高昂,均使私贩裹足不前。

此外,苏俄所施行之经济政策难有改善之希望,因此项经济政策实与苏联共产政体关系密切,共相终始,此项政策一时不能改革。如此,则损蚀华岸税收者,不在两国间少数人之私贩行动,而在苏俄远东贸易公司主动有组织之私运也。该公司为苏俄之国家贸易机关在满洲(东三省)北部负责贸易之机构,专司输出俄货及采购华货各贸易,倘有私运行为,华方实难察觉。

以俄货私运入华境一事而论,华方沿黑龙江岸一带因天然地势之关系,更无道路及铁道之便利,货物由此运至兴安岭以南富庶之区,殊觉困难;然因华方现行进口税率甚高,将俄货私运虽有交通困难,且运费高昂,但其中或者仍有利可图,亦未可知。

究其事实,华方可虑者,非在贩运私货之可能与否,而在军火及违禁或限制之物品,倘有巨量输入情事,华方无法制止,此为最可虑者也。

再以私运华货入俄境一事而论,华方边界既无周密巡防之设施,倘该公司蓄意私贩,即使俄币(卢布)在华如此低落,且俄方亦无相当市场,此等情事亦不能令其行动稍有收敛。此后,苏俄远东贸易公司一举一动颇堪注意。该公司现已得省政府之许可在大黑河设立分公司,每次进出口货物在未行起运之前,均须请省政府批准明令黑河市政筹备处转行海关后,再行输运。

查现在小贩私运货物虽未全行消失,但数量甚微,无关大体。在此隆冬之际,俄方农民和难民私逃来华者多有牵得牲畜俱来,未经报税,并有华民将皮货私运至俄国兑换黄金。然此种情事,即使巡防再周密,亦无法遏止。苏俄现有如此之严密边防,亦无法避免此类事件。然牲畜之私运将来必随俄方田地私有制度同归消失，而皮货之私运，若无俄政府支持，其数量亦不至如何之巨。俄方皮货过去私运来华颇多，然现今俄人以猎为生者，因力不能置猎具药品，均已放弃其所业，故此项私运今已不复见。

6. 由上述所陈各事可知，沿边设立海关分关一事因近八年来边界情况之变迁，问题殊属复杂。华境严密之巡防实非必需，然据观察，有甚多特殊之原因对于边界防务亦须时加注意，尤不可任数千里之国界上毫无边防措施。兹以为，为今之计，应先择可与兴安岭以南之富庶区域联络交通之地点设立海关分关，借以扩充海关管理之范围。各分关现执行之职责，首在观察各处之情形，随时报告再行提议。关于管理办法等事，便于设立分关之地点如下：

黑龙江上游：

漠河：距离大黑河 520 英里

连崟：距离大黑河 450 英里

倭西门：距离大黑河 280 英里

呼玛河：距离大黑河 170 英里

三道卡：距离大黑河 50 英里

黑龙江下游：

奇克特：距离大黑河 85 英里；查此处之四境，土地均称肥沃富饶，且与墨尔根（嫩江）和龙门等处修有平坦道路，交通便利。

乌云县：距离大黑河 180 英里；此处农产甚为丰富。

朝阳镇：距离大黑河 260 英里

萝北县：距离大黑河 350 英里

兆兴镇：距离大黑河 385 英里

中兴镇：距离大黑河 430 英里

查瑷珲关原设立两分卡，一在上游卧牛河，一在下游小黑河，各距大黑河约 5 英里，但自苏俄严行封锁边境以后，贩运私货之事逐渐减少，该两分卡业于 1927 年奉总税务司署第 111337 号令指示暂行停办。此外，瑷珲关此前于梁家屯设立分卡，后因种种事故，业于 1924 年经前瑷珲关税务司致总税务司署第 187 号呈中请准该卡停止稽征，该地情形依旧殊无充足理由再请重开。

在设立海关分关之议以外，当有一项办法似可选择。华方可仿苏俄之办法，指定数处相当地点，非经由该各指定地点处，不得自由贸易。唯此项办法必须与军队通力合作，方收实效,诚恐近时难以施行也。

在沿黑龙江边界上,有两处重要区域必须特加注意,一为自大黑河起至乌云县止,一为自萝北县起至松黑两江合流处止。前一段区域包括奇克特及乌云县等处,四境土地皆肥沃富饶,且与墨尔根(嫩江)、讷河及龙门等处均有平坦道路,交通便利。至于萝北县至松黑两江合流处,此一段可达富锦,而富锦物产丰厚,倘有贩运私货情事,亦可由此运往哈尔滨及其他大城市。

将来中俄两国恢复交通及贸易之时,该处须设立水路巡防往来稽查,然此项时期为日尚远。即使苏俄经济政策骤变,以西伯利亚各处现今之萧条景象,若求其恢复旧观,当需时日也。华方之发展固可独自进行,若一旦铁路通达沿江各处,海关于管理上亦应注意,然此项事实发生渺茫,似不必急之深虑。现今所筹计者,仅为于关键处留其余地,以待将来发展宏大规模之边防设施而已。另查华岸往来货物,非运入松花江者,海关概免征税。

7. 为明晰本地特殊情势起见,另函附寄地图两份:

地图1:满洲(东三省)北部地势及国界,以一英寸代一百俄里为比例

地图2:黑龙江华俄两岸形势,以一英寸代四十俄里为比例

唯遗憾地图中之中国地名未能皆照本署之命令使用罗马拼音标注。

8. 兹附报告汉文译本,一式三份。

> 您忠诚的仆人
>
> 周骊(C. H. B. Joly)
>
> 瑷珲关署理税务司

附录

沿黑龙江各税卡现用人员税收贸易各情形列表

（自额尔古纳河之洛古河起至松黑两江合流处止）

表1

税卡名称	现用人员				贸易状况	每年税收以1929年为凭哈大洋（元）
	局长或分局局长	巡差	司事	稽查		
一、黑龙江上游						
漠河区						
总局						
漠河	1+	3	1	1	运往华岸之土货如木筏、木料、木桦、木耳、皮货、鹿茸、蘑菇等类；由大黑河或松花江各口岸运来之食品及日用品。	6000.00 §
分局						
洛古河	1*	1			运往华岸之土货如木筏、木料、木桦、木耳、皮货、鹿茸、蘑菇、药材、黑松油等类；由大黑河或松花江各口岸运来之食品及日用品。	300.00
额钦哈达	1*	1				700.00
乌苏力	1*	1				200.00
巴尔嘎力	1*	1				150.00
连卡	1*	2	1			1000.00
阿穆尔站	1*	1				250.00
开库康	1*	1				400.00
欧浦或倭西门区						
总局						
倭西门	1+	2	1	1	运往华岸之土货如粮食、木筏、木料、木桦、木耳等类；由大黑河或松花江各口岸运来之食品及日用品；有少数马匹随同难民由俄岸私渡来华。	3000.00 §

表2

税卡名称	现用人员				贸易状况	每年税收以1929年为凭哈大洋（元）
	局长或分局局长	巡差	司事	稽查		
分局						
安罗卡	1*	1			运往华岸之土货如粮食、木筏、木料、木柈、木耳等类；由大黑河或松花江各口岸运来之食品及日用品；有少数马匹随同难民由俄岸私渡来华。	400.00
依西肯	1*	1				1600.00
呼玛河区						
总局						
古站	1+	2	2	1	运往华岸之土货如松油、木筏、木料、木柈、鹿茸、皮货、药材等类；由大黑河或松花江各口岸运来之食品及日用品。	4000.00§
分局						
安干卡					运往华岸之土货如木筏、木料、木耳、松油、欧洲越桔、药物材、鹿茸、皮货等类；由大黑河或松花江各口岸运来之食品及日用品。	200.00
西尔根奇	1*	1				300.00
察哈彦	1*	1				1000.00
湖通河	1*	1				500.00
呼玛河	1	2	1		运往华岸之土货如松油、木筏、木料、木柈、鹿茸、皮货、药材等类；由大黑河或松花江各口岸运来之食品及日用品。	2000.00§
二、黑龙江中游						
瑷珲区						
总局						

表3

税卡名称	现用人员				贸易状况	每年税收以 1929 年为凭哈大洋（元）
	局长或分局局长	巡差	司事	稽查		
大黑河	1	6	5	4	由上游运来及运往黑龙江及松花江各口岸之土货；由哈尔滨或松花江各口岸运来之食品及日用品；特准出口运往西伯利亚之大豆；由［布拉戈维申斯克Blagovestchensk］运来之少数烟酒。	25000.00 §
分局						
满洲屯	1	2	1	1	运往黑龙江或松花江各口岸之土货如木筏、木桦、皮货、木耳、粮食等类；由大黑河或松花江各口岸运来之食品及日用品。	500.00
卧牛河	1	1			在冬季用雪橇来往华岸运输干草、马料或皮货。	150.00
瑷珲	1	2	1	1	由黑龙江上游运来及运往黑龙江或松花江各口岸之土货；由哈尔滨或松花江各口岸运来之食品及日用品。	12000.00 §
大五家子	1	1		1	运往黑龙江及松花江各口岸之土货如粮食、鹿茸、木耳等类；有少数马匹随同难民由俄岸私渡来华。	2000.00
四季屯	1	1				

注：（1）卧牛河厘金税卡由十月中旬起开至次年四月中旬止；当地原设有海关分卡一处，业于1927年暂行停办（参阅呈文§6）。

（2）瑷珲区内尚有山神府和三家子内地分卡二处。山神府分卡由十月中旬起开至次年四月中旬止，征收草料及皮货等物之税；三家子分卡随同面粉厂开办之时起开办，征收该厂所用粮食及小麦之税。此二卡所收之税款每年约350银圆。

表4

税卡名称	现用人员				贸易状况	每年税收以1929年为凭哈大洋（元）
	局长或分局局长	巡差	司事	稽查		
三、黑龙江下游						
奇克特区						
总局						
奇克特	1+	2	1	1	运往黑龙江及松花江各口岸之土货如粮食、木耳、皮货、鹿茸等类；由哈尔滨或松花江各口岸运来之食品及日用品；有少数马匹随同难民由俄岸私渡来华；特准出口运往西伯利亚之大豆。	4000.00§
分局						
嘎巴亮子	1	2			运往黑龙江及松花江各口岸之土货如粮食、木耳、皮货、鹿茸等类；由哈尔滨或松花江各口岸运来之食品及日用品；有少数马匹随同难民由俄岸私渡来华。	1500.00§
车陆	1	1				500.00§
上道干	1	1				200.00§
乌云区						
总局						
乌云	1+	2	1	1	运往黑龙江及松花江各口岸之土货如粮食、木耳、皮货、鹿茸等类；由哈尔滨或花江各口岸运来之食品及日用品；有少数马匹随同难民由俄岸私渡来华；特准出口运往西伯利亚之大豆。	6000.00§
分局						

表5

税卡名称	现用人员				贸易状况	每年税收以1929年为凭哈大洋（元）
	局长或分局局长	巡差	司事	稽查		
常家屯	1	2			运往黑龙江及松花江各口岸之土货如粮食、木耳、皮货、鹿茸等类；由哈尔滨及松花江各口岸运来之食品及日用品；有少数马匹随同难民由俄岸私渡来华。	2000.00 §
佛山区						
总局						
朝阳镇	1+	2	1	1	运往黑龙江及松花江各口岸之土货如粮食、木耳、皮货、鹿茸等类；由哈尔滨及松花江各口岸运来之食品及日用品；有少数马匹随同难民由俄岸私渡来华。	3500.00 §
萝北区						
总局						
萝北	1	4	1	1	运往黑龙江及松花江各口岸之土货如粮食、木耳、皮货、药材等类；由哈尔滨或松花江各口岸运来之食品及日用品。	9000.00 §
分局						
太平沟	1	3	1		运往黑龙江及松花江各口岸之土货如粮食、木耳、皮货、药材等类；由哈尔滨或松花江各口岸运来之食品及日用品。	3000.00 §
兆兴镇	1*	1				600.00
中兴镇	1	2				400.00

说明：+ 征收局局长一员系由县长兼代，该区内所收之捐税各款，均交至黑龙江省政府财政厅。

＊ 本卡卡官兼代征收分局局长，所收捐税各款交至总局。

§ 此款含无关本报告之各项捐税在内，难以按照种类分析。

此抄件发送至滨江关税务司。

录事：陈培因　三等二级税务员

专题三

梁家屯分卡管理及裁撤

1. 为呈报梁家屯分卡裁撤理由事

LIANGCHIAT'UN BARRIER: arguments for and against the retention of, submitting; the abolition of, recommending.

Aigun   3rd. September, 1924.

Entered in Card-Index.

Replied to in No. 201.

Sir,

1.   I have the honour to acknowledge receipt of your despatch No. 187/99,950 (with reference to my despatch No. 64 and your despatch No. 79/91,277) :

informing me that the Chambers of Commerce at Aigun and Taheiho have complained to the Shui-wu Ch'u of the unsatisfactory working of the 12 Regulations governing the taxation of goods passing the Liangchiat'un Barrier (whereby this office exempts from taxation all native cargo and such foreign cargo as is provided with duty payment proof but collects duty on all foreign cargo unprovided with duty payment proof) and that they have given 4 reasons for advocating the abolition of the Liangchiat'un Barrier; and instructing me to study and report on the question;

and, in reply, to state that, as directed, I have gone into this question with my Superintendent

who

The Inspector General of Customs,

Peking.

who agrees with me that the Liangchiat'un Barrier should be completely and definitely abolished.

2.   The decision of this office to establish a system of control inland started as a temporary measure in 1909 when it was found necessary to regulate trade between the 100 li free zone and the hinterland, and Liangchiat'un, a village 50 li from Aigun and 125 li from Taheiho, was selected as the site for our barrier because it was on the main Aigun-Tsitsihar trade route and obviously the place where the Customs would be best able to keep in close touch with everything which came into the Aigun District. There are a number of back roads by which the Liangchiat'un Barrier can be evaded, but this main trade route offers infinitely greater capacity for the transportation of cargo cheaply and rapidly than any of the other routes and it is the one which is generally used.   At Liangchiat'un we have, as it were, our grip on the jugular vein of the district and so long as we refuse to

relax

relax this grip we are able to make our control a fairly effective instrument. It must therefore be admitted that a Customs Barrier at Liangchiat'un, while it may have tended to direct a certain amount of trade to other and far less convenient roads, has undoubtedly increased our control and acted as a deterrent against smuggling. In brief, it has been a winning card.

3.   It would be idle to attempt to minimise the great difficulties with which we should have been faced if the Liangchiat'un Barrier had been abolished when it was the practice of this office to collect duty on both foreign and native cargo, inwards and outwards, arriving at Liangchiat'un. The disappearance from the scene of the extraordinary control we had exercised inland would have made it necessary for us to rely upon our patrols to see that all cargo, foreign and native, entering and leaving the district, reported at the Custom House for examination and payment of duty, and this would naturally have meant a step

from

from something relatively easy to something relatively hard. The abolition of the Liangchiat'un Barrier to-day will mean that during the winter season this office will have to surrender its claim to collect duty on all cargo other than dutiable goods in postal parcels and Chinese cargo sent to, and foreign cargo imported from, Siberia. This means that a port which for some considerable while past has been unable even to balance its budget, let alone find a surplus for remittance to your revenue account, may have to sacrifice the greater part of its winter collection. But it does not follow from this that we ought to stay at Liangchiat'un. Obviously there remains the question of what is right and just and I venture the opinion that we exercise at Liangchiat'un a wholly unjustifiable authority. It is my argument that in functioning there we overstep the limit of fair customs procedure as understood in other customs districts and that most of the revenue which we now collect during the winter months is money to which we can establish no legal claim.

4.

4.	The Aigun and Taheiho Chambers of Commerce have been agitating for the removal of the Liangchiat'un Barrier at more or less regular intervals ever since its establishment in 1909 and now that the problem has come into the foreground a 7th. time I submit that the question should be approached from a new angle without any pre-possessions in favour of the view that revenue interests justify us in treating the public's side of this question as negligible. It was in 1922 that the Chambers of Commerce made representations in Peking for the 6th. time with a view to re-moving our barrier and on this occasion their representations were not wholly unsuccessful. The situation was modified and a new Agreement arrived at which provided that native cargo, and cargo of foreign origin with proof of duty payment, should be passed free of duty, and that duty should be collected only on foreign cargo unprovided with duty payment proof. This naturally placed merchants in circumstances far more advantageous than was

formerly

formerly the case, but the Chambers of Commerce made it clear at the time that acceptance of the new Agreement should not be taken to mean that they had signed away their right of further protest, or that they had in any way abandoned their hope of securing the removal of the barrier at Liang-chiat'un.   As a matter of fact they have never made any attempt to veil their dislike of the present system and the agreement has really been little more than an agreement to disagree.

5.	No one will attempt to deny the need and the right of a frontier port to exercise the most careful and most persistent watchfulness over the movement of cargo, but control should be effected with due regard to the just claims of the public and in fairness to the local community it must be realised that our procedure at Liangchiat'un is obtrusive. However plausible the defence of a system may be, when that system proves in practice to be unjust and irregular it surely follows that the case for its retention at once breaks down.

Now

Now it cannot be pretended that our activities at Liangchiat'un are in conformity with established precedent in other customs districts and I therefore argue that the continued existence of our barrier there is possible only at the price of acquiescence in a policy which is shown to be irregular by reason of the alteration which it effects on the whole relation of this Custom House to the public. I submit that the real case is rather that customs regulations everywhere should ensure equal treatment to all people alike and that we must not get into the way of depriving a man of his rights just because he happens to be living in a district where customs control is difficult to exercise. The status of a merchant has been definitely fixed by treaties and it is not our business to determine whether he is to purchase foreign goods or native goods. Except in the case of contraband cargo and cargo covered by special regulations, he should be his own master in such a matter, but this he obviously is not so long as we have the right

to

to challenge him to produce his goods for inspection at a place 125 li away from the Custom House. The inconvenience resulting from this vexatious and irresponsible restriction on goods entering and leaving the Aigun District overland via Liangchiat'un falls upon the individual citizen and I submit that it is high time that the long-established rights of the latter were fully restored.

6.   The Aigun and Taheiho Chambers of Commerce now advance four reasons for demanding the abolition of the Liangchiat'un Barrier and although they have what, in my opinion, is a very good case there are a few comments which I beg leave to submit. I will take their letter of complaint point by point.   Their first point is: The subsequent refund of duty collected on cargo arriving at Liangchiat'un proves that in some instances goods of native origin have been wrongly passed as of foreign origin.   The answer to this is: It is becoming increasingly difficult to distinguish between certain articles of foreign type made in

China

China and the bona-fide foreign-manufactured articles
and delay caused by misunderstandings and disputes
has generally been due to the action of the merchants
themselves or of their representatives in withholding
from the examiners assistance in the form of
documentary proof which the latter had a right to
expect. Such disputes as have occurred have arisen
out of perfectly honest and apparently inevitable
mistakes and all such mistakes have been promptly
settled on receipt of proof that the goods in
question have been manufactured in China. It is
therefore contended that this office has made as
successful an effort as was possible to work
effectually the rules in force and that it has
acted without unnecessary provocation, yet with the
firmness required to prevent attempts to render the
regulations different from their design. **Their**
second point is: The Customs have no right to
function at Liangchiat'un now that the duty-free
zone no longer exists. This is conceded.
Their third point is: (a) Most of the cargo
imported

imported overland is intended for local consumption;
(b) Cargo to and from Siberia will naturally pass
through Taheiho; (c) Foreign goods brought into this
district overland **via** Liangchiat'un have paid duty
elsewhere and these should no longer be taxed now
that native cargo is released free of duty; and
(d) A barrier at Liangchiat'un cannot possibly stop
smuggling across the ice in the winter. The answer
to this is: (a) It is impossible to say how
much of the cargo imported overland is consumed
locally and if the private affairs of merchants are
a matter solely for the merchants themselves this
question should not concern us; (b) The argument
that the proper place for cargo to and from Siberia
to arrive at is Taheiho is true, but its very
truth emphasises the complete improbability that this
will always be the case. The suggestion is, of
course, that all cargo to and from Russian territory
will be sent for examination to the Custom House
and that nobody will smuggle, but we can hardly
accept such an assumption. The broad and in-
disputable fact is that the length of our frontier
is

is an insuperable obstacle to its proper defence,
but I venture the opinion that this does not justify
us in hampering and obstructing merchants 125 **li**
away from the frontier and it seems to me that it
is the most natural thing in the world for the
Chambers of Commerce to protest that we have no
right to exploit a position of difficulty to the
disadvantage of individual citizens by forcing the
latter to become in a special and particular manner
identified with Customs preventive measures; (c) The
argument that foreign and native cargo coming into
this district overland **via** Liangchiat'un should be
treated alike seems to be a fair one.   This point
is further referred to in §7 (i); and (d) In former
days when duty was collected on all cargo arriving
at Liangchiat'un, inwards and outwards, our barrier
there palyed an important part in stopping smuggling
in the winter but since the introduction of the
present system its sphere of action has been much
curtailed.   <u>Their fourth point is:</u>   The Customs
should rely for preventive measures upon their patrols
and barriers.   This is conceded.

7.

7.   To sum up: The arguments hitherto advanced
in favour of the retention of the Liangchiat'un
Barrier are as follows:-

(a) It is an imperative necessity to provide
for the safety of the national revenue and
private interests must if necessary be
sacrificed to this end;

(b) The geographical situation of the port
compels this office to handle cargo entering
the district as near to its source as
possible and unless this is done the
defence of essential revenue interests must
become impracticable;

(c) A barrier at Liangchiat'un enables the
Customs to keep in close touch with almost
everything which enters the Aigun District
and is the only constructive plan for
grappling with illicit trade;

(d) The permanent retention of a Customs
staff at Liangchiat'un alone makes it
possible to secure a fair equipoise between
national and private interests;

(e) Those who advocate the abolition of the
Liangchiat'un Barrier underrate the importance of preventing a frontier district
from being used as a jumping-off ground
for smugglers;

(f) A bargain is better than a situation in
which one side gives and the other takes
all and if eventually it should be decided
to close the barrier at Liangchiat'un our
withdrawal should be conditional on assent
being obtained to the collection of duty
on cargo arriving at Aigun and Taheiho
from places on the Chinese side of the
Amur;

(g) A broad view of this problem should
have as its fundamental basis both the
protection of the <u>status quo</u>, whereby a
portion of territory inland is brought
under Customs control, and the right of
the Customs to tax Amur river-borne cargo
which has hitherto been passed free by
this office notwithstanding the abolition
in 1914 of the 100 **li** duty free zone;

(h) If it is decided to abolish the barrier
at Liangchiat'un and at the same time to
allow river-borne traffic to remain untaxed
the result must inevitably be the break up
of the Aigun Customs District; and

(i)

(i) While it may be permissible to exempt from taxation all native goods and such foreign goods as may be provided with proof of duty payment, foreign cargo which arrives at Liangchiat'un without duty payment proof should certainly pay duty to this office;

unconditional

The case for the abolition of the Liangchiat'un Barrier may be stated thus:-

(a) The arguments in favour of the retention of the barrier do not contain one suggestion of any real readiness to consider interests other than those of the Customs and it is now time to look at the position from the point of view of the trader whose side of the case deserves as much consideration as does that of the Customs;

(b) A barrier at Liangchiat'un is a measure of doubtful respectability vis--à--vis the local authorities because we are appropriating to Customs control a portion of territory where complete political and economic control should rest exclusively with the territorial officials;

(c) The abolition of the barrier would remove a cause of friction, local merchants being hostile to its continuance, not only because they desire freedom of trade, but because the system in force actually penalises traders by imposing in certain circumstances an extra charge on foreign cargo which is not paid elsewhere;

(d) The Liangchiat'un Barrier has gradually become a cloak for the exercise of Customs authority in a way that was never intended and we have no right to subordinate moral considerations to the one end of revenue collection;

(e) It cannot be admitted that in order to check illicit trade in smuggling the right of the Customs to control cargo should be extended to a distance of 125 li from the Custom House because a proposal of this kind involves departure from the accepted principle that the limit of Customs jurisdiction is the Customs harbour and that taxation of cargo beyond that distance is the prerogative of the territorial authorities;

(f) The Liangchiat'un Barrier was an emergency measure designed to meet extraordinary circumstances and its existence was justifiable only as a temporary expedient;

(g)

(g) The position of trade in this district is exceedingly disquieting and since future prospects are to a great extent interlocked with the situation on the Russian side of the Amur fundamental conditions are not likely to improve for some considerable while; so long as the present difficult circumstances prevail the exemption of trade from further taxation is a necessary and vital necessity and the proposal to collect duty on Amur river-borne traffic (to which reference will be made in a further report) can not be recommended and should not be entertained for the present;

(h) It should not be the object of a Custom House to get as much revenue as possible to the exclusion of all other considerations and in the case of a frontier port a rigid distinction should be made between the problem of revenue collection, the function of the Customs, and the wider problem of frontier defence, the function of the territorial authorities; and

(i) An objection to the present rules governing the overland traffic in this district is the unevenness of their operation. It is submitted that there can be no reason to suppose that foreign cargo which enters the district via Liangchiat'un is any less likely to have paid duty than native cargo; that it is a moral certainty that it has paid before arriving at our barrier and that a great deal of it has paid more than once. It is possible that some of it may have escaped taxation altogether at a maritime custom house (and that payment in consequence is due at this end) but it seems arguable whether the convenience of acting without proof on what in some few cases may be within the bounds of possibility is not far outbalanced by the hardship that such action entails in the majority of cases when duty has been collected elsewhere.

8.   The unevenness of the operation of our regulations to which reference is made above is noticeable in our treatment of Foreign cargo exported overland via Liangchiat'un.   It is the practice of this office to require foreign cargo exported

via

Via Liangchiat'un to Harbin and places in the interior, e.g. Kerosene Oil, Cigarettes, Shovels, etc., sent to the gold mines in this district, either to produce proof of payment of import duty or to pay a full import duty before it is released, the idea being that all foreign cargo unprovided with duty payment proof must have been smuggled in from Siberia. Obviously cargo which arrives here from Siberia should pay to us an import duty, but I submit that we have no right to collect an import duty on foreign cargo purchased locally for export overland. We can hardly argue that foreign goods offered for sale in the local shops did not pay duty on importation without exposing ourselves to ridicule and even if these have escaped taxation we have surely no right to expect any chance purchaser to pay what it was our business to see that some one else paid. No one can be compelled to apply for an Inward Transit Pass and if a merchant should decide to send foreign cargo inland past our barrier without customs documents he should be at liberty to do so. It happens that this office

has

has not yet been asked to issue an Inward Transit Pass but if application were to be made for one port practice would require us to tell applicant that unless he could prove to our satisfaction that his goods had paid a full import duty he himself would have to pay this duty in addition to transit dues. And this would be irregular because the issue of a transit pass against payment of half the duty levied on original importation can be claimed as a treaty right.

It is always possible to make out some sort of case for a particular arbitrary act but on the wider ground of right an arbitrary act is open to question, and it is on this ground that I have taken up my stand against the retention of our Liangchiat'un Barrier. I hold that we are wrong in the methods which we are adopting for the control of cargo entering and leaving the district overland via Liangchiat'un, believing these to be a violation of lawful customs procedure and contrary to the principle that every merchant is entitled to his meed of justice. I submit that

the

the demand for our withdrawal from Liangchiat'un is a demand of obvious justice and that we have no right to seek to get out of this piece of fairness to the public on the plea that the abolition of our barrier will be detrimental to revenue interests.   The moral I draw here is to repeat exactly what I have maintained earlier in this report.   Liangchiat'un is a relic, which ought as quickly as possible to disappear, of the 100 li free zone period. If, as I argue is the case, our present system stands condemned, no attempt should be made to bolster it up and we should make our exit from Liangchiat'un at once.

I append a statement showing how the revenue collection of this port would have been affected if foreign cargo entering and leaving the district overland via Liangchiat'un during the winters of 1922/1923 and 1923/1924 had been released free of duty.   The loss during 1922/1923 would have amounted to Hk.Tls. 5,350; and that during 1923/1924 to Hk.Tls. 7,001.

11.

11.   A Chinese version of this report, from which §8 is being omitted, will be forwarded at an early date.

I have the honour to be,

Sir,

Your obedient Servant,

R. &. Hlingchunty

Commissioner.

REFERENCES.	
DESPATCHES.	
From I.G.	To I.G.
Commrs.No.	Port No.
TO HARBIN.	FROM HARBIN.
623/34,972	518 602
902/42,708	854 1195
977/44,757	2187
1242/53,091	FROM AIGUN.
2305/79,216	32
2568/84,137	36
TO AIGUN.	64
17/87,300	95
42/89,154	153
79/91,277	(154)
106/93,288	(158)
118/94,270	(171)
(154/97,060)	
(161/97,311)	
172/98,648	
(174/98,763)	
(183/99,682)	
187/99,950	

APPENDIX.

Statement showing the extent to which the Revenue Collection during the winters of 1922/1923 and 1923/1924 would have been affected if Foreign Cargo entering and leaving the Aigun District overland via Liangchiat'un had been released free of duty.

CHINESE FLAG.

	Import Direct Hk.Tls.	Import Coast Hk.Tls.	Export Direct Hk.Tls.	Export Coast Hk.Tls.	Coast Trade Hk.Tls.	Total Hk.Tls.
Winter Collection, 1922/1923: (i.e.from Nov.1922 to Apr.1923)						
Total Collection:	1,001.489	5,954.622	4,106.383	3,110.616	609.470	14,782.580
deduct Postal Parcel Collection:	...	605.056	...	3,065.637	609.470	4,280.163
Nett Overland Collection: (i.e. to and from Russia and to and from Interior via Liang-chiat'un)	1,001.489	5,349.566	4,106.383	44.979	...	10,502.417
Winter Collection, 1923/1924: (i.e.from Nov.1923 to Apr.1924)						
Total Collection:	1,270.462	7,493.885	281.491	3,843.536	289.229	13,178.603
deduct Postal Parcel Collection	...	492.659	...	3,836.393	289.229	4,618.281
Nett Overland Collection: (i.e. to and from Russia and to and from Interior via Liang-chiat'un)	1,270.462	7,001.226	281.491	7.143	...	8,560.322

a.)

a) By "Import Direct" is meant duties collected on Foreign Goods imported from Russia.

b) By "Import Coast" is meant duties collected on Foreign Goods imported from and exported to Interior via Lienchiat'un, or on Postal Parcels imported from various places.

c) By "Export Direct" is meant duties collected on Native Goods exported to Russia.

d) By "Export Coast" is meant duties collected on Postal Parcels exported to various places.

e) By "Coast Trade" is meant duties collected on Postal Parcels imported from and exported to various places.

Note: The collection of duty on Native Goods imported and exported overland was discontinued as from 1st November, 1922.

x This figure represents the duty collection on Foreign Cargo imported and exported overland via Lienchiat'un - i.e. the sum which would not have been collected if the Lienchiat'un Barrier had not been in existence.

Prepared by:

Jotipan Chen
3rd Assistant, B.

CUSTOM HOUSE,

Aigun/Tahaiho, 3rd September, 1924.

R. J. C. Aliaguly
Commissioner.

呈总税务司署 187 号文　　　　　　　　　　　　瑷珲关 1924 年 9 月 3 日

尊敬的海关总税务司（北京）：

1. 根据总税务司署第 187/99950 号令（参阅瑷珲关第 64 号呈及总税务司署第 79/91277 号令）：

"瑷黑商会向税务处投诉称，瑷珲关稽征由陆路经过梁家屯来往货物办事章程十二条（即土货与有完税凭照之洋货即行免税，无完税凭照之洋货仍在纳税章程之内）办理欠善，并列举四项理由，呈请将梁家屯分卡裁撤；请详细考察各情形后呈交报告。"

兹汇报，本署已与海关监督详细商酌，均认为梁家屯分卡应完全裁撤。

2. 查本关在内地稽征货物办法始于 1909 年，本为一种临时办法，用以稽征由百里免税区域来往内地之货物。梁家屯位置齐瑷贸易通道之半，离瑷珲五十里，离大黑河一百二十五里，为海关设卡最宜之地，凡输入瑷珲境内各物，均在掌握中，故于该处设立分卡。梁家屯附近小路数道，由此而行，可偷越该处分卡，但该屯主路利便大宗输运，且运费低，时间速，故为常用之路。海关在梁家屯地方设卡可握本境之咽喉，长此以往，则势力颇为稳固。因此，该分卡之设虽不免有少数货物取较远之路而行，然本关由此查验势力亦增，走私行为更受威慑。简言之，梁家屯分卡确为本关争得优胜之地位。

3. 按照本关惯例，凡洋土各货经过梁家屯，无论运入运出，均行征税，该卡一经撤去，本关则立现困难，在内地稽征货物之优势亦就此消减，只能依靠巡缉卫兵查洋土各货入口或出口时曾否报由本关查验纳税，不免舍易而就难也。此外，该卡裁撤后，本关对于冬季来往洋土货物，除邮政包裹应税货物，与出口西伯利亚之土货及由西伯利亚进口之洋货外，均不能再行征税。本关税收已有数月入不敷出，若冬季税收再因此而损失大半，则更无盈余汇至海关总税务司税收账户。然上列种种不能成为梁家屯分卡留存之理由。兹以为，本关在梁家屯执行职务完全无此权力，且出乎海关办事准则之外，为他关所为见，而本关冬季税收大半均无权利征收。

4. 自 1909 年设立梁家屯分卡以来，瑷黑商会屡次要求裁撤该卡，今既为第七次要求，兹认为，此案不能有所偏见，应从新的角度考虑，不能再以保护税收利益为由，置人民之理由而不顾。1922 年瑷黑商会第六次向北京方面呈请裁撤该卡，所得结果尚不尽如人意，于是海关与该商会议定办法，凡土货及有完税凭照之洋货免缴关税，不过洋货无完税凭照者仍须纳税。此种办法于商人方面实较以前更为有利，但该商会当时声明此种协定并不代表其会放弃再行呈请裁撤梁家屯分卡之权利与希望。据事实观之，该商会等厌恶现行办法未曾不露表示之态度，故此项协定不过彼此争持之片纸空谈而已。

5. 查边界海关对于稽查来往货物应有采取严厉手段之必要，此人所共认者也，唯海关方面亦须体察商情而行之。梁家屯分卡办事手续操之太过。任何制度，无论有多合理，一旦于实践中变得不公平、不正常，便再无存续之必要。梁家屯分卡之存在与办事宗旨有所不合，且为他关未有之先例，若继续留存，商人与海关之关系亦会有所变更。兹认为，海办事章程对于商民应取同一待遇，断不能因本关稽查不易，便对本埠商民权利另有限制。商人对于海关之义务已于协定上明白规定，而商人购买洋货或土货，除违禁品有专章规定之货物外，自有主权。若离本关125里之远，本关仍有强迫货物运至该处查验之权，商人权利未免受限。本关于梁家屯设卡管理经由陆路进出瑷珲关区之货物，已为商民带来不便，此非负责任之行为，故此提议，归还商民该项权利。

6. 查瑷黑商会等提出四项理由，主张裁撤梁家屯分卡所据言辞颇近情理，唯内有四点不能不解释者也，谨将该商会等所呈各理由逐一解释如下：

商会第一条理由：本关将在梁家屯征收税款发还，足证有时以土货误为洋货。

解释：现在中国制造洋式货物与真正在外洋制造品之分别渐感困难，海关验货员有检查来往货物单据之权，货商或其代理人每每不将单据交出以致彼此有所争执，迟延时日。查以前各次发生误会实出不得已，原无他意存在，本关接到来函复称该货系于中国制造后，均立即秉公办理。由此可见，本关不惮烦劳以期所订章程之实行，避免众商集怨，唯对于所订章程，凡有更变其原来宗旨之举动，本关决意抵抗之。

商会第二条理由：百里免税区域业已取消，梁家屯分卡无存在之必要。

解释：此条理由充足，似可承认。

商会第三条理由：(1)以陆路运来货物多半行销本埠；(2)凡货物由西伯利亚进口或出口至西伯利亚自然经过大黑河；(3)洋货未运来本埠以前业已完纳关税，今土货既已免税，洋货更无征税之必要；(4)梁家屯分卡在冬季封江时不能杜绝黑龙江上下游之私运。

解释：(1)由陆路运来货物行销本埠者若干，实难知其确数，此问题乃商人本身之事，与本关无涉；(2)货物由西伯利亚进口或出口至西伯利亚自然经过大黑河一说，虽言之成理，然不能以为永远如此；以为凡运往俄境或由俄境运来之货物全行前来海关查验，而无人走私，诚不足信者也。毫无疑问，沿江一带广长数千里，防范走私事属不易，然若以防范不易而于离边境125里之遥与商贾不便，殊属不公，故商会等以本关不应因边防困难不撤梁家屯分卡而强迫商人遵守防范走私条例导致商民有所不利为由屡次抗议，乃势所必然也；（3）该商会以陆路运来本埠货物无论洋土应受同等待遇之理由甚为充足，此款将另详于本呈第7条（9）中；（4）从前本关对于由梁家屯出入货物均行征税时，该卡冬季为杜绝私运之主要地点，然现行办法施行后，该卡势力甚为减少。

商会第四条理由：本关稽查货物应依靠分卡与巡缉卫兵。

解释：此条理由充足，似可承认。

7. 总之历来存留梁家屯分卡之理由有九，略述如下：

（1）维持国家税收至为重要，为保持国家税收，宁可牺牲他人之私利；

（2）本埠因位置关系，凡输入瑷珲境内之货物，不得不于靠近运出之处检查，否则无以保持国家税收；

（3）瑷珲关在梁家屯设立分卡，凡输入瑷珲境内各货，归该卡范围者几占全数，故该卡之设立乃为防止私运之唯一方法；

（4）瑷珲关派遣关员常驻梁家屯分卡，所以使国家权利与个人权利相平均；

（5）赞成裁撤梁家屯分卡者，实不知国家对于私贩以边境为走私之孔道实有取缔之必要也；

（6）为免一方面独得利益，而彼方面独受损失起见，不若彼此交换条件，譬如将梁家屯分卡裁撤，商人理应承担交纳黑龙江华岸来往瑷黑两埠货物关税之义务；

（7）本问题之大纲不特保守，以往情形将内地之一部分永远在海关管辖之下，且瑷珲关亦有征收黑龙江来往货物之权，然该项货物自1914年百里免税区域取消后，并未征税；

（8）若将梁家屯分卡裁撤又不征收黑龙江来往货税，势必使瑷珲关税收一落千丈；

（9）凡土货及有完税凭照之洋货经过梁家屯分卡既免征关税，则无完税凭照之洋货当然纳税。

梁家屯分卡应无条件裁撤各理由有九，陈述如下：

（1）保留梁家屯分卡所持各理由仅顾及海关利益，本案商人权利应与海关权利受到同等重视；

（2）梁家屯分卡存在，则内地之一部分就政治与经济上而言本应完全由地方官管制，却由海关代管，故该卡之存在对于地方官方面是否留一污点亦有疑问；

（3）本埠商民反对梁家屯分卡之存在，不独因其对贸易自由之渴望，还因梁家屯分卡办事手续亦有苛征之情例，如洋货有时或加以重征，此乃各处所为见者，苟该卡一裁，则商民抵抗之点亦去矣；

（4）梁家屯分卡渐渐假借执行各种职务出乎设立之初意，海关无权为税收罔顾道义；

（5）海关为防偷漏起见应扩张关权至于总关125里以外以管辖货物，此说甚为欠解，因海关主权只能操于本埠港口之内，凡本港以外货物之征税，乃地方官之权，此人所公认者也；

（6）梁家屯分卡之设，乃紧急计划，以迎合当时特别情形，而该卡存在之理由亦为暂时之设施而已；

（7）本埠商业正处恐慌时代，贸易之转移多以俄岸情形之变化而定，贸易之起色无期；于此凋零时代，有免征关税之必要，故此征收黑龙江华岸来往货物税之议现在不能实行，故不提议；

（8）海关不能只顾以多收税款为目的，不顾一切情形，边界海关应分明税收问题与海关之职务，并边境之国防及地方官之权限；

（9）由陆路来往本埠货物现行章程所反对者，即在办法不公平。譬如由陆路经梁家屯运入之货物，土货业已纳税，而洋货则反然，此种理想实为无理；就道德上而言，洋货均已完税又重征关税者居多。洋货未在他处海关完税者应在本关缴纳，当系实情，当然其中逃税者或有一二，而海关一概以未完税论。此种办法，海关所得利益与已完税货物所受之困苦是否相偿，仍有待商榷。

8. 梁家屯分卡办事手续不公，主要涉及由陆路经梁家屯运出之洋货征税。本关惯例，凡洋货由陆路经梁家屯运至哈尔滨或内地他处者，如供本地金矿区所用之煤油、香烟、铁铲等，若无完税凭照，均须交纳进口正税，因凡无完税凭照之洋货均被视为自西伯利亚走私入境。自西伯利亚运入之洋货自应交纳进口正税，然兹认为，本关并无对在本埠购买并由陆路运出之洋货征收进口税之权。如果说本埠所售洋货未纳进口税，那么于本关工作而言，无疑为一种嘲讽；即使辩称入境时有逃税者，亦为本关失查，实不应强迫买主支付本应由他人所纳之税款。本关从未强迫商人申请洋货入内地半税单照，商人经梁家屯分卡运送洋货至内地时可自主决定是否申请。迄今尚未有申请者，若有申请，按照本关惯例，凡洋货无完税凭照者，除子口税外还需缴纳进口正税。然此办法并不合理，因按照条约规定，最初进口时交纳半税即可申请入内地半税单照。

9. 凡事虽皆可通过独断强制手段解决，然一旦涉及权利之事，难免会引发质疑，故此反对继续保留梁家屯分卡。兹认为，本关对由陆路经梁家屯出入货物所施行之办法有违海关正当办事手续，于商民不公。裁撤梁家屯分卡之要求当为平允，海关不能以税收有损为由，而对商民有所推诿。梁家屯分卡乃百里免税时代之遗物，至于今日，应即裁撤。若如以上所述，现行办事手续果然不当，本关应立即撤出梁家屯。

10. 兹附瑷珲关1922/1923年及1923/1924年封江期间税收报表，以示梁家屯分卡如果裁撤,海关将损失之税收数目。据表可之,1922/1923 年封江期间,海关所受损失为海关两 5350 两,1923/1924 年封江期间,海关所受损失为海关两 7001 两。

11. 此报告中文版本中已将第 8 条删去,将尽快呈送。

您忠诚的仆人

贺智兰（R. F. C. Hedgeland）

瑷珲关税务司

瑷珲关致总税务司署第 187 号呈附录

瑷珲关 1922/1923 年及 1923/1924 年封江期间税收报表

—— 以示梁家屯分卡如果裁撤,海关将损失之税收数目

	挂中国旗轮船					
	进口	复进口	出口	复出口	复进口／复出口	总计
	海关两	海关两	海关两	海关两	海关两	海关两
1922/1923 年（即自 1922 年 11 月至 1923 年 4 月）封江期间税收						
总计:	1001.489	5954.622	4106.383	3110.616	609.470	14782.580
扣除邮政包裹税收:	–	605.056	–	3065.637	609.470	4280.163
陆路净税收:（即经梁家屯来往俄国及内陆）	1001.489	* 5349.566	4106.383	44.979	–	10502.417
1923/1924 年（即自 1923 年 11 月至 1924 年 4 月）封江期间税收						
总计:	1270.462	7493.885	281.491	3843.536	289.229	13178.603
扣除邮政包裹税收:	…	492.659	…	3836.393	289.229	4618.281
陆路净税收:（即经梁家屯来往俄国及内陆）	1270.462	* 7001.226	281.491	7.143	–	8560.322

1)"进口"项下为对自俄境进口之洋货所征税款。

2)"复进口"项下为对经梁家屯来往内地之洋货所征税款,及对自各地进口之邮政包裹所征税款。

3)"出口"项下为对出口至俄境之土货所征税款。

4)"复出口"项下为对出口至各地之邮政包裹所征税款。

5）"复进口及复出口"项下为对来往各地之邮政包裹所征税款。

注：自1922年11月1日起，已停止对由陆路来往之土货征税。

＊为对由陆路经梁家屯来往之洋货所征税款，即梁家屯分卡如果裁撤，海关将损失之税收数目。

编制人：叶元章　三等帮办后班

贺智兰（R. F. C. Hedgeland）瑷珲关税务司

1924年9月3日，瑷珲关/大黑河

2. 为批准梁家屯分卡关闭各安排事

[4.—29]

No. 217   COMMRS.

Aigun   No.102,129

INSPECTORATE GENERAL OF CUSTOMS,

PEKING, 24th February 1925.

Entered in Card-Index.

Sir,   Replied to in No. 219.

    I have to acknowledge receipt of your despatch No. 203 :

reporting, with reference to previous correspondence concerning the Liangchiatun Barrier, that this Barrier ceased to function on the 1st November 1924; detailing the arrangements made in regard to buildings, furniture and Staff; requesting authority for an expenditure of $150.00 incurred thereon; reporting that you have sold a quantity of Service firewood and a number of logs and planks confiscated some years ago; stating that you have a junior foreign officer available for transfer; recommending that the two Boatmen/Guards formerly employed at Liangchiatun be retained for duty elsewhere; and raising, with reference to a suggestion made by your predecessor, the question of introducing the

the taxation of river-borne cargo arriving at and sent from Aigun and Taheiho to and from places on the Chinese side of the Amur :

and, in reply, to state as follows :

1.   The arrangements made by you in connection with the closing of this Barrier are approved and the expenditure incurred, i.e. $150.00, is sanctioned.

2.   You are requested to report further concerning your suggestion to use the furniture formerly at this Barrier in the Outdoor Staff Quarters at Aigun, forwarding a list of the articles in question together with a list of the furniture now supplied to the Outdoor Staff Quarters.

3.   You are further requested to report what has become of the sum of $42.00 received from the sale of confiscated logs, etc.

4.   It has been noted that you now have a

junior

The Commissioner of Customs,

    A I G U N.

Junior Foreign officer in excess of requirements and arrangements will be made to transfer a junior officer from your District in the near future.   The services of the two Boatmen/Guards may be retained.

5.   With reference to your remarks concerning the introduction of taxation of river-borne cargo transported between Aigun and other places on the Chinese side of the Amur, I have to say that, although provision is made in the Aigun Customs Provisional Regulations for the collection of Coast Trade Duties on native goods moving between Aigun and other trade marts, it is questionable whether such collection would be in accordance with the principles under which the Maritime Customs function at the trade marts in Manchuria, for I believe that it was originally intended that we should confine ourselves to the frontier, taxing only trans-frontier trade and keeping our fiscal hands off native trade within the three eastern provinces altogether.   Moreover,

a movement is in progress for the abolition of Coast Trade Duties, and it would not, in any case, be desirable in inaugurate a system leading in the opposite direction.

　　　　I am,

　　　　　　Sir,

　　　　Your obedient Servant,

　　　　　　　　　　Inspector General.

致瑷珲关第 <u>217/102129</u> 号令　　　　　总税务司署 1925 年 2 月 24 日,北京

尊敬的瑷珲关税务司:

第 203 号呈收悉:

"呈报梁家屯分卡已于 1924 年 11 月 1 日关闭;详述房屋、家具及职员安排;请
示核销撤卡费用 150.00 银圆;汇报已出售海关几年前罚没充公的大量木桩及原木、
木板;说明有一名洋籍资历较浅的职员可供调任;建议两位原梁家屯分卡水手卫兵
留任他职;依据前瑷珲关税务司建议,就'是否要对抵达瑷珲关(大黑河)和自瑷珲关
(大黑河)寄送的,往来阿穆尔河中国境内河域(即黑龙江)江运货物征税'提出疑问。"

现批复如下:

1. 批准梁家屯分卡关闭安排,撤卡支出即 150 银圆,予以报销。

2. 请详细说明将原梁家屯分卡家具分配给瑷珲关外班职员宿舍使用的建议,并汇报梁
家屯分卡家具清单及已提供给外班职员宿舍的家具清单。

3. 请汇报罚没充公原木等物品售卖所得 42.00 银圆的明细。

4. 本署已登记原梁家屯分卡有一名洋籍初级职员待职,即将安排为其调职。两名水
手 / 卫兵的职务可保留。

5. 关于瑷珲关与黑龙江(中国境内)沿岸各地之间江运货物的征税事宜,兹告知,尽管
《瑷珲关海关暂行条例》规定,向瑷珲关与其他贸易市场之间往来的土货征收复进口半税,
但因职责范围原应仅限于边境,只可对过境贸易征税,不得插手东三省境内贸易,所以此
类征收是否属于海关在满洲里贸易市场职能尚待商榷。而且,目前正在策划废除土货复
进口半税,因此无论如何不能反其道而行。

您忠诚的仆人

安格联(F. A. Aglen)

海关总税务司

图东、图西分卡的设立及关闭

1. 为汇报图东及图西分卡开设事

10 Enclosures.

LIANGCHIAT'UN BARRIER: opening of two Barriers near
寬 Taheiho for purpose of checking international
trade,reporting; Statement of Expenditure,Plans
and Photographs,submitting; remarks.

153.

I.G.   Aigun   11th. March, 1924.

Replied to in No. _____.

Sir,

1.   I have the honour to refer to your

Despatch No. 118/94,270 (in reply to Aigun No. 95):

LIANGCHIAT'UN BARRIER: proposal to
establish two Barriers in vicinity
of Taheiho for purpose of checking
international trade sanctioned by
Shui-wu Ch'u ; initial expenditure up
to Hk.Tls. 1,200 and annual expenditure
up to Hk.Tls. 800 to be appropriated
from Revenue Collection ;

and to report that these two Barriers have been

established at a total cost of ($1,494.22 at 156.65

=) Hk.Tls. 953.860 - Hk.Tls. 479.987 for the Upper

Barrier at Wo Niu Ho and Hk.Tls. 473.873 for the

Lower Barrier at Hsiao Hei Ho.

2.   I append a detailed statement showing (1) expenditure incurred in connection with the establishment
of the two Barriers, and (2) the estimated monthly

expenditure

The Inspector General of Customs,

Peking.

Entered in Card-Index.

expenditure.

3.   The general appearance of the two Barriers
can be seen from the Plans and Photographs which
go forward to your address under separate cover.

res:10
3.-19a
3.-36

4.   The two Barriers are built on similar
lines and their general plan follows closely that
of the ordinary Siberian Log-House.   The
material used is thoroughly sound and workmanlike,
and it is anticipated that our new stations will
prove durable and efficient for the purpose for
which they are intended.   The internal arrangements provide suitable office accommodation and
living quarters for one Officer and three Boatmen-
Guards.   The outbuildings afford stabling for
two horses and each piece of property is enclosed
by a fence measuring 65' by 35'.

5.   The Upper Barrier has been established
at Wo Niu Ho (卧牛河) at the foot of a hill
near the river bank, some 16 li above Taheiho.
It faces Upper Blagovestchensk and is close to the

terminus

terminus of the main road from Taheiho. The Lower Barrier has been erected on an island opposite the mouth of the river Zeya, 2 <u>li</u> from Hsiao Hei Ho（小黑河）and 12 <u>li</u> Ta Hei Ho. The site of each Barrier is a commanding one.

6.   The staff at each Barrier consists of a Chinese Tidewaiter and two Boatmen-Guards who carry out their duties under strict supervision. The Tidesurveyor pays a surprise visit to each Barrier once a week. A Foreign Officer from the Head Office, accompanied by a Boatman-Guard, visits each Barrier twice a week to inspect and take charge of the patrol for the day. A Daily Report of Occurrences is kept by the Chinese Tidewaiter and sent every week to the Tidesurveyor.

7.   As a general rule the Upper (Wo Niu Ho) Barrier Patrol -Chinese Tidewaiter and Boatman-Guard- proceeds daily by sledge to a point not further than 20 <u>li</u> above the Barrier, but on three occasions Ma Ch'ang（马廠）, a small village 40 <u>li</u> from Ta Hei Ho has been visited. On return of the patrol

patrol to the Barrier the second Boatman-Guard leaves on horseback to patrol the country for a distance of 10 <u>li</u> in the direction of Ta Hei Ho. Here his beat ends, the lower section being patrolled from the Head Office. The patrol from the Lower (Hsiao Hei Ho) Barrier goes daily down river as far as Ch'ang Fa T'un（长发屯）, 10 <u>li</u> below the Barrier, but it sometimes happens that a visit is paid to Ka Lun Shan（卡偷山）, a village 15 <u>li</u> below the Barrier. On return of the patrol to the Barrier the section between the Barrier and Ta Hei Ho is patrolled by a mounted Boatman-Guard whose beat takes him as far as the Ta Hei Ho Public Park, 8 <u>li</u> from the Lower Barrier and 4 <u>li</u> from Head Office.

8.   Nine seizures of a total value of <u>Hk.Tls.</u> 394 have been made at the Upper Barrier, and five of a total value of <u>Hk.Tls.</u> 1,671 at the Lower Barrier. No requests have been received at the Head Office for permission to pass export cargo through either of the Barriers, but 23 applications have been handed in by representatives of two foreign firms to

cover

cover the arrival of skins from Siberia through the Upper Barrier.   The value of these skins amounts to Hk.Tls. 10,254.

9.   The two Barriers have not as yet accomplished anything very great and while it may be held that the period since they commenced to function - the 21st. of September, 1923, in the case of the Lower Barrier and the 15th. of October, 1923, in the case of the Upper Barrier - is too brief to justify confident predictions upon their final success or failure, the expectation that all we are likely to achieve with their help is to keep smugglers at a somewhat greater distance from the Custom House by declaring a wider margin of patrolled region does not seem to me to be at all unreasonable.

10.   It is well known that the main traffic routes along the river bank are in the grip of gangs of soldiers who add to their pay by helping people to break the law, and whose natural inclinations are to impede us as much as they can.   The soldiers, whose interest in illicit trade is apparently connived

at

at by their officers, look upon a smuggler as a personal necessity and hate us cordially because our policy is inconsistent with their aims and intentions. In the forefront we have to place the maintenance of friendly relations with the military authorities and since the most important of the smuggling ventures are cut and dried from the start there is a continuous and ever-recurring chance that some act on the part of our frontier guards, or some almost inadvertent accident, may cause what the military would be certain to regard as vexatious overlapping of interests.   It is thus obvious that the necessity of avoiding all friction balks us of our free action and in the special circumstances of this district our power of effecting reform must be considered very limited.   The natural consequence is an encouragement to illicit trade which tends to dissipate our authority and the fact that to all intents and purposes we are functioning along the river on sufferance rather than by right naturally places us in a most unsatisfactory position.   Customs authority can be expected to increase only in proportion

as

as those who are now directly concerned in exploiting lawlessness are brought under control, and in the existing political situation this is not likely to happen by any but very gradual stages.

I have the honour to be,

Sir,

Your obedient Servant,

R. F. Chengelunb

Commissioner.

APPENDIX.

AIGUN DESPATCH NO. 153 TO I.G.

APPENDIX.

Statement of expenditure incurred in connection with the establishment near Taheiho of two Barriers for the purpose of checking international trade.

(I.G. No. 118/94,270)

(Audit Secretary's S/O Memorandum of 13th. November,1923)

WO NIU HO (UPPER) BARRIER.
(Opened 15th. October, 1923)

(a) Initial Expenditure (as already reported in Revenue Account.)

1923.		$ 156.65	Hk.Tls. 100
Oct.19.	Cost of constructing Barrier (Rev.A/c.Oct.1923:Sch.2(b):Vr.3)	650.00	414.938
Oct.29.	Official Inventory (Rev.A/c.Oct.1923:Sch.2(b):Vr.5)	80.60	51.452
Nov.13.	Bath Tub (Rev.A/c.Nov.1923:Sch.2(b):Vr.3)	11.00	7.022
Dec.29.	Petty Cash Expenditure,Dec.Qr.1923] (Rev.A/c.Dec.1923:Sch.2(b):Vr.6)	10.30	6.575
		751.90	479.987

(b) Maintenance Expenses (as already reported in Revenue Account.)

1923.		$ 156.65	Hk.Tls. 100
Oct.29.	15 sajens firewood (to cover period ending 30th.April,1924) (Rev.A/c.Oct.1923:Sch.2(b):Vr.4)	61.50	39.259
1924.			
Jan.31.	2½ cases Kerosene Oil (Rev.A/c.Jan.1924:Sch.2(b):Vr.4)	19.50	12.448
		81.00	51.707

(c) Estimated future monthly expenditure.

(c) Estimated future monthly expenditure.

During 7 winter months:-

	$ 156.65	Hk.Tls. 100
Salary of Chinese Tidewaiter (4th.A)		$450.00
Special Allowance for Tidewaiter		$ 15.00
Uniform Allowance for Tidewaiter		$ 4.17
Two Boatmen-Guards at Hk.Tls. 11		$ 22.00
Fodder for two horses -30 poods Hay -15 poods Oats		$ 9.00
Kerosene Oil -1 tin	4.20	2.68
Firewood -2½ Sajens at $4.50	11.25	7.18
Petty Cash Expenditure		10.00
		19.86

$ Paid from A/c. A.

During 5 summer months:-

	$ 156.65	Hk.Tls. 100
Salary of Chinese Tidewaiter (4th.A)		$ 45.00
Special Allowance for Tidewaiter		$ 15.00
Uniform Allowance for Tidewaiter		$ 4.17
Two Boatmen-Guards at Hk.Tls. 11		$ 22.00
Fodder for 2 horses -15 poods Hay -7½ poods Oats	5.63	$ 3.75
Benzine for launch -8 visits at 4 gallons -32 gallons at $1.50/48.00		$ 36.00
Engine Oil -8 visits at ½ gallon -4 gallons at $1.80	7.20	$ 4.80
Kerosene Oil -1 tin	4.20	2.68
Petty Cash Expenditure	15.66	10.00
		12.68

$ Paid from A/c. A.

HSIAO HEI HO (LOWER) BARRIER.

HSIAO HEI HO (LOWER) BARRIER.
(Opened 21st.September, 1923)

(a) Initial Expenditure (as already reported in Revenue Account.)

		$ 156.65	Hk.Tls. 100
1923.			
Sept.28.	Cost of constructing Barrier (Rev.A/c.Sept.1923:Sch.2(b):Vr.3)	651.50	415.895
Sept.28.	Official Inventory (Rev.A/c.Sept.1923:Sch.2(b):Vr.5)	72.00	45.963
Sept.29.	Petty Cash Expenditure Sept.1923 (Rev.A/c.Sept.1923:Sch.2(b):Vr.6)	6.30	4.022
Nov.13	Bath Tub (Rev.A/c.Nov.1923:Sch.2(b):Vr.3)	11.00	7.022
Dec. 29.	Petty Cash Expenditure Dec.Qr.1923 (Rev.A/c.Dec.1923:Sch.2(b):Vr.6)	1.52	0.971
		742.32	473.873

(b) Maintenance Expenses (as already reported in Revenue Account.)

		$ 156.65	Hk.Tls. 100
1923.			
Sept.28.	22½ sajens firewood (to cover period ending 30th.April,1924) (Rev.A/c.Sept.1923:Sch.2(b):Vr.4)	96.75	61.762
1924.			
Jan. 31.	2½ cases Kerosene Oil (Rev.A/c.Jan.1924:Sch.2(b):Vr.4)	19.50	12.448
		116.25	74.210

(c) Estimated future monthly expenditure.

153

(c) Estimated future monthly expenditure.

During 7 winter months:-

	$ 156.65	Hk.Tls. 100
Salary of Chinese Tidewaiter (3rd.A)		$ 65.00
Special Allowance for Tidewaiter		$ 15.00
Uniform Allowance for Tidewaiter		$ 4.17
Two Boatmen-Guards at Hk.Tls. 11		$ 22.00
Fodder for two horses -30 poods Hay -15 poods Oats		$ 9.00
Kerosene Oil - 1 tin	4.20	2.68
Firewood - 2½ Sajens at $4.50	11.25	7.18
Petty Cash Expenditure		10.00
		19.86

$ Paid from A/c. A.

During 5 summer months:-

	$ 156.65	Hk.Tls 100
Salary of Chinese Tidewaiter (3rd.A)		$ 65.00
xxSpecial Allowance for Tidewaiter		$ 15.00
Uniform Allowance for Tidewaiter		$ 4.17
Two Boatmen-Guards at Hk.Tls.11		$ 22.00
Fodder for two horses -15 poods Hay -7½ poods Oats	5.63	$ 3.75
Benzine for launch -8 visits at 4 gallons 32 gallons at $1.50	48.00	$ 36.00
Engine Oil -8 visits at ½ gallon 4 gallons at $1.80	7.20	$ 4.80
Kerosene Oil - 1 tin	4.20	2.68
Petty Cash Expenditure	15.66	10.00
		12.68

$ Paid from A/c.A.

TOTAL EXPENDITURE INCURRED TO DATE IN CONNECTION
WITH THE ESTABLISHMENT OF UPPER (WO NIU HO) AND
LOWER (HSIAO HEI HO) BARRIERS.

TOTAL EXPENDITURE INCURRED TO DATE IN CONNECTION
WITH THE ESTABLISHMENT OF UPPER (WO NIU HO) AND
LOWER (HSIAO HEI HO) BARRIERS.

	Hk. Tls. 100
(a) INITIAL EXPENDITURE:-	
Upper (Wo Niu Ho) Barrier	479.987
Lower (Hsiao Hei Ho) Barrier	473.873
Total (a) Initial Expenditure	953.860
(b) MAINTENANCE EXPENSES:-	
Upper (Wo Niu Ho) Barrier	51.707
Lower (Hsiao Hei Ho) Barrier	74.210
Total (b) Maintenance Expenses	125.917
Sum Expended..........HK.TLS.....1,079.777	
Sum Authorised........HK.TLS.....1,200,000	
Sum Unexpended........HK.TLS.......120,223	

ESTIMATED ANNUAL EXPENDITURE.

(1) 7 Winter Months-

Hk.Tls. 19.86 x 7(months) = Hk.Tls.139.02
Hk.Tls.139.02 x 2(Barriers)= ,,   278.04

(2) 5 Summer Months-

Hk.Tls. 12.68 x 5(months) = Hk.Tls. 63.40
Hk.Tls. 63.40 x 2(Barriers)= ,,   126.80

Estimated Annual Expenditure Hk.Tls.404.84

Sanctioned Annual Expenditure .. 800.00

(Assistant)

True Copy:-
Commr.

REFERENCES.	
From I.G. Commrs.No.	To I.G. Port No.
17/87,300	23
42/89,154	32
68/90,437	36
79/91,277	55
106/93,288	84
118/94,270	95

呈总税务司署 153 号文 　　　　　　　　　　　　　　瑷珲关 1924 年 3 月 11 日

尊敬的海关总税务司（北京）：

1. 根据总税务司署第 118/94270 号令（回复瑷珲关第 95 号呈）：

"梁家屯分卡：税务处已批准于大黑河附近增设两处分卡以便检查跨江运输之提议；初期经费海关两 1200 两（上限）及年度经费海关两 800 两（上限）均由江捐税收支出。"

兹报告，该两处分卡已建设完成，总计支出海关两 953.860 两（按海关两 100 两 =156.65 银圆的汇率计算，即 1494.22 银圆），其中图西（卧牛河）分卡为海关两 479.987 两，图东（小黑河）分卡为海关两 473.873 两。

2. 兹附一份详细报表，据报表可知（1）设立两处分卡所产生之费用及（2）每月预计支出费用。

3. 另函附寄可示两处分卡整体外观之平面图及照片。

4. 该两处分卡建造方式大体相同，整体结构与传统西伯利亚木屋相似，建造所用皆为标准材料，房屋应会经久耐用，满足预期需求。内部布局可为 1 名关员及 3 名水手兼卫兵提供舒适的办公及居住空间；外部附属建筑可作两匹马的马厩之用；两处关产皆围有 65 英尺 ×35 英尺的围栏。

5. 图西分卡设于卧牛河靠近江岸的山脚下，位于大黑河上游约 16 里处，与布拉戈维申斯克（Blagovestchensk）上游站相对，靠近通往大黑河主路之尽头。图东分卡设于结雅河河口对岸的内陆之地，与小黑河相距 2 里，与大黑河相距 12 里。两处分卡均处视野开阔之地。

6. 两处分卡各驻有 1 名华籍铃子手和 2 名水手兼卫兵，其工作一直受到严格监督，每周不仅会有头等总巡突击检查一次，还会有一名洋籍关员携一名水手兼卫兵检查两次，该洋籍关员会监督并管理当日的巡缉工作。华籍铃子手须编写每日报告，并按周发送至头等总巡查看。

7. 按照惯例，图西（卧牛河）分卡的华籍铃子手和一名水手兼卫兵每日会乘雪橇向分卡上游巡缉 20 里，但亦有三次行至距大黑河 40 里的小村庄马厂巡查。待两人巡缉结束返回后，另外一名水手兼卫兵再骑马向分卡下游大黑河方向巡缉 10 里，余下路程由大黑河总关负责巡缉。图东（小黑河）分卡每日的巡缉范围，下游至距分卡 10 里的长发屯，偶尔亦会至 15 里处的村庄卡伦山，上游至距分卡 8 里，距大黑河 4 里的大黑河公园处，由一名陆路卫兵负责。

8. 图西分卡共没收货物 9 次，价值总计海关两 394 两，图东分卡共没收货物 5 次，价值总计海关两 1671 两。截至目前，大黑河总关尚未收到出口货物欲通过该两处分卡之申请，但已有两家外国公司代表递交了 23 份关于其自西伯利亚进口之皮货须通过图西分卡之申请，此等皮货价值总计海关两 10254 两。

9. 虽然图西、图东分卡尚无突出成效，但两处分卡运行时间过短（图东分卡于 1923 年 9 月 21 日开设，图西分卡于 1923 年 10 月 15 日开设），目前难以判定最终结果，且，两处分卡设立后，巡缉范围相继扩大，的确有助于使走私者远离海关。

10. 众所周知，黑龙江沿岸运输的主要路线皆由士兵所控制，他们通过帮助他人违法通行谋取暴利，更是要尽一切可能妨碍海关工作，而其上级显然对此等行为持纵容之态度；他们视走私为私人需要，对海关心怀怨恨，只因海关政策与其主张及目的背道而驰。然海关仍需于表面上与军方维持友好关系，不过，由于海关阻断了走私要道，走私之事已日渐销迹，海关卫兵的行动，甚至是一些无意的偶然事件，在军方看来，都可能是侵犯其利益之行为。由此可见，若要避免冲突，海关之行动必然会受到阻碍，而且，瑷珲关区情况又较为特殊，海关施行改革的力度十分有限。长此以往，非法贸易昌盛，海关权力渐衰。而海关之所以能够沿江巡缉防范走私，皆因他人的勉强同意，而非正当权利使然这一事实，足以证明海关处境不容乐观。海关权力唯有待至利用法律漏洞牟利之人得到控制之时方得扬眉，而于当前的政治环境下，此事只能逐步解决。

您忠诚的仆人

贺智兰（R. F. C. Hedgeland）

瑷珲关税务司

瑷珲关致总税务司署第 153 号呈附录

为检查跨江贸易于大黑河附近增设两处分卡的费用报表

（根据总税务司署第 118/94270 号令）

（根据会计科税务司 1923 年 11 月 13 日机要通函）

卧牛河（图西）分卡

（开设于 1923 年 10 月 15 日）

一、初期经费（参见税收账户报告）

1923 年		名目	银圆	海关两（两）
月	日		156.65 银圆 = 海关两 100 两	
10	19	建造费用： ［税收账户/1923 年 10 月/费用项目 2（b）/传票字号 3］	650.00	414.938
10	29	官方家具清单： ［税收账户/1923 年 10 月/费用项目 2（b）/传票字号 5］	80.60	51.452
11	13	浴盆： ［税收账户/1923 年 11 月/费用项目 2（b）/传票字号 3］	11.00	7.022
12	29	1923 年第四季度小额现金支出： ［税收账户/1923 年 12 月/费用项目 2（b）/传票字号 6］	10.30	6.575
		合计：	751.90	479.987

二、维护费用（参见税收账户报告）

1923年		名目	银圆	海关两（两）
月	日		156.65银圆 = 海关两100两	
10	29	15俄丈①木桩（将用至1924年4月30日）： ［税收账户/1923年10月/费用项目2（b）/传票字号4］	61.50	39.259
1924年				
1	31	2.5箱煤油： ［税收账户/1924年1月/费用项目2（b）/传票字号4］	19.50	12.448
		合计：	81.00	51.707

三、每月预计支出

冬季7个月	银圆	海关两（两）
	156.65银圆 = 海关两100两	
华籍（四等前班）钤子手薪俸：		450.00
钤子手特殊津贴：		15.00
钤子手制服津贴：		4.17
两名水手兼卫兵薪俸：每名海关两11两		22.00
两匹马所需饲料：30普特干草；15普特燕麦		9.00
注：以上由A账户支出		
煤油：1罐	4.20②	2.68
木桩：2.5俄丈，每俄丈4.5银圆	11.25	7.18
小额现金支出：		10.00
小计：		19.86

---

① sajen是俄国的非公制长度单位，约合2.14米，其中文有沙绳/撒身或俄丈两种译法，此处翻译为俄丈。

② 原文为44.20，参照上下文，误，修改为4.20。

续表

夏季5个月	银圆	海关两（两）
		156.65银圆＝海关两100两
华籍（四等前班）钤子手薪俸：		45.00
钤子手特殊津贴：		15.00
钤子手制服津贴：		4.17
两名水手兼卫兵薪俸：每名海关两11两		22.00
两匹马所需饲料：15普特干草；7.5普特燕麦	5.63	3.75
汽艇用汽油：出航8次/每次4加仑/共32加仑/每加仑1.50银圆	48.00	36.00
汽艇用机油：出航8次/每次0.5加仑/共4加仑/每加仑1.80银圆	7.20	4.80
注：以上由A账户支出		
煤油：1罐	4.20	2.68
小额现金支出：	15.66	10.00
小计：		12.68

小黑河（图东）分卡

（开设于1923年9月21日）

一、初期经费（参见税收账户报告）

1923年		名目	银圆	海关两（两）
月	日		156.65银圆＝海关两100两	
9	28	建造费用： [税收账户/1923年9月/费用项目2（b）/传票字号3]	651.50	415.895
9	28	官方家具清单： [税收账户/1923年9月/费用项目2（b）/传票字号5]	72.00	45.963
9	29	1923年第三季度小额现金支出： [税收账户1923年9月：第2（b）项下：第6号传票]	6.30	4.022

1923 年		名目	银圆	海关两（两）
月	日		156.65 银圆 = 海关两 100 两	
11	13	浴盆： [税收账户/1923 年 10 月/费用项目 2（b）/传票字号 3]	11.00	7.022
12	29	1923 年第四季度小额现金支出： [税收账户/1923 年 12 月/费用项目 2（b）/传票字号 6]	1.52	0.971
		合计：	742.32	473.873

二、维护费用（参见税收账户报告）

1923 年		名目	银圆	海关两（两）
月	日		156.65 银圆 = 海关两 100 两	
9	28	22.5 俄丈木桩（将用至 1924 年 4 月 30 日）： [税收账户/1923 年 9 月/费用项目 2（b）/传票字号 4]	96.75	61.762
1924 年				
1	31	2.5 箱煤油： [税收账户/1924 年 1 月/费用项目 2（b）/传票字号 4]	19.50	12.448
		合计：	116.25	74.210

三、每月预计支出

冬季 7 个月	银圆	海关两（两）
		156.65 银圆 = 海关两 100 两
华籍（三等前班）铃子手薪俸：		65.00
铃子手特殊津贴：		15.00
铃子手制服津贴：		4.17
两名水手兼卫兵薪俸：每名海关两 11 两		22.00
两匹马所需饲料：30 普特干草；15 普特燕麦		9.00
注：以上由 A 账户支出		

续表

冬季7个月	银圆	海关两（两）
	156.65 银圆 = 海关两 100 两	
煤油：1 罐	4.20	2.68
木桦：2.5 俄丈，每俄丈 4.5 银圆	11.25	7.18
小额现金支出：		10.00
小计：		19.86
夏季5个月		
华籍（三等前班）铃子手薪俸：		65.00
铃子手特殊津贴：		15.00
铃子手制服津贴：		4.17
两名水手兼卫兵薪俸：每名海关两 11 两		22.00
两匹马所需饲料：15 普特干草；7.5 普特燕麦	5.63	3.75
汽艇用汽油：出航 8 次 / 每次 4 加仑 / 共 32 加仑 / 每加仑 1.50 银圆	48.00	36.00
汽艇用机油：出航 8 次 / 每次 0.5 加仑 / 共 4 加仑 / 每加仑 1.80 银圆	7.20	4.80
煤油：1 罐	4.20	2.68
注：以上由 A 账户支出		
小额现金支出：	15.66	10.00
小计：		12.68

图西（卧牛河）分卡及图东（小黑河）分卡自开设以来费用支出总表

名目	海关两（两）
一、初期经费：	
图西（卧牛河）分卡：	479.987
图东（小黑河）分卡：	473.873
小计：	953.860

续表

名目	海关两（两）
二、维护费用：	
图西（卧牛河）分卡：	51.707
图东（小黑河）分卡：	74.210
小计：	125.917
两项支出总计：	1079.777
批准支出总计：	1200.000
余额总计：	120.223

预计每年支出

（1）冬季7个月	海关两（两）
每月预计支出：	19.86
7个月共计：	139.02
两处分卡合计：	278.04
（2）夏季5个月	
每月预计支出：	12.68
5个月共计：	63.40
两处分卡合计：	126.80
每年预计支出	404.84
批准每年支出	800.00

制表：叶元章四等帮办前班（司账）

该抄件内容真实有效，特此证明：

确认人签字：贺智兰（R. F. C. Hedgeland）瑷珲关税务司

2. 为报告图东及图西分卡的日常工作事

Memorandum.

Tidesurveyor's Office
Taheiho, 1st March, 1926.

To
The Assistant in Charge
Aigun Customs District.

Sir.

I have the honour to submit a report on the functioning of the Woniuho and Hsiao-He-ho Barriers as follows.

During the past year these Barriers have done practically nothing worth mentioning or commenting on. In my memo of the 28th, October 1924. I stated that these Barriers had not been given a fair chance to show satisfactory results owing to the stagnancy of trade with Russia and various other reasons, one of the most important being the opposition of the Chinese Military out-posts stationed at various points along the frontier who protected the Smugglers and Merchants and in return received their regular 10% on value of all goods smuggled across the frontier.

In 1922., Mr. Boezi the then Acting Commissioner, commenced the mounted patrol system, and mounted patrols were sent out day and night patrolling the foreshore in both directions from Taheiho Custom House, and on one occasion Mr. Lankin, Officer of the patrol, attempted to detain some Russian smugglers who had crossed the frontier from the Russian side with several bags of valuable skins, but the Chinese Soldiers interfered and threatened to fire on our patrols if they insisted on molesting the smugglers and also informed Mr. Lankin that they knew very well that it was the Customs patrols. Mr.Boezi continually complained to the local Military Authorities, but without satisfactory result, he then approached the Tao-Yin on the matter, at the same time suggesting the opening of the Barriers. It was not until the early part of 1923., when trade had become so bad that there was practically nothing crossing the frontier in that the local Military authorities agreed to give us the Military Pass-word daily, our patrols from that time on functioning day and night along the foreshore without hindrance from the Chinese Soldiers.

The opening of these Barriers no doubt gave the Chinese Customs a certain amount of prestige and did away with illicit traffic across the frontier in their vicinities, and they have now been functioning for over two years, but in my opinion they have not come up to the standard of effective control as was expected, serving only as Scare-crows, the merchants and smugglers still finding it profitable to pay the extra cost of transportation of their goods to some further point up or down the river for destination across the frontier, thus avoiding our Barriers and the high Russian Customs Tariffs.

This profitable illicit traffic with the Russian side was short lived, corporative stores began to open up in Blagovestchensk and gradually the Russian authorities adopted a firm resolution to monopolize foreign trade protecting their country against domination of foreign capital by raising their tariffs, closing the frontier, and in order to guard themselves against further importation of foreign goods, they re-enforced their Coastguards and Customs Patrols to double the former strength with good equipments patrolling an area of over ten miles each direction of Blagovestchensk and when they shoot they shoot to kill no matter whether of Russian or Chinese nationality.

During the winter 1924-5., I have seen women and and children shot to death whilst attempting to cross the river by unofficial roads, and their bodies have remained on the ice where they fell for several days before the parents or relatives could get permission to remove the bodies for burial.

With

With such stringent measures taken by the Russian authorities to stamp out the smuggling of foreign goods into their territory our Barriers and Patrols are rendered almost useless as the Russian authorities are doing the work for us, and as there is little hope of the frontier opening to trade with the present Government in power as it would mean the reducing of their tariffs and be detrimental to the development of the country's productive powers, I beg to suggest that the Woniuho and Hsiao-Ho-ho Barriers be closed until the frontier opens to trade again.

Under present trade conditions at this port the upkeep of these Barriers are only a waste of Service funds. If they are closed and only one Boatman is retained at at each Barrier to look after service property the running expenses of these Barriers will be reduced Hk.Tls.2I06.00, per year as follows.

Yearly running expenses of the Woniuho and Hsiao-Ho-ho Barriers.

Salaries for two Chinese Tidewaiters per year	Hk.Tls.I500.00
Uniform allowance " " " "	" " I20.00
Salaries for four Boatman/Guards " "	" " 528.00
Firewood 2/3rds cost paid by Service " "	" " 60.00
Kerosene Oil 24 Tins " "	" " 60.00
Fodder for 5 Patrol Horses " "	" " I37.00
Miscellaneous expenses " "	" " 20.00
	Total 2425.00

Yearly expenses with only one Boatman/Guard as Watchman at each Barrier.

Salaries for two Boatman:guards per year	Hk.Tls. 264.00
Firewood 2/3rds cost paid by Service "	" " 40.00
Kerosene Oil 6 Tins "	" " I5.00
	Total 3I9.00

We have at present seven horses for patrol work, five of these can be dispensed with and two kept for patrolling foreshore

foreshore within the harbour limits during the winter months.

Yours obediently,

(signed)   Actg.Tidesurveyor & Harbour Master.

通函

由：	致：
监察课	瑷珲关区代理税务司
大黑河,1926 年 3 月 1 日	

尊敬的裴德生(C. M. Petterson)先生：

兹呈交卧牛河及小黑河分卡的日常工作报告。

过去一年,以上两分卡并无可提及或评述之处。本人于 1924 年 10 月 28 日之通函中表示,鉴于与俄贸易停滞不前及其他多种原因,其中最重要的一点是反对中方军队前哨基地沿边境在各地驻扎,走私者及商人通常将走私利润的 10% 上缴军队,而后者为其供保护,因此卧牛河分卡及小黑河分卡并未获得同样的机会以期能得到满意的结果。

1922 年,当时的瑷珲关署理税务司包安济(G.Boezi)先生设立了陆路巡缉队。巡缉队负责从大黑河海关大楼沿堤岸两侧日夜巡逻。一次,巡缉队队员兰金(V. Z. Lankin)先生试图扣押从对岸穿过边境的一些俄籍走私者,携带着几袋贵重的皮毛,但中方军队介入其中并威胁称若巡缉队坚持骚扰走私者的话将向其开火,并告知兰金先生军队很清楚巡缉队隶属海关。包安济先生向当地军方表达海关对此事的不满,结果并不令人满意,随后包安济先生试图与道尹就此事进行商谈,并建议开放分卡。但 1923 年贸易低迷,走私几近停止,当地军方才向海关发布了军队每日暗号,自那时起,海关巡缉队才可以沿堤岸两侧日夜巡逻而不受军方阻挠。

分卡的开放毫无疑问为海关赢得一些声誉,且消除其管辖区域之跨境非法运输,分卡现已正常工作超过两年时间,但本人认为分卡并未达到对该地区进行有效管理的预期,而仅仅作为一个象征。商人和走私者仍通过黑龙江上下游较远的地点将货物走私至河对岸,虽为此需支付额外的运输费用,但过中国分卡及俄海关的高额关税则属仍有利可图。

向俄国走私非法货物利润颇丰但为期较短,布拉戈维申斯克开始创办合作社,俄国政府也逐渐实行强硬条例以垄断对外贸易,并通过提高关税、关闭边境保护本国免受外国资本控制。此外,为避免国外货物进一步进入俄国,俄国重新启用了海岸巡防及海关巡缉队,配备精良的装备,人数为之前的两倍,以布拉戈维申斯克为中心以超过 10 里为半径向外进行巡逻。无论走私者是俄国国籍还是中国国籍,沿岸卫队或海关巡稽队都有权射杀。

1924 年至 1925 年冬季,本人目睹了妇女和儿童尝试经非官道跨江时被射杀,在其家人获得许可将遗体带走,但在举行葬礼之前遗体一直留在冰面上,无人移动。

俄国政府采取如此严格的措施以杜绝国外货物通过走私的方式进入俄国。鉴于俄方执行力度之大,中国海关及巡缉队位同虚设。此外,与现执政政府进行贸易往来的可能性非常小,这意味着运输量减少,且对生产力发展造成损害,为此本人建议贸易再次开放前关闭卧牛河分卡及小黑河分卡。

以瑷珲关目前的贸易状况,维持分卡不过是浪费资金,若将分卡关闭并于每一分卡留任一名水手看管关产,每年分卡的费用将减少海关两2106两,细则如下所示:

卧牛河及小黑河两处分卡年度支出	
	海关两（两）
2名华籍钤子手薪俸	1500.00
2名华籍钤子手制服津贴	120.00
4名水手兼卫兵薪俸	528.00
薪柴费用（海关支付三分之二）	60.00
煤油费（24罐）	60.00
草料（5匹巡缉马）	137.00
杂项支出	20.00
总计:	2425.00
两处分卡仅各派一名水手兼卫兵担任巡役之年度支出	
2名水手兼卫兵薪俸	264.00
薪柴费用（海关支付三分之二）	40.00
煤油费（6罐）	15.00
总计:	319.00

目前瑷珲关拥有7匹马用于巡逻工作,其中5匹可以卖掉,剩下2匹可于冬季负责在港口范围内巡逻堤岸。

您忠诚的仆人

博韩（G. E. Baukham）

署理头等总巡及理船厅

3. 为报告图东分卡和图西分卡现状事

DOCKET: BARRIERS, UPPER AND LOWER: transfer of part of staff
at, to Head Office for time being, owing to practical
cessation of smuggling; recommending.

300.

I.G.

Aigun, 26th January, 1927.

Sir,

I have the honour to report to you on the
present status of the Upper and Lower Barriers and
to request your instructions as to the policy to
be followed under existing frontier conditions. In
this connection the following paragraph copied from
my predecessor's Handing-over-memo (forming an
enclosure to Aigun despatch No. 288 to I. G.) is
of pertinent interest:

    4. Frontier control:

      "My predecessor in his S/O. letter
    "No. 55 recommends the closing of the
    "Upper and Lower Barriers so long as
    "Russia keeps her own frontier closed
    "and guarded. The Inspector General
    "wishes the matter to be thoroughly
    "investigated and reported on by
    "despatch to the Inspectorate (vide
    "I. G. S/O. letter dated 21st June, 1926)
    "I am of opinion that as far as the
    "open-river season is concerned the
                 "Barriers

"Barriers could safely be closed; but
"as I have no actual experience of
"the conditions obtaining during the
"winter-season, when smuggling is rife,
"I have not the necessary data to
"write a report on this subject. It
"must be remembered that once the
"Barriers are closed, it may be
"difficult to obtain permission from
"the provincial authorities to
"re-establish them, were the frontier
"again opened to trade".

The Barriers were originally opened in 1923 as
an offset to the closing of the Liangchiat'un
Barrier. I. G. despatch No. 118 notifies this office
of the approval of the Shui-wu Ch'u to the step
and instructs that reports are to be submitted as
soon as the Barriers have been established; and
after they have functioned for twelve months. Aigun
despatch No. 153 to I. G. reports the establishment
of the Barriers and states that while they are not
doing much in the way of actual seizures their
moral effect is of help in preventive work.

                 At

The Inspector General of Customs,

    Peking.

At this time the Staff at each Barrier consisted of a Chinese Tidewaiter and two Boatmen/Guards. Two Foreign Tidewaiters were detached two days each week to take charge of the patrols.

Early in 1923, through a combination of circumstances, the frontier was closed to trade. As a consequence there was great activity amongst the smugglers on the Chinese side and our patrols constantly came up against the military who looked on this trade as a source of income. During the last two years, however, the Soviet authorities have taken the strictest precautions to prevent goods crossing the frontier in either direction and have lined their side of the Amur with troops who get a bounty for every smuggler shot. The result has been that smuggling has almost ceased and even the Chinese military have lost all interest in the traffic.

What little smuggling there is consists of carrying goods from China to Russia as the latter
                                                    country

country no longer produces anything that China wants except furs and gold which commodities are smuggled into China at points distant from here. And of the goods smuggled to Russia some 90% may be said to consist of articles of foreign type such as piece goods, matches, sugar, thread, cigarettes, knick-knacks, etc., etc., which have already paid duty. I have visited many contraband shops myself and have verified this from the stocks on their shelves. Spirit is practically the only commodity on which we are losing export duty. More recently the fall of the trouble has caused the contraband shops still further loss of trade and it is now said that out of some 30 such shops along the river at various intervals just above and below Taheiho only 6 are now open.

It will not be surprising, therefore, when I report that, though the patrols have been kept up as usual, the seizures for the past year have been practically nil, a result discouraging to the
                                                    Staff

Staff concerned. As I cannot foresee any change in present conditions I would now recommend that the activities of the two Barriers be curtailed for the time being, the Chinese Tidewaiter and a Boatman/Guard being withdrawn from each leaving a Boatman/Guard (with horse) at each Barrier to maintain the property and report any unusual occurrences.

This practical closing of the Barriers would further necessitate the abandonment of the present system of checking junks and rafts. No loss would result, however, as only River Dues are concerned and they are so small that no junk or raft would take the time and trouble to evade them.

In advocating the above step I concur in the views of my immediate predecessors that, for reasons of "face" and a possible difficulty in re-opening them if once closed, the Barriers should not be entirely abandoned.

The question now arises as to what the saving

would

would be if the Barriers ceased preventive work. The first consideration would be the matter of Staff and after thoroughly studying the situation I am forced to say that I cannot see that any net reduction in the Staff would eventuate. At the time of the establishment of the Barriers the Taheiho Staff (concerned with this report, and excluding Aigun, Liangchiat'un and the Upper and Lower Barriers) consisted of:

	1923	1927
Tidesurveyor	1	1
Examiners	2	2
Foreign Tidewaiters	5	2
Foreign Watcher	1	-
Chinese Watchers	3	3

It will be seen from these figures that the Taheiho Foreign Staff has been greatly reduced since 1923 and that there are now only two Foreign Tidewaiters on duty at the Taheiho Office. To my mind, and in the opinion of the Acting Tidesurveyor, this strength is not sufficient for boarding duty, searching steamers, duty along the bund

and

and night duty. I would propose, therefore, to retain
the two Chinese Tidewaiters, to be released at the
Barriers, for strengthening the Taheiho Staff especially
in preventive work. Of the two Boatmen/Guards also
to be released they would be absorbed by the demand
for additional hands in the launch and gig, the
Staff now being two under strength in this department.

With regard to the upkeep of the Barriers and
the patrols, a certain amount of saving could be
effected. At present we have seven patrol horses.
I would recommend that three only be retained to
keep up communications and make an occasional patrol -
one horse at each barrier and one at the Head
Office. The reductions in Staff and horses as
suggested would make the following difference in
yearly expenses:

	Present Exp.	Proposed Exp.
Firewood	$ 90	$ 60
Kerosene Oil	90	25
Fodder	420	180
Miscellaneous	30	15
	630	280

Showing

Showing a gain of some $350 per year - the above
items are paid from Revenue Account. The principal
gain would not be in expenditure, however, but in
the increased efficiency of the Taheiho Staff.

In conclusion, if you approve my recommendations
I have the honour to request your permission to
make the dispositions indicated and to dispose of
four of the patrol horses - for a sum estimated at
$240.

I have the honour to be,

Sir,

Your obedient Servant,

Acting Commissioner.

REFERENCES.

From I. G.	To I. G.
106/93,266	95
118/94,270	153
172/96,648	Aigun S/O No.55
I.G. S/O of	
21/6/1926.	

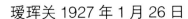
呈总税务司署 <u>300</u> 号文　　　　　　　　　　瑷珲关 1927 年 1 月 26 日

尊敬的海关总税务司（北京）：

兹报告图东分卡和图西分卡现状，恳请总税务司署按边境现状指示瑷珲关应遵循的方针政策。瑷珲关前任税务司的工作移交书（瑷珲关致总税务司署第 288 号呈附件）中列有与此相关之内容：

"4. 边境管控：

瑷珲关前任税务司在其第 55 号机要文件中建议，只要俄国设卡封锁边境，便可关闭图西及图东分卡。总税务司署希望瑷珲关彻查此事，并呈报海关总税务司（参见总税务司署 1926 年 6 月 21 日机要文件）。兹建议，航运季开通之前，图西、图东分卡皆可放心关闭；然因本署尚未于冬季（走私猖獗）管理过本口岸，资料不足，难以撰写报告。而且，一旦关闭图西、图东分卡，待边境贸易再次开放，瑷珲关重设分卡恐难再获得省政府批准。"

图西、图东分卡设立于 1923 年，其目的是为抵消梁家屯分卡被关闭所产生的影响。总税务司署第 118 号令已知会瑷珲关，对于税务处此举表示赞成，并指示图西、图东分卡一经开设，立即呈文报告；在分卡运作 12 个月后再次呈文报告。瑷珲关致总税务司署第 153 号呈报告已开设图西、图东分卡，并说明分卡虽实际查获无几，但确有防患之效。

现两处分卡各有 1 名华籍稽查员及 2 名水手／卫兵。每周另有两天派遣 2 名钤子手负责巡缉。

1923 年初，因环境等综合因素，边境贸易关闭。走私者开始在中国边境猖獗行动，中国军方亦在利用走私交易牟利，瑷珲关巡缉队与军方之间冲突不断。在过去的两年里，苏维埃政府已采取严格措施，防止往来货物跨边境走私，并于黑龙江俄岸驻扎军队，奖赏击毙走私者，走私因此几近消失，中国军方也不再因走私获利。

鉴于俄国除毛皮和金子以外，不再生产中国所需物资，因此现存之少量货物走私皆是从中国走私到俄国，俄国所产之毛皮和金子仍于其他地点（距此地较远）走私入中国境内。走私至俄国的货物 90% 均为洋式货物，如布匹、火柴、糖类、线、香烟及摆件等等。本署亲自查看各走私品商铺后，已证实商铺货架上的此类洋式货物均已完纳税款，因此瑷珲关未征出口税之货物实际上仅为酒精一项。近来，由于走私减少，走私品商铺生意持续亏损，据称大黑河上游及下游黑龙江沿岸各处 30 家走私品商铺中，现仅余 6 家仍在营业。

正因如此，虽然巡缉队一如既往坚守岗位，但过去一年里实际查获却为零。鉴于难以预测事态发展之动向，本署建议暂停图西、图东分卡目前的巡缉活动，两处分卡各撤走一名华籍稽查员及一名水手／卫兵，只留一名水手／卫兵（配一匹马）负责看守关产，并报告异常之情况。

既然图西、图东分卡已几乎处于关闭状态，检查民船和木筏之惯例亦可中止，毕竟此检查惯例仅涉江捐一项。民船和木筏需缴纳之江捐数额较小，定不会为了逃避江捐而浪费时间，招惹麻烦。

本署与瑷珲关前任税务司意见相同，考虑到海关之立场以及关闭后再重开图西、图东分卡可能受阻等因素，不建议完全关闭该两处分卡。

若停止分卡目前工作，则需考虑哪些为可节省之开支项。首先，关于职员精简问题，本署仔细研究当前形势后，发现无法精简职员，只能作调配之安排。图西、图东分卡开设之时，瑷珲关于大黑河驻地之职员（关于此报告，不包括瑷珲分关、梁家屯分卡和图西、图东分卡）包括：

	1923 年	1927 年
头等总巡／监察长	1	1
验货	2	2
洋籍稽查员	5	2
洋籍巡役	1	—
华籍巡役	3	3

由上述可知，自 1923 年以来大黑河洋籍职员已大幅精简，目前瑷珲关于大黑河驻地的在职洋籍稽查员仅有两名。本税务司及署监察长均认为，人手不足，难以完成登船检查、搜索轮船、沿堤岸值守以及夜巡等工作。因此本署建议将图西、图东分卡撤走的两名华籍稽查员留在大黑河，以补充大黑河人手，加强预防性工作。此外，鉴于在汽艇和小艇上工作的职员人数不足（仅两名职员），故将图西、图东分卡撤走的两名水手／卫兵派遣至此。

在维护图西、图东分卡及巡缉所方面，可节省一笔开支。当前用于巡缉之马匹有 7 匹。故本署建议仅留下 3 匹以作通信之用，及偶尔一次的巡缉，其中每个分卡一匹马，另有一匹留于瑷珲关总关。按照提议调配人员及马匹后，年度经费支出变化如下：

	当前经费支出	提议后经费支出
	银圆	银圆
薪柴	90	60
煤油	90	25
饲料	420	180
杂项	30	15
总计	630	280

上述款项由税收账户支出,每年将节省约350银圆。然主要益处并非减少经费支出,而是以此提高大黑河职员工作效率。

望批准本署做出上述部署,并处理4匹巡缉用马(预计价值240银圆)。

您忠诚的仆人

铎博赉(R. M. Talbot)

瑷珲关署理税务司

专题五

瑷珲关因局势紧张被迫转移、关停及重新开放

1. 为汇报暂时关闭瑷珲关并撤离职员事

Custom House,

Aigun (Harbin), 29th November, 1929.

EVACUATION OF PORT: temporary closing of Aigun Customs and
evacuation of Staff, in accordance with instructions, reporting.

Sir,

    I have the honour to acknowledge the receipt
on the 5th November of telegraphic instructions
transmitted through the Harbin Commissioner:

        Aigun Staff to be evacuated and the port
        treated as a sub-station of Harbin for the
        time being:

and to report that the evacuation has been completed.

    On the receipt of the above instructions I
called on the Taoyin/Superintendent informing him
of your instructions and requesting his cooperation.
He readily approved the proposed step stating that
he would wire the Tsitsihar Authorities for military
escort on our journey to Tsitsihar. On the 7th
November I wrote him officially that the Staff was
being evacuated and asked for protection on the
journey as well as for the Staff remaining in
Taheiho and Aigun. He replied on the 9th instant
acknowledging the receipt of my letter and inquiring
from whence the Superintendent's Allowance would be
sent. My reply of the same date stated that I
would know about the continued issuing of his
                                Allowance

The Inspector General of Customs,

    S H A N G H A I.

Allowance until I reached Harbin. Copies of these
three letters are appended for your information.
At the same time the Superintendent and myself
issued a joint notification that the collection of
revenue was suspended for the time being.

    I explained to the Lower Employees that
by your instructions the transferable Staff of the
port was being evacuated to Harbin, and that I
expected them to remain in care of the Customs
property as they were natives of the place. To my
agreeable surprise they readily consented to remain.
The November pay had been issued on the 7th
instant prior to the evacuation and, after
consultation with the Harbin Commissioner, I decided
to issue to those remaining their December pay.
I further append a copy of an Order I issued on
leaving Aigun. It will be noted that I propose
therein to issue Hk.Tls.10 each to Watchers Yu Fu-
shou (于福寿) and Ko Chin-chiu (郭敬九) placed
in charge of property at Taheiho and Aigun
respectively. I trust that this action will meet
with your approval. I feel that the arrangements
I made for looking after Customs property will
work out satisfactorily provided there is no
fighting or looting.

    The furniture in the Commissioner's House was
moved to a house in the Old Customs Compound for,
as the Commissioner's house is leased property, I felt
it would be safer if stored on official premises
and also less likely to be used if Taheiho
was occupied. The lease of the Commissioner's
House expires on the 1st June, 1930, and 6
                              months'

months' rent, i.e. $600, is payable on the 1st
December, 1929. As it is the only suitable house
in Taheiho for a Commissioner's residence and has
just been completely done up I would recommend
that it be kept on. A T'ingch'ai, Coolie and
Gatekeeper are living in the servants' quarters to
look after the property.

The lease of the Custom House at Aigun
expires on the 15th May, 1931, and 6 months' rent
in advance, $250, was due on the 15th November,
1929, but had not been claimed before I left.
I do know if the landlord is now in Taheiho.

With the exception of the Commissioner's
furniture, all inventories were left in the houses
to which they belong. Certain articles of crockery
and glassware on the inventory of the Commissioner's
house were broken and have been indented for from
the Works Department by myself, to be sent to
the Harbin Commissioner for keeping until the Staff
returns to Aigun.

As the cost of transportation was so high
between Taheiho and Harbin, owing to the abnormal
conditions, I only permitted to be taken the less
bulky and more necessary personal effects. Much
belonging to the Staff was left behind in the
Customs House to be sent for later when it can
be transported under normal conditions.

In the way of archives I took all
correspondence between Aigun and the Inspectorate and
the ports, as well as the records from the
Accounts, Secretary's, Writer's, Tidesurveyor's,

General

General and Returns Offices. I also took the
seals, code books, typewriters, etc., etc., so
that everything required for carrying on the
functions of the Aigun Office is now in Harbin.
All bonds guaranteeing Customs employees signed by
local merchants are now probably useless, as all
shops have been closed.

In evacuating I first concentrated the
Staff and luggage at Liangchiat'un. This move was
completed on the 10th instant. My party consisted
of 14 adults, 9 children and 7 servants, a total
of 30. In addition we had to allow for carrying
from 3 to 6 soldiers as escort. Personal effects
and luggage amounted to 200 poods equal to some
7,200 pounds. With so many passengers and so
much luggage it was necessary to make two trips
between Liangchiat'un and Mergen, where additional
cars were obtained and the journey continued. The
first contingent left Liangchiat'un on the 15th
instant and arrived in Harbin on the 22nd via
Tsitsihar. The second party did not get through
until the 27th instant. The journey was a cold
one, native inns were uncomfortable and the danger
from hunghutze was very real. However, all
difficulties were safely surmounted, the protection
furnished by the Authorities on the road proving
effective. Many other parties were robbed. Owing
to the attacks by the Soviet in the vicinity of
Manchouli and Hailar considerable demoralization
existed at the Railway Station at Tsitsihar and
great difficulty was found in getting accommodation
on the train. Thanks to the assistance of the
Chinese

Chinese Railway officials, however, we were eventually able to leave for Harbin.

The cost of the evacuation was necessarily very dear as all transport was engaged by civilians retiring on Harbin. A statement of the amount spent is being prepared and will be handed to the Harbin Commissioner. Roughly speaking the total cost will be local $4,000 which includes the cost of transporting the archives.

This despatch will supplement my Handing-Over-Memorandum written, for the most part, before I left Aigun. A copy is being handed to the Harbin Commissioner.

I have the honour to be,
Sir,
Your obedient Servant,

(Signed) F. L. Dalbel

Acting Commissioner.

Appendix.

ORDER NO. 1,3 2.

CUSTOM HOUSE,
Aigun/Taheiho, 5th November, 1929.

AIGUN CUSTOMS TEMPORARILY CLOSED: INSTRUCTIONS AS TO CARRYING ON UNTIL ITS RE-OPENING:

Instructions have been received from the Inspector General that the Aigun Customs is to be closed temporarily and the Commissioner, Chinese Indoor and Foreign and Chinese Outdoor Staff withdrawn to Harbin. The Lower Miscellaneous Staff is to remain to take care of the Customs property and carry on certain routine while the Customs is closed.

The Tidesurveyor has been instructed to issue a roster assigning the different employees remaining to occupy certain definite quarters. Each employee will be responsible for the contents of the buildings they occupy. Whilst living on these quarters they will be furnished with firewood and kerosene oil at Service expense.

Pay for December will be advanced to those employees remaining and arrangements will be made for the issue of further pay as it falls due.

Mr. Yu Fu Shou (于福寿), as Senior Watcher, will be in charge of the Customs Staff remaining and all Customs property at Aigun, Taheiho and Liangchiat'un and the Upper and Lower Barrier, while the Custom House is closed and will receive an extra allowance of Hk.Tls. 15.00 per month for this added responsibility. Likewise Ko Chin Chiu (郭敬九) Watcher will be in charge at Aigun and Liangchiat'un and will also receive an allowance of Hk.Tls. 15.00 per month. However he will be subordinate to Mr. Yu Fu Shou and will report to him for instructions. I have reported to the Superintendent

that

that Yu Fu Shou has been left in charge of Aigun
Customs property. The latter is to report to him for
advice and assistance when it is necessary.

The two Customs horses will be left with two
carts and fodder provided. Boatman Wang Chin Tsai(王进财)
will be in charge of the horses and is instructed to
take particular care of them.

A daily attendance book is to be kept and the
Tidesurveyor is to arrange for the keeping of daily
meteorological readings and the regular despatch of the
telegram concerned. He is also to arrange for Mr. Yu
Fu Shou to keep a Report Book in which is to be
entered daily anything of importance occuring of either
Service or general interest. He is to forward weekly
to the Chief Tidesurveyor, Harbin, copies of his entries
in his Daily Report Book. Stationery is to be provided
for this purpose.

The Senior Watcher Yu Fu Shou will also be
provided with an advance of 100.00 for Petty Cash
Expenditure and a careful record is to be kept of all
expenditure made, and vouchers secured, and it is to be
understood that only the most necessary expense is to
be incurred. Any not justified will have to be refunded
later. A monthly report is to be made to the Chief
Tidesurveyor, Harbin, of expenditure made and balance
remaining in hand.

In case of extreme danger Customs premises may
be evacuated and the Staff may retire to a place of
safety, but are to return as soon as possible when it
is safe to do so. Before leaving, however, Mr. Yu Fu
Shou is to report to the Superintendent or to the
Sun Ling Fu,

Sun Ling Fu, if the Superintendent is absent, requesting
protection for the Customs property and Staff. Mr. Mo
Chin Thiu is to take similar steps at Aigun if it
becomes necessary to evacuate. At the same time Mr. Yu
is to notify the Harbin Customs. If Customs premises
are vacated they are first to be securely closed up and
locked; their contents will remain as they are. The
families of those remaining may be sent to Hsangchiat'un
and occupy official quarters there.

Finally I have to add that the loyalty of those
employees remaining at these ports is fully appreciated
by myself and I shall recommend their names to the
Inspector General that they may be specially rewarded at
the time of the reopening of the Customs.

(signed) R.W. Talbot,
Acting Commissioner.

True copy:

Unclassed Assistant.

CUSTOM HOUSE.

S/O No. 122. **Aigun (Harbin)** 28th Nov., 19 29.

Dear Mr. Maze,

My last S/O dated the 30th October described the growing acuteness of the situation at Taheiho owing to the imminent freezing of the Amur and the difficult situation the place was in owing to its isolation. On the 3rd November I wired you recommending that, for the purposes of information and instructions regarding evacuation, Aigun might be considered a sub-station of Harbin for the time being. On the 5th November I received a wire from the Harbin Commissioner, transmitting your telegraphic instructions, that the Staff was to be evacuated to Harbin and Aigun was to be considered as a sub-station for the present. While I had not anticipated that these instructions would arrive so soon, and rather felt that I appeared to be quitting under fire, I must confess that I felt a certain amount of relief that I no longer had the responsibility of providing for the safety of the Staff.

Just

F. W. Maze, Esquire,

etc., etc., etc.,

Shanghai.

Just before the receipt of the evacuation orders I had been waited on by the Manager of the Bank of China and had been informed by him that the Bank was leaving at once for Harbin. They were practically without funds but by good luck I got some $2,400 from Messrs. Kunst & Albers who were also closing up. With this money and with the assistance of a loan by the Bank of China from the Provincial Bank I managed to collect enough to pay the Staff their November pay before leaving and to have a balance left for the expense of evacuation.

I called on the Taoyin directly after the order for evacuation arrived and informed him that you had decided to withdraw the Staff temporarily, intimating that your decision was probably prompted by the fact that there would be no collection in Aigun this winter under any circumstances, and received his full approval of the contemplated step. In the course of the next two days I addressed him about the matter saying that the Staff was being transferred to Harbin and that for the time being Aigun was to be considered as a sub-station of Harbin. At the same time I arranged for and issued a joint

notification

notification to the effect that the collection of
revenue was temporarily suspended.   He acknowledged
the receipt of my despatch and inquired from what
source his allowance would be paid in the future.
My reply was that I had no definite instructions
regarding that point but that I would receive information when I arrived at Harbin.

The next few days were busy ones preparing for
the evacuation.   I managed to arrange with a local
Russian garage to put two old motorbusses in order
as all cars were engaged far ahead and many were
being commandeered by the military.   I had my own
car, a small one for 5 passengers, which was also
available.   The party to /evacuated consisted of

	Adults	Children	Servants
Acting Commissioner	1		2
Tidesurveyor Smith	2	3	1
Examiner Snow	1		1
Clerk Wang Te Mao	2	1	
" Chang Yuan Yang	2	2	1
Writer Yang Tsun-hou	1		1
Ho-shui-yüan Li Yung-p'o	2	3	
Chinese Tidewaiter Wang Liang	1		
" " Wang Hua Cheng	2		1
	14	9	7
		30	

In

In addition there were archives and personal effects to
the amount of 200 poods = 7,200 pounds.   The amount
that could be carried in the way of luggage was very
small and I limited each one to the necessities only
all bulky personal effects and furniture being left
behind.   From the archives I took all despatches, S/Os,
Memoranda, etc., from the Inspectorate and ports, the
accounts for this and the two previous years, revenue
returns, the important General Office records and
registers, the archives of the Writer's office, the
necessary records for preparing this years returns,
Customs seals, typewriters, code books, etc. etc. leaving
practically only printed instructions.   As the
Commissioner's house was leased I stored the official
furniture from it in the Married Examiner's House in
the old Customs Compound considering it would be safer
there.   The rest of the inventory I left where it was.
The safe in the Commissioner's Office was left open.
Several days were employed in these preparations boxes
being moved to Liangchiat'un Barrier as fast as they
were packed.   The Staff was also concentrated there
waiting for the word to move.

When I had completed all preparations on the 8th
November, the Taoyin/Superintendent unexpectedly requested

an

an interview and inquired as to the future of Aids
and what was to be done with the balance in Aids
A/c. I informed him that it was my intention to
transfer everything to Harbin and to carry on from
there for the time being. He then told me that he
had decided that the Aids Commission must dispense with
Mr. Ignatieff's services owing to the fact that Aids
activities had ceased and to the likelihood that when
the present troubles were readjusted an entirely new
agreement might be made as to the navigation of, and
upkeep of Aids on, the Sino-Soviet frontier rivers.
The Taoyin proposed to give Mr. Ignatieff 3 months pay
in lieu of notice and expressed the hope that he
could be reengaged if the services of a Technical
Adviser to Aids were again required. At the same time
he requested that the balance in Aids of some $6,600
be handed over to him that he might carry on while
the Customs was away and in view of the fact that
some new arrangements might be made by the Provincial
Authorities for the continuation of the present work.
I informed the Taoyin that I could understand his
attitude and that of the Commission regarding the
continued employment of Mr. Ignatieff and that after
paying him three months pay as requested I would report
the

the action taken to you. With regard to the closing
of Aids accounts, however, I told him that I did not
dare to do this without first obtaining your instructions
as it meant the practical severing of connections
between the Aids Commission and the Customs. At the
same time I inquired regarding the repayment of the
advance of $15,000 outstanding from Sungari Aids A/c.
now that the question of the closing of Aids A/c. was
being brought up. He assured me that if the Amur
Aids could not repay this advance the Heilungchiang
Authorities would; the balance in Aids was not a large
one and was needed by himself to carry on with during
the present crisis. I told him I would think the
matter over and reply the next day, when I wrote him
that as there were still certain payments to be made
from Aids and that as the accounts were packed I would
prefer that the question remain open until I arrived
at Harbin and had received your instructions. He was
not at all staisfied with this reply and after a
rather stormy interview in which he stated that he had
already informed the Provincial Authorities that he
considered he should take over the balance in Aids I
finally agreed to give him $4,500 to carry on with
Aids account to remain open for the time being.
At

At the beginning of the arrangements for evacuation I informed the **Lower Staff** that as they were natives of the place I would expect them to remain and look after the property after my departure. I had consulted the Harbin Commissioner about this and he suggested that I advance them December in addition to their November pay. On their agreeing to stay (willingly, I should record) I gave them their December pay. I placed Watcher Yu Fu Shou (于福寿) in charge of the Staff and property at Taheiho and instructed him to keep a daily report book, extracts from which were to be sent weekly to the Chief Tidesurveyor at Harbin. He was also to keep the meteorological readings and send off the daily telegram and was given an advance of $100 for Petty Cash expenditure. For the added responsibility **he** was expected to assume he would receive a special allowance of Hk.Tls.10 per month. I also took the liberty of placing Watcher Ko Chin Chiu (郭敬九) in charge of the property at Aigun sub-station and at Liangchiat'un also with an allowance of Hk.Tls.10 per month. I had no time to refer this question of allowances to you and trust that you will consider my action justified under the circumstances. Two horses and carts, with fodder, Customs property, were left in the care of

the

the Staff to be used in the case of an emergency. Different employees were assigned to different Customs properties with the understanding that firewood and kerosene would be funished by the Customs and they would be responsible for the buildings they occupied. I left Taheiho with the feeling **that all** would be well cared for unless the place was occupied by Soviet troops or looted by Chinese soldiers.

Having only two motorbusses and my passenger car the evacuation had to be carried out in two moves. I left Liangchiat'un on the 16th instant with the first lot taking the women and children in my car. We were provided with military escorts enroute by orders of the Governor and though the route was infested with Hutze we were undisturbed. From Nohoting to Tsitsihar I travelled with General Ch'eng Chih-yüan (陈志远) who took a seat in one of our cars and sent ahead a car with 20 soldiers to protect the party. The journey of 5 days from Liangchiat'un to Tsitsihar in the cold and stopping at native inns was far from comfortable but as we arrived safely at Tsitsihar we cannot complain. On trying to leave there we had considerable difficulty in continuing on to Harbin as the activities of Soviet army in the vicinity of Manchouli and Hailar had

completely

completely disorganized the Chinese military and civilians who were fleeing as fast as they could to Harbin. Only the friendly assistance of the Chinese officials of the C.E. Ry. enabled us to get away from Tsitsihar. I arrived with my party on the 22nd instant and the balance of the Staff with luggage put in an appearance on the 27th after a very tiring journey. In view of what is happening at present at Manchuria I have the feeling that we got away from Taheiho just in time.

The Handing-Over-Memo which I have prepared was written for the most part before I left Taheiho. It touches very little on the evacuation of the place but should be found useful when the Customs resumes its functions there. Prior to 1922 Aigun was a sub-station of Harbin. To my mind, if the joint upkeep of Aids is abolished and trade conditions do not improve at the end of the present misunderstanding Aigun could continue to remain a sub-station if a senior Foreign Assistant is sent there in charge. If conditions revert to what they were before the present unpleasantness, however, the former status of Aigun might well be restored.

I am preparing despatches reporting the evacuation of Aigun, the severance of the relations between the

Aids

Aids commission and the Technical Adviser and the transfer of the Aids balance to Harbin.

A copy of this S/O is being handed to the Harbin Commissioner.

Yours truly,

呈总税务司署 <u>450</u> 号文　　　　　　　　　　瑷珲关 1929 年 11 月 29 日

尊敬的海关总税务司（上海）：

11 月 5 日总税务司署电令收悉（由滨江关税务司转交）：

"撤离瑷珲关职员并将瑷珲关暂时视为滨江关分关。"

兹报告撤离工作已完成。

收到上述指令后，本署请求道尹兼海关监督进行协助，道尹兼海关监督表示同意本署提议的方案并将发电报至齐齐哈尔当局，以保证本署职员在前往齐齐哈尔的路途中能够有军队的保护。11 月 7 日，本署书面告知道尹兼海关监督，瑷珲关职员已开始撤离，希望撤离及留守职员均能够得到保护。11 月 9 日，道尹兼海关监督回复已收到本署信函，并询问海关监督津贴的发放事宜。本署于同日回复，抵达滨江关之后，方能知晓其海关监督津贴发放事宜。兹附三封信函副本，以供总税务司署参考。同时海关监督与本署发布了联合通知，暂时停收税费。

本署向低职级职员解释道，根据总税务司署指令，瑷珲关可调任职员已开始撤离至哈尔滨，由于低职级职员为本地人，所以希望他们可以留下看管关产。他们欣然同意。在撤离前，职员 11 月的薪俸已于 11 月 7 日发放。本署在与滨江关税务司商谈后，决定给留下的职员发放 12 月薪俸。兹附上本署在撤离瑷珲关时所发布谕令的抄件。本署提议鉴于巡役于福寿和郭敬九分别负责管理瑷珲关于大黑河和瑷珲两处驻地的关产，两人各发放海关两 10 两，相信总税务司署会予以批准。兹认为，只要没有战争或抢劫事件，按照本署之安排，瑷珲关关产必会受到妥善的保管。

鉴于税务司住所为租用关产，不如海关自有关产安全，遂已将税务司住所的家具移至旧海关大院房屋，且一旦大黑河被侵占，这些家具也将无所用处。税务司住所租期将于 1930 年 6 月 1 日到期，6 个月的租金即 600 银圆，应于 1929 年 12 月 1 日交付。由于该住所是大黑河唯一适合税务司的房屋，且已整修翻新，故本署建议继续租用该住所，可以由居住在职员宿舍的一名听差、一名苦力和一名门役照管一应关产。

瑷珲关海关办公楼租期至 1931 年 5 月 15 日，按租约规定应于 1929 年 11 月 15 日预付 6 个月租金 250 银圆。但本署在离关前并未接到交付房租的要求，据悉房主现正在大黑河。

除税务司的家具，其余物品均留在原房屋。税务司住所的部分陶器和玻璃器具已破损，本署已在工务科重新定制，并将在职员返回瑷珲关之前先寄至滨江关税务司保存。

因局势动荡，大黑河与滨江关之间的运输费用高昂，故本署仅携带小件行李和必要的随身物品,职员们则将大部分物品留在海关,待一切恢复正常再行运送。

本署携至哈尔滨的档案包括所有瑷珲关与总税务司署及其他口岸的往来信件,以及会计股、文案房、汉文科文书股、监察课、统计课的记录,除此之外还有印章、密码簿、打字机等等一切瑷珲关正常运作所需之物。所有的商铺都已关门,因此所有经本地商人签订的海关职员担保书现应已无用。

为便于撤离,本署首先命职员携其行李于梁家屯集合,并于11月10日集合完毕。该批撤离职员包括14名成年人、9名孩子及7名仆人,共计30人,另需3到6名士兵沿途护送。撤离职员的随身物品及行李共计200普特(约合7200磅)。因撤离职员及行李较多,从梁家屯至墨尔根需分两批运送,于墨尔根又得一些车辆后,方继续行进。首支分队已于11月16日自梁家屯出发,途经齐齐哈尔,并于22日抵达哈尔滨。第二支分队则直至11月27日方才抵达。本次行程虽经历了气温较低、当地旅店不安全以及遭遇红胡子(土匪)袭击等一系列的危险,但幸得政府派人沿途保护,最终都得以平安度过。不过其他很多队伍都遭遇了抢劫。由于满洲里及海拉尔邻近地区遭到苏维埃的攻击,齐齐哈尔火车站十分混乱,火车上亦难以寻得膳宿之地,幸得中国铁路职员相助,瑷珲关一行人等才得以顺利抵达哈尔滨。

由于所有运输点所雇用的都是滨江关的退休人员,因此撤离费用非常昂贵,约合哈大洋4000银圆(包括档案运输费),该费用明细表将上交至滨江关税务司。

此呈可作本署撤离瑷珲关之前所呈工作移交书的补充文件,抄件已发送至滨江关税务司。

您忠诚的仆人

铎博赛(R. M. Talbot)

瑷珲关署理税务司

瑷珲关第 <u>1300</u> 号谕令　　　　　　　瑷珲关／大黑河 1929 年 11 月 9 日

（瑷珲关暂时关闭：复开瑷珲关前的举措）

兹已收到总税务司的指示：瑷珲关暂时关闭，华籍内班职员与华洋外班职员撤离至滨江关，关产及日常事务暂由低职级杂项职员管理。

监察长已下达指示，要求编制一本花名册，以安排职员入住固定的宿舍，居住期间，职员将对宿舍的物品负责；同时宿舍还会配备火柴和煤油，费用由海关部门报销。12 月的薪酬将会预支给这些职员。由于税金降低，其他薪酬的发放也将陆续安排。

高等巡役于福寿先生将负责管理瑷珲关职员以及瑷珲关、大黑河、梁家屯分卡、图西与图东分卡的所有关产，由于目前海关正处于闭关时期，上述职责皆属于附加职责，故每月将为于先生发放额外津贴海关两 10.00 两。同样，巡役郭敬九先生将负责管理瑷珲关与梁家屯分卡；每月亦将为其发放额外津贴海关两 10.00 两。不过郭先生为于先生之下属，遇事向于先生报告并等候指令。于福寿先生接管瑷珲关关产一事，本署已向海关监督报告。必要时，郭敬九先生可以向于福寿先生报告，请示意见或寻求帮助。

海关会将两匹马和两辆手推车留下，并提供饲料，由水手王进财负责管理，并对马匹进行特别照看。需保留一本签到簿，由监察长负责安排日常气象及相关电报常规令文的阅读。报告簿则由于福寿先生保管，并记录海关的重要事项或受到普遍关注的问题，且须每周向滨江关总监察长呈交报告簿的副本（海关会为其提供信纸）。

此外，为高等巡役于福寿预支 100.00 银圆。此虽为小额现金，但仍须仔细记录每一项支出并附上相关凭据。需要注意的是，该笔款项应只用于必要的开支。任何未能证实的开支，后期都须退还。兹向滨江关总监察长呈交关于开支及余额的月报告一份。

若发生紧急情况，海关房屋中的职员将撤离至安全地带，但须在关口恢复安全时尽快返回。在撤离之前，须先由于福寿先生向海关监督或司令部报告；若海关监督不在，则须以保护职员及海关关产的安全为先。如果确有撤离的必要，郭敬九先生亦可在瑷珲关采取相应措施，同时由于先生通知滨江关。若海关房屋完好，屋中的家居物品将不做转移，职员家属则将被接送至梁家屯分卡，并住进海关宿舍。

最后,对于上述口岸的职员之忠诚任事,本署深表感激,并会将这些职员的姓名呈报总税务司署,提请于海关复开之时予以特殊奖赏。

铎博赉(R. M. Talbot)

瑷珲关署理税务司

此抄件内容真实有效,特此证明。

录事: 罗作福　未列等额外帮办

第 122 号半官函　　　　　　　　　1929 年 11 月 28 日　于瑷珲关（哈尔滨）

（铎博赉① 致梅乐和② 函）

尊敬的梅乐和先生：

　　本人于上一封 10 月 30 日半官函中汇报称，黑龙江江面即将完全结冰，届时大黑河将孤立无援，该地区的形势愈发严峻，处境愈发艰难；又于 11 月 3 日向阁下发送电报提议，为便于收发撤离相关信息和指令起见，暂将瑷珲关视为滨江关分关；后于 11 月 5 日收到滨江关税务司电报，内称阁下电令将瑷珲关关员撤至哈尔滨，暂时将瑷珲关视为滨江关分关。从未料到阁下的指令会下达得如此之快，反而觉得自己的离开可能会招致责难，不过不得不承认，得知不必再为瑷珲关关员的安全承担责任，确有如释重负之感。

　　在收到阁下撤离指令之前，中国银行大黑河支行经理一直在等待本人，并告知银行将立即迁至哈尔滨。当时中国银行已无资金，所幸本人从即将关门的孔士洋行借来约 2400 银圆，另在中国银行的帮助下，从东三省银行借来一笔贷款，两笔款项刚好足够于撤离之前为关员支付 11 月的薪俸，还可有剩余钱款支付撤离大黑河的路费。

　　本人收到撤离指令后立即与道尹会面，告知总税务司已决定让瑷珲关关员暂时撤离大黑河，暗称或许是考虑今年冬季瑷珲关无税可征，总税务司方会有此决定。道尹对此表示全力支持。随后两日，本人又向道尹致函说明此事，告知瑷珲关关员将撤至哈尔滨，瑷珲关暂时被视为滨江关分关。与此同时，本人与海关监督发布联合公告，说明瑷珲关暂时停止征税工作。道尹回函告知已收悉本人函文，询问海关监督津贴日后将如何支付。本人回复称，目前尚无明确指令，待抵达哈尔滨后应会收到消息。

　　接下来几日，本人便一直忙于准备撤离大黑河之事。当地所有汽车在很久之前便都已被租借出去，其中还有很多已被军方征用。所幸本人在当地一家由俄国人开设的汽车修理厂租到了两辆旧客运汽车以供撤离使用。此外，本人自己还有一辆汽车，可搭载 5 名乘客。撤离队伍明细如下所示：

---

　　① 铎博赉（R. M. Talbot）时任瑷珲关署理税务司
　　② 梅乐和（F. W. Maze）时任总税务司

	成人	儿童	仆人
署理税务司	1		2
监察长施密(H. A. Smith)先生	2	3	1
验货员斯诺(H. W. Snow)先生	1		1
税务员王德懋先生	2	1	
税务员张远扬先生	2	2	1
汉文文牍员杨存厚先生	1		1
核税员李永坡先生	2	3	
华籍稽查员王良先生	1		
华籍稽查员王化纯先生	2		1
合计:	14	9	7
总计:		30	

此外还有瑷珲关档案及关员个人物品需要运输,总重量为200普特①(合7200磅)。个人物品方面,因此次撤离车队可运载的行李数量十分有限,本人已下令每人仅可携带生活必需品上路,大件个人物品和家具都暂时留在大黑河。档案方面,决定携带的有:瑷珲关与总税务司署和其他各口往来公文、半官函、通函等,今年及前两年的账簿,税收统计表,总务课记录簿和登记簿,文书股档案,编制今年统计表所需资料,海关印章,打字机,密码本等,留下的实际仅有一些印谕。鉴于税务司住所为租赁关产,为安全起见,室内官方家具都已存放于旧海关办公楼大院已婚验货员宿舍之中,其他家具仍留于原处。另外税务司办公室的保险柜空出后未再上锁。各项准备工作占用了数日时间,所有物品装箱完毕后便立即运往梁家屯分卡。全体关员亦前往梁家屯分卡集合,等待撤离至哈尔滨的命令。

11月8日所有准备工作完毕后,道尹兼海关监督突然提出与本人会面,商议中俄黑龙江水道委员会日后工作及航路标志账户余额的处理办法。本人表示计划暂时将瑷珲关一应事务转移至哈尔滨继续办理。道尹表示,鉴于黑龙江水道委员会相关工作已经停止,待当前危机解除后,中苏双方很有可能会就边界河道的航运及水道委员会相关事宜重新签

---

① Pood,或译作"布特",是俄制重量单位,1普特合16.38千克。

订协议,因此决定黑龙江水道委员会与易保罗(P. I. Ignatieff)先生解除合同,提议为其直接发放 3 个月的薪俸,并表示日后黑龙江水道委员会若仍有设立航务专门顾问一职之需要,再将之召回。道尹还提出,鉴于黑龙江省政府可能会下令继续开展黑龙江航路标志工作,其或许会于海关搬离后接手相关事务,因此要求接管黑龙江水道委员会账户约 6600 银圆的余额。

本人回复称,关于易保罗先生任用之事,可以理解道尹和黑龙江水道委员会的立场,待按要求为其发放三个月薪俸后,会将此事呈报总税务司;至于关闭黑龙江水道委员会账户一事,本人断不敢在未有总税务司指示的情况下擅自应允,因为此举意味着黑龙江水道委员会与海关的关系将就此中断;同时向其询问黑龙江水道委员会账户关闭后,此前从松花江航路标志账户所借的 15000 银圆应当作何处理。

道尹承诺,如果黑龙江水道委员会账户无法归还此笔借款,黑龙江省政府将代为偿还,并称黑龙江水道委员会账户余额数目不大,需要于危机爆发期间交由其掌管。鉴于此,本人便回称需要考虑此事,明日再行回复;次日遂向道尹致函,说明黑龙江水道委员会账户还有一些款项需要支付,但瑷珲关账簿都已打包完毕,因此此事须待本人抵达哈尔滨并得到总税务司指示后再行解决。道尹对此回复十分不满,随即又与本人进行会谈。会谈期间争论颇为激烈,道尹表示其已向黑龙江省政府报告称自己应可接管黑龙江水道委员会账户的余额。因此本人最终同意将黑龙江水道委员会账户余额中的 4500 银圆交给道尹,且暂不关闭账户。

在撤离工作准备之初,本人便向低职级关员说明,鉴于他们皆为大黑河当地人士,希望他们可于本人撤离后留在本地照看海关关产。关于此事,本人业已向滨江关税务司征询意见,其建议除 11 月薪俸外,还应为他们预先支付 12 月的薪俸。各低职级关员答允后(均为自愿,特此记录),本人便为他们预支了 12 月的薪俸,并对日后工作做出了相应安排。其中,巡役于福寿将负责管理大黑河的关产和留守关员,填写每日报告簿,每周向滨江关总监察长呈交报告,记录气象读数,发送每日电报等。对于此等超出其原本职责范围的工作,于福寿先生每月将得享海关两 10 两特殊津贴。此外,本人还交与其 100 银圆,用于小额现金支出。巡役郭敬九将负责管理瑷珲和梁家屯两地的关产,为此每月将得享海关两 10 两的特殊津贴。由于时间紧迫,未能提前呈报特殊津贴一事,但是相信阁下会认同本人在特殊情形下所采取的措施。

本人另为留守关员留下了两匹马、两辆运货马车及草料,以备不时之需。各关员已被分派到各处关产,皆明晰须为自己所看护的关产负责,亦知晓日常所需薪柴和煤油将由海关提供。兹相信，本人离开后，只要大黑河未被苏联军队占领，未遭中国士兵劫掠，海关关产便可安然无恙。

由于此次撤离的交通工具只有两辆客运汽车和本人的私人汽车，因此所有人员需分成两批进行撤离。本人于11月16日随第一批撤离队伍离开梁家屯。乘坐本人汽车的均为妇女和儿童。途中虽有土匪强盗出没，但是因为黑龙江省政府已命军方沿途护送，撤离队伍并未受到袭击。自讷河廷至齐齐哈尔一段，陈志远将军与撤离队伍同车而行，并派遣一辆载有20名士兵的汽车在前面引路，保护撤离队伍的安全。吾等自梁家屯出发后，经过5日方抵达齐齐哈尔，途中不仅需要克服寒冷天气，夜晚亦只能居住在沿途的小旅店当中，可以说毫无舒适可言，但既然已经安全抵达齐齐哈尔，此番艰辛也无何抱怨之处。不过，由于苏联军队在满洲里和海拉尔地区频繁活动，齐齐哈尔地区的中国士兵和平民已方寸大乱，都希望可以尽快逃往哈尔滨，因此撤离队伍在前往哈尔滨之时面临了诸多难题。所幸中东铁路的中国官员为撤离队伍施以援手，帮助吾等成功离开了齐齐哈尔。第一批撤离队伍于11月22日抵达哈尔滨；第二批撤离队伍在经历了疲倦不堪的旅程后，携带行李于11月27日抵达哈尔滨。现今满洲地区局势混乱，兹认为，瑷珲关关员们撤离大黑河的行动十分及时。

本人在离开大黑河之前便已完成了移交职务备忘录的大部分内容，其中关于撤离大黑河一事的内容着墨不多，但所述之事于海关重返大黑河行使职能之时应会有所助益。兹认为，瑷珲关既然早于1922年之前便为哈尔滨关的分关，那么如果当前中苏危机结束后，联合维护黑龙江水道委员会一事被迫取消，大黑河地区的贸易状况也未有所改善，建议瑷珲关继续作为滨江关的分关行使职能，唯须指派一名洋籍超等帮办至大黑河负责各项事务；但如果当前危机结束后，大黑河地区的状况仍与危机爆发之前一样，建议仍保留瑷珲关独立关的地位。

本人已开始撰写呈文汇报瑷珲关关员撤离大黑河事，黑龙江水道委员会与航务专门顾问解除合同事及黑龙江水道委员会账户余额已汇至哈尔滨事。

此函抄件将交给滨江关税务司。

您真挚的

铎博赉（R. M. Talbot）

2. 为呈送撤离期间职员从瑷珲关至滨江关的费用事

TRAVELLING EXPENSES: incurred during evacuation of Staff from Aigun to Harbin: statement of submitted.

460

I.G.

Aigun (Harbin) 30th December, 1929.

Sir,

    I have the honour to enclose, in duplicate, a Statement of Expenditure drawn up by Mr. R. M. Talbot, formerly Acting Commissioner at Aigun, for the Expenditure, amounting to H.$4,038.80 (= HK.Tls.2,892.53), incurred in evacuating the Aigun Staff from Taheiho to Harbin in accordance with your telegram of 5th November, 1929. It is to be noted that this statement does not include the personal expenses of the individual members of Staff which will be submitted separately.

    I also enclose, in duplicate, a transportation account, supported by explanations and a letter addressed to the Harbin Commissioner, made out by Mr. Chipourin of Taheiho and Tsitsihar, who states that he has been insufficiently paid and claims H.$1,133.80 more.

    It is unfortunately impossible for me to give a definite decision on the alleged underpayment. With the exception of 1 Clerk and 1 Lushih, who travelled in the second and first parties, respectively, and of Mr. Ignatieff, the Technical Adviser to the Amur Aids Commission, who travelled in advance of both, the entire Staff had been transferred before my arrival

Enc. No.1
(in duplicate)

Enc. No.2
(in duplicate)

THE INSPECTOR GENERAL OF CUSTOMS.

SHANGHAI.

arrival. But it appears, as acknowledged by Mr. Chipourin in his letter to the Harbin Commissioner (Vide Enclosure No.2), that the arrangement between Messrs. Talbot and Chipourin was a verbal and indefinite one which, of course, I have no means of checking. Mr. Ignatieff, however, considers that Mr. Chipourin's claim is by no means unreasonable. He says that motor-buses at that time were charging $35 per head from Taheiho to Tsitsihar for a complement of 30 persons, i. e. $1,050; whereas Mr. Chipourin reckons $65 (his item No.1) from Taheiho to Liangchiatsun plus $350 (his item No.5) from Liangchiatsun to Mergen plus $350 (his item No.11) from Mergen to Tsitsihar plus one-quarter, say, of the $1,158 for benzine and tyres (Statement, sub-vouchers Nos. 1 and 2) = $1,054. Moreover, public vehicles were driven by anyone posing as a chauffeur, whereas Mr. Chipourin left his work and family and personally attended to our transportation as far as Tsitsihar.

    Mr. Chipourin might be taken at his word and his account for the first and second trips submitted to Messrs. Smith and Snow, respectively, before being passed by you; on the whole, however, it seems probable that Mr. Chipourin is acting straightforwardly and that his accounts are correct, the more so as Mr. Talbot is said to have acknowledged before his departure that it was possible that Mr. Chipourin might have been underpaid to some extent.

    I have the honour to be,

Sir,

Your obedient Servant,

Hopkins

Acting Commissioner.

[D.—8]　　A I G U N *Customs,*　　ACCOUNT

30th November, 1929 .　Schedule :　　Voucher No.

Authority,　　　　　Pay.

　　　　　　　　　　Commissioner.

STATEMENT of Payments by Mr. E.M.Talbot, Acting Commissioner for evacuation of Aigun Customs Staff
From　　Taheiho　　to　　Harbin.

Amounting to

I CERTIFY that the following charges were incurred solely on account of the Public Service, and that no Vouchers beyond those annexed were procurable.

(Signed) E. M. Talbot

Acting Commissioner.

Date 1929	No. of Sub-Voucher.	PARTICULARS.	CURRENCY. [$ 150 = Hk.Th 100]	Hk.Th.	OBSERVATIONS.
		Expenditure for evacuation of Aigun Staff from Taheiho to Harbin.			
		(1) General expenses of evacuation, and expenses of first party from Taheiho to Harbin.			
Nov. 7	1.	Messrs. Kunst & Albers:Motor car tires and tubes	398	00	considered as part hire of motor cars.
" 9	2.	Asiatic Petroleum Co.:40 cases benzine @$19.00 per case	760	00	
	3.	Tsoyin's office: Taxes on freight and passengers to Nohoting	105	00	
" 10	4.	Tsoyin's Office:Road tax on 20 passenger tickets @$1.00	20	00	
		Ferry charges for various motor cars crossing Gansa river at different times	18	50	
" 11		Hire horses for towing car back to Liangchiat'un after breaking down	10	00	
		Ferry charges for Commr's car to Aigun and return on official business	4	00	
" 12		Advance for food for Liangchia- t'un military escorts	10	00	
" 12		Gratuities to police at Liangchiat'un	10	00	
	5.	4th Cl.Tw'tr. Wang Hua Chun: cart hire from Aigun to Liangchiat'un	10	00	
		carried forward	1,345	50	

Date 1929	No. of Sub-Voucher.	PARTICULARS.	CURRENCY. [$ 150 = Hk.Th 100]	Hk.Th.	OBSERVATIONS.
		Brought forward	1,345	50	
November 10		Advance for food for 3 Sanchang soldiers to Mergen	15	00	
" 16		Charges for inn at Sanchang for the party	8	00	
"		Mergen: inn charges for entire party	7	20	
	6.	Mergen: 2 telegrams (1) Shilnikoff Tsitsihar pochemu chapurin ne otveshaet Chapurin Talbot	2	85	
	7.	(2) Chapurin Tsitsihar ozidaem dva mashina otveshai Chapurin	2	25	
" 17		Benzine for motor cars	54	00	Motor cars were changed at Mergen
"		Cash to Chapurin for motor hire	300	00	
" 18	8.	Motor car Mergen to Tsitsihar	360	00	
"	9.	Mergen, telegram to Tsitsihar: Custos Harbin leaving today for Tsitsihar with first half of party Talbot	3	64	
"		Mergen: inn charges for self and Smith's family	5	00	
"		Mergen: garage hire	1	50	
"		" : inn charges for Chinese staff	10	00	
"		Nohoting: inn charges for Chi. staff	4	00	
"		Nohoting: Board & lodging for self & Mr. Actg. T'yor Smith's family and gratuities to official servts	20	00	
" 19		Nohoting: gratuities to 3 Sanchang soldiers	30	00	These soldiers had to make their own way back to San- chang
"	10.	Tai Nan Chen: Benzine Tsitsihar: 1 tin benzine	20	00	
" 20	11.		8	50	
"		Chapurin: part payment for motor truck Mergen to Tsitsihar	500	00	
"	12.	Mr. Actg.T'yor Smith: Medical attendance on his family en route	3	00	
"		Gratuity to chauffeur	15	00	
"		Nohoting: 1 case benzine	18	50	
"		Tsitsihar R-way station: Coolie hire for baggages	8	00	
"		Porters for luggage at Harbin	9	00	
"		Cartage " " to Custom House	6	00	
"		Yaganoff: motor car hire from Taheiho to Tsitsihar station (small car)	200	00	
"		Inn fee for Chi. & For. Staff at Tsitsihar city	12	60	
"		Two motor cars for Chi. staff from Tsitsihar city to Ong-ong- hsi R-way station	18	00	
"		Coolie hire for discharging baggages	3	40	
"		Inn fee for Chinese Staff at Tsitsihar R-way station	6	10	
"	13.	Tsitsihar: telegram (urgent): Harbin urgent Chinese director Chinese eastern railway please send one mixed and one third class cars for evacuating Taheiho Custom Taheiho Customs Commr.	24	51	
		Carried forward	3,042	55	

DATE. 1929.	No. OF SUB-VOUCHER.	PARTICULARS.	CURRENCY. ($ 150 = Hk.Tls 100)		Hk.Tls	OBSERVATIONS.
		Brought forward	3,042	55		
November 21	14.	Telegram fee at Hsiao Hao Tse: Custos Harbin arriving this evening seven fifteen Talbot	2	47		
" "	15.	Tsitsihar station: hotel charges for one night for self, T'yor Smith and family and 1 servant	22	60		
" "		Tsitsihar Rly.Station: Passenger tickets: 11 2nd cl. tickets @ $ 11.05	121	55		
" "		3 half 2nd cl. tickets @ $6.65	19	95		
" "		4 3rd cl. tickets @ $6.65	26	60		
" "		R-way charges for luggages	70	70		
" 20	16.	Coolie hire at Tsitsihar station	18	00		Text vide below
" "		Telegram to Mergen:	4	07		
						Note; for the evacuation of the Staff a
		Expenses of Second party from Liangchiat'un to Harbin.				motor car bus and motor
" 22		Gratuity to 2 Liangchiat'un soldiers	20	00		truck were engaged at Taheiho. These
" "		Inn at Sanchang	2	00		two trucks first made
" "		" " Ssunhang	10	00		several trips between Taheiho
" 23	17.	Telegram to Chepurin: Urgent Chepurin Tsitsihar neotpravlai sdusam otvechai (reply paid)	8	45		and Liangchiat'un afterwards proceeding from
" 24		Inn at Mergen	8	00		Liangchiat'un
" "		Garage hire	2	00		to Mergen and returning to
" "		Carriage hire for visiting Magistrate at Nohoting	1	50		Liangchiat'un thence return-
" 25		Gratuity for 3 soldiers from Sanchang to Nohoting	35	00		ing again to Mergen and
" "		Inn at Nohoting and tip to Nightwatchman	11	00		then continu- ing to Tsitsi-
" "		Guide to Tsitsihar, strange road	15	00		har. In addition
" "		Inn, while hiring guide and making repairs	1	70		another motor bus and motor
" "		Gratuity for 3 soldiers from Nohoting	20	00		truck were used by first party
" 26	18.	Passenger car Mergen to Tsitsihar	325	00		from Mergen to Tsitsihar. The
" "		Motor truck (baggage) from Tsitsihar to Ong-ong-hsi	25	00		Commr.chauffeur, who has his own
" "		Hotel expenses at Tsitsihar, Chinese and For. Staff	11	00		car, also transported 5
" "		Station coolies discharging baggage from truck	6	00		passengers from Liangchiat'un to Tsitsihar.
" 27		Railway station: 4 2nd cl. tickets @ $ 11.05	44	20		
		5 3rd cl. tickets @ $ 6.65	33	25		
" "		Freight for baggages Tsitsihar to Harbin	95	00		
" "		Coolie hire at Tsitsihar station	19	00		
" "	19.	Telegram to Harbin: Talbot Customs Harbin arriving 7.20 p.m. Snow	1	21		
" "		Porters & Cartage of baggages to Custom House	16	00		
			4,038	80		
					2,692 53	

呈总税务司署 460 号文　　　　　　　　瑷珲关/滨江关 1929 年 12 月 30 日

尊敬的海关总税务司（上海）：

根据 1929 年 11 月 5 日总税务司署电报指示，瑷珲关已从大黑河撤离至哈尔滨，撤离费用共计黑龙江大洋 4038.80 元（海关两 2692.53 两），兹附瑷珲关前署理税务司铎博赍（R.M.Talbot）先生编制的撤离费用报表（一式两份）。但瑷珲关职员的个人支出并未纳入该报表之中，将会单独呈文报告。

兹附查普林（Chipourin）先生往返于大黑河及齐齐哈尔两地的交通账目，内附账目说明及查普林先生致滨江关税务司的信函（各一式两份）。查普林先生称仍需为其报销哈大洋 1133.80 元，但本署无法决定是否要报销其申请金额。

在本人到任之前，已撤离全部职员。在大批职员撤离之前，已有一名税务员及一名录事已分别于第二批及第一批先行撤离，而黑龙江水道委员会专门顾问易保罗（P. I. Ignatieff）先生则早于这两批人员撤离之前就已动身。查普林先生在其致滨江关税务司的信函（参见附件 2）中表示，铎博赍先生只是与其达成口头协议，并无明确安排，但本人无法予以核实。然而，易保罗先生认为查普林先生的额外报销申请绝非无理之举，因为当时自大黑河至齐齐哈尔的汽车票价为每人 35 银圆，载满 30 人共计 1050 银圆；而查普林先生称，自大黑河至梁家屯需要 65 银圆（见查普林先生交通账目说明第 1 项），自梁家屯至墨尔根需要 350 银圆（见查普林先生交通账目说明第 3 项），自墨尔根至齐齐哈尔需要 350 银圆（见查普林先生交通账目说明第 11 项），此外还需支付汽油与轮胎费（1258 银圆）的四分之一，共计 1054 银圆。何况当时，查普林先生舍其工作与家人，运送海关职员直至齐齐哈尔。

本署可以将查普林先生的账目及说明分别交予施密（Smith）先生和斯诺先生（Snow）核实之后，再呈交至贵署；但总体看来，查普林先生行事公正，编制的账目应当准确。据悉，铎博赍（R.M.Talbot）先生更是于离开之前承认，或许确实未足额支付查普林先生之费用。

您忠诚的仆人

富乐嘉（H. G. Fletcher）

瑷珲关署理税务司

录事：张远扬　三等二级税务员

瑷珲关致总税务司署第 460 号呈附件 1

差旅报销单

瑷珲关 账户：

1929 年 11 月 30 日 费用项目 传票字号：

授权依据：	提交人： 瑷珲关署理税务司

署理税务司铎博赉（R. M. Talbot）撤离瑷珲关职员

出发地点 　大黑河　 到达地点 　哈尔滨　

报销金额＿＿＿＿＿＿＿＿＿＿＿＿＿＿＿＿＿＿

兹证明，下表均为公务相关费用，再无其他费用。

铎博赉（R. M. Talbot）

瑷珲关署理税务司

日期		子传票字号	摘要	金额				备注
1929				银圆 150		海关两 100 两		
			瑷珲关职员自大黑河撤离至哈尔滨的费用					
			（1）撤离费用总计及自大黑河至哈尔滨的第一批撤离费用					
11	7	1	孔士洋行：汽车轮胎及内胎	398	00			
11	9	2	亚细亚石油公司：40 箱轻质汽油，每箱 19.00 银圆	760	00			
11	9	3	道尹公署：运送货物及乘客前往讷河的税费	105	00			
11	9	4	道尹公署：20 名乘客票税，每人 1 银圆	20	00			
11	10		汽车借助渡船过河费用	18	50			
11	11		雇佣马匹将故障车拖回梁家屯	10	00			
11	12		税务司的车因公务往返瑷珲关的轮渡费用	4	00			
11	13		预支 2 支梁家屯军队护卫的粮费	10	00			
11	13		梁家屯警察赏钱	10	00			
11	13	5	四等稽查员王化纯：雇车从瑷珲关至梁家屯	10	00			
11	15		三名三站士兵前往墨尔根的预支粮费	15	00			
11	16		三站旅店费用	8	00			
11	16		墨尔根：旅店费用	7	20			
11	16	6	墨尔根：电报（1）	2	85			
11	16	7	墨尔根：电报（2）	2	25			
11	17		汽车轻质汽油	54	00			
11	17		向查普林支付现金以雇佣其汽车	300	00			墨尔根换车
11	18	8	从墨尔根到齐齐哈尔的汽车费	380	00			
11	18	9	从墨尔根发电报至齐齐哈尔	3	64			
11	18		墨尔根：施密（Smith）先生及家人旅店费用	6	00			

日期	子传票字号	摘要	金额		备注
1929			银圆 150	海关两 100 两	
11 18		墨尔根：车库租金	1	50	
		墨尔根：华籍职员旅店费	10	00	
11 18		讷河：华籍职员旅店费	4	00	
11 18		讷河：署监察长施密（Smith）先生及家人的船票费和膳宿费，以及差役的赏钱	20	00	
11 19		讷河：三名三站士兵的赏钱	30	00	士兵需自行返回三站
11 19	10	轻质汽油	20	00	
11 19		齐齐哈尔：一桶轻质汽油	8	50	
11 20	11	向查普林支付部分雇佣汽车的费用（自墨尔根至齐齐哈尔）	500	00	
11 20	12	署监察长施密先生：途中家人的医疗护理费用	3	00	
11 20		汽车司机的赏钱	15	00	
11 20		讷河：一箱轻质汽油	18	00	
11 20		齐齐哈尔火车站：雇佣苦力搬运行李	8	00	
11 20		哈尔滨门役搬运行李费	9	00	
11 20		货车运送行李至海关的费用	6	00	
11 20		雇佣汽车自大黑河至齐齐哈尔站（小型汽车）	200	00	
11 20		华洋籍关员在齐齐哈尔的旅店费	12	60	
11 20		雇佣2辆汽车从齐齐哈尔运送华籍关员至车站	18	00	
11 20		雇佣苦力卸行李	3	40	
11 20		华籍关员在齐齐哈尔火车站的旅店费	6	10	
11 20	13	齐齐哈尔：电报（紧急）费	24	51	
11 21	14	电报费	2	47	

日期		子传票字号	摘要	金额		备注
1929				银圆 150	海关两 100 两	
11	21	15	齐齐哈尔站：署监察长施密先生及家人和一位仆人一晚的旅店费	22	60		
11	21		齐齐哈尔火车站：乘客票：11 张二等票,每张 11.05 银圆	121	55		
11	21		3 张二等半价票每张 6.65 银圆	19	95		
11	21		4 张三等票,每张 6.65 银圆	26	60		
11	21		铁路运送行李费	70	70		
11	21		在齐齐哈尔站雇佣苦力	18	00		
11	25	16	发送电报至墨尔根	4	07		
			自梁家屯至哈尔滨的第二批撤离费用			
11	22		打赏 2 名梁家屯士兵	20	00		
11	22		三站：旅店费	2	00		
11	22		四站：旅店费	10	00		
11	23	17	发送电报至查普林	8	45		
11	24		墨尔根：旅店费	8	00		
11	24		车库租金	2	00		
11	24		在讷河雇佣马车拜访地方长官的费用	1	50		
11	25		从三站到讷河,打赏 3 名士兵	35	00		
11	25		讷河：旅店费以及打赏更夫	11	00		
11	25		陌生路段至齐齐哈尔的向导费用	15	00		
11	25		修车期间的旅店费	1	70		
11	25		打赏来自讷河的 3 名士兵	20	00		
11	26	18	自墨尔根至齐齐哈尔的车费	325	00		
11	26		从齐齐哈尔至车站的行李运输费	25	00		
11	26		华洋籍职员在齐齐哈尔的旅店费	11	00		
11	26		在车站雇佣苦力卸行李	6	00		
11	27		火车站：4 张二等票,每张 11.05 银圆	44	20		

| 日期 | | 子传票字号 | 摘要 | 金额 | | | 备注 |
1929				银圆 150		海关两 100 两	
11	27		5 张三等票,每张 6.65 银圆	33	25		
11	27		铁路运送行李费	95	00		
11	27		在齐齐哈尔站雇佣苦力	19	00		
11	27	19	发送电报至滨江关	1	21		
11	27		运送行李至海关的门役及货车运费	16	00		
			银圆总计	4038	80		
			海关两总计			2692	53

　　说明：为撤离职员,于大黑河租用一辆公共汽车和一辆载重卡车,两辆车首先将职员分批自大黑河运至梁家屯,又分批自梁家屯运至墨尔根,最后继续分批自墨尔根运至齐齐哈尔。除此之外,在墨尔根又雇用了一辆公共汽车和载重卡车,将第一批撤离人员运至齐齐哈尔。署理税务司的司机用自己的车将 5 名撤离人员自梁家屯运至齐齐哈尔。

3. 为瑷珲关职员返回大黑河及海关重新开放事

STAFF: number and personnel of: certain reduction in Outdoor
But none in Indoor advocated. All Staff to be in Harbin
by 30th April, dependant, however, on further telegraphic
advice in re. Suggestions re seniority towards leave and
size of family of Chinese appointees.

481.

I. G.   Aigun (Harbin) 24th March, 1930.

Registered

Sir,

1.   With reference to my despatch No.454, § 6;

            Suggesting the number and personnel
            of the Staff required on the return
            of this Office to its normal
            habitat at Tahaiho:

I have the honour to remind you that river traffic
will probably reopen at the beginning of May. It
is necessary for the Staff to travel by the first
steamer that proceeds from Harbin to Aigun, in
order to collect the duties thereon.   My telegram
of 14th March apprised you of the fact that the
Aigun Superintendent was remaining in Harbin
endeavouring to arrange with the Russian authorities
for Chinese vessels to ply on the Amur. At an
interview on the 21st March he told the Harbin
Commissioner and myself that the Soviets have
practically agreed to Chinese shipping re-entering
the Amur immediately on the opening of navigation.
He promised to inform me immediately the question
was decided definitely. If all goes well, it is
necessary that the whole of the Staff should be
in Harbin by 30th April. I propose to refer to
this despatch by telegram as soon as the

                                        Superintendent

THE INSPECTOR GENERAL OF CUSTOMS,
    SHANGHAI.

Superintendent has arranged matters satisfactorily.

2.   I previously suggested 4 Clerks (or 1
Assistant and 3 Clerks) instead of the 1
Assistant and 4 Clerks who were on the Staff
during the years 1925 - 9. That suggestion was
made when it was possible that we should return
to Aigun before the opening of navigation and
before I had been enabled to gain a close
personal insight into much of the work to be
performed.   Now I beg leave to retract it. I
do not see how the work can be carried on without
the 1929 total of 1 Assistant and 4 Clerks (or
5 Clerks, if you prefer it), this total of 5
having been reduced from 6 on 1st January, 1926
owing to bad trade, a factor that has thus been
discounted in advance.   It must be remembered that
the collection and accounting of River Dues, together
with all the reports and returns, with their
Chinese translations, depending on or arising
therefrom, to say nothing of the diplomatic work
which the framing of Aids Agreements etc. invariably
throws on our hands, entail a vast amount of
clerical labour and the expenditure of much time
foreign to the ordinary Custom House routine. My
predecessor, speaking from long experience, recommends
no diminution of the linguist Indoor Staff, vide
Aigun despatch No.452, enclosure 1, § 6. As for
his suggestion to dispense with the Ho-shui-yuan,
I would mention that that employee is now taking
the place of the Writer who is on Inspectorate

                                        leave

leave and also that I would like time to see
for myself whether the move that is now being
made in the direction of a more general use of
the Chinese language will render it necessary to
use him partly for calculating duties and writing
Duty Memos, acts which, strange to relate, have
hitherto been performed solely by the Linguist.

I therefore ask for the former total of
5 Assistants and Clerks in any combination you
approve. Should experience show that this number
can be reduced, I shall not hesitate to apprise
you of the fact, either reporting specially or
taking advantage of an application for long leave
to effect reduction. At present there are 2
Clerks here, one of whom has applied for
Inspectorate leave, _vide_ my despatch No.476, and
two are appointed from 1st May, _vide_ your despatch
No.519/126,721.

3.   In this connexion I would advise that
Chinese be not appointed to Aigun unless they
have a considerable period to run before becoming
entitled to Inspectorate leave: Aigun is a very
unpopular port with our Chinese colleagues, leave
is almost sure to be applied for as soon as
due, travelling is expensive, and replacements take
a long time. Young men, and men with small
families, are likely to be happier and better
workers than their opposite numbers.

4.   As regards the Out-door Staff, I do not
withdraw from the reductions and personnel advocated
in my despatch No. 464, § 6. From all I can
hear, their number has lately been in excess of
                                    strict

strict requirements. Should experience _in situ_
prove this assumption to be incorrect, I shall
inform you accordingly and request help.

I have the honour to be,
Sir,
Your obedient servant,

(H. G. Fletcher)
Acting Commissioner.

CUSTOM HOUSE.

S/O No. 222   A I G U N 9th June 1930.

Dear Mr. Maze,

   RETURN TO AIGUN (TAHEIHO): As reported in my
despatch No. 488 we all arrived here safely on 30th May.
Up to the last moment it was not certain that the
steamer would leave Harbin, but she finally did so on
16th. She, the S. S. "Suchow", is the worst steamer of the
semi-official Tung-pei Company's fleet, only 2nd class
accomodation being available. This was entirely taken up
by our Staff. At the junction of the Sungari and Amur
Rivers at Lahasusu, considerable trepidation was again
evident: but we emerged into the latter River without
incident and nothing untoward occurred throughout the
tremendous length of the voyage which occupied 15 days,
whereas the fast steamers compass it in 7. The
Superintendent very kindly came to the wharf to meet us
and took a photograph. He has since had the whole of
the Staff to dinner and is very affable.
                                                   The

W. Maze, Esquire,
Inspector General of Customs,
      etc., etc., etc.,
         S H A N G H A I.

   The Custom House was re-opened on the
following day, the 31st, all preparations for doing
so having been made on board. Various instructions
contained in your despatches and Circulars during the
past 6 months, instructions which could not possibly
be attended to in Harbin, are gradually being complied
with and it is hoped that our list thereof will soon
assume less formidable proportions than it does at
present, but things are somewhat difficult for us at
the moment, since only 1 member of the transferrable
Staff, In-door and Out-door, has ever been in the port
before. To make matters worse, the whole of the
Tidesurveyor's archives and the inventories, which we
expected to find here, have disappeared and we are now
instituting enquiries in every direction with a view to
their speedy recovery.

                              Yours truly,

CUSTOM HOUSE.

S/O No.131   A I G U N   30th June   30.

Dear Mr. Maze,

　　　　　I write a formal letter to let you know that
nothing happens. The Amur Aids Annual Agreement is not
consummated and does not show any signs of being so.
No transfrontier trade has actually taken place yet. Both
sides would like to have it, but pride and regulations
so far forbid. Russia desires it most and the Mayor
is inclined to barter permission in exchange for other
advantages which the Russian representative is probably
not in a position to grant. Very friendly relations
exist between the Customs, Russian Consulate, Superintendent
and Mayor, and other local officials. Though it is
amusing to see the Taoyin and Russian Consul, say,
strolling about arm in arm at a party and then to hear
the acrid remarks they make about each others conduct in
some official case. Russia, for instance, does not allow
emigration to this side of the river. When a case of
flight occurs, as it sometimes does, the Russian

                                                authorities

W. Maze, Esquire,
Inspector General of Customs,
        etc., etc., etc.
            S H A N G H A I.

authorities, when they get to know of it, claim
extradition and are prepared to trump up all kinds of
civil charges against the unfortunate man in order to
get him back to the other side and shoot him as an
example to others. The usual quota of Chinese steamers
is arriving here from Harbin. The Staff is well and
happy.

                    Yours truly,

呈总税务司署 <u>481</u> 号文 瑷珲关（哈尔滨）1930 年 3 月 24 日

尊敬的海关总税务司（上海）：

补充瑷珲关第 464 号呈第 6 节之内容：

"需要迁回大黑河住所的瑷珲关职员人数及职员人选建议。"

兹汇报，5 月初瑷珲关航运可能将重新开通，因此有必要让相关职员乘坐由滨江关出发的第一艘轮船前往瑷珲关，以便能够及时开展征税工作。海关监督仍在滨江关同俄国政府协商有关中国船只在黑龙江上的航运事宜（参见瑷珲关 3 月 14 日电呈）。3 月 21 日双方会晤时，海关监督告知滨江关税务司及本署，俄国政府已同意航运开通后，华籍船只可于黑龙江上航行；且俄国政府承诺，双方一经签署明确协议，会立即通知本署。若一切顺利，所有职员将在 4 月 30 日前全部抵达滨江关，故本署建议海关监督，与俄方的协议一经签署，请立即通过电报的形式予以发布。

本署曾经建议，不再依循 1926 年至 1929 年期间的人员配置（一名帮办与四名税务员），而是只设置四名税务员（或一名帮办与三名税务员）。当时作此建议，是考虑到有关职员能够于航运季开始之前及时返回瑷珲关，本署亦可提前完成对所需工作的了解；但就目前来看，今年若不继续沿用 1929 年的人员配置，即一名帮办与四名税务员（或五名税务员），工作恐怕很难顺利展开。1926 年 1 月 1 日，受贸易低潮影响，职员从原来的六名缩减至五名。但本署目前的工作内容，不仅涉及江捐征收、江捐账单，各种报告、报表，以及相应的中文译本，还涉及拟订与《航路标志协议》相关的外交工作，这些工作需要大量的税务人员，外事与海关的日常办公亦需花费大量时间。前任瑷珲关税务司根据长期的工作经验，建议不要缩减会多国语言的内班职员（参阅瑷珲关第 452 号呈 1 号附件）。至于前任瑷珲关税务司所提出的免除核税员一职的建议，本署需说明，目前该核税员已接替正在休假的汉文文牍员之职；同时考虑到目前使用汉语的工作增多，是否需要该职员同时承担起计算税款及填写税款缴纳证的职责（之前一直由通事独立负责），本署也需斟酌。

故本署向海关总税务司申请五名职员，并请裁定税务员及帮办的人数。即使有先例表明可以裁减人数，但本署必须说明，实际上只当有特殊情况或休假申请时，才会出现人员减少的情况。目前瑷珲关只有两名税务员，而其中一名已申请休假（参阅瑷珲关第 476 号呈），5 月 1 日起将有另外两名税务员就职（参阅总税务司署第 519/126721 号令）。

本署建议不再任命华籍职员至瑷珲关任职，除非其任职后要经过很长时间才有申请休假的资格。瑷珲关是一个非常不受华籍职员欢迎的口岸，一旦具备了申请休假的资格，他们便会立即提出休假申请，如此一来，不但有高昂的差旅费需要海关支付，还会因接任一事耽误很长时间。相对来说，年轻人和拥有小家庭的工作人员，其工作状态会更好一些。

关于外班职员，本署仍坚持瑷珲关第464号呈（第6章）所述的缩减职员之提议。据本署所知，现有职员人数已严重超过实际所需。若后期的实际工作情况证明本署所知有误，本署将向海关总税务司做出新的汇报。

您忠诚的仆人

富乐嘉（H.G.Fletcher）

瑷珲关署理税务司

录事：张远扬　三等二级税务员

第 130 号半官函　　　　　　　　　　　　1930 年 6 月 9 日于瑷珲关

（富乐嘉^①致梅乐和^②函）

尊敬的梅乐和先生：

为返回瑷珲关（大黑河）事：

如瑷珲关第 488 号呈中所述，瑷珲关全体关员已于 5 月 30 日安全抵达大黑河。此次乘坐的是东北航务局最为破旧的一艘轮船"苏州（Suchow）"号，只有二等舱可选，而且在开船之前一直都不确定能否驶离哈尔滨，所幸终于 5 月 16 日顺利出发。不过在行至松花江和黑龙江交汇处的拉哈苏苏时，轮船出现了严重的颠簸情况，好在还是安全驶入了黑龙江。整段航程并未有何意外事件发生，用时共计 15 日，但乘坐快船只需 7 日。瑷珲关关员抵达大黑河时，海关监督已在码头热情迎接，还一起合影留念，随后又邀请所有关员参加接风宴席，态度十分友善。

5 月 31 日，海关办公楼重新开放，一应准备工作已由关员于乘船期间完成。过去六个月间总税务司署令文及通令的各项指示及未能于哈尔滨处理完毕的指令现已着手办理，希望工作内容可以尽快不再如此艰巨。但是当前的情况着实有些棘手，内班外班调任关员中仅有 1 名曾于大黑河口岸任职，更为糟糕的是，原以为存放于大黑河的监察长档案和清单全部无影无踪。现下已开始四处搜寻，希望可以尽快找到。

您真挚的

富乐嘉（H. G. Fletcher）

---

① 富乐嘉（H. G. Fletcher）时任瑷珲关署理税务司
② 梅乐和（F. W. Maze）时任总税务司

第 131 号半官函　　　　　　　　　　　1930 年 6 月 30 日于瑷珲关

（富乐嘉① 致梅乐和② 函）

尊敬的梅乐和先生：

　　特此致函告知大黑河地区目前无事发生。年度黑龙江航路标志协议尚未签署，亦未有将要签署之迹象。跨境贸易还未开展，尽管中苏双方皆有此意向，但碍于国家规定与民族尊严，仍无法重新开始。苏方对开展跨境贸易的需求更为迫切，不过黑河市政筹备处处长希望通过允许此事来换取其他有利条件，但苏联代表目前可能无法满足其要求。现阶段，海关、苏联领事、海关监督兼黑河市政筹备处处长及其他地方官员之间的关系均非常友好。不过看到黑河市政筹备处处长与苏联领事上一秒还在宴会上挽手闲叙，下一秒却在正式会谈中针锋相对，的确颇有戏剧之感。比如，苏联方面禁止中国移民来至黑龙江华岸，但偶尔亦会有私逃事件发生，苏联当局发现后便会要求引渡私逃者，通过强加各种民事罪行将之带回俄岸枪毙，以警示他人。目前轮船定期自哈尔滨来到大黑河；瑷珲关关员们业已安顿下来，生活顺遂。

　　　　　　　　　　　　　　　　　　　　　　您真挚的

　　　　　　　　　　　　　　　　　　　　　　富乐嘉（H. G. Fletcher）

---

① 富乐嘉（H. G. Fletcher）时任瑷珲关署理税务司
② 梅乐和（F. W. Maze）时任总税务司

第二部分

人事管理

专题六

历任税务司任免

1. 为瑷珲海关分关改为独立关，任命头等帮办后班包安济先生为署理税务司事

No. 1   COMMRS.

Aigun   No. 85,630

INSPECTORATE GENERAL OF CUSTOMS,

PEKING, 6th September, 1921.

Sir,

1.   I have to inform you that the Shui-wu Ch'u having agreed to the proposal to change the status of Aigun from that of a sub-station of the Harbin Customs to that of a separate Customs establishment, I have decided to carry the scheme into effect from 1st October 1921, and hereby appoint you Acting Commissioner (1st Assistant B) with pay at the rate of Hk.Tls.350.00 plus 100.00 (Acting Allowance) a month from that date.

2.   As Commissioner of Aigun you are to obey the orders of myself and myself alone, but while you will administer your district independently from the Harbin Commissioner, the latter will act for some time to come in an advisory capacity and you are to refer to him for guidance when necessary.

3.   For the sake of continuity and in order not

G. Boezi, Esquire,

   Acting Commissioner of Customs,

     A I G U N .

not to complicate matters, the Harbin Customs will continue to render the Aigun Returns and Accounts until the end of the current year, but from 1st January 1921 they are to be rendered directly by the Aigun Customs, thereby completing the separation of the two offices.

4.   You will continue to issue to yourself and to your staff the special allowance authorised in I. G. despatch No.2514/83,369 to Harbin, under the conditions stated in the said despatch.

5.   You will address me semi-officially every fortnight as well to supplement your despatches as to keep me informed of interesting or important occurrences at your port or in its vicinity - occurrences which it might be expedient to bring to my notice, but which could not properly form the subject of official correspondence.

6.   The Statistical Secretary is being instructed to send you a copy of the Service

(Jordan)

(Jordan) telegraphic code, which you are in future to use when communicating with the Harbin or other Commissioners or myself by telegram, and you are to register your code address, "Custos, Aigun", with the Telegraphic Administration.

7.   Your retention of this appointment will depend on the requirements of the Service and on your own character, conduct and general efficiency.

        I am,

           Sir,

     Your obedient Servant,

    For Inspector General.

致瑷珲关第 <u>1/85630</u> 号令　　　　　　　　总税务司署　　1921 年 9 月 6 日,北京

尊敬的瑷珲关署理税务司包安济（G. Boezi）先生：

谨告知,中方税务处已同意将瑷珲关从哈尔滨关下属分关改设为独立关的提议,并且我已批准该方案于 1921 年 10 月 1 日起生效,现特任命您担任署理税务司（头等帮办后班）,从即日起,发放月薪海关两 350.00 两及津贴海关两 100.00 两（代理津贴）。

作为瑷珲关税务司,您需遵守我一人的命令。虽然您可以不听从哈尔滨关税务司命令独立管理关区,但哈尔滨关税务司在一段时间内仍有顾问资格,必要时可向他咨询意见。

为了工作的连贯性和进展顺利,哈尔滨关将会继续掌管瑷珲关纳税申报和账户,直至本年年底。但从 1922 年 1 月起,此类事宜将由瑷珲关直接管理,由此顺利完成两个公署的分立。

根据总税务司署致哈尔滨关第 2514/83369 号令所述,您可继续按照该令授权核发您及您下属员工的特殊津贴。

您需要每两周 "半官方性" 地向我致函,补充说明您呈文中的未尽事宜,随时告知我您所辖港口或其邻近之所发生的趣闻或要事,这些内容涉及需要我了解但不宜列入官方通信之中。

我已指示统计科给您发送一份海关（乔氏）电报代码副本,将来您可以使用该代码通过电报与我联络,或者与哈尔滨关税务司或其他税务司联络。您需要向电报管理局登记电报挂号机构 "Custos, Aigun（瑷珲关）"。

本职位留用与否既取决于海关岗位要求,也取决于您自己的个人品行与工作能力。

您忠实的仆人

包罗（C. A .Bowra）

受海关总税务司委托签发此文

2. 为包安济先生将管理权转交至贺智兰先生事

[4—11]

No. 111   COMMRS.

Aigun   No. 93,604

INSPECTORATE GENERAL OF CUSTOMS,

PEKING, 23rd March, 1923.

SIR,

1.—I have to authorise you to make over charge to Mr. R. F. C. Hedgeland , appointed Commissioner ; you will then proceed to Peking as soon as possible.

2.—When surrendering charge you will supply your successor with a carefully prepared memorandum (of which a copy is to be sent to myself), explanatory of any unfinished work in hand and of any peculiarities of official duty in your district,—suggestive of the line of conduct most likely to conduce to the preservation of pleasant relations with community and officials, Foreign and Chinese,—giving full information respecting any non-Customs business which Chinese officials or local circumstances place in the Commissioner's hands,—and containing whatever miscellaneous hints your own experience may lead you to regard as calculated to be of use to any officer on assuming charge at your port, etc., etc., etc.

3.—Your pay will be discontinued at Aigun on the 30th April, 1923, and your Charge Allowance from date of handing over charge.

I am,

Sir,

Your obedient Servant,

Inspector General.

G. Boezi, Esquire,

Acting Commissioner of Customs,

AIGUN.

[4—1]

No. 112   COMMRS.

Aigun   No. 93,605

INSPECTORATE GENERAL OF CUSTOMS,

PEKING, 23rd March, 1923.

SIR,

1.—I have to inform you that I have selected you to take charge of the Customs establishment at Aigun , and I hereby appoint you Commissioner there, and require you, as such, to obey the orders of myself and myself only.

2.—You will assume charge of the establishment on, or as soon as possible after, the 16th April, 1923 ; salary will be payable to you at the rate of Haikwan Taels Nine Hundred a month from the 16th April, 1923, or from date of reporting for orders at Shanghai if later than that date.

3.—You will be careful to acquaint yourself thoroughly with the correspondence that has passed between your office and the Inspectorate General, and you will take special pains to be guided in the conduct of business by the instructions contained in Circulars.

4.—You will endeavour to cultivate and maintain friendly relations with all officials, Native and Foreign, and you will give such assistance to merchants and mercantile enterprise as your position admits of, in view of existing regulations.

5.—The Superintendent is being acquainted with your appointment.

6.—You will address me semi-officially every fortnight, as well to supplement your despatches as to keep me informed of interesting or important occurrences at your port or in its vicinity—occurrences which it might be expedient to bring to my notice, but which could not properly form the subject of official correspondence.

7.—Your retention of this appointment will depend on the requirements of the Service and on your own character, conduct, and general efficiency.

I am,

Sir,

Your obedient Servant,

Inspector General.

R. F. C. Hedgeland, Esquire,

Commissioner of Customs,

AIGUN.

CUSTOM HOUSE,

Aigun / Taheiho, 31st May, 1923.

Sir,

1.—In accordance with the instructions of your Despatches Nos. 111 /93,604 and 112 /93,605:

Aigun Customs: transfer of charge of; Mr. G.Boezi to be succeeded by Mr. R.F.C. Hedgeland:

the undersigned have the honour to report that transfer of charge has been to-day duly effected.

2.—The cash balances of the several Accounts handed and taken over are as follows:—

Account A		Hk.Tls.	4,887.79
	B	"	972.51
	C	"	---
	D	"	22,962.36
	N	"	---
Local Moneys Account		"	8,165.06 *
Maritime Customs Revenue Account		"	1,407.814
Native	"	"	---
Tonnage Dues Account		"	---

* River Dues & c., below included in A/c. N.

3.—Enclosed herewith is the statement (copy of which is being sent to the Engineer-in-Chief) called for by Circular No. 2708, concerning the changes which have taken place during the period of charge of the outgoing incumbent in the standard official Inventories, including those of the officially furnished quarters at branch or sub offices or stations.

The Inspector General of Customs.

PEKING.

Entered in Card-Index.

(2)

4.—The standard official Inventories have been checked with the articles in the various Service buildings and, having been found to be in agreement, have been signed as correct.

5.—As required by Service rules, the articles of crockery and glassware in the Commissioner's house broken and or lost during the period of charge of the outgoing incumbent have been replaced.

6.—A copy of the handing-over-charge memorandum prepared by Mr. G. Boezi is enclosed herewith.

7.—The copy of the Inspectorate Telegraphic Code (Jordan's) has been handed over and a receipt given.

8.—The semi-official correspondence has been duly handed over.

9.—The lists of books, etc., in the official libraries (including the Examiner's Reference Library) of this office have been checked and found to be short of certain books, as per list enclosed.

10.—The official card index is up to date.

11.—The office file of property records, together with the copies of the relative title-deeds, have been duly checked and handed over, and we certify that these documents are complete and up to date.

We have the honour to be,

Sir.

Your obedient Servants,

G. Boezi

Acting Commissioner (outgoing).

R.F. Chengcheun

Commissioner (incoming).

CUSTOM HOUSE,

AIGUN 15th. June 19 23.

SIR,

1.—This Despatch will be handed to you by Mr. G. Boezi, 1st.Assistant A , transferred to ~~your port~~ Peking by the Inspector General.

2.—Mr. Boezi 's pay has been issued to Charge Alice. to 31st.May,1923. him to the 30th. April, 1923 : ~~E~~ . He was relieved from duty here on 31st. May, 1923 and a passage has been provided for him to Harbin together with a mileage allowance of $241 (to Peking).

3.—While in this Office Mr. Boezi has been in charge of the Aigun Customs. Contributions have been collected to the 30th. April, 1923.Mr.Boeziwill leave for Peking on the 17th. instant.

4.—The usual Memo. of Service is herewith enclosed.

I am,

Sir,

Your obedient Servant,

R. F. Meyer....

Commissioner of Customs.

Chief Secretary,
~~Commissioner of Customs,~~
Inspectorate General of Customs,
Peking.

Entered in Card-Index.

致瑷珲关第 <u>111/93604</u> 号令　　　　　总税务司署　1923 年 3 月 23 日,北京

尊敬的瑷珲关代理税务司包安济(G. Boezi)先生:

　　1. 兹授权将您手中的管理权转交至新任命的税务司贺智兰(R. F. C. Hedgeland)先生;完成交接后,请尽快出发前往北京。

　　2. 在您离任之前,需要为继任者认真准备一份移交书(抄送我一份副本),说明目前手中尚未完成的工作以及本关工作职责的特殊性,给出有助于与华洋职员维持良好关系的行为建议,提供全面详尽的非海关业务资料,便于税务司掌握华籍职员情况或当地局势,并且根据您的经验,添加一些您认为对税务司有益的提示等等。

　　3. 您在瑷珲关的薪俸发放截至 1923 年 4 月 30 日。另外,您的职务津贴自管理权移交之日起停发。

您忠诚的仆人

安格联(Francis Arthur Aglen)

海关总税务司

签章: 总税务司署

致瑷珲关第 112/936054 号令　　　　　总税务司署　1923 年 3 月 23 日，北京

尊敬的瑷珲关税务司贺智兰（R. F. C. Hedgeland）先生：

1. 谨通知，指定您负责瑷珲关海关事务，任命您担任瑷珲关税务司，且仅遵守我一人的命令。

2. 您需于 1923 年 4 月 16 日或此日期后尽快就职；自 1923 年 4 月 16 日起月薪为海关两 900.00 两，若在上海报到时晚于此日期，则以报到之日为准。

3. 您需认真了解并熟悉瑷珲关与海关总税务司之间的通信，处理事务时应尽力参照通令中包含的指示。

4. 您需努力与所有华洋职员培养并保持良好关系，根据现行规定，为商人及商行提供职责范围内的帮助。

5. 海关监督已知悉此项任命。

6. 您需要每两周"半官方性"地向我致函，补充说明您呈文中的未尽事宜，随时告知我您所辖口岸或其邻近之所发生的趣闻或要事，这些内容涉及需要我了解但不宜列入官方通信之中。

7. 本职位留用与否既取决于海关岗位要求，也取决于您的个人品行与工作能力。

您忠诚的仆人

安格联（Francis Arthur Aglen）

海关总税务司

签章：总税务司署

[B.–I4]

　　　　　　　璦珲关 / 大黑河 1923 年 5 月 31 日

尊敬的海关总税务司（北京）：

1. 根据总税务司署第 111/93604 号令及第 112/93605 号令：

　　"璦珲关：移交管理权；包安济（G. Boezi）先生正式将管理权移交给贺智兰（R. F. C. Hegeland）先生。"

兹报告，职务交接自今日起生效。

2. 各账户现金余额交接明细如下：

账户 A	海关两（两）	4887.79
账户 B	海关两（两）	972.51
账户 C	海关两（两）	
账户 D	海关两（两）	2262.36
账户 N	海关两（两）	
地方公款清账	海关两（两）	8165.06*
海关税收账户	海关两（两）	1407.814
常关税收账户	海关两（两）	
船钞账户	海关两（两）	

说明：＊江捐账户：已并入 D 账户中。

3. 根据总税务司署第 2078 号通令，兹附交接报表（抄件已发送至总营造司），内容包括：交接期间官方物品的变化情况，包括海关各部门、各分关或分卡住房家具情况。

4. 已照标准官方清单对海关各址物品进行核查，并在确认无误后签字。

5. 根据海关相关规定，已更换交接期间税务司房屋内损坏或丢失的陶器和玻璃器皿。

6. 随函附寄包安济先生的工作移交书抄件。

7. 已上交总税务司署电报代码［乔氏（Jordan's）］副本及收据。

8. 半官函已及时移交。

9. 璦珲关图书馆书籍清单（包括二等验货参考书）已核查完毕，按照随附数目清单，发现缺少部分书籍。

    10. 官方卡片索引为最新版本。

    11. 关产记录文件及相关所有权证书已核查并移交，兹证实文件完整且为最新版本。

您忠诚的仆人

包安济（G. Boezi）

瑷珲关署理税务司（即将离任）

贺智兰（R. F. C. Hedgeland）

瑷珲关税务司（新任）

[F.-20]

呈总税务司署 124 号文　　　　　　　　　　瑷珲关 / 大黑河 1923 年 6 月 15 日

尊敬的总税务司署（北京）总务科税务司：

　　1. 此呈文由头等帮办前班包安济（G. Boezi）先生转交至贵署，奉总税务司命令，包安济先生已调任至北京。

　　2. 包安济先生之薪俸发放至 1923 年 4 月 30 日，职务津贴发放至 1923 年 5 月 31 日。其已于 1923 年 5 月 31 日从瑷珲关卸任，已向其发放至哈尔滨的旅费及里程津贴 241 银圆（至北京）。

　　3. 在本关，包安济先生任瑷珲关署理税务司，其储金缴纳至 1923 年 4 月 30 日；包安济先生将于 6 月 17 日前往北京。

　　4. 随函附寄常规《关员履历表》。

您忠诚的仆人

贺智兰（R. F. C. Hedgeland）

瑷珲关税务司

3. 为贺智兰先生正式将管理权移交给裴德生先生事

[B.—14]

No. 240.

I. G.

CUSTOM HOUSE.

Aigun   16th. October, 192 5

For enclosure see separate cover

~~ENCLOSED~~

SIR,

1.—IN accordance with the instructions of your Despatches Nos. 255 / 104,944 and 256 / 104,945,

Aigun   Customs : transfer of charge of; Mr. R.F.G.Hedgeland, to be succeeded by Mr. C.M.Petterson ;

the undersigned have the honour to report that transfer of charge has been to-day duly effected.

2.—The cash balances of the several Accounts handed and taken over are as follows :—

Account A	. . . . . .	Hk.Tls.	2,376.82
„ B	. . . . .	„	934.25
„ C	. . . . .	„	-.-
„ D	. . . . .	„	10,114.39
„ N	. . . . .	„	-.-
Local Moneys Account #	. . . .	„	7,564.82
Maritime Customs Revenue Account	„	4,838.773	
Native	. . . .	„	-.-
Tonnage Dues Account	. . . .	„	-.-
		„	
		„	
		„	

#River Dues A/c. Already included in A/c.D.

3.—Enclosed herewith is the statement (copy of which is being sent to the Engineer-in-Chief) called for by Circular No. 2708, concerning the changes which have taken place during the period of charge of the outgoing incumbent in the standard official Inventories, including those of the officially furnished quarters at branch or sub offices or stations.

THE INSPECTOR GENERAL OF CUSTOMS,
PEKING.

(2)

4.—The standard official Inventories have been checked with the articles in the various Service buildings and, having been found to be in agreement, have been signed as correct.

5.—As required by Service rules, the articles of crockery and glassware in the Commissioner's house broken and/or lost during the period of charge of the outgoing incumbent ~~xxxxxxxxx~~ are being placed.

6.—A copy of the handing-over-charge memorandum prepared by Mr. Hedgeland is enclosed herewith.

7.—The copy of the Inspectorate Telegraphic Code (Jordan's) has been handed over and a receipt given.

8.—The semi-official correspondence has been duly handed over.

9.—The lists of books, etc., in the official libraries (including the Examiners' Reference Library) of this office have been checked and found to be correct.

10.—The official card index is up to date.

11.—The office file of property records, together with the copies of the relative title-deeds, ~~is incomplete~~(vide Handing-over-charge Memo) ~~xxxxxxxxxxxxxxxxxxxxxxxxxxxxxxxxxxxxxxxx~~

12.—The banks in which Service and Revenue moneys are deposited have been duly notified of the present transfer of charge and that, acting under the Inspector General's instructions, the incoming Commissioner will, until further notice, sign cheques on the official Accounts.

We have the honour to be,

SIR,

Your obedient Servants,

R.F.C.Hedgeland
Commissioner (outgoing).

(incoming).
Assistant-in-Charge,
temporarily.

CASH IN SAFE.

1. Fine on S. S. "Kwangchi" for concealing arms on
   board. Seizure Report No. 116 of 20th. October,
   1922. Hk.Tls. 250.00 @ 156.63 = $391.63

2. Subscriptions paid in advance for purchase of
   Customs Returns:

   (a) Heiho Chamber of Commerce......$ 15.60

   (b) Mr. Shimomura..................$ 0.60

   N.B. To be brought to account $ 16.20
         after publications received   _____
         and distributed. $407.83

The sum of $407.83 handed over by Mr.
R. F. C. Hedgeland, Commissioner, and taken over by
Mr. C. M. Patterson, Assistant-in-Charge on
October, 1925.

R. F. C. Hedgeland
Commissioner.

C. M. Patterson
Assistant-in-Charge (temporarily).

CUSTOM HOUSE.
Aigun/Taheiho, 16th. October, 1925.

AIGUN NO. 240 TO I.G.

ENCLOSURE 1.

STANDARD OFFICIAL INVENTORIES.

(1) NEW ARTICLES ADDED TO INVENTORIES OF OFFICIALLY
FURNISHED QUARTERS.

A. COMMISSIONER'S HOUSE (RENTED).

Standard Furniture Grade 11.

Drawing Room:

Carpet, Green axminster	1
Chairs with arms	2
" without arms	3
" . Easy	2
Card table	1
Table	1
" . Sutherland	1
Cakestand	1
Teapoy	1

Dining Room:

Hall Table, Stained Oak	1
Carpet, Brown Axminster	1
Curtains, brown Repp	2
Dinner Set: Soup Plates	12
Meat "	36
Pudding "	24
Dessert "	12
Cheese "	12
Meat Dish: 9"	1
10"	1
12	1
14	1
16	1
18	1
Vegetable Dishes	4
Fish Dish with strainer	1
Sauce Tureens and ladies	2
Fruit Dishes	3

Breakfast

Breakfast Set:	Cups & Saucers	12
	Plates	12
	Egg Cups	6
Tea Set:	Cups & Saucers	12
	Plates	12
	Cake Dishes	3
	Slop Basin	1
	Milk Jug	1
Kitchen Set:	Baking Dishes	6
	Pie Basins	3
	Pudding Bowls	2
Glassware:	Port Glasses	12
	Sherry "	12
	Claret "	12
	Champagne "	12
	Hock "	12
	Liqueur "	12
	Custard "	12
	Tumblers	12
	Ice Plates	12
	Finger Bowls	12
	Claret Jug	1
	Tankard Jug	1
	Decanters	2
	Cut Glass Dish -10"	1
	" " " - 8"	1
	" " " - 6"	1
	Jam Pots & Covers	2
	Butter dish with cover and strainer	1
Dinner Wagon; Stained Oak		1

Study:

Carpet, brown Axminster	1
Chairs, Morris	2
Book Case	1
Curtains	2

Bedroom No. 1:

Chair	1
Toilet Set:	Jug	1
	Basin	1
	Slop Pail	1
	Soap Dish	1
	Chamber Pot	1
	Tooth brush cup	1

Bedroom No. 2:

| Dressing Table, Stained Oak with Mirror | 1 |
| Washstand | 1 |

Chest

Chest of Drawers, Stained Oak	1
Towel Horse " "	1
Bedside Table " "	1
Chair " "	1
Toilet Set:	Jug	1
	Basin	1
	Slop Pail	1
	Soap Dish	1
	Chamber Pot	1
	Tooth brush cup	1

Bedroom No. 3:

Toilet Set:	Jug	1
	Basin	1
	Slop Pail	1
	Soap Dish	1
	Chamber Pot	1
	Tooth brush cup	1
Washstand, stained Oak		1
Chest of Drawers, stained Oak		1
Wardrobe, stained Oak with mirror		1
Dressing Table, stained Oak with mirror		1
Chair, stained Oak		1
Towel Horse, stained Oak		1

Bathroom No. 1:

Bathtub, Enamelled	1
Bath Tray, Zinc-lined	1
Linen Press	1
Glass Shelf	1

Bathroom No. 2:

| Bath Tray, Zinc-lined | 1 |
| Glass Shelf | 1 |

Hall:

Chair, Stained Oak	1
Foot Scraper	1
Ice Chest	1

Kitchen:
| Sink | 1 |

2.

B. NEW CUSTOM HOUSE AND QUARTERS.

Officers Quarters:

Bedroom No. 1.

Wardrobe, Oak Stained	1	From Liangchiatun	
Toilet Set	1	,,	,,

Bedroom No. 2.

Bedstead, Iron	1	,,	,,
Mattress	1	,,	,,
Bedside Table, Oak Stained	1	,,	,,
Wardrobe, ,, ,,	1	,,	,,
Washstand, ,, ,,	1	,,	,,
Toilet Set	1	,,	,,

Bedroom No. 3.

Bedstead, Complete with bolster and mattress	1	,,	,,

Bathroom No. 1.

Bath, Zinc	1		
Bath Tray, Cement	1		
Grating, Wooden	1		
Shaving Mirror	1	,,	,,

Bathroom No. 2.

Boiler with Water gauge and Control Pointer	1		
Bath, Zinc	1		
Bath Tray, Cement	1		
Grating, Wooden	1		

Hall.

Wall Lamp	1	From Liangchiatun	
Footscraper, Iron	1	,,	,,
Coir Mat	1	,,	,,

Mess

Mess Room.

Dinner Set	6	From Liangchiatun	
Tea Cups	6	,,	,,
Tea Saucers	6	,,	,,
Coffee Cups	2	,,	,,
Coffee Saucers	4	,,	,,
Tumblers	6	,,	,,
Wine Glasses	5	,,	,,
Liqueur Glasses	6	,,	,,
Salt Cellars	2	,,	,,
Table Knives	6	,,	,,
,, Forks	6	,,	,,
,, Spoons	6	,,	,,
Dessert Knives	6	,,	,,

Customs Offices:

General and Examiner's Offices.

Desk	1	,,	,,
Cash Box	1	,,	,,
Table	1	,,	,,
Stationery Box	1	,,	,,
Howe Scale, Platform	1	,,	,,
Notice Boards	2	,,	,,
Steel Yards	2	,,	,,
Searching Lantern	1	,,	,,
,, Iron	1	,,	,,
Alcoholmeter	1	,,	,,

Commissioner's Office:

Book Case	1	,,	,,

C.

C. OLD CUSTOM HOUSE (Occupied by Foreign Out-door Staff).

Unmarried Officers' Quarters.

Room No. 1:

Dining Table	1	From Liangchiatun
Filter	1	" "

Room No. 2:

Chest of Drawers	1	" "
Table Lamp	1	" "

Bathroom:

Bath Tub, Soochow	1	" "
Washstand, Oak Stained	1	" "
Toilet Set, one set	3	" "
Shaving Mirror	1	" "

(2) OLD ARTICLES REPAIRED OR RENOVATED.

AIGUN/NO. / TO I.G.
ENCLOSURE 1.
STANDARD OFFICIAL INVENTORIES.

(2) ARTICLES REPAIRED OR RENOVATED.

COMMISSIONER'S HOUSE.

Date of Purchase.

Easy Chairs, soft wood painted white	6	1912
Settee, soft wood painted white	1	1912

These were in a very bad condition but they have been renovated at a cost of $44 and are now thoroughly serviceable.

(3) ARTICLES BROKEN AND REPLACED.

(3) ARTICLES BROKEN AND REPLACED.

COMMISSIONER'S HOUSE (RENTED).

Standard Furniture Grade 11.

Dining Room.

Glassware:

Decanter.............1

(4) ARTICLES LOST, BROKEN, DISCARDED, OR OTHERWISE
DISPOSED OF WITHOUT REPLACEMENT.

(4) ARTICLES LOST, BROKEN, DISCARDED, OR OTHERWISE

DISPOSED OF WITHOUT REPLACEMENT.

DISCARDED AS BEING USELESS.

COMMISSIONER'S HOUSE:

(Old Furniture).

Drawing Room.		Date of Purchase.
Table, Painted White.........1.....................1912		
Carpet, Blue..................1..................1913		
Book Shelf, Painted White.....1.....................1911		

Dining Room.

Carpet, Red................1...................1918		
Dinner Service............12 broken plates and		
	52 spoons & Forks of	
	cheapest possible quality	
	left behind by former	
	Senior Assistant.........1920	

Hall.

Table, Small White............1.....................1914

Bedroom No. 2.

Washstand, Tiled top.........1.................1911

Toilet Set...................3 broken pieces........1920

Chest of Drawers, painted
white................... 1911

Carpet, Blue................. 1913

Study.

Carpet, Blue................. 1913

Chairs, Bentwood.............3 1911

N.B. The above articles were all perfectly useless.
Vide Aigun No. 129/I. G. and Engineer-in-Chief's
comments for description of the old furniture in
the Commissioner's House.

ARTICLES BROKEN WITHOUT REPLACEMENT.

ARTICLES BROKEN WITHOUT REPLACEMENT.

Glassware:

Sherry Glasses.......................2
Port   " 2
Liqueur   " 4
Ice Plates.........................2
Butter Dish........................1
Jam Pots...........................2
Tumblers...........................3
Champagne Glasses..................3
Hock   " 3
Claret Glass.......................1

Commissioner.

CUSTOM HOUSE.
Aigun/Tsheihs, 16th. October, 1925.

[B-I4]

呈总税务司署 <u>240</u> 号文 瑷珲关 1925 年 10 月 16 日

尊敬的海关总税务司（北京）：

1. 根据总税务司署第 255/104944 号令及 256/104945 号令：

"瑷珲关：移交管理权；贺智兰（R. F. Hedgeland）先生正式将管理权移交给裴德生（C. M. Petterson）先生。"

兹报告，职务交接自今日起生效。

2. 各账户现金余额交接明细如下：

账户 A	海关两（两）	2376.82
账户 B	海关两（两）	934.25
账户 C	海关两（两）	…
账户 D	海关两（两）	10114.39
账户 N	海关两（两）	…
地方公款清账 *	海关两（两）	7564.82
海关税收账户	海关两（两）	4838.773
常关税收账户	海关两（两）	…
船钞账户	海关两（两）	…

说明：* 江捐账户：已并入 D 账户中。

3. 根据总税务司署第 2078 号通令，兹附交接报表（抄件已发送至总营造司），内容包括：交接期间官方物品之变化情况，包括海关各部门、各分关或分卡住房家具情况。

4. 已照标准官方清单对海关各址物品进行核查，并在确认无误后签字。

5. 根据海关相关规定，已更换交接期间税务司房屋内损坏或丢失的陶器及玻璃器皿。

6. 随函附寄贺智兰先生的工作移交书抄件。

7. 已上交总税务司署电报代码［乔氏（Jordan's）］副本及收据。

8. 半官函已及时移交。

9. 瑷珲关图书馆书籍清单（包括二等验货参考书）已核查无误。

10. 官方卡片索引为最新版本。

11.关产记录文件及相关所有权证书抄件不完整（参见工作移交书）。

12.已及时向海关经费及税款存放银行说明税务司管理权移交事宜,及新任税务司需待总税务司署的进一步指示,方能于公款项下签署支票。

您忠诚的仆人

贺智兰（R. F. C. Hedgeland）

璦珲关税务司（即将离任）

裴德生（C. M. Petterson）

璦珲关暂行代理税务司（新任）

保险箱现金明细

名目	金额		备注
	海关两	银圆	
1. 罚金			
"光驰（Kwangchi）"号轮船私藏武器罚金 （按照海关两 100 两 =156.65 银圆计）	250.00	391.63	参阅 1922 年 10 月 20 日第 116 号海关查获货物报告；
合计：		391.63	
2. 购买海关统计表／册预付款			待海关统计表／册刊行下发后登记入账；
（1）黑河商会		15.60	
（2）下村（Shimomura）先生		0.60	
合计：		16.20	
总计：		407.83	

该 407.83 银圆已由税务司贺智兰（R. F. C. Hedgeland）先生于 1925 年 10 月移交暂行代理税务司裴德生（C. M. Petterson）先生管理。

贺智兰

瑷珲关税务司

（即将离任）

裴德生

瑷珲关暂行代理税务司

（新任）

1925 年 10 月 16 日，瑷珲关／大黑河

瑷珲关致总税务司署第 240 号呈附件 1

标准官方清单

表 1

1. 增加至清单的新物品：

（1）税务司住所（租赁）（二级标准家具）

客厅：

绿色阿克明斯特（Axminster）地毯	1	
扶手椅	2	
无扶手椅	3	
躺椅	2	
牌桌	1	
桌子	1	
萨瑟兰（Sutherland）桌	1	
蛋糕架	1	
茶几	1	

餐厅：

着色橡木玄关桌	1	
棕色阿克斯明斯特地毯	1	
棕色棱纹窗帘	2	
晚餐餐具：汤盘	12	
肉盘	36	
布丁盘	24	
甜点盘	12	
奶酪盘	12	
9.5 英寸肉菜盘	1	
10.5 英寸肉菜盘	1	
12 英寸肉菜盘	1	
14 英寸肉菜盘	1	
16 英寸肉菜盘	1	

表2

18 英寸肉菜盘	1	
蔬菜盘	4	
带滤网的鱼盘	1	
调味盘及女侍	2	
水果盘	3	
早餐餐具：杯子＆茶托	12	
盘子	12	
鸡蛋杯	6	
茶具：茶杯＆茶托	12	
盘子	12	
蛋糕盘	3	
倒残茶的浅碟	1	
牛奶壶	1	
厨房用具：烘焙盘	6	
馅饼盘	3	
布丁碗	2	
玻璃器具：葡萄酒杯	12	
雪利酒杯	12	
红葡萄酒杯	12	
香槟酒杯	12	
霍克酒杯	12	
利口酒杯	12	
蛋奶糕杯	12	
大玻璃杯	12	
冰盘	12	
洗指碗	12	
红葡萄酒壶	1	
啤酒壶	1	

表3

玻璃瓶	2	
10 英寸刻花玻璃盘	1	
8 英寸刻花玻璃盘	1	
6 英寸刻花玻璃盘	1	
果酱罐＆盖子	2	
黄油盘（带盖子及滤网）	1	
手推餐车：着色橡木	1	
书房：		
棕色阿克明斯特地毯	1	
莫里斯椅	2	
书柜	1	
窗帘	2	
1号卧室：		
椅子	1	
盥洗室设施：水壶	1	
脸盆	1	
污水桶	1	
皂盒	1	
夜壶	1	
刷牙杯	1	
2号卧室：		
着色橡木梳妆台（带镜子）	1	
盥洗台	1	
着色橡木衣柜	1	
着色橡木毛巾架	1	
着色橡木床头柜	1	
着色橡木椅	1	
盥洗室设施：水壶	1	
脸盆	1	

表4

污水桶	1	
皂盒	1	
夜壶	1	
刷牙杯	1	

3号卧室：

盥洗室设施：水壶	1	
脸盆	1	
污水桶	1	
皂盒	1	
夜壶	1	
刷牙杯	1	
着色橡木盥洗台	1	
着色橡木抽屉柜子	1	
着色橡木衣柜（带镜子）	1	
着色橡木梳妆台（带镜子）	1	
着色橡木椅	1	
着色橡木毛巾架	1	

1号浴室：

搪瓷浴缸	1	
锌衬浴盘	1	
亚麻布熨烫机	1	
玻璃隔板	1	

2号浴室：

锌衬浴盘	1	
玻璃隔板	1	

门厅：

着色橡木椅	1	
刮擦鞋用具	1	
冰柜	1	

表5

厨房：		
水槽	1	

（2）新海关办公楼及职员宿舍

① 职员宿舍：

1号卧室：		
着色橡木衣柜	1	购自梁家屯
盥洗室设施	1	购自梁家屯

2号卧室：		
铁制床架	1	购自梁家屯
床垫	1	购自梁家屯
着色橡木床头柜	1	购自梁家屯
着色橡木衣柜	1	购自梁家屯
着色橡木盥洗台	1	购自梁家屯
盥洗室设施	1	购自梁家屯

3号卧室：		
床架,带靠枕及床垫	1	购自梁家屯

1号浴室：		
锌制浴缸	1	
胶结材料洗漱盘	1	
木制栅栏	1	
剃须镜	1	购自梁家屯

2号浴室：		
带水位表及指示针的锅炉	1	
锌制浴缸	1	
胶结材料洗漱盘	1	
木制栅栏	1	

门厅：		
壁灯	1	购自梁家屯
铁制刮擦鞋用具	1	购自梁家屯

表6

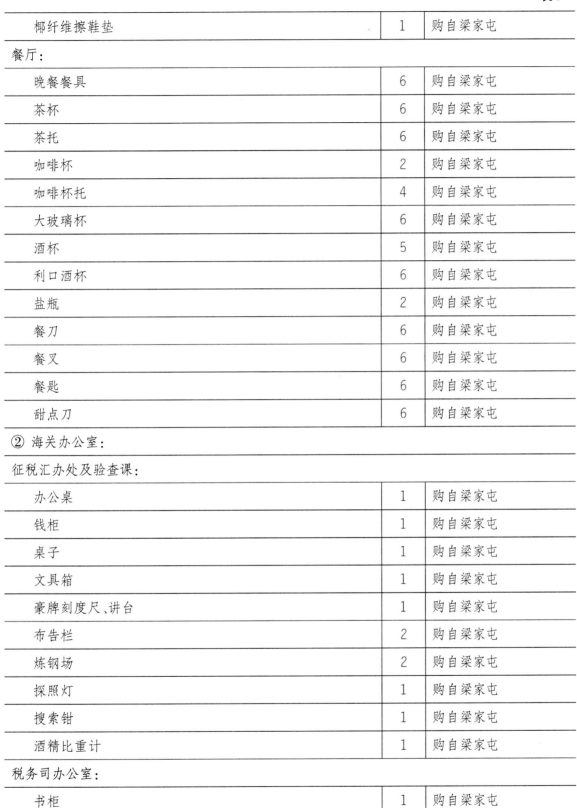

椰纤维擦鞋垫	1	购自梁家屯
餐厅:		
晚餐餐具	6	购自梁家屯
茶杯	6	购自梁家屯
茶托	6	购自梁家屯
咖啡杯	2	购自梁家屯
咖啡杯托	4	购自梁家屯
大玻璃杯	6	购自梁家屯
酒杯	5	购自梁家屯
利口酒杯	6	购自梁家屯
盐瓶	2	购自梁家屯
餐刀	6	购自梁家屯
餐叉	6	购自梁家屯
餐匙	6	购自梁家屯
甜点刀	6	购自梁家屯
② 海关办公室:		
征税汇办处及验查课:		
办公桌	1	购自梁家屯
钱柜	1	购自梁家屯
桌子	1	购自梁家屯
文具箱	1	购自梁家屯
豪牌刻度尺、讲台	1	购自梁家屯
布告栏	2	购自梁家屯
炼钢场	2	购自梁家屯
探照灯	1	购自梁家屯
搜索钳	1	购自梁家屯
酒精比重计	1	购自梁家屯
税务司办公室:		
书柜	1	购自梁家屯

表7

（3）旧海关住址（由洋籍外班职员使用）

未婚职员宿舍：

1号房间：

餐桌	1	购自梁家屯
过滤器	1	购自梁家屯

2号房间：

带抽屉的柜子	1	购自梁家屯
台灯	1	购自梁家屯

浴室：

苏州浴盆	1	购自梁家屯
着色橡木盥洗台	1	购自梁家屯
盥洗用具，一套	3	购自梁家屯
剃须镜	1	购自梁家屯

2. 已修理或修复的旧物品：

税务司住所（租赁）（二级标准家具）

重漆白色木制安乐椅	6	购于1912年
重漆白色木制长椅	1	购于1912年

注：此等物品此前已破损不堪，经修复后（花费44银圆），已完全可用。

3. 更换破损物件：

税务司住所（租赁）（二级标准家具）

餐厅：

玻璃器具：玻璃瓶	1	

4. 遗失／破损／丢弃／无替换品之物件：

税务司住所（租赁）（二级标准家具）

（1）旧家具

客厅：

表8

白漆桌	1	购于 1912 年
蓝色地毯	1	购于 1913 年
白漆书架	1	购于 1911 年

餐厅：

红色地毯	1	购于 1918 年
晚餐餐具：破损盘子	12	购于 1920 年,由前超等帮办所置
破损勺子、叉子	52	

门厅：

小白桌	1	购于 1914 年

2 号卧室：

瓦顶盥洗台	1	购于 1911 年
盥洗室设施	3	购于 1920 年
白漆带抽屉的柜子	1	购于 1911 年
蓝色地毯	1	购于 1913 年

书房：

蓝色地毯	1	购于 1913 年
弯木椅	3	购于 1911 年

注：上述物件已彻底无用（参阅瑷珲关致总税务司署第 129 号呈及总营造司关于瑷珲关税务司住所旧家具之意见）。

（2）无替换品之物件

玻璃器具：		
雪利酒杯	2	
葡萄酒杯	2	
利口酒杯	4	
冰盘	2	
黄油盘	1	
果酱罐	2	
大玻璃杯	3	
香槟酒杯	3	

表9

霍克酒杯	3	
红葡萄酒杯	1	

贺智兰(R. F. C. Hedgeland)

瑷珲关税务司

1925 年 10 月 16 日,瑷珲关 / 大黑河

4. 为裴德生先生正式将管理权移交给瑚斯敦先生事

[A.—35]

No. 282   COMMRS.

Aigun   No. 106,885.

12 APR 1926
Registered.

INSPECTORATE GENERAL OF CUSTOMS,

PEKING, 30th March 1926.

INDEXED

SIR,

1.—I have to authorise you to make over charge to Mr. J.H.W. Houstoun , appointed Commissioner ; you will then proceed on transfer to Harbin.

2.—When surrendering charge you will supply your successor with a carefully prepared memorandum (of which a copy is to be sent to myself), explanatory of any unfinished work in hand and of any peculiarities of official duty in your district,—suggestive of the line of conduct most likely to conduce to the preservation of pleasant relations with community and officials, Foreign and Chinese,—giving full information respecting any non-Customs business which Chinese officials or local circumstances place in the Commissioner's hands,—and containing whatever miscellaneous hints your own experience may lead you to regard as calculated to be of use to any officer on assuming charge at your port, etc., etc., etc.

3.—Your pay will be discontinued at Aigun on 30th April 1926, and your Acting Allowance on the date on which you surrender charge.

I am,

Sir,

Your obedient Servant,

Inspector General.

C.M. Patterson , Esquire,

Assistant-in-charge, temporarily,

AIGUN.

[A.—1]

No. 283   COMMRS.

Aigun   No. 106,887.

12 APR 1926
Registered.

INSPECTORATE GENERAL OF CUSTOMS,

PEKING, 30th March 1926.

INDEXED

SIR,

1.—I have to inform you that I have selected you to take charge of the Customs establishment at Aigun , and I hereby appoint you Commissioner there, and require you, as such, to obey the orders of myself and myself only.

2.—You will assume charge of the establishment on, or as soon as possible after, the 16th April 1926 ; salary will be payable to you at the rate of Haikwan Taels 1,000 a month from the 16th April 1926, or if later: from the date on which you reported for orders at Shanghai.

3.—You will be careful to acquaint yourself thoroughly with the correspondence that has passed between your office and the Inspectorate General, and you will take special pains to be guided in the conduct of business by the instructions contained in Circulars.

4.—You will endeavour to cultivate and maintain friendly relations with all officials, Native and Foreign, and you will give such assistance to merchants and mercantile enterprise as your position admits of, in view of existing regulations.

5.—The Superintendent is being acquainted with your appointment.

6.—You will address me semi-officially every fortnight, as well to supplement your despatches as to keep me informed of interesting or important occurrences at your port or in its vicinity—occurrences which it might be expedient to bring to my notice, but which could not properly form the subject of official correspondence.

7.—Your retention of this appointment will depend on the requirements of the Service and on your own character, conduct, and general efficiency.

I am,

Sir,

Your obedient Servant,

Inspector General.

J.H.W. Houstoun Esquire,

Commissioner of Customs,

AIGUN.

[B.—14]

Registered.

No. 264
I. G.

CUSTOM HOUSE,

Aigun, 15th May, 192 6

SIR,

1.—In accordance with the instructions of your Despatches Nos. 282 / 106,886 and 283 / 106,887 :

Aigun Customs: transfer of charge of; Mr. C.M.Petterson

to be succeeded by Mr. J.H.W.Houstoun :

the undersigned have the honour to report that transfer of charge has been to-day duly effected.

2.—The cash balances of the several Accounts handed and taken over are as follows :—

Account **A**		Hk.Tls.	7,901.77
„ **B**		„	132.77
„ **C**		„	....
„ **D**		„	4,280.68
„ **N**		„	....
Local Moneys Account *		„	282.57
Maritime Customs Revenue Account		„	2,706.210
Native		„	....
Tonnage Dues Account		„	....
		„	....
		„	....
		„	....

* River Dues A/c already included in A/c D .

3.—Enclosed herewith is the statement (copy of which is being sent to the Engineer-in-Chief) called for by Circular No. 2708, concerning the changes which have taken place during the period of charge of the outgoing incumbent in the standard official Inventories, including those of the officially furnished quarters at branch or sub offices or stations.

THE INSPECTOR GENERAL OF CUSTOMS,
PEKING.

(2)

4.—The standard official Inventories have been checked with the articles in the various Service buildings and, having been found to be in agreement, have been signed as correct.

5.—As required by Service rules, the articles of crockery and glassware in the Commissioner's house broken and/or lost during the period of charge of the outgoing incumbent have been replaced. are being

6.—A copy of the handing-over-charge memorandum prepared by Mr. Petterson is enclosed herewith.

7.—The copy of the Inspectorate Telegraphic Code (Jordan's) has been handed over and a receipt given.

8.—The semi-official correspondence has been duly handed over.

9.—The lists of books, etc., in the official libraries (including the Examiners' Reference Library) of this office have been checked and found to be correct. (This office has never been supplied with I.G.Circulars Nos. 638-832)

10.—The official card index is up to date.

11.—The office file of property records, together with the copies of the relative tide-deeds, is incomplete (vide Handing-over charge Memo been duly checked over and verified and the documents are complete and up-to-date

12.—The banks in which Service and Revenue moneys are deposited have been duly notified of the present transfer of charge and that, acting under the Inspector General's instructions, the incoming Commissioner will, until further notice, sign cheques on the official Accounts.

We have the honour to be,

SIR,

Your obedient Servants,

Examiner (outgoing).
Assistant in charge, temporarily

Commissioner (incoming).

Enclosure No.1: Aigun Despatch No.264/I.G.

STANDARD OFFICIAL INVENTORIES.

1. New Articles added to Inventories.

    a) Commissioner's Office. - 1 typewriter table with single
                                 compartment for stationery.
    b) Accountant-Secretary's Office.- 1 typewriter table with
                                 double compartments for station-
                                 ery.
    c) General Office. - 2 field telephones - private system-
                                 (from seizures).

2. Old articles repaired or renovated.

Commissioner's House.
    a) Drawing Room. - 12 chair covers redyed.

    b) Study.-   4 pair curtains redyed blue(once
                      discarded and now again added to list)

    c) Bedroom No.3.- 1 box spring, mattress, and bolster
                      repaired and re-covered.

3. Broken Articles to be Replaced.

Commissioner's House.
    a) Dining Room.   2 sherry glasses.
                         1 champagne glass.
                         1 claret glass.
                         1 tumbler.
                         1 dinner plate.
                         1 pudding plate.
                         2 tea cups.

4. Articles discarded.

Commissioner's House.
    a) Dining Room. -   2 discoloured baking dishes.

    b) Bathroom No.2.- 1 old commode.

    Note: Aigun Despatch No.240/I.G.: Enclosure No.1: List of
           Articles broken without replacement, Replaced by Mr.
           P.F.C.Hedeeland, Commissioner.

Custom House.   Assistant in charge, temporarily.
Aigun/Taheiho, 15th May, 1936.

致瑷珲关第 <u>282/106886</u> 号令　　　　　总税务司署　1926 年 3 月 30 日，北京

尊敬的瑷珲关暂行代理税务司裴德生（C. M. Petterson）先生：

　　兹授权将您手中的管理权转交至新任税务司瑚斯敦（J. H. W. Houstoun）先生；您将被调任至哈尔滨。

　　在您离任之前，需要为继任者认真准备一份移交书（向我抄送一份副本），说明目前手中尚未完成的工作以及本关该工作职责的特殊性，给出有助于与中外职员维持良好关系的行为建议，提供全面详尽的非海关业务资料，便于税务司掌握华籍职员情况或当地局势，并且根据您的经验，添加一些您认为对税务司有益的提示等等。

　　您在瑷珲关的薪俸发放截至 1926 年 4 月 30 日。另外，您的代理津贴自管理权移交之日起停止发放。

您忠诚的仆人

安格联（F. A. Aglen）

总税务司

（签章：海关总税务司）

致瑷珲关第 <u>283/106887</u> 号令　　　　　　总税务司署　1926 年 3 月 30 日,北京

尊敬的瑷珲关税务司瑚斯敦(J. H. W. Houstoun)先生,

谨通知,指定您负责瑷珲关海关事务,任命您担任瑷珲关税务司,且仅遵守我一人的命令。

您需于 1926 年 4 月 16 日或此日期后尽快就职;从 1926 年 4 月 16 日起月薪为海关两 1000.00 两,若在上海的报到日期晚于此日期,则以报到之日为准。

您需认真了解并充分熟悉瑷珲关与总税务司署之间的通信,处理事务时应尽量参照通令中的指示。

您需努力与所有华洋职员培养并保持良好关系,根据现行规定,为商人及商行提供职责范围内的帮助。

海关监督已知悉此项任命。

您需要每两周 "半官方性" 地向我致函,补充说明您呈文中的未尽事宜,随时告知我您所辖口岸或其邻近之所发生的趣闻或要事,这些内容需要我了解但不宜归入官方通信之中。

本职位留用与否既取决于海关岗位要求,也取决于您的个人品行与工作能力。

您忠诚的仆人

安格联(F. A. Aglen)

总税务司

(签章: 海关总税务司)

[B-I4]

呈总税务司署 264 号文　　　　　　　　　　瑷珲关 1926 年 5 月 15 日

尊敬的海关总税务司（北京）：

1. 根据总税务司署第 282/106886 号令及 283/106887 号令：

　　"瑷珲关：移交管理权；裴德生（C. M. Petterson）先生正式将管理权移交给瑚斯敦（J. H. W. Houstoun）先生。"

兹报告，职务交接自今日起生效。

2. 各账户现金余额交接明细如下：

账户 A	海关两（两）	7901.77
账户 B	海关两（两）	132.77
账户 C	海关两（两）	...
账户 D	海关两（两）	4280.00
账户 N	海关两（两）	...
地方公款清账 ＊	海关两（两）	282.57
海关税收账户	海关两（两）	2706.210
常关税收账户	海关两（两）	...
船钞账户	海关两（两）	...

说明：＊江捐账户：已并入 D 账户中。

3. 根据总税务司署第 2078 号通令，兹附交接报表（抄件已发送至总营造司），内容包括：交接期间官方物品之变化情况，包括海关各部门、各分关或分卡住房家具情况。

4. 已照标准官方清单对海关各址物品进行核查，并在确认无误后签字。

5. 根据海关相关规定，已更换交接期间税务司房屋内损坏或丢失的陶器和玻璃器皿。

6. 随函附寄裴德生先生的工作移交书抄件。

7. 已上交总税务司署电报代码［乔氏（Jordan's）］副本及收据。

8. 半官函已及时移交。

9. 瑷珲关图书馆书籍清单（包括二等验货参考书）已核查无误。（瑷珲关未曾收到总税务司署第 638 号至 832 号通令）。

10. 官方卡片索引为最新版本。

11. 关产记录文件及相关所有权证书抄件不完整（参见工作交接书）。

12. 已及时向海关经费及税款存放银行说明税务司管理权移交事宜，及新任税务司需待总税务司署的进一步指示，方能于公款项下签署支票。

您忠诚的仆人

裴德生

瑷珲关暂行代理税务司

（即将离任）

瑚斯敦

瑷珲关税务司（新任）

瑷珲关致总税务司署第 264 号呈附件

标准官方清单

1. 增加至清单的新物品：

（1）瑷珲关税务司办公室	1 张打字机桌及一个放信纸的隔间
（2）会计课兼文书课	1 张打字机桌及放信纸的双重隔间
（3）征税汇办处	2 部野战电话——私人系统（罚没物品）

2. 已修理或修复的旧物品：

税务司住所

（1）客厅	12 把重漆的椅子
（2）书房	4 套蓝色窗帘（丢弃后现重新列入清单）
（3）3 号卧室	已修理或修复的一盒弹簧，一张床垫及靠枕。

3. 更换破损物件：

税务司住所

（1）餐厅	2 个雪利酒杯
	1 个香槟酒杯
	1 个红葡萄酒杯
	1 个不倒翁
	1 个餐盘
	1 个布丁盘
	2 个茶杯

4. 丢弃物件：

税务司住所

（1）餐厅	2 个褪色的烘烤盘
（2）2 号浴室	1 个旧盥洗台

　　说明：瑷珲关致总税务司署第 240 号呈：附件 1：无替换品之破损物品清单：此等破损物品已由瑷珲关税务司贺智兰（R. F. C. Hedgeland）先生置换。

裴德生（C. M. Petterson）

瑷珲关暂行代理税务司

1926 年 5 月 15 日　瑷珲关 / 大黑河

5. 为瑚斯敦先生正式将管理权移交给铎博赍先生事

15 JULY 1926
Registered.

No. 301   COMMRS.   INSPECTORATE GENERAL OF CUSTOMS,

Aigun   No.108,279.   PEKING,   2nd July 1926.

Pensions No. 1990.

INDEXED

Sir,

1.   With reference to your telegram of 10th
April 1926, transmitted through the Shanghai
Commissioner :

                requesting permission to retire
                under the terms of Circular No. 3397 :

to the Inspector General's telegram of 12th
April in reply :

                informing you that you would be
                permitted to retire :

and to I. G. despatch No. 296/107,992, Pensions
No. 1946 :

                requesting you to notify the date
                on which you wish to retire :

I have now to acknowledge the receipt of your
despatch No. 269 :

                stating that you desired to retire
                on 16th October 1926 :

                                    and,

.W. Houstoun, Esquire,
Commissioner of Customs,
    A I G U N.

and, in reply, to inform you that your
withdrawal will become operative on the 16th
October 1926.

2.   Arrangements for your relief from duty
on 15th October 1926 will accordingly be made,
and you are requested to note that your pay
and allowances (if any) will cease on that date,
and that the benefits under Circulars Nos. 3006
and 3262 will then become payable to you.

3.   A retiring allowance, calculated to the
15th October 1926, will be issued to you at
the same time.

4.   Purchase of Annuity.   You are requested
to inform me as soon as possible of the name
of the insurance company you have selected for
the payment of the annuity which the Service
will purchase on your behalf.   Two proposal
forms of the company concerned, with the required
particulars duly filled in, signed and dated,
                                    should

should be procured and forwarded to me at the same time.   In this connection I must ask you to note that the Service can incur no responsibility for any possible loss resulting from a delay in your choice of an insurance company.

5.   You are further requested to note that the only forms of annuity that are permissible under the existing Superannuation and Retirement Rules are the ordinary "Immediate" annuity and the "Impaired" annuity.

6.   I have also to request you to furnish me with a statement of the name of the bank or address to which you wish your Silver Benefit and Retiring Allowance to be sent, or of any other disposition you would wish me to make of these moneys.

7.   I have to request you to note that your contributions are to be collected in full up to, and including, 15th October, and that

your

your contribution for the period 1st to 15th October is Hk. Tls. 30.00.   You should forward Form B.-41 in time to reach this Office before the date of your withdrawal.

    I am,

        Sir,

        Your obedient Servant,

        Officiating Inspector General,
        ad interim.

310

COMMRS.

28 SEP 1926

INSPECTORATE GENERAL OF CUSTOMS,

igun   No. 109,394.   PEKING, 16th September 1926. 310/I.G.

SIR,

1.—I have to authorise you to make over charge to
Mr. R. M. Talbot, appointed **Acting Commissioner
(Chief Assistant B)**; you will then retire from the Service as
instructed in my despatch No.301/108,279, Pensions No.1990.

2.—When surrendering charge you will supply your successor with a carefully prepared memorandum (of which a copy
is to be sent to myself), explanatory of any unfinished work
in hand and of any peculiarities of official duty in your
district,—suggestive of the line of conduct most likely
to conduce to the preservation of pleasant relations with
community and officials, Foreign and Chinese,—giving full
information respecting any non-Customs business which Chinese
officials or local circumstances place in the Commissioner's
hands,—and containing whatever miscellaneous hints your own
experience may lead you to regard as calculated to be of
use to any officer on assuming charge at your port, etc.,
etc., etc.

3.—Your pay will be discontinued at **Aigun**
on **15th October 1926.**

4. I take this opportunity to express the Inspector
General's appreciation of your faithful services over a long
term of years and the hope that you will enjoy a long and
ppy period of retirement.   I am,

Sir,

Your obedient Servant,

Officiating Inspector General, ad
interim.

J. H. W. Houstoun, Esquire,

Commissioner of Customs,

AIGUN.

311

COMMRS.

28 SEP 1926

INSPECTORATE GENERAL OF CUSTOMS,

Aigun   No. 109,395.   PEKING, 16th September 1926. 311/I.G.

SIR,

1.—I have to inform you that I have selected you to take
charge of the Customs establishment at **Aigun**
and I hereby appoint you **Acting Commissioner (Chief Assistant B)** there,
and require you, as such, to obey the orders of myself and
myself only.

2.—You will assume charge of the establishment on, or if
absolutely necessary before, ~~as soon as possible after,~~ the **15th October 1926**; salary will
be payable to you at the rate of Haikwan Taels **550.00**
a month from the **1st October 1926, plus an**
Acting Allowance of **Hk.Tls.150 a month from the date of assuming charge.**

3.—You will be careful to acquaint yourself thoroughly
with the correspondence that has passed between your office
and the Inspectorate General, and you will take special pains
to be guided in the conduct of business by the instructions
contained in Circulars.

4.—You will endeavour to cultivate and maintain friendly
relations with all officials, Native and Foreign, and you will
give such assistance to merchants and mercantile enterprise
as your position admits of, in view of existing regulations.

5.—The Superintendent is being acquainted with your
appointment.

6.—You will address me semi-officially every fortnight,
as well to supplement your despatches as to keep me informed
of interesting or important occurrences at your port or in its
vicinity—occurrences which it might be expedient to bring
to my notice, but which could not properly form the subject
of official correspondence.

7.—Your retention of this appointment will depend on
the requirements of the Service and on your own character,
conduct, and general efficiency.

I am,

Sir,

Your obedient Servant,

Officiating Inspector General, ad
interim

R. M. Talbot, Esquire,

Acting Commissioner of Customs,

AIGUN.

[R—14]

No. 288.
I. G.

CUSTOM HOUSE,

Aigun , 12th October, 1926.

Sir,

1.—In accordance with the instructions of your Despatches
Nos. 310 / 109,394 and 311 / 109,395

Aigun Customs: transfer of charge of; Mr. J. H. W. Houstoun
to be succeeded by Mr. E. M. Talbot :

the undersigned have the honour to report that transfer of charge has been to-day
duly effected.

2.—The cash balances of the several Accounts handed and taken over are
as follows:—

Account A . . . . Hk.Tls. 2,251.62
„ B . . . . „ 139.25
„ C . . . . „ . . .
„ D . . . . „ 14,980.47
„ N . . . . „ . . .
Local Moneys Account* . . . . „ 6,251.84
Maritime Customs Revenue Account „ 4,628.089
Native „ . . . . . . „ . . .
Tonnage Dues Account . . . . „ . . .
„ . . .
„ . . .
„ . . .

*River Dues A/C. already included in A/C. D.

3.—The banks in which Service and Revenue moneys are deposited have
been duly notified of the present transfer of charge and that, acting under the
Inspector General's instructions, the incoming Commissioner will, until further notice,
sign cheques on the official Accounts.

Officiating
The Inspector General of Customs,
PEKING.

(2)

Enclosure No. 1.

4.—Enclosed herewith is the statement (copy of which is being sent to the
Engineer-in-Chief) called for by Circular No. 2708, concerning the changes which
have taken place during the period of charge of the outgoing incumbent in the
standard official Inventories, including those of the officially furnished quarters at
branch or sub offices or stations.

5.—The standard official Inventories have been checked with the articles in
the various Service buildings and, having been found to be in agreement, have been
signed as correct.

6.—As required by Service rules, the articles of crockery and glassware in the
Commissioner's house broken and/or lost during the period of charge of the outgoing
incumbent have been replaced.

Enclosure No. 2.

7.—A copy of the handing-over-charge memorandum prepared by
Mr. Houstoun is enclosed herewith.

8.—The copy of the Inspectorate Telegraphic Code (Jordan's) has been
handed over and a receipt given.

9.—The semi-official correspondence has been duly handed over.

10.—The lists of books, etc., in the official libraries (including the Examiners'
Reference Library) of this office have been checked and found to be correct.
(This Office has never been supplied with I.G.Circulars Nos.
638-832)

11.—The official card index is up to date.

12.—The office file of property records, together with the copies of the relative
title-deeds, is incomplete (vide Aigun No. 264 to I. G.)

We have the honour to be,

Sir,

Your obedient Servants,

J. H. W. Houstoun,
Commissioner (outgoing).

Acting Commissioner (incoming).

Aigun No. 288 to O.I.G.

Enclosure No.1.

STANDARD OFFICIAL INVENTORIES.

1. New Articles added to Inventories:

        N I L.

2. Old Articles repaired or renovated:

    Commissioner's House:
       a) Bedroom No. 1.-   1 mattress, recovered.
       b) Bedroom No. 2.-   1 mattress, recovered.

3. Broken Articles to be replaced:

    Commissioner's House:
       a) Dining Room.-   1 pudding plate.
                              1 tea cup.
                              1 champagne glass.
                              1 finger bowl.
                              2 sherry glasses
                              1 port wine glass.

4. Articles discarded:
    Commissioner's House:
       a) Dining Room.-   2 vegetable dishes, discoloured.
                              3 baking dishes, discoloured.

                                    J. R. S. Houstoun,
                                        Commissioner.

CUSTOM HOUSE,
Aigun, 12th October, 1926.

致瑷珲关第 <u>301/108279</u> 号令　　　　　　　　总税务司署　1926 年 7 月 2 日, 北京

尊敬的瑷珲关税务司瑚斯敦（J. H. W. Houstoun）先生：

　　1. 根据 1926 年 4 月 10 电呈（经由江海关税务司转交）：

　　"根据第 3397 号通令条款, 请求批准退休"

　　总税务司 4 月 12 日电令：

　　"通知准予您退休"

　　总税务司署第 296/107992 号令, 第 1946 号养老储金：

　　"请您确定退休时间"

　　第 269 号呈收悉：

　　"您希望于 1926 年 10 月 16 日退休"

　　现批复如下：兹通知, 您于 1926 年 10 月 16 日正式退休。

　　2. 安排您自 1926 年 10 月 15 日起卸职, 您的薪俸及津贴（如有）将于此日停止发放, 根据第 3006 号通令及第 3262 号通令, 相关抚恤金届时将发放给您。

　　3. 截至 1926 年 10 月 15 日的酬劳金亦于此日发放给您。

　　4. 购买年金如您选定购买年金的保险公司, 请尽快告知我处此保险公司名称, 海关将代为购买年金。同时, 须向我处提交两份该公司的保险单, 并填入规定细节, 签署姓名及日期。对此, 您须知悉, 若是由于您推迟确定保险公司名称的时间造成的损失, 海关不承担任何责任。

　　5. 请知悉, 现行"养老（退休）储金规定"许可的年金形式仅为常规"即时"年金及"削减"年金。

　　6. 请您向本署提交一份明细表, 写明您的银款抚恤金及酬劳金收款银行名称和地址, 或这些钱款的其他处置方式。

　　7. 您需缴纳储金至 10 月 15 日（包含）, 您第一阶段自 10 月 1 日至 15 日应缴纳储金额为海关两 30.00 两。在您卸职前, 请将表 B.—41 及时上交至本署。

您忠诚的仆人

易纨士（A. H. F. Edwardes）

暂代代理海关总税务司

致瑷珲关第 <u>310/109394</u> 号令　　　　总税务司署　1926 年 9 月 9 日,北京

尊敬的瑷珲关税务司瑚斯敦（J. H. W. Houstoun）先生,

　　1. 兹授权将您手中的管理权转交至新被任命的署理税务司（超等帮办后班）铎博赉（R. M. Talbot）先生；随后您需根据总税务司署第 301/108279 号令及第 1990 号养老储金指令自瑷珲关退休。

　　2. 在您离任之前,需要为继任者认真准备一份移交书（向我抄送一份副本）,说明目前手中尚未完成的工作以及本关该工作职位的特殊性,给出有助于与华洋职员维持良好关系的建议,提供全面详尽的非海关业务资料,便于税务司掌握华籍职员情况或当地局势,并且根据您自己的经验,添加一些您认为对税务司有益的提示等等。

　　3. 您在瑷珲关的薪俸发放截至 1926 年 10 月 15 日。

　　4. 您在长年累月的工作中,尽职尽力,谨借此机会转达总税务司的赞赏及感激之情,希望您退休后生活愉快,安度晚年。

您忠诚的仆人

易纨士（A. H. F. Edwardes）

暂代代理海关总税务司

致瑷珲关第 <u>311/109395</u> 号令　　　　　总税务司署　　1926 年 9 月 16 日, 北京

尊敬的瑷珲关署理税务司铎博赛 (R. M. Talbot) 先生:

1. 谨通知, 指定您负责瑷珲关海关事务, 任命您担任瑷珲关署理税务司 (超等帮办后班), 且仅遵守我一人的命令。

2. 您需于 1923 年 4 月 16 日或必要时在此日期前, 尽快就职; 自 1926 年 10 月 1 日起月薪为海关两 550.00 两, 并自就任之日起, 每月发放代理津贴海关两 150.00 两。

3. 您需认真了解并充分熟悉瑷珲关与总税务司署之间的通信, 处理事务时应尽力参照通令中包含的指示。

4. 您需努力与所有华洋职员培养并保持良好关系, 根据现行规定, 为商人及商行提供职责范围内的帮助。

5. 海关监督已知悉此项任命。

6. 您需要每两周 "半官方性" 地向我致函, 补充说明您呈文中的未尽事宜, 随时告知我您所辖口岸或其邻近之所发生的趣闻或要事, 这些内容需要我了解但不宜列入官方通信之中。

7. 本职位留用与否既取决于海关岗位要求, 也取决于您的个人品行与工作能力。

您忠诚的仆人

易纨士 (A. H. F. Edwardes)

暂代代理海关总税务司

[B-I4]

呈总税务司署 288 号文　　　　　　　　　　**瑷珲关 1926 年 10 月 12 日**

尊敬的代理海关总税务司（北京）：

1. 根据总税务司署第 310/109394 号令及第 311/109395 号令：

"瑷珲关：移交管理权；瑚斯敦（J. H. W. Houstoun）先生正式将管理权移交给铎博赉（R. M. Talbot）先生。"

兹报告，职务交接自今日起生效。

2. 各账户现金余额交接明细如下：

账户 A	海关两（两）	2251.82
账户 B	海关两（两）	139.25
账户 C	海关两（两）	…
账户 D	海关两（两）	14980.47
账户 N	海关两（两）	…
地方公款清账 ★	海关两（两）	8251.84
海关税收账户	海关两（两）	4828.089
常关税收账户	海关两（两）	…
船钞账户	海关两（两）	…

说明：＊江捐账户：已并入 D 账户中。

3. 已及时向海关经费及税款存放银行说明税务司管理权交接事宜，及新任税务司需待总税务司署的进一步指示，方能于公款项下签署支票。

4. 根据总税务司署第 2078 号通令，兹附交接报表（抄件已发送至总营造司），内容包括：交接期间官方物品之变化情况，包括海关各部门、各分关或分卡住房家具情况。

5. 已照标准官方清单对海关各址物品进行核查，并在确认无误后签字。

6. 根据海关相关规定，已更换交接期间税务司房屋内损坏或丢失的陶器和玻璃器皿。

7. 随函附寄瑚斯敦先生的工作移交书抄件。

8. 已上交总税务司署电报代码［乔氏（Jordan's）］副本及收据。

9. 半官函已及时移交。

10. 瑷珲关图书馆书籍清单（包括二等验货参考书）已核查无误。（瑷珲关未曾收到总税务司署第 638 号至 832 号通令）。

11. 官方卡片索引为最新版本。

12. 关产记录文件及相关所有权证书抄件不完整（参见瑷珲关致总税务司署第 264 号呈）

您忠诚的仆人

瑚斯敦

瑷珲关税务司

（即将离任）

铎博赉

瑷珲关署理税务司（新任）

瑷珲关致总税务司署第 288 号呈附件

标准官方清单

增加至清单的新物品：	
无	
已修理或修复的旧物品：	
税务司住所	
（1）1 号卧室	修复一张床垫
（2）2 号卧室	修复一张床垫
更换破损物品：	
税务司住房	
（1）餐厅	1 张布丁盘
	1 个茶杯
	1 个香槟酒杯
	1 个洗指碗
	2 个雪利酒杯
	1 个葡萄酒杯
丢弃物品：	
税务司住所	
（1）餐厅	2 个褪色的蔬菜盘
	3 个褪色的蔬菜盘

瑚斯敦（J. H. W. Houstoun）

瑷珲关税务司

1926 年 10 月 12 日, 瑷珲关

6. 为铎博赉先生正式将管理权移交给富乐嘉先生事

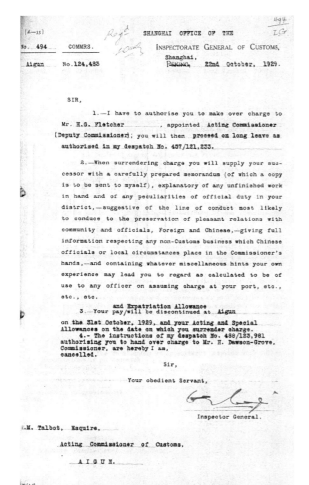

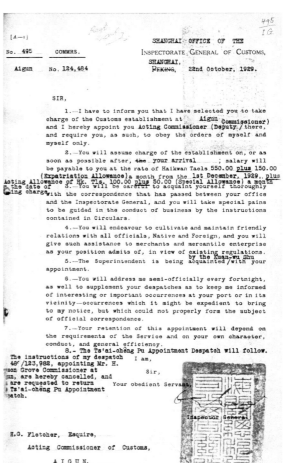

[B.—14]

No. 6929 (Harbin)
No. 452 (Aigun)

I. G.

CUSTOM HOUSE,

AIGUN(HARBIN)____, 16th December, 192 9.

SIR,

1.—In accordance with the instructions of your ~~telegram~~ telegram of the 4th November, 1929 ~~despatch~~ despatch ~~No.~~ and No.495 /124,484 :

AIGUN Customs: transfer of charge of, Mr. P. G. S. Barentzen

to be succeeded by Mr. H. G. Fletcher :

the undersigned have the honour to report that transfer of change has been to-day duly effected.

2.—The cash balances of the several Accounts handed and taken over are as follows :—

Account A	.	.	.	.	Hk. Tls. 7,159.39
" B	.	.	.	.	" 341.73
" C	.	.	.	.	" . . .
" D	.	.	.	.	" 1,015.36
" N	.	.	.	.	" . . .
Local Moneys Account		.	.	.	" . . .
Maritime Customs Revenue Account			.	.	" 65,831
Native " "		.	.	.	" . . .
Tonnage Dues Account		.	.	.	" . . .
Additional Duty and surtax Account				.	" 148,970
Amur River Dues Account			.	.	" 1,970.60

3.—Enclosed herewith is the statement (copy of which is being sent to the Engineer-in-Chief) called for by Circular No. 2708, concerning the changes which have taken place during the period of charge of the outgoing incumbent in the standard official Inventories, including those of the officially furnished quarters at branch or sub offices or stations.

THE INSPECTOR GENERAL OF CUSTOMS,
~~PEKING~~
SHANGHAI.

(2)

not
4.—The standard official Inventories have been checked with the articles in with the exception of the Inventory of the the various Service building ~~xxxxxxxxxxxxxxxxxxxxxxxxxxxxxxxxxx~~ Commissioner's house which is stated in Aigun/Harbin despatch ~~xxxxxxxxxxxxxx~~ No.452 to have been found to be in agreement. The inventories are not to hand in Harbin.
5.—As required by Service rules, the articles of crockery and glassware in the Commissioner's house broken and/or lost during the period of charge of the outgoing incumbent ~~xxxxxxxxxxxxxx~~ are as stated by Mr. R. M. Talbot to be in course of replacement, but nothing is known in Harbin either as to the sufficiency of these replacements or as to the condition of the remaining articles.6.—A copy of the handing-over-charge memorandum prepared by Mr. R. M. Talbot was enclosed ~~herewith~~ in Aigun/Harbin despatch No. 452/I.G.

7.—The copy of the Inspectorate Telegraphic Code (Jordan's) has been handed over and a receipt given. Also one copy of Slater's Code.

8.—The semi-official correspondence has been duly handed over.

9.—The lists of books, etc., in the official libraries (including the Examiners' are as stated in Aigun/Harbin despatch No.452 to Reference Library) of this office have been checked ~~xxxxxxx~~ by Mr.R. M. Talbot and found correct, but neither books nor catalogues are to hand in Harbin.

10.—The official card index is up to date.

11.—The office file of property records, together with the copies of the relative title-deeds, have been duly checked and handed over, and we certify that these documents are complete and up to date.
12. The Banks in which Service and Revenue moneys are deposited have been duly notified of the present transfer of charge and that, acting under the Inspector General's instructions the incoming Commissioner will, until further notice, sign cheques on the official accounts.
13. The instructions of I.G. Circular No.3863/II regarding the collection and filing of information relative to trade, etc. for the purpose of the ~~We have the honour to be,~~ Trade and Decennial
Reports are said by Mr. R. M. Talbot SIR,
in Aigun/Harbin despatch No.452/I.G.
to have been duly carried out but the
data is not to hand in Harbin.

Your obedient Servants,

Commissioner (outgoing).

Acting Commissioner (incoming).

BALANCE SHEET FOR THE PERIOD
1ST TO 15TH DECEMBER, 1929.

A/C. A:		Hk.Tls.7,135.39
A/C. B:	" "	239.73
A/C. D:	" "	2,385.90
	" "	9,761.02

Cash in:
Bank of China, Harbin (Taheiho Branch Office):

Hk.Tls. A/c.:*		HK.Tls.	...
Dollar A/c : $3,504.15 @ 150		" "	2,336.09
River Dues A/c: $2,055.90 @ 150		" "	1,370.60
Hongkong & Shanghai Bank, Shanghai:			
S'hai Tls.A/c: Sh.Tls.7,464.76 @ 111.40		" "	8,700.86
Safe: Hk.Tls.0.15		" "	.15
		" "	10,407.70
Difference:			
Less cheque No.1008 drawn but not yet			
cashed for $970.02 @ 150		- " "	646.68
		" "	9,761.02

* As per Bank Pass Books.
$ As per cheque book of Hongkong & Shanghai Bank.

Handed over by:

[signature]

Commissioner.

Taken over by:

[signature]

Acting Commissioner.

Prepared by:

[signature]

3rd Clerk B.

CUSTOM HOUSE,
Aigun(Harbin), 16th December, 1929.

致瑷珲关第 <u>494/124483</u> 号令　　　　　总税务司署（上海）　1929 年 10 月 22 日

尊敬的瑷珲关署理税务司铎博赛（R. M. Talbot）先生：

　　1. 兹授权将您手中的管理权移交至新任命的署理税务司（副税务司）富乐嘉（H. G. Fletcher）先生；根据第 457/121233 号令批准，您可以开始休长假。

　　2. 在您离任之前，需要为继任者认真准备一份移交书（向我抄送一份副本），说明目前手中尚未完成的工作以及本关该工作职责的特殊性，给出有助于与中外职员良好关系的行为建议，提供全面详尽的非海关业务资料，便于税务司掌握华籍职员情况或当地局势，并且根据您的经验，添加一些您认为对税务司有益的提示等等。

　　3. 您在瑷珲关的薪俸及离国津贴发放截至 1929 年 10 月 31 日。另外，您的代理津贴及特殊津贴自管理权移交之日起停止发放。

　　4. 我署第 488/123981 号令所载指令授权您移交管理权至税务司克勒纳（H. Dawson-Grove）先生的事宜就此取消。

您忠诚的仆人

梅乐和（F. W. Maze）

海关总税务司

致瑷珲关第 <u>495/124484</u> 号令　　　　　总税务司署（上海）　1929 年 10 月 22 日

尊敬的瑷珲关署理税务司富乐嘉（H. G. Fletcher）先生：

1. 谨通知，指定您负责瑷珲关海关事务，任命您担任瑷珲关署理税务司（副税务司），且仅遵守我一人的命令。

2. 您需于 1929 年 12 月 1 日或此日期后尽快就职；自此日起每月薪俸海关两 550 两及离国津贴海关两 150 两；自就任之日起，每月发放代理津贴海关两 100.00 两及特殊津贴 50 两。

3. 您需认真了解并充分熟悉瑷珲关与总税务司署之间的通信，处理事务时应尽力参照通令中包含的指示。

4. 您需努力与所有华洋职员培养并保持良好关系，根据现行规定，为商人及商行提供职责范围内的帮助。

5. 海关监督将通过财政部关务署了解你的委任事宜。

6. 您需要每两周"半官方性"地向我致函，补充说明您呈文中的未尽事宜，随时告知我您所辖口岸或其邻近之所发生的趣闻或要事，这些内容需要我了解但不宜归入官方通信之中。

7. 本职位留用与否既取决于海关岗位要求，也取决于您的个人品行与工作能力。

8. 随函附上财政部委任令。

9. 我署第 489/123982 号令所载指令授权您移交管理权至税务司克勒纳（H.Dawson-Grove）先生的事宜就此取消，您需将财政部委任令交回我署。

您忠诚的仆人

梅乐和（F. W. Maze）

海关总税务司

呈总税务司署 <u>457（3929）</u>号文 　　　　　瑷珲关 1929 年 12 月 16 日

尊敬的海关总税务司（上海）：

1. 根据总税务司署 1929 年 11 月 4 日电报及第 495/124484 号令：

"瑷珲关：移交管理权；滨江关税务司巴闰森（P.G.S.Barentzen）先生正式将管理权移交给富乐嘉（H.G.Fletcher）先生。"

兹报告，职务交接自今日起生效。

2. 各账户现金余额交接明细如下：

账户 A	海关两（两）	7135.39
账户 B	海关两（两）	239.73
账户 C	海关两（两）	
账户 D	海关两（两）	1015.30
账户 N	海关两（两）	
地方公款清账	海关两（两）	
海关税收账户	海关两（两）	65.831
常关税收账户	海关两（两）	
船钞账户	海关两（两）	
附加税账户	海关两（两）	148.470
黑龙江江捐账户	海关两（两）	1370.60

3. 根据总税务司署第 2078 号通令，兹附交接报表（抄件已发送至总营造司），内容包括：交接期间官方物品的变化情况，包括海关各部门、各分关或分卡住房家具情况。

4. 标准官方清单还未送交海关各址核查，无须核查税务司住房清单（参阅瑷珲关第 452 号呈）。清单目前还未移交至滨江关。

5. 据铎博贲（R. M. Talbot）先生所述，根据海关法规章则，在交接期间，税务司住房中破损及遗失的陶器与玻璃器具将被替换，但对可用于替换之物件的充裕情况及现有物件的情况，滨江关一无所知。

6. 铎博贲先生的工作移交书已随函附寄于瑷珲关致总税务司署第 452 号呈中。

7. 已上交总税务司署电报代码［乔氏（Jordan's）］副本及收据。附斯莱特（Slater's）电报代码副本。

8. 半官函已及时移交。

9. 瑷珲关图书馆书籍清单（包括验货员参考书）已载于瑷珲关第 452 号呈中，经铎博赉先生核查无误，但书籍及书录都尚未移交至滨江关。

10. 官方卡片索引为最新版本。

11. 关产记录文件及相关所有权证书已核查并移交，兹证实文件完整且为最新版本。

12 已及时向海关经费及税款存放银行说明税务司管理权移交事宜，及新任税务司需等待总税务司署的进一步指示，方能于公款项下签署支票。

13. 铎博赉先生于瑷珲关致总税务司署第 452 号呈中汇报，已根据总税务司署第 3863 号通令（第 2 章），收录《最近十年各埠海关报告》所需的贸易等相关信息，但数据尚未移交至滨江关。

您忠诚的仆人

巴闰森

滨江关税务司（即将离任）

富乐嘉

瑷珲关署理税务司（新任）

1929 年 12 月 16 日　瑷珲关（滨江关）

1929 年 12 月 1 日至 15 日期间

资产负债表

账户 A	海关两（两）	7135.39
账户 B	海关两（两）	239.73
账户 D	海关两（两）	2385.90
共计：	海关两（两）	9761.02

现金账户：

中国银行,哈尔滨分行,（大黑河支行）

海关两账户	海关两（两）	
银圆账户：3504.13 银圆 （150 银圆 = 海关两 100 两）	海关两（两）	2336.09
江捐账户：2005.90 银圆 （150 银圆 = 海关两 100 两）	海关两（两）	1370.60
汇丰银行（上海分行）		
上海规平银账户：上海规平银 7464.76 两 （上海规平银 111.40 两 = 海关两 100 两）	海关两（两）	6700.86
保险箱：		
	海关两（两）	0.15
共计：	海关两（两）	10407.70
差额：		
扣除第 1008 号支票 970.02 银圆 （尚未兑现）（150 银圆 = 海关两 100 两）	海关两（两）	646.68
共计：	海关两（两）	9761.02

依据：银行收支簿 / 汇丰银行支票簿

制表：张远扬　三等二级税务员

移交人：巴闰森

滨江关税务司

接管人：富乐嘉

瑷珲关署理税务司

7. 为富乐嘉先生正式将管理权移交给周骊先生事

[B—14]

No. 515
I. G.

CUSTOM HOUSE,

A I G U N ,14th October 1920.

SIR,

1.—In accordance with the instructions of your Despatches Nos 552 / 130,025 and 553 / 130,026 :

Aigun Customs: transfer of charge of; Mr. H. G. Fletcher to be succeeded by Mr. C. H. B. Joly :

the undersigned have the honour to report that transfer of charge has been to-day duly effected.

2.—The cash balances of the several Accounts handed and taken over are as follows :—

Account A	. . . . .	Hk.Tls. 3,227.58
" B	. . . . .	" 247.89
" C	. . . . .	" ...
" D	. . . . .	" 7,734.10
" N	. . . . .	" ...
Local Moneys Account	. . . .	" ...
Maritime Customs Revenue Account	.	" 3,069,933
Native " "	. . .	" ...
Tonnage Dues Account	. . .	" ...
Additional Duty and Surtax Account		" 2,421.019
Amur River Dues Account	. . .	" 3,566.36

3.—Enclosed herewith is the statement (copy of which is being sent to the Engineer-in-Chief) called for by Circular No. 2708, concerning the changes which have taken place during the period of charge of the outgoing incumbent in the standard official Inventories, including those of the officially furnished quarters at branch or sub offices or stations. This statement includes a list of the discrepancies between the Inventories (except that of the Commissioner's House)on file at time of evacuation on 9th November 1929 and the articles actually on hand on reopening of port on 31st May 1920.

THE INSPECTOR GENERAL OF CUSTOMS,
PEKING.
SHANGHAI.

(2)

4.—The standard official Inventories have been checked with the articles in the various Service buildings and, having been found to be in agreement, ~~have been~~ ~~signed as correct~~ except in/far as modified by the statement of the preceding paragraph, have been rewritten and signed as correct. Copies are being forwarded to the Architect.

5.—As required by Service rules, the articles of crockery and glassware in the Commissioner's house broken and/or lost during the period of charge of the outgoing incumbent have been replaced.

6.—A copy of the handing-over-charge memorandum prepared by Mr. H. G. Fletcher is enclosed herewith.

7.—The copy of the Inspectorate Telegraphic Code (Jordan's) has been handed over and a receipt given. Also a copy of Slater's Code, and two copies Marine Code.

8.—The semi-official correspondence has been duly handed over.

9.—The lists of books, etc., in the official libraries (including the Examiners' Reference Library) of this office have been checked and found correct with the exception of those books now reported in Enclosure No.3 which were found missing ~~on~~ return from evacuation.

10.—The official card index is up to date.

11.—The office file of property records, together with the copies of the relative title-deeds, have been duly checked and handed over, and we certify that these documents are complete and up to date.

12. The Banks in which Service and Revenue moneys are deposited have been duly notified of the present transfer of charge and that, acting under the Inspector General's instructions, the incoming Commissioner will, until further notice, sign cheques on the official accounts.

13. The instructions of I.G.Circular No.3863, II, regarding the collection and filing of information relative to trade, etc., for the purpose of the Trade and Decennial Reports have been duly carried out.

We have the honour to be,

SIR,

Your obedient Servants,

(H.G.Fletcher)
Acting Commissioner (outgoing).

(C.H.B.Joly)
Acting Commissioner (incoming).

呈总税务司署 515 号文　　　　　　　　　　瑷珲关 1930 年 10 月 14 日

尊敬的海关总税务司（上海）：

1. 根据总税务司署第 552/130025 号及 553/130026 号令：

"瑷珲关：移交管理权：瑷珲关署理税务司富乐嘉（H. G. Fletcher）先生正式将管理权移交给周骊（C. H. B. Joly）先生。"

兹报告，职务交接自今日起正式生效。

2. 各账户现金余额交接明细如下：

账户 A	海关两（两）	3227.56
账户 B	海关两（两）	247.89
账户 C	海关两（两）	…
账户 D	海关两（两）	7724.10
账户 N	海关两（两）	…
地方公款清账	海关两（两）	…
海关税收账户	海关两（两）	3069.933
常关税收账户	海关两（两）	…
船钞账户	海关两（两）	…
附加税账户	海关两（两）	2421.019
黑龙江江捐账户	海关两（两）	3566.86

3. 根据总税务司署第 2708 号通令，兹附交接报表（抄件发送至总营造司），内容包括：交接期间官方物品的变化情况，包括海关各部门、各分关或分卡住所家具情况。此外，还包括一份根据 1929 年 11 月 9 日瑷珲关撤离时所载标准官方家具清单（不含税务司住所）及 1930 年 5 月 31 日大黑河口岸重新开放时的既有物品编制之物品变动表。

4. 已照标准官方清单对海关各址物品进行核查，根据上述变动修订后，已重新确认并签字。修订后的清单抄件已发送至建筑师。

5. 根据海关相关规定，已更换交接期间税务司住所内损坏或丢失的陶器及玻璃器具。

6. 兹附富乐嘉先生的工作移交书抄件。

7. 已上交总税务司署电报代码［乔氏（Jordan's）］副本及收据。附电报代码斯莱特

（Slater's）副本一份及海务代码（Marine Code）副本两份。

8. 半官函已即时移交。

9. 除返回口岸后经查丢失之书籍外（参见附件 3），瑷珲关图书馆书籍清单（包括验货员参考图书馆）已核查无误。

10. 官方卡片索引已更至最新。

11. 关产记录文件及相关产权证书已核查并移交，兹证实文件完整且为最新版本。

12. 已及时向海关经费及税款存放银行说明税务司管理权移交事宜，及新任税务司需待总税务司署的进一步指示，方能于公款项下签署支票事。

13. 根据总税务司署第 3863 号通令（第二辑）指示，已及时收录《最近十年各埠海关报告》所需的贸易等相关信息。

您忠诚的仆人

富乐嘉

瑷珲关署理税务司（即将离任）

周骊

瑷珲关署理税务司（新任）

8. 为按照洋籍职员与华籍职员平等之原则，重组海关职员事

STAFF: CHINESE MISCELLANEOUS OUTDOOR: recommendations as
to revised scale of pay for, and schedule of special
allowances to be issued to, as called for by I.G.
Circ. No.3,873, forwarding.

418.

I. G.　　　　　　　　　Aigun　　　6th May, 1929.

Registered,
ENCLOSED

Sir,

1.　　　With reference to I. G. Circular No. 3,873
notifying the reorganisation of the Service on a
basis of equality between Chinese and foreign
employees, and with particular reference to § 6 of
that Circular and to § 3 (f) of its Enclosure No.
2;

　　　　　　　that the scale of pay of the
　　　　　Chinese Miscellaneous Outdoor
　　　　　Staff be readjusted so that the
　　　　　maximum pay received shall be
　　　　　increased by from $15 to $20
　　　　　per month, the maximum not to
　　　　　be reached before the completion
　　　　　of 25 years of service; and
　　　　　that at the same time a scale
　　　　　of special allowances, where
　　　　　required, be recommended;

I have the honour to append my recommendations as
to a revised scale of pay and a schedule of
special allowances to be issued to the Aigun
Chinese Miscellaneous Outdoor Staff.

2.　　　Appendix No. 1 embodies my suggestions as
　　　　　　　　　　　　　　　　　to

THE INSPECTOR GENERAL OF CUSTOMS,
SHANGHAI.

to how the scale of pay of the employees concerned
might well be readjusted. By way of comparison
I have shown both the proposed scale of pay and
the present one notified in I. G. despatch No.
302/108,299. In drawing up the new scale I found
some difficulty in certain cases in reconciling it
with the various limitations laid down. I have
introduced for your consideration a double scale of
pay after the 15th year one reaching the increased
maximum of $15 and the other $20. The smaller
limit would be for less capable, but still deserving
employees. I have also ventured to introduce a
probationary period of 6 months before an employee
will be confirmed in his appointment. While this
may not be in accordance with the instructions of
the Circular that promotions shall be annual it
seems to me to follow its spirit in that advances
in future are to be by selection. New employees
will be more carefully scrutinised during their
probationary period and would not be taken on at
once for life, regardless of their capabilities, as
is apt to be the case now.

3.　　　Appendix No. 2 shows the special allowances
I would propose be issued to the Chinese staff of
lower rank and gives a comparison of the pay now
enjoyed by the Aigun staff and that as proposed
with allowances. The special allowances I would
　　　　　　　　　　　　　　　　　recommend

recommend are as follows:

Watchers, T'ingch'ai and
Carpenter: Hk.Tls.5.00 per month.

Boatmen/Guards, Office
Coolies, Gatekeepers,
and Nightwatchmen: Hk.Tls.4.00 per month.

House Coolies: Hk.Tls.3.50 per month.

4. I further solicit your authority to issue an additional allowance of Hk.Tls.2 per month to the No. 1 Boatman to differentiate his position and to compensate him for certain expenses he must incur in keeping up an appearance commensurate with his added responsibilities. The present Head Boatman now receives the same pay as two other Boatmen - Hk.Tls.15 per month.

5. I would still advocate the issue of a winter outfit allowance of Hk.Tls.25 to Native Watchers, to be granted once on appointment, as recommended in Aigun despatch No. 407, in addition to the special allowance. In a despatch to follow I wish to bring to your attention the advisability of raising the limit of pay of Hk.Tls.18 now applying to Native Watchers for the issue of uniform allowances (I. G. Circular No. 2,723).

6. In support of the recommendations made above I would refer you to my despatch No.406 recommending the continued issuing of the Special Manchurian Allowance to this port and to my despatch No. 407 just

just mentioned suggesting that a winter outfit allowance be issued to the Foreign Outdoor Staff and certain members of the Chinese Staff. What I say in these despatches about the high prices for food and clothing in this remote and extremely cold port applies equally as well to the lower ranks of Chinese employees.

I have the honour to be,
Sir,
Your obedient Servant.

Acting Commissioner.

Appendix

Appendix No. 1.

PROPOSED INCREASES IN SCALE OF PAY FOR AIGUN CHINESE MISCELLANEOUS OUTDOOR STAFF.

(I. G. Circular No.3873 § 6)

No. of Years Served	Watchers Old Scale Hk.Tls.	Watchers Proposed Scale Hk.Tls.	Boatmen/Guards Old Scale Hk.Tls.	Boatmen/Guards Proposed Scale Hk.Tls.	Tingch'ai Old Scale Hk.Tls.	Tingch'ai Proposed Scale Hk.Tls.	Office Coolies Gatekeepers Nightwatchmen Old Scale Hk.Tls.	Office Coolies Gatekeepers Nightwatchmen Proposed Scale Hk.Tls.	House Coolies Old Scale Hk.Tls.	House Coolies Proposed Scale Hk.Tls.	Carpenters Old Scale Hk.Tls.	Carpenters Proposed Scale Hk.Tls.
6 months	..	18		12		13		12	..	11	..	16
1 year	18	20	12	13	13	14	12	13	11	12	16	17
2 years	19	22	13	14	14	15	13	14	12	13	17	18
3 years	20	24	14	16	15	16	14	15	13	14	18	19
4 years	22	25	15	17	16	17	14	16	14	15	18	20
5 years	22	26	15	18	16	18	15	17	15	16	19	21
6 years	24	27	16	19	17	19	16	18	15	17	20	22
7 years	24	28	16	20	17	20	16	19	16	18	20	23
8 years	26	29	17	22	18	21		20	16	20	21	24
9 years	26	30	18	23	19	22		21		20	21	25
10 years	28	31	19	24	20	23	17	22	17	21	22	26
11 years	28	32	20	25	21	24	17	23	17	22	22	27
12 years	30	33	20	26	22	25	17	24	17	23	23	28
13 years	30	34	21	27		26	17		17		23	29
14 years	32	35	21			27	17		16		24	30
15 years	32	36	22		21	28	17	24	16	23	24	31
16 years	34	37	22	27	22	28	16	24	16	24	26	32
17 years	34	38	22	28	22	29	16	24	16	24	26	33
18 years	36	39	22	28	22	30	16	25	16	24	26	34
19 years	36	40	22	29	22	31	16	25	16	25	27	35
20 years	38	41	22	29	22	32	16	26	16	25	27	36
21 years	38	42	22	30	22	33	16	26	16	26	27	37
22 years	38	43	22	30	22	34	16	27	16	27	27	38
23 years	38	44	22	31	22	35	16	28	16	28	27	39
24 years	38	45	22	31	22	35	16	29	16	29	27	39
25 years	38	46	21	31	22	36	16	29	16	30	26	40
26 years	38	47	21	31	22	36	16	30	16	30	26	40
27 years	38	48	21	31	22	36	16	30	16	30	26	40
28 years	38	48	21	31	22	36	16	30	16	30	26	40
29 years	38	48	21	31	22	36	16	30	16	30	26	40
30 years	38	48	21	31	22	36	16	30	16	30	26	40

CUSTOM HOUSE.

Aigun, 2nd May, 1929.

(signature) Acting Commissioner.

Appendix No.2.

STATEMENT SHOWING COMPARATIVE INCREASE IN PROPOSED NEW SCALE OF PAY FOR CHINESE MISCELLANEOUS OUTDOOR STAFF TOGETHER WITH SUGGESTED SCALE OF SPECIAL ALLOWANCE.

(I. G. Circular No.3873 § 6)

No. of years served	No. on Staff	Old Pay		Proposed Pay		Proposed Allowance		Increase for each employee	Remarks
		Rate	Amount issued	Rate	Amount issuable	Rate	Amount issuable		
		Hk.Tls.	Hk.Tls.	Hk.Tls.	Hk.Tls	Hk.Tls.	Hk.Tls.	Hk.Tls.	
					Watchers.				
2	1	19	19	22	22	5.00	5.00	8.00	
3	1	20	20	24	24	5.00	5.00	9.00	
7	1	24	24	28	28	5.00	5.00	9.00	
10	1	26	26	31	31	5.00	5.00	10.00	
12	1	28	28	33	33	5.00	5.00	10.00	
					Boatmen/Guards.				
2	2	13	26	14	28	4.00	8.00	5.00	
3	1	14	14	15	15	4.00	4.00	5.00	
4	2	14	28	16	32	4.00	8.00	6.00	
5	2	15	30	17	34	4.00	8.00	6.00	
6	2	15	30	18	36	4.00	8.00	7.00	
6	1	16	16	18	18	4.00	4.00	6.00	Formerly mounted courier, now made Boatman with 6 years seniority.
					T'ingch'ai.				
7	1	17	17	20	20	5.00	5.00	8.00	
9	1	18	18	22	22	5.00	5.00	9.00	Due for promotion but will be passed over
				Office Coolies, Gatekeepers, Nightwatchmen.					
4	1	14	14	16	16	4.00	4.00	6.00	
7	1	16	16	19	19	4.00	4.00	7.00	
11	2	17	34	22	44	4.00	8.00	9.00	This increase could be spread over 2 years.
					House Coolies.				
4	1	13	13	15	15	3.50	3.50	5.50	
					Carpenters.				
9	1	21	21	25	25	5.00	5.00	9.00	
							99.50 2.00		Proposed Allowance to be issued to No1 Boatman now paid Hk.Tls. 15.00 per month.
TOTALS:			394		462		101.50		

Acting Commissioner.

CUSTOM HOUSE.

Aigun, 2nd May, 1929.

279

呈总税务司署 <u>418</u> 号文 　　　　　　　　　　　　瑷珲关 1929 年 5 月 6 日

尊敬的海关总税务司（上海）：

根据总税务司署第 3873 号通令：

"按照洋籍职员与华籍职员平等之原则，重组海关职员。"

及总税务司署第 3873 号通令［（第 6 章节和附件 2 第 3 章节（f）项］：

"调整华籍杂项外班职员薪俸，最高涨幅 15 至 20 银圆，但只有于海关任职满 25 年者，薪俸方可按最高涨幅调整；请根据需要制定特殊津贴发放表。"

兹附本署对瑷珲关华籍杂项外班职员薪俸调整及特殊津贴发放之建议。

本署于附录 1 中提出对瑷珲关华籍杂项外班职员薪俸的调整建议，并将建议薪俸金额与现行薪俸金额（总税务司署第 302/108299 号令所附）以对比的形式呈现于列表中。在拟定新的薪俸表时，本署发现有不同的限额规定，比如按照规定，职员任职满 15 年后，其薪俸的涨幅最高可达 15（虽能力较差，但仍具备相应资格者）或 20 银圆，因此便难以决定应如何调整薪俸。除此之外，本署提议职员在被正式任用之前应有 6 个月的试用期，虽然这可能与总税务司署第 3783 号通令指示（按年度晋升）相左，但本署认为应该在尊重通令的基础上，再加以选拔机制来擢升职员。新职员在试用期将受到严格考察，无论其能力如何，都不会立即被任用。

本署于附录 2 中提出对瑷珲关华籍杂项外班职员特殊津贴的发放建议，并将瑷珲关现行薪俸、建议薪俸及特殊津贴以对比的形式呈现于列表中。本署建议的特殊津贴如下所示：

巡役、听差及木匠	每月海关两海关两 5.00 两
水手、卫兵、差役、门役及更夫	每月海关两 4.00 两
宅役	每月海关两 3.50 两

恳请批准，每月为一级水手发放额外津贴海关两 2 两，以便与其他职级职员有所区分，并补贴其日常工作之外的附加工作。目前水手长的月薪与其他两名水手相同，均为每月海关两 15 两。

本署亦提议为华籍巡役发放冬季装备津贴海关两 25 两，在其就职后立即发放（如瑷珲关第 407 号呈所示），但不包括特殊津贴在内。华籍巡役的制服津贴最低限额为海关两

18两（参阅总税务司署第 2723 号通令），本署欲于下一封呈文中申请适当增加此限额。

本署于瑷珲关第 406 号呈提议本口岸应继续发放满洲特殊津贴，并于瑷珲关第 407 号呈提议为洋籍外班职员及部分华籍职员发放冬季装备津贴，但鉴于口岸地处偏僻且极度寒冷，食物与衣物的物价甚高，兹申请对华籍低级职员亦给予同等津贴。

您忠诚的仆人

铎博赉（R. M. Talbot）

瑷珲关署理税务司

附录 1

瑷珲关华籍杂项架外班职员薪俸上调建议

（根据总税务司署第 3873 号通令第 6 章节）

任职年数	巡役 现行薪俸(海关两)	巡役 建议薪俸(海关两)	水手/卫兵 现行薪俸(海关两)	水手/卫兵 建议薪俸(海关两)	听差 现行薪俸(海关两)	听差 建议薪俸(海关两)	差役、门役及更夫 现行薪俸(海关两)	差役、门役及更夫 建议薪俸(海关两)	宅役 现行薪俸(海关两)	宅役 建议薪俸(海关两)	木匠 现行薪俸(海关两)	木匠 建议薪俸(海关两)
6个月	…	18	…	12	…	13	…	12	…	11	…	16
1年	18	20	12	13	13	14	12	13	11	12	16	17
2年	19	22	13	14	14	15	13	14	12	13	17	18
3年	20	24	14	15	15	16	14	15	13	14	18	19
4年	20	25	14	16	15	17	14	16	13	15	18	20
5年	22	26	15	17	16	18	15	17	14	16	19	21
6年	22	27	15	18	16	19	15	18	14	17	19	22
7年	24	28	16	19	17	20	16	19	15	18	20	23
8年	24	29	16	20	17	21	16	20	15	19	20	24
9年	26	30	17	21	18	22	16	21	16	20	21	25
10年	26	31	17	22	18	23	16 17	21	16	20	21	26
11年	28	32	18	23	19	24	16 17	22	16	21	22	27
12年	28	33	18	24	19	25	16 17	22	16 17	21	22	28
13年	30	34	19	25	20	26	16 17	23	16 17	22	23	29
14年	30	35	19	26	20	27	16 17	23	16 17	22	23	30
15年	32	36	20	27	21	28	16 17	24	16 17	23	24	31

任职年数	巡役		水手/卫兵		听差		差役、门役及更夫		宅役		木匠	
年数	现行薪俸 海关两	建议薪俸 海关两	现行薪俸 海关两	建议薪俸 海关两	现行薪俸 海关两	建议薪俸 海关两	现行薪俸 海关两	建议薪俸 海关两	现行薪俸 海关两	建议薪俸 海关两	现行薪俸 海关两	建议薪俸 海关两
16 年	32	38	20	27	21	28	16	24	16	23	24	32
17 年	34	39	21	28	22	28	16	24	16	23	25	33
18 年	34	40	21	28	22	29	16	24	16	24	25	34
19 年	36	41	21	28	22	29	16	25	16	24	26	35
20 年	36	42	22	29	22	30	16	25	16	24	26	36
21 年	38	43	22	29	22	30	16	25	16	25	26	37
22 年	38	44	22	29	22	30	16	25	16	25	27	38
23 年	38	45	22	30	22	31	16	26	16	25	27	38
24 年	38	46	22	30	23	31	16	26	16	25	27	39
25 年	38	47	22	30	23	31	16	26	16	25	27	39
26 年	38	48	22	31	23	32	16	26	16	26	27	40
27 年	38	49	22	31	23	32	16	26	16	26	27	40
28 年	38	50	22	31	23	32	16	26	16	26	27	40
29 年	38	51	22	31	23	32	16	26	16	26	27	40
30 年	38	52	22	31	23	32	16	26	16	26	27	40

铎博赛（R. M. Talbot）
瑷珲关署理税务司
瑷珲关，1929 年 5 月 2 日

附录2

瑷珲关华籍杂项外班职员薪俸上调及特殊津贴发放建议

（根据总税务司署第3873号通令第6章节）

任职年数	职员等级	现行薪俸		建议薪俸		建议津贴		职员薪俸增额	备注
		发放比率	发放金额	发放比率	发放金额	发放比率	发放金额		
		海关两	海关两	海关两	海关两	海关两	海关两	海关两	
巡役									
2	1	19	19	22	22	5.00	5.00	8.00	
3	1	20	20	24	24	5.00	5.00	9.00	
7	1	24	24	28	28	5.00	5.00	9.00	
10	1	26	26	31	31	5.00	5.00	10.00	
12	1	28	28	33	33	5.00	5.00	10.00	
水手/卫兵									
2	2	13	26	14	28	4.00	8.00	5.00	前陆路马差现任职水手（附6年工龄）
3	1	14	14	15	15	4.00	4.00	5.00	
4	2	14	28	16	32	4.00	8.00	6.00	
5	2	15	30	17	34	4.00	8.00	6.00	
6	2	15	30	18	36	4.00	8.00	7.00	
6	1	16	16	18	18	4.00	4.00	6.00	
听差									原晋升事宜将不再予以考虑
7	1	17	17	20	20	5.00	5.00	8.00	
9	1	18	18	22	22	5.00	5.00	9.00	
差役、门役及更夫									
4	1	14	14	16	16	4.00	4.00	6.00	此增薪额度延续2年
7	1	16	16	19	19	4.00	4.00	7.00	
11	2	17	34	22	44	4.00	8.00	9.00	
宅役									
4	1	13	13	15	15	3.50	3.50	5.50	提议一级水手每月发放津贴海关两15.00两
木匠									
9	1	21	21	25	25	5.00	5.00	9.00	
							99.50		
							2.00		
总计：		394		462		101.50			

铎博赉（R. M. Talbot）

瑷珲关署理税务司

瑷珲关，1929 年 5 月 2 日

专题七

瑷珲关华籍关员清册

RECORD: *Revenue.*   DEPARTMENT: *Native Staff.*

RECORD.	REMARKS.
Wang Tê-mas （王德懋） Native of Chihli	1st Clerk B A.
Born on Kuang hsü, 19th year, 8th moon, 23rd day. (2nd October, 1893.)	Superannuation and Retirement Scheme Contribution.
1 Oct. 1921: appointed 3rd Clerk, A in the Aigun Customs @ Hk.Tls. 70 a month (Status of Aigun Customs changed to an independent office - I.G. Desp No. 1/85,620)	Security Bond cancelled 14.1.1926 (7-53)
1 Nov. 1921: Promoted to be 2nd Clerk, B @ Hk.Tls. 80 a month (Gazette No. 289-Special)	Amended here date of R/A - 31st Mar. 1931 (Circ 3704 & audit note 47)
1 June 1922: Promoted 2nd Clerk, A @ Hk.Tls. 100 a month (Cir. No. 3814, II)	
1923 May 14: received Hk.Tls 1200.00 Retiring Allowance for 1st duodec. - decennial period, 22 Jan. 1912 to 16 April, 1923 (I.G. No. 117/44 269 of 1923 to Aigun).	
1 June, 1925: Promoted 2nd Clerk B @ HK.Tls. 115 a month (Sp. Gazette No. 338)	
1st July 1926: Pay increased from Hk.Tls. 115 to Hk.Tls. 130 a month (Circ 3704-Revised Scale).	
1st June, 1929: Promoted 2nd Clerk A @ Hk $ 130 a month (Gazette No. 300, Special)	
1st May 1929: Pay changed from HK.Tls. 150 to HK.Tls. 170 (I.G. Circular No. 3882. II)	See Page 18.

RECORD: *Revenue*   DEPARTMENT: *Native Staff.*

RECORD.	REMARKS.
See page 3	
Wang Tê-mas （王德懋）	2nd Clerk A.
1st Dec. 1929: Pay ceased on transfer to Tientsin (I.G. telegram 25.11.29 and desp. No. 125,064)	10th December 1929 Released from duty
1st February, 1930 Re-appointed to Aigun (I.G. desp. No. 125,754)	27th January, 1930 Reported for duty
1st June 1930 Promoted to be 1st Clerk B with pay at the rate of Hk.Tls.190 p.m. (Sp. Gaz 412)	APR 14 1931 Received Hk.Tls. 2.09 per Hk.Tls 3,320.00 representing Rd No 2 from 17.4.1929 - 31.3.1931 (I.G No.589/11716) ref/2138
1st October, 1932: Pay ceased on transfer to Shanghai (I.G. telegram No 16 of 21st September 1932)	Released from duty on 7 OCT 1932 post previously closed
1st November, 1932: appointed as clerk in charge (1st class B) temporarily, (I.G. desp. No. 142576)	Reported for duty on

Left page

RECORD: Revenue. DEPARTMENT: Native Staff.

RECORD.	REMARKS.
Yang Ts'un-hou (杨存厚) Native of Chihli. Born on: Kuang Hsü 3rd year 11th moon, 28th day. (12th January, 1878) (born Szechwan)	Tuchili Tsunking Consular Sub examination and Retirement scheme contributor
1 Oct. 1921: appointed Tuchili in the Aigun customs @ Hk.Tls. 30 a month. (Status of Aigun customs changed to an independent office – I.G. Despatch No. 1/85,620)	(Security Bond verified in Hochi)
1 Jan. 1922: Pay increased from Hk.Tls. 30 to Hk.Tls. 35 a month. (I.G. Cir. No. 2986 + Commr's Order No. 860)	
1 May 1922: appointed Writer in the Aigun customs @ Hk.Tls. 40 a month. (I.G. Desp. No. 4/69,536)	Writer
1 May 1923: Pay increased from Hk.Tls. 40 to Hk.Tls. 55 a month. (I.G. Circular No. 3429 + Commr's Order)	1st May 1923: Pay increased from HK$ 70 to HK$ 75 a month (I.G. Circular No. 3429, 3704 and Commr's Order No. 1/80/5)
15 August 1924: Received Hk.Tls. 660.00 Retiring Allowance for 1st decennial - Andecennial period. 31st July, 1913 to 23rd July, 1924 (I.G. Despatch No. 156/99,973 (914 Aigun)	Amended date of R A 7.12.32 (See Aigun No. 4.6
1 May 1925: Pay increased from Hk.Tls. 55 to Hk.Tls. 60 a month (I.G. Circular No. 3429 + Commr's Order No. 1/124)	
1st July 1926: Pay increased from Hk.Tls. 60 to Hk.Tls. 70 a month (Cir. 3704 - Revised Scale)	
14 July 1926: Special allowance of Hk.Tls. 10.00 a month related to dissage (24 to apart to surplus a 105) (Cir. No. 3709)	
1 March 1929: Pay increased to Hk.Tls. 90 a month (I.G. Circular No. 3911)	See page 19.

Right page

see page 6

RECORD: Revenue DEPARTMENT: Native Staff.

RECORD.	REMARKS.
Yang Ts'un-hou (杨存厚)	Writer.
1st Dec. 1929: Granted 6 months' leave on full pay and instructed to report for duty at Aigun on expiry of his leave (I.G. despatch No. 125, 140)	
1st March 1929: Pay increased to Hk.Tls. 90 p.a. (vide I.G. Cir. No. 3911)	
1st March 1931 Pay increased from 90 to 700 (I.G. 577/112,35)	13-5-30 reported for duty after return from leave B.A. Hk @ 1000 (best of period of leave) incad from 1-3-29. From 1-3-31, B.A. Hk. the ceases. I.G. No. 578/32,866)
1st October 1932: Pay ceased on transfer to Shanghai (I.G. telegram No. 16 of 21/9/32)	Relieved from duty on 7 OCT 1932 post provisionally closed.

RECORD: _Revenue_   DEPARTMENT: _Native Staff._

RECORD.	REMARKS.
Chen Pei-yin (陳培因)	3rd Clerk B
Native of Foochow	Superannuation and Retirement
Born on: Kuang Hsü 33rd year, 11th moon, 21st day	Scheme Contributor
(5th January 1907	
1st May 1930: appointed 3rd Clerk B at	Reported for duty on 30/4/30
HK.Tls. 115.00 a month on	Security Bond retained in
transfer from _Foochow_	Foochow. Security bond retained
(I.G. despatch No. 519/12/47/61)	in Foochow became worthless (IG
1st May 1931: Appointed 4th Assistant A @ HK.Tls. 150	No. 570/133,113) New bond signed
a month (G. Gaz. No. 424)	by 陳 培因 and 黃 誼生 retained in
	Amoy Office (from 2½/Chpte 146/h)
	22/9/ bond released No. 4354
Granted four months' leave (on full pay)	
from 1st September 1932. On expiry of leave	
Mr. Chen will report for orders at Tientsin.	
(I. G. No. 658/141,561).	

RECORD: _Revenue_   DEPARTMENT: _Native Staff._

RECORD.	REMARKS.
Chen Chang-an (陳長安)	Watcher.
Family home: Heilungkiang, Aigun Hsien 黑龍江愛琿縣	
Born on: Kuang Hsü 16th year, 3rd moon, 8th day	Bond No. 8 secured for $50.
(26th Apr. 1890)	verified 20.12.25
1st August 1923: appointed Native Watcher @ HK.	
Tls. 16 a month (Order No. 892).	
1. August, 1924: Pay increased to HK.Tls. 18.	
a month (Order No. 979)	
1st June, 1926: Pay increased to HK.Tls. 20	
a month (order no. 1059)	
1st July, 1926: Pay increased from HK.Tls. 20 to	
HK.Tls. 22 per month (Order No. 1063)	
Revised scale I.G.309/303/163,299	
The above increase of Pay withdrawn	
(Order No. 1075) I.G. Despatch No.	
309/109,333.	
1st December, 1926: Pay increased from HK.$20	
to HK.$22.00 a month (Order	
No. 1088)	
1. Dec. 1928: Pay increased from HK.$22	1/4/29 transferred to Tsed
to HK.Tls. 24 a month (order	Granted 7 days leave
No.)	22/10/30 to 29/10/30.
1/8/29 Pay increased to HK.Tls. 25 p.m. (Order 1272)	
1/12/29 Pay HK.Tls. 26 p.m. (order 1305)	
1/12/29 Pay increased HK.Tls. 27.00 p.m. (Order 1349)	
1/12/31 Pay increased to HK.Tls. 28.00 p.m. (Order 1892)	

[F.—9]

RECORD: *Revenue* **DEPARTMENT:** *Native Staff.*

RECORD.	REMARKS.
Fan Chin Tsao 樊金濤 *Native of Tientsin*	1st Class Tidewaiter. S & R scheme contributor.
Born 25/5/1900	
10th April 1931 Appointed to Aigun on transfer from Shanghai (on leave till the 9–4–31) as 1st Class Tide @ HK Tls. 115 a month	Reported for duty. 20/5/31 Transferred to pin 1/8/32
1st October, 1932. Pay ceased on transfer to Shanghai (I.G. telegram No 16 of 21/9/32)	Released from duty on ⁷ OCT 1932 post provisionally closed
1st November 1932 Appointed as Senior Out-door Staff officer (1st Class Tidewaiter) temporarily. (I.G. desp. No. 143577)	Reported for duty on

RECORD: *Revenue* **DEPARTMENT:** *Native Staff.*

RECORD.	REMARKS.
Kung Fan-Chao (孔繁詔)	Tingchai
Family Home: Chong Hsien, Chihli 直隸滄縣	Bond No. 11 secured for $50.
Born on : K.H. 19th year, 1st moon, 11th day (27th Feb. 1893)	received 20.12.25
18.Nov.1922: Appointed Boatman/Guard @ HK.Tls. 11 a month (Order No. 905)	Bond renewed on 19th November, 1928.
19.Mar.1923: Reclassed Boatman/Guard @ HK. Tls. a month (Order No. 917)	
27.Apr.1923: Appointed Office Coolie @ HK.H. 11 a month (Order No. 922)	
1.May, 1923: Promoted Tingchai @ HK. Tls. 12 a month. (Order No. 927)	
1.May, 1925: Pay increased to HK Tls. 13 a month (Order No. 1015).	
1.July, 1926: Pay increased from HK Tls.13 to HK Tls. 15 per month (Order No. 1063): Revised scale. I.G.Desp. 302/08299)	
13th Dec. 1926: Pay increased from HK.$ 12.00 to HK.$ 16 a month (Order No. 1088)	
1 Dec 1928 Pay increased from HK.H. 16 to HK 14.4.18 (Order No. 1267)	
1/5/29 Pay increased to HK Tls 19 p.m (Order No. 1272)	
1/12/29 Pay increased to $20 p.m (Order 1303)	
1/12/30 " " " HK Tls 21.00 p.m (Order 1849)	
1/12/31 " " " HK Tls. 22.00 p.m (Order 1892)	

[F.—]

RECORD: Revenue   DEPARTMENT: Native Staff. Outdoor

RECORD.	REMARKS.
P'ei Kuei-chün (裴貴春)	Carpenter
Family home: Chang-li Hsien, Chihli.	Bond No 22 secured for $50
Born Kuang Hsü, 6th year 12th moon 2nd day.	realized 20.12.25
(3. Jan. 1881).	
1920 April 7th: Appointed Carpenter at Aigun Taheiho Customs with pay at	
Hk.Tls. 12.00 per month. (Comm. Order No.373)	
1920. April 7th: Pay increased to Hk.Tls 14.00 per month	
(Circular No 3054 Harbin Order 252)	
1923 Jan.1st: Pay increased from Hk.Tls.14 to Hk.Tls.15 per month (Order No.865)	
1924 Jan.1st: Pay increased from Hk.Tls.15 to Hk.Tls.16 per month (Order No.957)	
1925 Dec.1st: Pay increased from Hk.Tls.16 to Hk.Tls.17 per month (Order No.1038)	
1926 July 1st: Pay increased from Hk.Tls.17 to Hk.Tls.20 per month (Order No.1063) Revised scale: I.G. Desp. 302/108,299)	
1st June 1928: Pay increased from Hk.Tls.20 to Hk.Tls.21 a month (Order No.1191)	
1st June 1929: Pay $25 per month (Order/272.)	
" " 1930: increased $26 " (Order 1320)	
1st June 1931: " " " 27 " (. 1371)	
1st June 1932: " " " 28 " (. 1408)	

RECORD.	REMARKS.
Wei Fu-king (魏福典)	Boatman/Guard
Family home: Hsien Hsien Chihli 直隷獻縣	Bond no. 26 secured for $30 realized 30th Feb. 1946
Born on: K.H. 23rd year 5th moon thirteenth day	
(12th June 1897)	
13th Feb.1923: appointed Boatman @ Hk.Tls. 11 a month (Order No.913)	
19 Mar.1923: Reclassified Boatman/Guard @ Hk. Tls. 11 a month (Order No.917)	
13 Feb.1925: Pay increased to Hk.Tls.12 a month (Order No.1002)	
1st July 1926: Pay increased to Hk.Tls.14 per month (Order no.1063: Revised scale I.G.Desp. 302/108,299)	
1st June 1927: Pay increased to Hk.Tls.15 per month (Order No.1193)	
1st June 1929 " " " 16 " (" 1269)	
" " 1930 " " " 17 " (" 1320)	
1st June 1931 " " " 18 " (" 1371)	
1st June 1932 " " " 19 " (" 1408)	

RECORD:	DEPARTMENT: *Native Staff.*
RECORD.	**REMARKS.**

Continued from Page 93.

Tson Yui-Hwei (开玉官), Watches

1st Dec. 1927 Pay increased to HK.Tls. 19 a month (vide Order No. 1109)

1. Dec. 1928 Pay increased from HK.X. 19 to HK.Tls. 21 p.m. (Order No. 1266)

1/12/29 Pay to F.22 p.m. (Order 1305)

1/12/29 Pay to F.22 p.m. (Order 1305)

1/12/30 Pay increased to HK.Tls. 23.00 p.m. (Order No. 1349)

1/12/31 " " " 24.00 p.m. (Order 139.)

REMARKS: Granted sanitary leave from 5/1/31. (No. 1 boatman & the No. 6 watcher, interior, and from hisplaces provided a substitute to attend to boatman's work.) Returned to duty: 3. 4. 31.

RECORD: *Revenue*	DEPARTMENT: *Native Staff.*
RECORD.	**REMARKS.**

✓ Tao Tê-sheng (陶德盛) — Office Coolie.

Chinese born: Kwang Hsü 27th year 4th moon, 5th day (22nd May 1901).

REMARKS: Bond No. 18 secured for $20 — verified 20.12.25.

Family home: Tsinan Fu, Shantung 山東濟南府

1918 July 1st Appointed Office Coolie in the Aigun (Taheiho) Customs at Rs. 12.00 per month (Order No. 2787)

1919 Apr. 1st Pay revised from Rbs. 12. to HK.Tls. 6.50 per month. (Order No. 3163)

1919 June 1st Pay increased to HK.Tls. 7.00 per month (Order No. 3115.)

1920 Jan. 1st Pay revised to HK.Tls. 8.00 per month (Order No. 3321)

1920 Apr. 1st Pay increased to HK.Tls. 9.00 per month (Circular No. 3054 & Order No. 3536)

1922 Jan. 1st Pay increased from HK.Tls. 9 to HK.Tls. 12 per month (Order No. 868)

1924 Jan. 1st Pay increased from HK.Tls. 12 to HK.Tls. 13 per month (Order No. 951)

1925 Dec. 1st Pay increased from HK.Tls. 13 to HK.Tls. 14 per month (Order No. 1038)

1926 July 1st Pay increased from HK.Tls. 14 to HK.Tls. 16 per month (Order No. 1063); Revised scale 3 by Desp. 302/103, 297

1. Dec. 1928 Pay increased from HK.Tls. 16 to 77 (Order No. 1266)

1/12/29 Pay increased to HK.Tls. 19 p.m. (Order 1272)

1/12/30 " " " 20 p.m. (Order 1349)

Left page

√ ° Tsoon Lan-ting (鄂 田鸟)

Chinese Born Kwang Hsü, 12th year, 12th moon, 18th day. (Jan 12th 1887)

Family Home, Kwang Hsien, Shantung 山東 青岛

1924 Octob. 11th: Appointed Boatman/Guard at the Aiqun/Tabike Customs at H.K.$. 11.00 per month (Order No. 965)

1926 July 1st: Pay increased from H.K.$. 11 to H.K.$. 13 per month (Order no. 1063): Revised scale I.G. Desp. 303/108.299

14th Dec. 1926: Pay increased from H.K.$ 13.00 to H.K.$ 14.00 a month (Order No. 1088)

1. Dec. 1928 Pay increased from H.K.$ 14 to 15 (Order 1216)

1/3/29 Pay increased to H.K.$ 16 p.m. (Order 1272)

1/12/29 Pay to $17 p.m. (- 1308)

1/12/30 Pay increased to H.K.$.18.00 p.m. (Order No. 349)

1/12/31 " " " 19.00 p.m. (Order No. 1392)

Boatman/Guard

Bond No. 41 secured for $30.00

indized 20.12.25

1/3/29 transferred to Lower Barrier Warned for negligence (Order 1274)

Fined $1/00 for deserting his duties Order 1388

Right page

√ Kwang Shu-hsing (王 樹興)

Chinese Born Kwang Hsü, 13th year, 7th moon, 27th day (14th Sept. 1887)

Family Home, Loh Ting Hsien, Chili 直隸 樂亭 縣

1924 November 1st: Appointed Boatman/Guard at the Aiqun/Tabike Customs at H.K.$. 11.00 per month (Order No. 975)

1926 July 1st: Pay increased from H.K.$. 11 to H.K.$. 13 per month (Order No. 1063): Revised scale I.G. Desp. 303/108.299

1st Dec. 1926: Pay increased from H.K.$ 13.00 to H.K.$ 14.00 a month (Order No. 1088)

1. Dec. 1928 : Pay increased from H.K.$ 14 to 15. (Order No. 1216)

1 March 1929 Pay increased to $ 16 p.m (Order 1272)

1/12/30 Pay increased to H.K.$. 17.00 p.m. (Order No 349)

1/12/31 " " 18.00 p.m (Order No. 1392)

Boatman/Guard

Bond No. 42 secured for $30.00

indized 30th October 1926

1/1/29 transferred to Head Office from Lower Barrier

[F—4]

RECORD: *Revenue* **DEPARTMENT:** *Native Staff.*

RECORD.	REMARKS.
Yao Wên-shêng (姚文盛)	Night Watchman
Family Home: Anhui, yi hsien 安徽邑縣	
Born on: K.H. 11th year, 5th moon, 28th day	Bond No. 21 secured for $30—
(10th June 1885)	
1. Sept. 1922: Appointed Night watcher @ Hk.	Verified on 8.2.1926
Ho. 11 a month (Order No. 893)	
1. Sept. 1924: Pay increased from Hk Ho. 11 to	
Hk Ho. 12 per month (Order No. 995)	
1st June 1926: Pay increased to Ho Ho. 13	
a month (Order No. 1058)	
1st. July 1926: Pay increased from Hk Ho. 13 to Hk Ho. 14	
per month (Order No. 1063): Revised	
scale. J.G. Desp. 302/108,299)	
1st Dec. 1926: Pay increased from Hk. $14.00 to	
Hk. $ 14.00 a month (Order No. 1088)	
1. Dec. 1928: Pay increased from Hk Ho. 15	
to 16 (order No. 1216)	
1/3/29 Pay increased to $17 p.m. (Order No. 1272)	
1/12/29 " - " 18 p.m. (Order No. 1849)	

RECORD: *Revenue* **DEPARTMENT:** *Native Staff.*

RECORD.	REMARKS.
Chü Ts'ai (句財)	Boatman / Guard No. 1
Family Home: Lai Shui Hsien, Chihli 直隸涞水縣	
Born on: K.H. 18th year, 8th moon, 24th day	Bond No. 34 secured for $30.00
(14th October 1892)	Verified 26.10.26
4. May, 1923: Appointed Boatmen / Guard @ Hk.	
Ho. 11 a month (Order No. 926)	
4. May, 1925: Pay increased from Hk Ho. 11 to Hk Ho. 12	
a month (Order No. 1015)	
1st July, 1926: Pay increased from Hk Ho. 12 to Hk Ho. 14	
per month (Order No. 1063): Revised	
Scale, J.G. Desp. 302/108,299)	
1st Dec. 1926: Promoted No. 1 Boatman / Guard with	1/1 Pay Foreclass Hk Ho. 2 in addition
pay at Hk $14.00 a month (Order No. 1087)	of port AHS for being No. 1
1st June, 1927: Pay increased to Hk. Ho. 15 a month (Order No. 1168)	Boatman (Order No. 1268)
1. June 1929 " - " - " 16 (" - 1368)	
1. June 1929 - " - " 18 (" - 1292a)	Transferred to page 161
" " " 1930 " - " - 19 (" - 1381)	

Wang Te - shan (王德山)

Family home: Jenkiu Hsien, Chili (饶阳任丘县)
Born on: K.H. 21st year, 10ch day of 2nd moon (10th moon 1895)
7ch Feb. 1925: Appointed Boatman/Guard
@ HK Tls. 11.00 a month (Order No 1002)
1st July, 1926: Pay increased from HK Tls. 11 to HK Tls 13
per month (Order No. 1063): Revised
scale, I. G. Desp. 302/108, 299.)
1927 June 14: Pay increased from HK Tls. 13 to HK Tls. 14 per month
(Order #1129)
1929 June 1 Pay increased 15 HK Tls. a month (order 1261)
1929 March   "   "   - 16   (" 1272)
1930 June 1   "   "   17   (" 1320)
1931 June 1st "   "   - 18 (" 1371)
1932 " 1st   "   "   - 19 (- 1408)

	Boatman/Guard
	Bond No. 43 secured for $300
	verified 20.12.25
	1/1/29 transferred to Head Office from Upper Barrier
	See New Chin-Teku This records are in two books this year

RECORD: Revenue   DEPARTMENT: Native Staff.

RECORD.	REMARKS.
1 Yü Te-yuan (于德元)	Boatman/Guard
Born: K.H. 11th Year, 8h moon, 13th day (18 Sept 1885)	Bond No. 46 secured for $300
	verified 20.12.25
Family home: Yii Hsien, Pasting Fu, Chikli 玉林保定府	
18. April, 1925: Appointed Boatman/Guard at HK Tls. 11.00 a month. (Order No. 1011)	Boatman's work page 136
1st July, 1926: Pay increased from HK Tls. 11 to HK Tls. 13 per month (Order No. 1063): Revised scale: I. G. Desp. 302/108, 299.	
1927 June 1st: Pay increased from HK Tls. 13 to HK Tls. 14 per month (Order # 1129)	
1929 Jan 14: Pay increased 15 HK Tls. (Order # 1263)	1/1/29 transferred to Upper Barrier. Returned from barrier at opening of navigation Sealon
" " " " - .16 (" - 1272a)	
1930 " " " - .17 (" - 1320)	transferred to page 165.
2 Chin Ching-yueh (秦景悦)	House Coolie gatekeeper made office coolie from 1st Aug. 1925 I. G. No. 243/104.330
Born: K.H. 23rd year, 2nd moon, 22nd day (24 mar 1897)	Bond No. 47 secured for $30.00
	verified 20.12.25
Family home: Chao Yang Hsien, Chikli.	
10th May, 1925: Appointed House Coolie at HK Tls. 10.00 a month	
1st Aug. 1925: Appointed gatekeeper at HK Tls. 11. a month. I. G. No. 243/104.330.	
1st July, 1926: Pay increased from HK Tls. 11 to HK Tls. 13 per month (Order No. 1063): Revised scale: I.G. Desp. 302/108, 299.)	
1927, June 1st: Pay increased from HK Tls. 13 to HK Tls. 14 per month (Order # 1129)	Carried to page 124

Left card:

Chang Tien-chen (張殿辰):

Born: K. H. 20th year 2nd moon 24th day
(30th March 1894)

Family home: Paoting Hsien, Chihli (保定 縣)

1st Oct. 1925: Appointed House Coolie, Commissioner's House @ H.K. Tls 10 a month

1st July 1926: Pay increased from H.K. Tls 10 to H.K. Tls 11 per month (Order No 1063); Revised Scale I. G. Desp. 302/08, 299)

1st Dec. 1926: Pay increased from H.K. $11.00 to H.K. $12.00 a month (Order No. 1188)

1st Dec. 1927: Pay increased from H.K. $12 to H.K. $13 a month (Order No. 1273)

1/3/29 Pay increased to $14 p.m (Order No. 1272)
1/12/29 Pay increased to $16 (Order 1505)
1/12/31 Pay increased to H.K $17 p.m (Order 1892)

Remarks:

House Coolie, Commr's House.

Bond No. 51 secured for $30.00
verified 20.12.25

Gatekeeper Commr's House (Order No. 1273)
Granted 3 months' leave from 1/1/31
Substitute provided
Returned to Duty 05.1.31

Right card:

[F.—4]

RECORD: Revenue   DEPARTMENT: Native Staff.

RECORD.	REMARKS.

Tsou Chi-yü (鄒振吉)

Born: Kuang-hsü 27th year 12th Moon 7th Day (January Feb 1902)

Family home: 山東黃縣

16th January 1927: Appointed Boatman / Guard at H.K $12 a month (Order No. 1097)

1st June 1928: Pay increased from H.K $12 to H.K $13 a month (Order No. 1193)

1st Jan 1929: Pay increased to H.K.$14 (Order 1263)

1st July 1929: Transferred to the rank of Tingchai with pay at H.K. Tls. 15.00 per month (Order No. 1267)

1st June 1930 Pay increased to $16 (Order 1330)
1st June 1931 " " = $17 (Order 1371)
1st June 1932 " " = $18 (" 1460)

Remarks:

Boatman / Guard

Bond No. 95 secured for Bellew thirty.
verified 20th Jan 1927

1st Jan 1929 Transferred to Lower Service
1/5/29 Transferred to Head Office Tingchai

[F.—9]

RECORD: *Revenue*   DEPARTMENT: *Native Staff.*

RECORD.	REMARKS.
<u>Kuo Ching Chiu</u> (郭敬九)	<u>Native Watcher</u>
<u>Born</u>: Kuang-hsü 27 year 8th Moon, 1st day.	Bond no. 56. received for
(13th September, 1901)	$50.00
	Verified on 11th March, 1927.
<u>Family home</u>: 山東招遠縣.	
<u>12th March, 1927</u>: appointed Native Watcher	
with Pay at HK$18.00 a month (order no. 1111)	
<u>1st June, 1928</u>: Pay increased from HK$18 to	1/4/29 transferred to Engine
HK$19 a month (order no. 1191)	
<u>1. June 1929</u> Pay increased from HK$	
19 to 20 (order 1263)	
1 June 1929 Pay HK$21 (Order 12721)	
1 " 1930 " increased " $22 (" 1320)	
1 " 1931 " " " $23 (" 1371)	
1 " 1932 " " " $24 (" 1466)	

Name	Rank	Present		Date of Birth	First Appointment		
		Pay	Port Allowance		Rank	Date	Pay
Yü Fu Shou ch'i	N.Watcher	₹ 33	₹ 5	20y 11m 28d 24.12.94	N.Watcher	6. 7.17	R 18
Ch'u Ming- an	- do -	31	5	9y 8m 5d 5. 9.83	- do -	1.10.19	₹ 9
Ch'en Ch'ang kuei	- do -	28	5	16y 3m 8d 26. 4.90	- do -	1. 8.22	₹ 16
Tsou Yin- chiu	- do -	24	5	18y 5m 2d 27. 5.92	Boatman	20. 7.22	₹ 11
Kuo Ching-	- do -	23	5	27y 8m 1d 13. 9.01	N Watcher	12. 3.27	₹ 18
Chü Ts'ai	Boatman/Guard	20	6	18y 8m 24d 14.10.92	Boatman /Guard	4. 5.23	₹ 11
Wei Fu-hsing t'ing	- do -	18	4	23y 5m 13d 12. 6 97	Boatman	13. 2.23	₹ 11
Tsou Lan- hsing	- do -	19	4	12y 12m 18d 12. 1.87	Boatman -Guard	11.10 24	₹ 11
Wang Shu-	- do -	18	4	13y 7m 27d 14. 9.87	- do -	1.11.24	₹ 11
Wang Te-shan	- do -	18	4	21y 2m 10d 6. 3.95	- do -	7. 2.25	₹ 11
Yü Te-yuan ts'ai	- do -	18	4	14y 8m 13d 18. 9.88	- do -	18. 4.25	₹ 11
Wang Chin- chao	- do -	20	4	19y 1m 14d 2. 3.93	Mounted Courier	1. 1.23§	R 27
K'ung Fan- fen	T'ingch'ai	22	5	19y 1m 11d 27.2. 93	Boatman	18.11.22	₹ 11
Tsou Chen- shêng	- do -	17	5	27y 12m 7d 17. 1.02	Boatman /Guard	16. 1.27	₹ 12
T'ao Tê- shêng	Office Coolie	20	4	27y 4m 5d 22. 5.01	Off.Coolie	1. 7.18	R 12
Yao Wen- chen	N.Watchman	18	4	11y 4m 28d 11. 6.85	N.Watcher	1. 9.22	₹ 11
Chang Tien- yüeh	Gate Keeper	17	4	20y 2m 24d 30. 3 .94	Coolie House	1.10.25	₹ 10
Ch'in Ching- ch'un	House Coolie	17	3.50	23y 2m 22d 24. 3.97	- do -	10. 5.25	₹ 10
P'ei Kuei-	Carpenter	27	5	6y 12m 4d 3. 1.81	Carpenter	7. 4.20	₹ 12

§Joined Service 1.1.17 as Mounted Courier; appointed Boatman/Guard from 1.6.27; seniority from 1.1.23,vide remarks on Sept.Qr.,1929, A/c.A,Sch.1:3,Vr.10.
Complications between Chang Tien-ch'en and Ch'in Ching-yüeh: 10.5.25 Ch'in appointed House Coolie; 1.8.25 made Gatekeeper; 1.10.25 Chang appointed House Coolie;1930 made Gatekeeper; and at the same time Ch'in re-appointed House Coolie: see I.G.No. 104,330, and Commr's Order No.1273 of 1930.

All Boatmen were, since the Commr's Ordr No. 917, reclassified as Boatman/Guards.

Due to Promotion 1.3.3?

" " 1.12.3?

" " 1.6.33

" " 1.12.33

Name	Rank	Date of Birth (Kuang Hsü)	First Appointment Date	First Appointment Rank	Pay	Present Pay			Increase Next Date due	Pay	Remarks
						Pay	Inc. B.d. from which month	Pay			
Yü Fu Shou	Native Watcher	24.12.94(20y 11m 28d)	6. 7.17	Native Watcher	R.18	$33	$5	1.12.31	1.12.32	$34	
Ch'u Ming-ch'i	- do -	5. 9.85(6y. 8m 5d)	1.10.19	- do -	$ 9	$31	$5	1.12.31	1.12.32	$32	
Ch'en Ch'ang-an	- do -	23. 4.90(16y 3m 8d)	1. 8.22	- do -	$16	$28	$5	1.12.31	1.12.32	$29	
Tsou Yin kuei	- do -	27. 5.92(18y 5m 2d)	20. 7.22	Boatman	$11	$24	$5	1.12.31	1.12.32	$25	
Kuo Ching-chiu	- do -	13. 9.01(27y 8m 1d)	12. 3.27	Native Watcher	$18	$24	$5	1. 6.32	1. 6.33	$25	
Chü Ts'ai	Boatman/Guard	14.10.92(16y 8m 24d)	4. 5.23	Boatman/Guard	$11	$21	$6	1. 6.32	1. 6.33	$22	
Wei Fu-hsing	- do -	12. 6.97(23y 5m 13d)	13. 2.23	Boatman	$11	$19	$4	1. 6.32	1. 6.33	$20	
Tsou Lan-t'ing	- do -	12. 1.87(12y 12m 18d)	11.10.24	Boatman/Guard	$11	$19	$4	1.12.31	1.12.32	$20	
Wang Shu-hsing	- do -	14. 9.87(13y 7m 27d)	1.11.24	- do -	$11	$18	$4	1.12.31	1.12.32	$19	
Wang Te-shan	- do -	6. 3.95(21y 2m 10d)	7. 8.25	- do -	$11	$19	$4	1. 6.32	1. 6.33	$20	
Yü Te-yüan	- do -	18. 9.83(14y 3m 15d)	18. 4.25	- do -	$11	$19	$4	1. 6.32	1. 6.33	$20	
Wang Chin-ts'ai	T'ingch'ai	2. 3.93(19y 1m 14d)	1. 1.17	Mounted Courier	R.27	$20	$4	1. 6.31			
K'ung Fan-shao	T'ingch'ai	27. 2.93(19y 1m 11d)	18.11.22	Boatman	$11	$22	$5	1.12.31	1.12.32	$23	
Tsou Chen fen	- do -	17. 1.02(27y 12m 7d)	16. 1.27	Boatman/Guard	$12	$18	$5	1. 6.32	1. 6.33	$19	
T'ao Te-sheng	Office Coolie	22. 5.01(27y 4m 5d)	1. 7.18	Office Coolie	R.12	$20	$4	1.12.30	1.12.32	$21	
Yao Wen sheng	Night Watchman	11. 6.85(11y 4m 28d)	1. 9.22	Night Watchman	$11	$18	$4	1.12.30	1.12.32	$19	
Ch'in Ching-yüeh	House Coolie	24. 3.97(23y 2m 28d)	10. 5.25	House Coolie	$10	$17	$1	1. 6.31	1. 6.33	$18	
Chang Tien-ch'en	Gatekeeper	30. 3.94(20y 2m 24d)	1.10.25	House Coolie	$10	$17	$4	1.12.31	1.12.33	$18	
P'ei Kuei-ch'un	Carpenter	3. 1.81(6y 12m 4d)	7. 4.20	Carpenter	$12	$28	$1	1. 6.32	1. 6.33	$29	

关员清册

[F-9]　　　　　　　　　税课司：华籍职员

职员人事记录		备注
王德懋（Wang Tê-mao） 直隶 出生于光绪十九年八月二十三日（1893 年 10 月 2 日）		二等一级税务员 养老（退休）储金计划参保人
1921/10/1	任命为瑷珲关三等同文供事正前班,月薪海关两 70 两（瑷珲关改为独立关,见总税务司署第 1/85630 号令）	担保书于 1926 年 1 月 14 日撤销（F-52）
1921/11/1	擢升为二等同文供事副后班,月薪海关两 80 两（见第 289 号特别擢升公报）	修订酬劳金预计发放日期为 1931 年 3 月 31 日（见第 3704 号通令及第 47 次审计记录）
1922/6/1	擢升为二等同文供事后班,月薪海关两 100 两（见第 3314 号通令第 2 条）	
1923/5/14	发放第一阶段（每十年至十二年一次）自 1912 年 1 月 22 日至 1923 年 4 月 16 日的酬劳金海关两 1200.00 两（见 1923 年海关总税务公署致瑷珲关第 117/94249 号令）	
1925/6/1	擢升为二等同文供事中班,月薪海关两 115 两（见第 338 号特别擢升公报）	
1926/7/1	月薪自海关两 115 两增至海关两 130 两（见第 3704 号通令——薪酬等级表修订版）	
1928/6/1	擢升为二等一级税务员,月薪海关两 150 两（见第 380 号特别擢升公报）	
1929/5/1	月薪自海关两 150 两增至海关两 170 两（见总税务司署第 3882 号通令第 2 条）	

关员清册

[F-9]　　　　　　　　　税课司：华籍职员

职员人事记录		备注
王德懋（Wang Tê-mao）		二等一级税务员
1929/12/1	月薪自调任至津海关后停止发放（见总税务司署1929年11月25日电令及第125064号令）	1929年12月10日离职
1930/2/1	再次就任于瑷珲关（见总税务司署第510/125754号令）	1930年1月27日报到上任
1930/6/1	擢升为一等二级税务员,月薪海关两190两（见第412号特别擢升公报）	1931年4月14日发放上海海关两规平银2539.92两即海关两2280.00两,作为其第二阶段自1923年4月17日至1931年3月31日的酬劳金（见总税务司署第589/133933号令及第4335号通令）
1932/10/1	月薪自调任至江海关时停止发放（见总税务司署1932年9月21日第16号电令）	
1932/11/1	临时任命为一等二级税务员（见总税务司署第143876号令）	
		1932年10月7日离职,临时关闭口岸
		于　报到上任

关员清册

[F-9] 税课司：华籍职员

职员人事记录		备注
杨存厚（Yang Ts'un-hou） 直隶 出生于光绪二年十一月二十八日（1877年1月12日）		养老（退休）储金计划参保人
1921/10/1	任命为瑷珲关三等同文供事正前班,月薪海关两30两（瑷珲关改为独立关,见总税务司署第1/85630号令）	担保书保存于哈尔滨关
1922/1/1	月薪自海关两30两增至海关两35两（见海关总税务公署第2986号通令及第862号税务司谕）	
1922/5/1	任命为瑷珲关文案,月薪海关两40（见总税务司署第46/89536号令）	文案
1923/5/1	月薪自海关两40两增至海关两55两（见总税务司署第3429号通令第2条及第936号税务司谕）	
1924/8/18	发放第一阶段（每十年至十二年一次）自1913年7月31日至1924年7月23日的酬劳金海关两660.00两（见1924年海关总税务公署致瑷珲关第186/99873号令）	1928年5月1日 月薪自海关两70两增至海关两75两（见总税务司署第3429号通令、第3704号通令及第1185号税务司谕）
1925/5/1	月薪自海关两55两增至海关两60两（见总税务司署3429号通令第2条及第1014号税务司谕）	
1926/7/1	月薪自海关两60两增至海关两70两（见第3704号通令——薪酬等级表修订版）	修订酬劳金发放日期为1932年12月7日（见瑷珲关第416号呈）

职员人事记录	备注
1926/7/1　每月发放的特殊津贴海关两 10.00 两缩减至海关两 3.00 两,根据总税务司署第 3429 号通令及第 3704 号通令,下次增薪之日起停止减薪(见总税务司署第 811 号通令) 1929/3/1　月薪增至海关两 90 两(见总税务司署第 3911 号通令)	

关员清册

[F-9] 　　　　　　　　　税课司: 华籍职员

职员人事记录	备注
杨存厚(Yang Ts'un-hou)	汉文文牍员
1929/12/1　准予带薪休假六个月,休假结束后奉命前往瑷珲关报到上任(见总税务司署第 500/125140 号令)	1930 年 5 月 13 日休假结束后报到上任
1929/3/1　月薪增至海关两 90 两(见总税务司署第 3911 号通令)	自 1929 年 3 月 1 日起发放满洲里特别地区津贴海关两 10.00 两(休假期间无津贴),自 1931 年 3 月 1 日起,停止发放满洲里特别地区津贴,见总税务司署第 578/132844 号令
1931/3/1　月薪自自海关两 90 两增至海关两 100 两(见总税务司署第 577/132835 号令)	
月薪自调任至江海关时停止发放(见总税务司署 1932 年 9 月 21 日第 16 号电令) 1932/10/1	1932 年 10 月 7 日离职,口岸临时关闭

关员清册

[F-9] 税课司：华籍职员

职员人事记录		备注
李永坡（Li Yung-p'o） 直隶 出生于光绪十一年八月十七日（1885 年 9 月 25 日）		录事 养老（退休）储金计划参保人
1922/6/22	任命为瑷珲关录事,月薪海关两 20 两（见总税务司署第 46/89536 号令）	（担保书于 1926 年 1 月 7 日查实并存档于海关）
1923/5/1	月薪自海关两 20 两增至海关两 25 两（见海关总税务公署第 3429 号通令第 2 条及第 936 号税务司谕）	修订酬劳金发放日期为 1931 年 6 月 22 日（第 3873 号通令）（参见瑷珲关第 416 号呈）
1925/6/22	月薪自海关两 25 两增至海关两 30 两（见海关总税务公署第 3429 号通令及第 1020 号税务司谕）	1929 年 11 月 9 日转移至哈尔滨
1926/7/1	月薪自海关两 30 两增至 37 两（见海关总税务公署第 3704 号通令——薪酬等级表修订版）	1930 年 5 月 31 日返回瑷珲
1926/7/1	每月发放的特殊津贴海关两 10.00 两缩减至海关两 5.00 两,根据总税务司署第 3429 号通令及第 3704 号通令,下次增薪之日起停止减薪（见总税务司署第 307/109033 号令及总税务司署第 811 号通函）	自 1929 年 3 月 1 日起发放满洲里特别地区津贴（已发放海关两 5.00 两）。自 1931 年 3 月 1 日起仅发放满洲里特别地区津贴海关两 5 海关两（见总税务司署第 578/132844 号令）
1928/6/22	月薪自海关两 37 两增至海关两 42 两（见总税务司署第 3429 号通令、第 3704 号通令及第 1185 号税务司谕）	
1929/3/1	月薪自海关两 42 两增至海关两 47 两（见总税务司署第 3911 号通令）	1931 年 7 月 15 日收到海关两 624 两（第一阶段酬劳金）总税务司署致瑷珲关第 135701 号令

	职员人事记录	备注
1931/3/1	月薪自海关两 47 两增至海关两 52 两（见总税务司署第 577/132835 号令）	1931 年 7 月 22 日重订担保书（总税务司署第 4254 号通令）
1932/10/1	调任至江海关时停止发放薪俸（见 1932 年 9 月 21 日总税务司署第 16 号电令）	1932 年 10 月 7 日离职，口岸临时关闭。

关员清册

[F-9] 税课司：华籍职员

职员人事记录		备注
陈培因（Chen Pei Yin） 福州 出生于光绪三十二年十一月二十一日（1907年1月5日）		三等二级税务员 养老（退休）储金计划参保人
1930/5/1	任命为三等二级税务员（自闽海关调任），月薪海关两115.00两（见总税务司署第519/126761号令）	1930年4月30日报到上任 因担保书已失效将其保存在闽海关（见总税务司署第570/132112号令），经徐翔九及吴焚目签名的新担保书保存在瑷珲关（1931年1月15日将便条交回至总务科税务司）
1931/5/1	任命为四等一级帮办，月薪海关两150两（见第424号特别擢升公报） 准予自1932年9月1日起带薪休假四个月，休假结束后陈培因需前往津海关报到待命（见总税务司署第658/141561号令）	1931年7月22日退回担保书（见第4254号通令）

关员清册

税课司：华籍职员

职员人事记录		备注
于福寿（Yü Fu-shou） 山东登州府黄县 出生于光绪二十年十一月二十八日（1894年12月24日）		巡役 重订1号担保书，担保金为50银圆，1925年12月20日查实无误
1917/7/6	任命为瑷珲关巡役，月薪18.00卢布（见哈尔滨关第2468号命令）	
1918/11/1	月薪增至20卢布（见哈尔滨关第2900号命令）	
1919/4/1	月薪自20卢布缩减至海关两10.50两（见哈尔滨关第3163号命令）	
1919/10/1	月薪增至海关两11.00两（见哈尔滨关第3225号命令）	
1920/1/1	月薪自11.00海关两增至海关两13.00两（见哈尔滨关第3321号命令）	
1920/4/1	月薪增至海关两15两（见第3054号通令及哈尔滨关第3536号命令）	
1922/1/1	月薪自海关两15两增至海关两20两（见第865号命令）	
1924/1/1	月薪自海关两20两增至海关两22两（见第951号通令）	
1925/12/1	月薪自海关两22两增至海关两24两（见第1038号命令）	

职员人事记录		备注
1926/7/1	月薪自海关两 24 两增至海关两 26 两（见第 1063 号命令及总税务司署第 302/108299 号令——薪酬等级表修订版）	
1927/12/1	月薪自海关两 26 两增至海关两 28 两（见第 1459 号命令）	授命谴责其有开设赌场的嫌疑（见第 1354 号命令）
1929/3/1	月薪增至海关两 30 两（见第 1272 号命令）	
1929/12/1	月薪增至海关两 31 两（见第 1205 号命令）	
1930/12/1	月薪增至海关两 32 两（见第 1349 号命令）	
1931/12/1	月薪增至海关两 33 两（见第 1392 号命令）	
1932/9/30	口岸临时关闭时付清薪俸海关两 228 两（见总税务司署 1932 年 9 月 21 日第 16 号电报） 发放六个月的薪俸（见第 1417 号人事命令）	

关员清册

[F-9]

税课司：华籍职员

职员人事记录	备注
褚铭岐（Chu Ming Chi） 直隶顺天府 出生于光绪九年八月五日（1883年9月5日）	巡役 重订2号担保书,担保金为60银圆,1925年12月20日查实无误
1919/10/1　任命为巡役,月薪海关两9.00两（见哈尔滨关第3224号命令）	
1920/1/1　月薪自海关两9.00两增至海关两11.00两（见哈尔滨关第3321号命令）	
1920/4/1　月薪增至海关两14两（见第3054号通令及第3536号命令）	
1922/1/1　月薪自海关两14两增至海关两18两（见第865号通令）	
1924/1/1　月薪自海关两18两增至海关两20两（见第951号通令）	
1925/12/1　月薪自海关两20两增至海关两22两（见第1038号通令）	
1926/7/1　月薪自海关两22两增至海关两24两（见第1063号命令及总税务司署第302/108299号令——薪酬等级表修订版）	
1927/12/1　月薪自海关两24两增至海关两26两（见第1459号命令）	1932年9月30口岸临时关闭时日付清薪俸（见总税务司署1932年9月21日第16号电令）,发放六个月的月薪海关两216两（见第1417号人事命令）
1929/3/1　月薪增至海关两28两（见第1272号命令）	

职员人事记录		备注
1929/12/1	月薪增至海关两 29 两（见第 1305 号命令）	
1930/12/1	月薪增至海关两 30.00 两（见第 1349 号命令）	
1931/12/1	月薪增至海关两 31.00 两（见第 1392 号命令）	

关员清册

税课司：华籍职员

职员人事记录		备注
<div align="center">陈长安（Chên Ch'ang-an） 黑龙江瑷珲县 出生于光绪十六年三月八日（1890 年 4 月 26 日）</div>		巡役 重订 5 号担保书，担保金为 50 银圆，1925 年 12 月 20 日查实无误 1929 年 4 月 1 日调任至总关 准予自 1930 年 10 月 22 日至 1930 年 10 月 29 日休假七天
1922/8/1	任命为就地巡役，月薪海关两 16 两（见第 892 号命令）	
1924/8/1	月薪增至海关两 18 两（见第 979 号命令）	
1926/6/1	月薪增至海关两 20 两（见第 1059 号通令）	
1926/7/1	月薪自海关两 20 两增至海关两 22 两（见第 1063 号命令及总税务司署第 302/108299 号令——薪酬等级表修订版） 撤销上述加薪事宜（见第 1075 号令及总税务司署第 309/109333 号令）	
1926/12/1	月薪自海关两 20 两增至海关两 22 两（见第 1088 号命令）	
1928/12/1	月薪自海关两 22 两增至海关两 24 两（见第 1216 号命令）	
1929/3/1	月薪增至海关两 25 两（见第 1272 号命令）	
1929/12/1	月薪增至海关两 26 两（见第 1305 号命令）	
1930/12/1	月新增至海关两 27 两（见第 1349 号命令）	
1931/12/1	月薪增至海关两 28 两（见第 1392 号命令）	

关员清册

[F-9]　　　　　　　　　　税课司：华籍职员

职员人事记录		备注
樊金藻（Fan Chin Tsao） 天津 出生于 1900 年 5 月 25 日		一等稽查员 养老（退休）储金计划参保人
1931/4/10	任命为瑷珲关一等稽查员（自江海关调任），月薪海关两 115.00 两（休假至 1931 年 4 月 9 日）	1931 年 5 月 20 日报到上任 1932 年 4 月 1 调任至瑷珲关
1932/10/1	月薪自调任至江海关时停止发放（见总税务司署 1932 年 9 月 21 日第 16 号电令）	1932 年 10 月 7 日离职，口岸临时关闭
1932/11/1	临时任命为超等外班职员（一等稽查员）（见海关总税务司第 143877 号令）	于　报到上任

关员清册

　　　　　　　税课司：华籍职员

职员人事记录	备注
孔繁诏（K'ung Fan-chao） 直隶沧县 出生于光绪十九年一月十一日（1893 年 2 月 27 日）	听差 重订 11 号担保书,担保金为 50 银圆,1925 年 12 月 20 日查实无误 担保书于 1928 年 11 月 19 日重订
1922/11/18　任命为水手,月薪海关两 11 两（见第 905 号命令）	
1923/3/19　任命为水手 / 卫兵,月薪海关两 11 两（见第 917 号命令）	
1923/4/27　任命为差役,月薪海关两 11 两（见第 922 号命令）	
1923/5/1　任命为听差,月薪海关两 12.00 两（见第 927 号命令）	
1925/5/1　月薪增至海关两 13 两（见第 1015 号命令）	
1926/7/1　月薪自海关两 13 两增至海关两 15 两（见第 1063 号命令及总税务司署第 302/108299 号令——薪酬等级表修订版）	
1926/12/1　月薪自海关两 15 两增至海关两 16 两（见第 1088 号命令）	
1928/12/1　月薪自海关两 16 两增至海关两 17 两（见第 1216 号命令）	
1929/3/1　月薪增至海关两 19 两（见第 1272 号命令）	
1929/12/1　月薪增至海关两 20 两（见第 1305 号命令）	
1930/12/1　月薪增至海关两 21 两（见第 1349 号命令）	
1931/12/1　月薪增至海关两 22 两（见第 1392 号命令）	

关员清册

[F-9]　　　　　　　　　　　税课司：华籍职员

职员人事记录	备注
裴贵春（P'ei Kuei-ch'un） 直隶昌黎县 出生于光绪六年十二月四日（1881 年 1 月 3 日）	木匠 重订 22 号担保书, 担保金为 50 银圆, 1925 年 12 月 20 查实无误
1920/4/7　任命为瑷珲关 / 大黑河木匠, 月薪海关两 12.00 两（见哈尔滨关第 3378 号命及税务司谕令）	
1920/4/7　月薪增至海关两 14.00 两（见第 3054 号通令及哈尔滨关第 3536 号命令）	
1922/1/1　月薪自海关两 14 两增至海关两 15 两（见第 865 号命令）	
1924/1/1　月薪自海关两 15 两增至海关两 16 两（第 951 号命令）	
1925/12/1　月薪自海关两 16 两增至海关两 17 两（见第 1038 号命令）	
1926/7/1　月薪自海关两 17 两增至海关两 20 两（见第 1063 号命令及总税务司署第 302/108299 号令——薪酬等级表修订版）	
1928/6/1　月薪自海关两 20 两增至海关两 21 两（见第 1191 号命令）	
1929/6/1　月薪增至海关两 25 两（见第 2720 号命令）	
1930/6/1　月薪增至海关两 26 两（见第 1320 号命令）	
1931/6/1　月薪增至海关两 27 两（见第 1371 号命令）	
1932/6/1　月薪增至海关两 28 两（见第 1406 号命令）	

关员清册

[F-9]   税课司：华籍职员

职员人事记录		备注
魏福兴（Wei Fu Hsing） 直隶献县 出生于光绪二十三年五月十三日（1897年6月12日）		水手／卫兵 重订26号担保书，担保金为30银圆，1926年10月30日查实无误
1923/2/13	任命为水手,月薪海关两11两（见第913号命令）	
1923/3/19	再委任为水手／卫兵,月薪海关两11两（见第917号命令）	
1925/2/13	月薪增至海关两12两（见第1003号命令）	
1926/7/1	月薪增至海关两14两（见第1063号命令及总税务司署第302/108299号令——薪酬等级表修订版）	
1927/6/1	月薪增至海关两15两（见第1129号命令及总税务司署第302/108299号令）	
1929/6/1	月薪增至海关两16两（见第1269号命令）	
1930/6/1	月薪增至海关两17两（见第1320号命令）	
1931/6/1	月薪增至海关两18两（见第1371号命令）	
1932/6/1	月薪增至海关两19两（见第1406号命令）	

关员清册

[F-9]   税课司：华籍职员

职员人事记录		备注
	邹银贵（Tsou Yin-kwei）	准予自1931年1月5日起休假三个月（一水承担巡役的职责,邹银贵需提供一名替代者接替水手的工作）

1931年4月3日返职 |
1927/12/1	月薪增至海关两19两（见第1159号命令）	
1928/12/1	月薪自海关两19两增至海关两20两（见第1216号命令）	
1929/3/1	月薪增至海关两21两（见第1272号命令）	
1929/12/1	月薪增至海关两22两（见第1305号命令）	
1930/12/1	月薪增至海关两23两（见第1849号命令）	
1931/12/1	月薪增至海关两24两（见第1392号命令）	

关员清册

税课司：华籍职员

职员人事记录		备注
陶德胜（T'ao Tê-sheng） 山东济南府 出生于光绪二十七年四月五日（1901 年 5 月 22 日）		差役 重订 18 号担保书担,保金为 20 银圆,1925 年 12 月 20 日 查实无误
1918/7/1	任命为瑷珲关 / 大黑河差役,月薪海关两 12.00 两 （见哈尔滨关第 2787 号命令）	
1919/4/1	月薪自海关两 12.00 两缩减至海关两 6.50 两（见 哈尔滨关第 3163 号命令）	
1919/6/1	月薪增至海关两 7.00 两（见哈尔滨第 3115 号 命令）	
1920/1/1	月薪增至海关两 8.00 两（见哈尔滨关第 3321 号 命令）	
1920/4/1	月薪增至海关两 9.00 两（见第 3054 号通令及哈 尔滨关第 3536 号命令）	
1922/1/1	月薪自海关两 9 两增至海关两 12 两（见第 865 号 命令）	
1924/1/1	月薪自海关两 12 两增至海关两 13 两（见第 951 号命令）	
1925/12/1	月薪自海关两 13 两增至海关两 14 两（见第 1038 号命令）	
1926/7/1	月薪自海关两 14 两增至海关两 16 两（见第 1063 号命令及总税务司署第 302/108299 号令——薪 酬等级表修订版）	

职员人事记录	备注
1928/12/1　月薪自海关两 16 两增至海关两 17 两(见第 1216 号命令)	
1929/3/1　月薪增至海关两 19 两(见第 1272 号命令)	
1930/12/1　月薪增至海关两 20 两(见第 1349 号命令)	

关员清册

税课司：华籍职员

职员人事记录		备注
邹兰亭（Tsou Lan-t'ing） 山东黄县 出生于光绪十二年十二月十八日（1887 年 1 月 12 日）		水手／卫兵 重订 41 号担保书，担保金为 30.00 银圆，1926 年 12 月 20 日查实无误
1924/10/11	任命为瑷珲关／大黑河水手／卫兵，月薪海关两 11.00 两（见第 986 号命令）	
1926/7/1	月薪自海关两 11 两增至海关两 13 两（见第 1063 号命令及总税务司署第 302/108299 号命令——薪酬等级表修订版）	
1926/12/1	月薪自海关两 13 两增至海关两 14 两（见第 1088 号命令）	
1928/12/1	月薪自海关两 14 两增至海关两 15 两（见第 1216 号命令）	1929 年 3 月 1 日因其疏忽行为，调任至下级分卡（见第 1274 号命令）
1929/3/1	月薪增至海关两 16 两（见第 1272 号命令）	因渎职罚款 1.00 银圆（见第 1388 号命令）
1929/12/1	月薪增至海关两 17 两（见第 1305 号命令）	
1930/12/1	月薪增至海关两 18 两（见第 1349 号命令）	
1931/12/1	月薪增至海关两 19 两（见第 1392 号命令）	

<h1 style="text-align:center">关员清册</h1>

[F-9]　　　　　　　　　　　　　税课司：华籍职员

职员人事记录		备注
王树兴（Wang Shu-hsing） 直隶乐亭县 出生于光绪十三年七月二十七日（1887 年 9 月 14 日）		水手/卫兵 42 号担保书,担保金为 30.00 银圆,1926 年 10 月 30 日查实无误
1924/11/1	任命为瑷珲关/大黑河水手/卫兵,月薪海关两 11.00 两（见第 992 号命令）	1929 年 1 月 1 日自下级分卡调任至总关
1926/7/1	月薪自海关两 11 两增至海关两 13 两（见第 1063 号命令及总税务司署第 302/108299 号命令——薪酬等级表修订版）	
1926/12/1	月薪自海关两 13 两增至海关两 14 两（见第 1088 号命令）	
1928/12/1	月薪自海关两 14 两增至海关两 15 两（见第 1216 号命令）	
1929/3/1	月薪增至海关两 16 两（见第 1272 号命令）	
1930/12/1	月薪增至海关两 17 两（见第 1349 号命令）	
1931/12/1	月薪增至海关两 18 两（见第 1392 号命令）	

关员清册

税课司：华籍职员

职员人事记录		备注
姚文盛（yao Wên-shêng） 安徽黟县 出生于光绪十一年四月二十八日（1885年6月11日）		更夫 21号担保书,担保金为30银圆,1926年2月8日查实无误
1922/9/1	任命为更夫,月薪海关两11两（见第893号命令）	
1924/9/1	月薪自海关两11两增至海关两12两（见第995号命令）	
1926/6/1	月薪增至海关两13两（见第1059号命令）	
1926/7/1	月薪自海关两13两增至海关两14两（见第1063号命令及总税务司署第302/108299号令——薪酬等级表修订版）	
1926/12/1	月薪自海关两14两增至海关两15两（见第1088号命令）	
1928/12/1	月薪自海关两15两增至海关两16两（见第1216号命令）	
1929/3/1	月薪增至海关两17两（见第1272号命令）	
1930/12/1	月薪增至海关两18两（见第1849号命令）	

关员清册

[F-9]　　　　　　　　　　　税课司：华籍职员

职员人事记录		备注
句财（Chü Ts'ai） 直隶莱水县 出生于光绪十八年八月二十四日（1892 年 10 月 14 日）		水手／卫兵 30 号担保书,担保金为 30 银圆,1926 年 10 月 28 日查实无误
1923/5/4	任命为水手／卫兵,月薪海关两 11 两（见第 926 号命令）	
1925/5/4	月薪自海关两 11 两增至海关两 12 两（见第 1015 号命令）	
1926/7/1	月薪自海关两 12 两增至海关两 14 两（见第 1063 号命令及总税务司署第 302/108299 号令——薪酬等级表修订版）	
1926/12/1	擢升为水手／卫兵,月薪海关两 14 两（第 1087 号命令）	1929 年 3 月 1 日发放海关两 2 两的一水职位津贴（见第 1268 号命令）
1927/6/1	月薪增至海关两 15 两（见总税务司署第 302/108299 号令及第 1129 号命令）	
1929/6/1	月薪增至海关两 16 两（见第 1263 号命令）	
1929/6/1	月薪增至海关两 18 两（见第 1272a 号命令）	
1930/6/1	月薪增至海关两 19 两（见第 1320 号命令）	

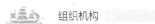

关员清册

[F-9]　　　　　　　　　　税课司：华籍职员

职员人事记录		备注
王德山（Wang Te-shan） 直隶任丘 出生于光绪二十一年十月二日（1895年3月6日）		水手／卫兵 43号担保书,担保金为30银圆,1925年12月20日查实无误
1925/2/7	任命为水手／卫兵,月薪海关两11两（见第1002号命令）	
1926/7/1	月薪自海关两11两增至海关两13两（见第1063号命令及总税务司署第302/108299号令——薪酬等级表修订版）	1929年1月1日自上级分卡调任至总关 参见王金德 （核税员李永坡先生之侄）
1927/6/1	月薪自海关两13两增至海关两14两（见第1129号命令）	
1929/6/1	月薪增至海关两15两（见第1263号命令）	
1929/3/1	月薪增至海关两16两（见第1272号命令）	
1930/6/1	月薪增至海关两17两（见第1320命令）	
1931/6/1	月薪增至海关两18两（见第1371号命令）	
1932/6/1	月薪增至海关两19两（见第1406号命令）	

关员清册

　　　　　　　　税课司：华籍职员

职员人事记录		备注
于德元（Yü Tê-yuan） 直隶保定府 出生于光绪十四年八月十三日（1888年9月18日）		水手/卫兵 46号担保书，担保金为30银圆，1925年12月20日查实无误
1925/4/18	任命为水手/卫兵，月薪海关两11两（见第1011号命令）	再任命，参见第65页
1926/7/1	月薪自海关两11两增至海关两13两（见第1063号命令及总税务司署第302/108299号令——薪酬等级表修订版）	1929年3月1日调任至上级分卡 在航行季节开始自分卡返回
1927/6/1	月薪自海关两13两增至海关两14两（见第1129号命令）	
1929/6/1	月薪增至海关两15两（见第1263号命令）	
1929/6/1	月薪增至海关两16两（见第1272a号命令）	
1930/6/1	月薪增至海关两17两（见第1320号命令）	

职员人事记录		备注
秦景岳(Ch'in Ching-yueh) 直隶朝阳县 出生于光绪二十三年二月二十二日(1897年3月24日)		宅役 自1925年8月1日任命为门役(见总税务司署第243/104330)
1925/5/10	任命为宅役,月薪海关两10.00两	47号担保书,担保金为30银圆,1925年12月20日查实无误
1925/8/1	任命为门役,月薪海关两11两(见总税务司署第243/104330)	
1926/7/1	月薪自海关两11两增至海关两13两(见第1063号命令及总税务司署第302/108299号令——薪酬等级表修订版)	
1927/6/1	月薪自海关两13两增至海关两14两(见第1129号命令)	

关员清册

税课司：华籍职员

职员人事记录		备注
张殿臣（Chang Tien-chén） 直隶保定 出生于光绪二十年二月二十四日（1894年3月30日）		税务司住房宅役 51号担保书,担保金为30银圆,1925年12月20日查实无误
1925/10/1	任命为税务司住房宅役,月薪海关两10两	
1926/7/1	月薪自海关两10两增至海关两11两（见第1063号命令及总税务司署第302/108299号令——薪酬等级表修订版）	
1926/12/1	月薪自海关两11两增至海关两12两（见第1088号命令）	税务司住房门役（见第1273号命令）
1927/12/1	月薪自海关两12两增至海关两13两（见第1459号命令）	准予自1931年1月1日起休假三个月
1929/3/1	月薪增至海关两14两（见第1272号命令）	提供接任人
1929/12/1	月薪增至海关两16两（见第1305号命令）	1931年3月25日返回原职位
1931/12/1	月薪增至海关两17两（见第1392号命令）	

关员清册

税课司：华籍职员

104.912		备注
秦景岳（Ch'in Ching-yueh） 直隶朝阳县 出生于光绪二十三年二月二十二日（1897年3月24日）		税务司住房宅役（见第1273号命令）
1929/6/1	月薪增至海关两15两（见第1263号命令）	
1930/6/1	月薪增至海关两16两（见第1272a号命令）	
1931/6/1	月薪增至海关两17两（见第1371号命令）	

关员清册

[F-9]　　　　　　　　　　税课司：华籍职员

职员人事记录		备注
邹振芬（Tsou Chin-fên） 山东黄县 出生于光绪二十七年十二月七日（1902 年 1 月 17 日）		水手 / 卫兵 55 号担保书,担保金为 30 银圆
1927/1/16	任命为水手 / 卫兵,月薪海关两 12 两（见第 1097 号命令）	1927 年 1 月 20 查实无误 1929 年 1 月 1 日调任至下级分卡
1928/6/1	月薪自海关两 12 两增至海关两 13 两（见第 1191 号命令）	1929 年 3 月 1 日调任至总关听差
1929/6/1	月薪增至海关两 14 两（见第 1263 号命令）	
1929/7/1	调职为听差,月薪海关两 15 两（见第 1267 号命令）	
1930/6/1	月薪增至海关两 16 两（见第 1320 号命令）	
1931/6/1	月薪增至海关两 17 两（见第 1371 号命令）	
1932/6/1	月薪增至海关两 18 两（见第 1406 号命令）	

关员清册

税课司：华籍职员

职员人事记录		备注
郭敬九（Kuo Ching-chiu） 山东招远县 出生于光绪二十七年八月一日（1901年9月13日）		就地巡役 56号担保书,担保金为50银圆,1927年3月11日查实无误 1929年4月1日调任至瑷珲关
1927/3/12	任命为就地巡役,月薪海关两18两（见第1111号命令）	
1928/6/1	月薪自海关两18两增至海关两19两（见第1191号命令）	
1929/6/1	月薪自海关两19两增至海关两20两（见第1263号命令）	
1929/6/1	月薪增至海关两21两（见第1272a号命令）	
1930/6/1	月薪增至海关两22两（见第1320号命令）	
1931/6/1	月薪增至海关两23两（见第1371号命令）	
1932/6/1	月薪增至海关两24两（见第1406号命令）	

瑷珲关低级职员薪俸一览表

姓名	现就任			出生日期	初任		
	职级	薪俸	口岸津贴		职级	就任日期	薪俸
于福寿	就地巡役	海关两 33 两	海关两 5 两	1894 年 12 月 24 日（光绪二十年十一月二十八日）	就地巡役	1917 年 7 月 6 日	18 卢布
褚鸣岐	就地巡役	海关两 31 两	海关两 5 两	1883 年 9 月 5 日（光绪九年八月五日）	就地巡役	1919 年 10 月 1 日	海关两 9 两
陈长安	就地巡役	海关两 28 两	海关两 5 两	1890 年 4 月 26 日（光绪十六年三月八日）	就地巡役	1922 年 8 月 1 日	海关两 16 两
邓银贵	就地巡役	海关两 24 两	海关两 5 两	1892 年 5 月 27 日（光绪十八年五月二日）	水手	1922 年 7 月 20 日	海关两 11 两
郭敬九	就地巡役	海关两 23 两	海关两 5 两	1901 年 9 月 13 日（光绪二十七年八月一日）	就地巡役	1927 年 3 月 12 日	海关两 18 两
句财	水手／卫兵	海关两 20 两	海关两 6 两	1892 年 10 月 14 日（光绪十八年八月二十四日）	水手／卫兵	1923 年 5 月 4 日	海关两 11 两
魏福兴	水手／卫兵	海关两 18 两	海关两 4 两	1897 年 6 月 12 日（光绪二十三年五月十三日）	水手	1923 年 2 月 13 日	海关两 11 两
邹兰亭	水手／卫兵	海关两 19 两	海关两 4 两	1887 年 1 月 12 日（光绪十二年十二月十八日）	水手／卫兵	1924 年 10 月 11 日	海关两 11 两
王树兴	水手／卫兵	海关两 18 两	海关两 4 两	1887 年 9 月 14 日（光绪十三年七月二十七日）	水手／卫兵	1924 年 11 月 1 日	海关两 11 两
王德山	水手／卫兵	海关两 18 两	海关两 4 两	1895 年 3 月 6 日（光绪二十一年二月十日）	水手／卫兵	1925 年 2 月 7 日	海关两 11 两
于德元	水手／卫兵	海关两 18 两	海关两 4 两	1888 年 9 月 18 日（光绪十四年八月十三日）	水手／卫兵	1925 年 4 月 18 日	海关两 11 两

姓名	现就任			出生日期	初任		
	职级	薪俸	口岸津贴		职级	就任日期	薪俸
王进才	水手/卫兵	海关两 20 两	海关两 4 两	1893 年 3 月 2 日（光绪十九年一月十四日）	陆路马差	1923 年 1 月 1 日 §	27 卢布
孔繁诏	听差	海关两 22 两	海关两 5 两	1893 年 2 月 27 日（光绪十九年一月十一日）	水手	1922 年 11 月 18 日	海关两 11 两
邹振芬	听差	海关两 17 两	海关两 5 两	1902 年 1 月 17 日（光绪二十七年十二月七日）	水手/卫兵	1927 年 1 月 16 日	海关两 12 两
陶德盛	差役	海关两 20 两	海关两 4 两	1901 年 5 月 22 日（光绪二十七年四月五日）	差役	1918 年 7 月 1 日	12 卢布
姚文盛	更夫	海关两 18 两	海关两 4 两	1885 年 6 月 11 日（光绪十一年四月二十八日）	更夫	1922 年 9 月 1 日	海关两 11 两
张殿臣	门役	海关两 17 两	海关两 4 两	1894 年 3 月 30 日（光绪二十年二月二十四日）	宅役	1925 年 10 月 1 日	海关两 10 两
秦景岳	宅役	海关两 17 两	海关两 3.50 两	1897 年 3 月 24 日（光绪二十三年二月二十一日）	宅役	1925 年 5 月 10 日	海关两 10 两
裴贵春	木匠	海关两 27 两	海关两 5 两	1881 年 1 月 3 日（光绪六年十二月四日）	木匠	1920 年 4 月 7 日	海关两 12 两

§ 1917 年 1 月 1 日于瑷珲关任陆路马差一职；自 1927 年 6 月 1 日就任水手/卫兵；自 1923 年 1 月 1 日起计算工龄，参见 1929 年第三季度账户 A，费用项目 1:3，传票字号 10 的备注。

张殿臣与秦景岳：1925 年 5 月 10 日秦景岳就任宅役；1925 年 8 月 1 日就任门役；1930 年就任门役；1925 年 10 月 1 日张殿臣就任宅役；同时秦景岳再次就任宅役：见总税务司署第 104330 号令及 1930 年第 1273 号税务司谕。

第 917 号税务司谕将所有的水手分类为水手/卫兵。

* 应晋升日 1932 年 6 月 1 日
o 应晋升日 1932 年 12 月 1 日
§ 应晋升日 1933 年 6 月 1 日
※ 应晋升日 1933 年 12 月 1 日

姓名	职级	出生日期（光绪年）	初任			现职薪俸			增薪		备注
			日期	职级	薪俸	薪俸	口岸津贴	发薪日期	日期	薪俸	
于福寿	就地巡役	1894年12月24日（光绪二十年十一月二十八日）	1917年7月6日	就地巡役	18卢布	海关两33两	海关5两	1931年12月1日	1932年12月1日	海关两34两	
褚鸣岐	就地巡役	1883年9月5日（光绪九年八月五日）	1919年10月1日	就地巡役	海关9两	海关两31两	海关5两	1931年12月1日	1932年12月1日	海关两32两	
陈长安	就地巡役	1890年4月26日（光绪十六年三月八日）	1922年8月1日	就地巡役	海关16两	海关两28两	海关5两	1931年12月1日	1932年12月1日	海关两29两	
邹银贵	就地巡役	1892年5月27日（光绪十八年五月二日）	1922年7月20日	水手	海关11两	海关两24两	海关5两	1931年12月1日	1932年12月1日	海关两25两	
郭敬九	就地巡役	1901年9月13日（光绪二十七年八月一日）	1927年3月12日	就地巡役	海关18两	海关两24两	海关5两	1932年6月1日	1933年6月1日	海关两25两	
句财	水手/卫兵	1892年10月14日（光绪十八年八月二十四日）	1923年5月4日	水手/卫兵	海关11两	海关两21两	海关6两	1932年6月1日	1933年6月1日	海关两22两	
魏福兴	水手/卫兵	1897年6月12日（光绪二十三年五月十三日）	1923年2月13日	水手	海关11两	海关两19两	海关4两	1932年6月1日	1933年6月1日	海关两20两	
邹兰亭	水手/卫兵	1887年1月12日（光绪十二年十二月十八日）	1924年10月11日	水手/卫兵	海关11两	海关两19两	海关4两	1931年12月1日	1932年12月1日	海关两20两	

姓名	职级	出生日期（光绪年）	初任			现职薪俸			增薪		备注
			日期	职级	薪俸	薪俸	口岸津贴	发薪日期	日期	薪俸	
王树兴	水手/卫兵	1887年9月14日（光绪十三年七月二十七日）	1924年11月1日	水手/卫兵	海关两11两	海关两18两	海关两4两	1931年12月1日	1932年12月1日	海关两19两	
王德山	水手/卫兵	1895年3月6日（光绪二十一年二月十日）	1925年2月7日	水手/卫兵	海关两11两	海关两19两	海关两4两	1932年6月1日	1933年6月1日	海关两20两	
于德元	水手/卫兵	1888年9月18日（光绪十四年八月十三日）	1925年4月18日	水手/卫兵	海关两11两	海关两19两	海关两4两	1932年6月1日	1933年6月1日	海关两20两	
王进才	水手/卫兵	1893年3月2日（光绪十九年一月十四日）	1917年1月1日	陆路马差	卢布27	海关两20两	海关两4两	1931年6月1日			
孔繁诏	听差	1893年2月27日（光绪十九年一月十一日）	1922年11月18日	水手	海关两11两	海关两22两	海关两5两	1931年12月1日	1932年12月1日	海关两23两	
邹振芬	听差	1902年1月17日（光绪二十七年十二月八日）	1927年1月16日	水手/卫兵	海关两12两	海关两18两	海关两5两	1932年6月1日	1933年6月1日	海关两19两	
陶德盛	差役	1901年5月22日（光绪二十七年四月五日）	1918年7月1日	差役	12卢布	海关两20两	海关两4两	1930年12月1日	1932年12月1日	海关两21两	

姓名	职级	出生日期（光绪年）	初任			现职薪俸			增薪		备注
			日期	职级	薪俸	薪俸	口岸津贴	发薪日期	日期	薪俸	
姚文盛	更夫	1885年6月11日（光绪十一年四月二十八日）	1922年9月1日	更夫	海关两11两	海关两18两	海关两4两	1930年12月1日	1932年12月1日	海关两19两	
秦景枞	宅役	1897年3月24日（光绪二十三年二月二十二日）	1925年5月10日	宅役	海关两10两	海关两17两	海关两3.50两	1931年6月1日	1933年6月1日	海关两18两	
张殿臣	门役	1894年3月30日（光绪二十年二月二十四日）	1925年10月1日	宅役	海关两10两	海关两17两	海关两4两	1931年12月1日	1933年12月1日	海关两18两	
裴贵春	木匠	1881年1月3日（光绪六年十二月四日）	1920年4月7日	木匠	海关两12两	海关两28两	海关两5两	1932年6月1日	1933年6月1日	海关两29两	

专题八

瑷珲关洋籍华籍关员履历表

MEMO. OF SERVICE.
[See Circular No. 23 of 1874.]

CHINESE MARITIME CUSTOMS.

Revenue DEPARTMENT: FOREIGN STAFF, *In-door*

NAME (in full)	CHINESE NAME	NATIONALITY
July Reel Henry Armagh	周驤	*British*

YEAR, MONTH, AND DAY OF BIRTH.	BIRTHPLACE.	MARRIED (with Date of Marriage) OR SINGLE.
1892 September 17th	*Diana*	*Married 3rd December 1909*

Appointed to	Revenue	Department: Foreign Staff.	In-door

On what Date.	To what Port.	In what Capacity.	On what Pay.	Authority.
2 Nov 1912, Shanghai	4th assistant B.	Hk.Tls. 125 per month.	70 years of 1912

CAREER IN SERVICE (FOREIGN STAFF. *In-door*)
FROM FIRST APPOINTMENT TO DATE OF PRESENT MEMO.

N.B.—The first "Port," etc., in this section will be the "Port," "Authority," "Capacity," and "Pay" entered in the section above; Promotions etc. while at each port are to be entered; the Pay is to be "Hk.Tls. per month," etc.

PORT.	AUTHORITY.	IN WHAT CAPACITY.	MONTHLY PAY. Hk.Tls.	TO WHAT DATE.	AUTHORITY.
Shanghai	70 of 1912	4th Assistant B	125	30 Sept 1913	43 of 1913

REMARKS.

1913 March 29 Awarded Certificate of Knowledge of the Chinese Language Class C ...

1919 May 16 Awarded Certificate of Knowledge of the Chinese Language Class B ...

Copies of Birth and Marriage Certificates forwarded to ...

Superannuation and Retirement Scheme Contributor.

1924 April 21 Awarded Certificate of Knowledge of the Chinese Language Class C ...

... Acting Allowance issued from ...

... Repatriation Allowance ...

1913, 200			
1922, 210			

Relieved from ...	... September 1930, for transfer to	Peiyun
Salary paid ...	... September 1930	
Passage paid ...		

Hankow 15th September 1930

Commissioner.

[F.—3]

MEMO. OF SERVICE.

(See Circular No 23 of 1874.)

CHINESE MARITIME CUSTOMS.

Revenue DEPARTMENT: FOREIGN STAFF, *Out door*

Name (in full)	Chinese Name	Nationality
Crossland, James Alfred	克忠闊	British

Year, Month, and Day of Birth.	Birthplace.	Married (with Date of Marriage) or Single.
1900, February 10th	Birkenhead	Married: 1st Sept, 1922

Appointed to	*Revenue* Department: Foreign Staff, *Out door*		
On what Date.	To what Port.	In what Capacity.	On what Pay.	Authority.

| 31 July 1920 | Hankow | Proby. Int. | Ht.Tls. 78 per month. | I.G. Circular 1700 2602 + 2912, II |

CAREER IN SERVICE (FOREIGN STAFF, *Out door*)

FROM FIRST APPOINTMENT TO DATE OF PRESENT MEMO.

N.B. The first "Port," etc., in this section will be the "Port," "Authority," "Capacity," and "Pay" entered in the section above ; Promotions, etc., whilst at each port are to be entered ; the Pay is to be " Ht.Tls. per month," etc.

Port.	Authority.	In what Capacity.	Monthly Pay.	To what Date.	Authority.
			Ht.Tls.		
Hankow	Circ 1700 2602+2912	Proby. Tidewaiter	75	20 Jan. 1921	3486 of 1921
"	3486 of 1921	4th Cl.	90	31 " 1922	11 Jany 1922 306
"	54 Jany 159 304	3rd "	100	27 Feb. 1923	" 280
"	" 300	2nd "	115	31 Mar. 1924	14140 of 1924
Harbin	3320 of 1924	" "	115	31 Oct. 1925	34 Jany 150 304
"	34 Jany 150 304	1st	130	" 1928	4068 of 1928
Shanghai	16 Aug 150 183	Asst. Examiner 9	105	28 Oct. 1929	Circ. 3570
"	Circ. 3570	" "	135 +20	8 Oct. "	
S.H.L.	2202 of 1929		135 +20	5 April 1930	2072/30/070
Aigun	823 of 1930	4th Examiner 9	135 +20	31 May 1930	Circ. 4590
"	Circ. 4590	"	135 +0	31 Oct. 1930	13601 of 1930
"	13601 of 1930	"	140 +65		

1906 / 4 22.

REMARKS:

Previous occupation : coal carter, 3 years. Gunner, (R.20) distillery, 2 years.

London Recruit

Superannuation and Retirement Scheme Contributor

With seniority from 21st July 1920

Officer's certificate of Identity No. 35 on new form (C-23) with photograph affixed, issued by Harbin Office on 27th July 1922

"Expatriation Allowance"

Leave curtailed to 5th April 1930 (I.G. No. 20002/125776 to Shanghai).

Copy of the "Handbook on classification of rice goods" by Mr. Torresani, issued by Shanghai Office.

Special Allowance at Ht.Tls 25th a month issued from 16.9.30 (the date on which he Crossland takes over duties of Senior O.D.S Officer I.G. desp No. 554/130,175 L.Aigun

1923, Aug. 16, (revised Ht.Tls. 1620) Retiring Allowance Pd 1st Sept initial period, 21.7.20 to 20.7.29 (13.9.30 2002, 20762 to Swatow bureau)

Reported from A.d.L 31st March 1930, for transfer to Aigun

Salary paid by this Office to 5th April 1930

Passage paid by this Office to Dairen

Mileage allowance $127.00 issued to Harbin via Dairen.

CUSTOM HOUSE.

Shanghai, 7th April 1930

B/o Commissioner

[F.—5]

MEMO. OF SERVICE.
[See Circular No. 23 of 1874.]

CHINESE MARITIME CUSTOMS.

Revenue   DEPARTMENT: CHINESE STAFF,   In-door

NAME: ROMANISED (in full).	NAME: CHINESE (in full: hsing, ming, and hao).
Ch'ang Fu Yuan	常 福 元 字 後 源

NATIONALITY.	YEAR, MONTH, AND DAY OF BIRTH. N.B.—Foreign and Chinese Calendars.	BIRTHPLACE.
Chinese	1901, October 13 / K.H. 27th Year, 9th Moon, 2nd Day.	Peking

FAMILY HOME	TITLES.
Peking	B.A. of the Yenching University

Appointed to   Revenue   Department: Chinese Staff,   In-door

On what Date.	To what Port.	In what Capacity.	On what Pay.	I.G.'s Despatch.
31.Oct.,1925	Kiaochow	Probationary Clerk.	Hk.Tls. 45 per month.	No. 2566 of 1925 to Kiaochow

CAREER IN SERVICE (CHINESE STAFF, Indoor ; FROM FIRST APPOINTMENT TO DATE OF PRESENT MEMO.

N.B.—The first "Port," etc., in this section will be the "Port," "I.G.'s Despatch," "Capacity," and "Pay" entered in the section above. Promotions, etc., while at each port are to be entered : the Pay is to be "Hk.Tls. per month," etc.

PORT.	No. OF I.G.'s DESPATCH.	IN WHAT CAPACITY.	MONTHLY PAY. Hk.Tls.	TO WHAT DATE PAID.	No. OF I.G.'s DESPATCH.
Kiaochow	2566 of 1925	Proby. Clerk	45	30.Oct.1926	2667 of 1926
"	2667 of 1926	3rd Clerk C	70	28.Feb.1929	Cir. No. 3932
"	Cir. 3932	4th " B	85		14.Aug.No.290
"	14.Aug.of 1930	3rd " B	115	30.Apr.1930	3207 of 1930
Aigun	525 of 1930	"	115	28 Feb. 1931	4 Aug.No.290
"	4.Aug.1930	" A	120		

REMARKS.

Previous Career : Teacher in the Tsui Wen Senior Middle School, Peking.

Dialects and/or languages spoken : Mandarin and English.

Security Bond filed in the Kiaochow Office.

Seniority from 31st October, 1925.

Retiring Allowance due on 9th January, 1933.

Superannuation And Retirement Scheme Contributor.

Contribution vouches $4.13.60. Statement (F.32) signed 18/4/31

	Received Hk.Tls.	Retiring Allowance for	second period.	to

Relieved from duty   22nd April,   19 30 for transfer to   Aigun

Passage allowance issued by this office to

Mileage Allce.of $55.00 for Tsingtao-Harbin issued by this Office.

Kiaochow CUSTOM HOUSE,

Tsingtao   21st April, 30.

R. L. Wade
Commissioner.

[P-5]

MEMO. OF SERVICE.
[See Circular No. 25 of 1874.]

CHINESE MARITIME CUSTOMS.

Revenue DEPARTMENT: CHINESE STAFF, In-door

NAME: ROMANISED (in full)	NAME: CHINESE (in full : hsing, ming, and hao).
Wang Tê-mao	王德懋 號 錫慶

NATIONALITY.	YEAR, MONTH, AND DAY OF BIRTH. N.B.—Foreign and Chinese Calendar.	BIRTHPLACE.
Chinese	1893 Oct. to Dec. 2nd Kuanghsü, 19th Year, 9th Moon, 23rd Day.	河北省 永平府

FAMILY HOME.	TITLES.
Kirin	Nil

Appointed to Revenue Department: Chinese Staff, In-door

On what Date.	To what Port.	In what Capacity.	On what Pay.	I.G.'s Despatch.
22 Jan. 1912	Harbin	Candidate Clerk	mm. 30 per month.	No. 883 of 1912 to Harbin

CAREER IN SERVICE (CHINESE STAFF, In-door) from FIRST APPOINTMENT TO DATE OF PRESENT MEMO.

N.B.—The first "Port," etc., in this section will be the "Port," "I.G.'s Despatch," "Capacity," and "Pay" entered in the section above ; Promotions, etc., while at each port are to be entered ; the Pay is to be "Hk.Tls. per month," etc.

Port.	No. of I.G.'s Despatch	In what Capacity.	Monthly Pay. Hk.Tls.	To what Date Paid.	No. of I.G.'s Despatch.
Harbin	883 of 1912	Candidate Clerk	30	21 Jan. 1913	993 of 1913
"	993. 1913	3rd Clerk D	40	30 Apr. 1916	1501. 1916
"	1501. 1916	" C	50	June 1919	3r. Gaz. 255
"	3r. Gaz. 255	" B	60	31 Oct. 1920	" 274
"	" 274	" A	70	30 Dec. 1921	2564 of 1921
Aigun	1 of 1921	"	"	Oct.	3r. Gaz. 239
"	3r. Gaz. 289	2nd D	80	31 May 1922	Circ. 3314
"	Circ. 3314	" C	100	1925	3r. Gaz. 333
"	3r. Gaz. 333	" B	115	30 Jun. 1926	Circ. 3704
"	Circ. 3704	" "	130	31 May 1928	3r. Gaz. 350
"	3r. Gaz. 350	" A	150	28 Feb. 1930	Circ. 3882
"	Circ. 3882	"	170	30 Nov.	"
Tientsin	8? 704 1930	"	170		
Aigun	510 of 1930	"	170	31 May	
"	Gaz.412 (49)	1st	8	170	

Mem. J.5.22

Left Form

MEMO. OF SERVICE.
[See Circular No. 23 of 1874.]

CHINESE MARITIME CUSTOMS.

Revenue DEPARTMENT: CHINESE STAFF, In-door

NAME: ROMANISED (in full):	NAME: CHINESE (in full: Assug, ming, and hao).
Chen Pei-yin	陳培因

NATIONALITY.	YEAR, MONTH, AND DAY OF BIRTH. N.B.—Foreign and Chinese Calendars.	BIRTHPLACE.
Chinese	1907, January 5th Kuanghsü 32nd Year 11th Moon 21st Day	Foochow

FAMILY HOME.	TITLES.
Peping	None

Appointed to Revenue DEPARTMENT: Chinese Staff, In-door

On what Date.	To what Port.	In what Capacity.	On what Pay.	L.G.'s Despatch.
4 July 1927,	Foochow	Chienhsi	Hk.Tls. 50 per month.	N. 3014 of 1927 to Foochow

CAREER IN SERVICE (CHINESE STAFF, In-door) FROM FIRST APPOINTMENT TO DATE OF PRESENT MEMO.

N.B.—The first "Port", etc., in this section will be the "Port," "L.G.'s Despatch," "Capacity," and "Pay" entered in the section above; Promotions, etc., while at each port are to be entered; the Pay is to be "Hk.Tls. per month," etc.

PORT.	NO. OF L.G.'s DESPATCH.	IN WHAT CAPACITY.	MONTHLY PAY.	TO WHAT DATE PAID.	NO. OF L.G.'s DESPATCH.
Foochow	N14 of 1927	Chien-hsi	Hk.Tls. 50	31 May 1928	Cir.No. 3806
"	Cir.No. 3806	Hsieh-hsi-ytan	60	3 Jul.1928	3518 of 1929
"	3518 of 1929	3rd Clerk B	85	26 Feb.1929	Cir.No. 3982
"	Cir.No.3982	4th " A	100	" "	Gaz.305 (Sp)
"	Gz.305 Sp)	3rd " B	115*	30 Apr.1930	3357 of 1930
Aigun	519 of 1930		115	30 " 1931	Gaz.434(4)
"	Gaz.434(Sp)	L/C Assistant A	150		

REMARKS.

SUPERANNUATION & RETIREMENT SCHEME CONTRIBUTOR.
Dialects and/or Languages spoken: Foochow,Shanghai,Mandarin, English and French
Seniority from 4th July 1927 (Cir.No.3733)
Bond for Hk.Tls.300 signed by 人林華 and 太和泰記, retained in Foochow Office. Date of birth as given is certified correct by guarantors.
*Receives Temporary Allowance (12½% of substantive pay) from 1st January 1930 (Vide L.G.Cir.No.4054)

Relieved	4th April 1930	for transfer to	Aigun

Passage allowance Dairen, together with a mileage allowance of $124.00 to Harbin.

CUSTOM HOUSE.
FOOCHOW 8th April 1930.

Commissioner.

Right Form

MEMO. OF SERVICE.
[See Circular No. 23 of 1874.]

CHINESE MARITIME CUSTOMS.

Revenue DEPARTMENT: CHINESE STAFF, In-door

NAME: ROMANISED (in full):	NAME: CHINESE (in full: Assug, ming, and hao).
Li Yung-Ko	李永坡 誦 鳳格

NATIONALITY.	YEAR, MONTH, AND DAY OF BIRTH. N.B.—Foreign and Chinese Calendars.	BIRTHPLACE.
Chinese	1885 September 28th Kuang Hsü 11th Year, 8th Moon, 17th Day	直隸任邱縣

FAMILY HOME.	TITLES.
直隸任邱縣	八等奇末

Appointed to Revenue DEPARTMENT: Chinese Staff, In-door

On what Date.	To what Port.	In what Capacity.	On what Pay.	L.G.'s Despatch.
22 June 1923,	Aigun	Lushih	Hk.Tls. 30 per month.	No. 46 of 1922 to Aigun

CAREER IN SERVICE (CHINESE STAFF, In-door) FROM FIRST APPOINTMENT TO DATE OF PRESENT MEMO.

N.B.—The first "Port", etc., in this section will be the "Port," "L.G.'s Despatch," "Capacity," and "Pay" entered in the section above; Promotions, etc., while at each port are to be entered; the Pay is to be "Hk.Tls. per month," etc.

PORT.	NO. OF L.G.'s DESPATCH.	IN WHAT CAPACITY.	MONTHLY PAY.	TO WHAT DATE PAID.	NO. OF L.G.'s DESPATCH.
Aigun	46 of 1922	Lushih	Hk.Tls. 30	30 Apr. 1923	Circ.No.3429
	Circ.No.3429		35	21 June 1923	
			30	30 June,1926	Cir.3704
"	Cir.3704	"	37	31 June 1929	Circ.3429
"			42	28 Feb. 1934	Circ.No 1411
"	Circ.No 1411		47	28 Feb. 1931	577/123 of 1931
"	577/123 of 1931	1/c Lupau	52		

REMARKS.

Bond for good behaviour and willingness to proceed wherever ordered, filed in Aigun Office with other Bonds. Examined by Canton Medical Officer and found physically fit. 1st July, 1926; Special allowance of Hk.Tls.10.00 a month reduced to Hk.Tls.5.00 and to cease upon receiving next increase of pay vide I.G.Cir.No.3429. (I.G.Desp.No.207/109.033)

Relieved from duty		19	for transfer to	

Passage allowance issued by this Office to

CUSTOM HOUSE.
Aigun/Luheiho 22nd June 1923

Acting Commissioner.

Security Bond returned (Vide Cir.4250)

[F.—5]

MEMO. OF SERVICE.
[See Circular No. 27 of 1874.]

CHINESE MARITIME CUSTOMS.

Revenue DEPARTMENT: CHINESE STAFF. *Out-door*

NAME: ROMANISED (in full).	NAME: CHINESE (in full: hsing, ming, and hao).		
Fan Chin Tsao	樊金溪	樊覺生	

NATIONALITY.	YEAR, MONTH, AND DAY OF BIRTH. N.B.—Foreign and Chinese Calendars.	BIRTHPLACE.
Chinese	1900, *May* 25th *Kuang Hsü* 26th Year, 4th Moon, 27th Day.	*Tientsin*

FAMILY HOME.	TITLES.
Hopeh	*None*

Appointed to *Revenue* Department: Chinese Staff. *Out-door*

On what Date.	To what Port.	In what Capacity.	On what Pay.	I.G.'s Despatch.
16. Oct. 1920	Tientsin	Cadet (Chn.) Tidewaiter Hk.Tls.	25. per month.	No. 3065. etc. Tientsin

CAREER IN SERVICE [CHINESE STAFF. *Out-door*] FROM FIRST APPOINTMENT TO DATE OF PRESENT MEMO.

N.B.—The first "Port," etc., in this section will be the "Port," "I.G.'s Despatch," "Capacity," and "Pay" entered in the section above; Promotions, etc., while at each port are to be entered; the Pay is to be "Hk.Tls. per month," etc.

PORT.	No. OF I.G.'s DESPATCH.	IN WHAT CAPACITY.	MONTHLY PAY. Hk.Tls.	TO WHAT DATE PAID.	No. OF I.G.'s DESPATCH.
Tientsin	Cir. 3065	Cadet (Chn.) Tidewaiter	25	15. April 1921	6117 of 1921
	6117 of 1921	4th Class	40	" Oct. 1922	6601 - 1922
	6601 - 1922	" " "	45	" 1924	7006 - 1924
	7006 - 1924	2nd " "	55	20 June 1926	Cir. 3701
	Cir. 3701	" " "	65	15. Oct. 1926	7628 of 1926
	7628 of 1926	" " "	72	" 1928	Cir. 3874
	Cir. 3874	1st " "	85	28. Feb. 1929	Cir. 3874
	Cir. 3874	Tidewaiter	95	30. April 1930	3422 of 1909
Shanghai	3422 of 1930		98	31 May 1930	Cir. 4091
	Cir. 4091		100	9. Feb. 1931	21148/1930
	21148/12072	(4 months' leave full class tidewaiter)	100	"	Tsg.4a1(4)
	Tsg.4a1(4)	(2 months' leave)	115	9 April	21500/123.462
Aigun	133.aa	4th Cl. Tsty.	115		

2000/1.2.

345

REMARKS.

"Seniority from 16. October 1920 (Cir. 3065).

Superannuation And Retirement Scheme Contribution.

Statement (S.-52) signed, Bond cancelled 5/1/29

1920, May 5, received Hk.Tls. 1140.00 Outfitting Allowance in lieu of deferred period 16. 10. 1920 to 16. 4. 1926 (35th No. 3057/12.7965 to Shanghai).

Relieved from duty ——— 19—, for transfer to *Aigun*

Passage allowances issued by this Office to *Tientsin*

CUSTOM HOUSE,

Shanghai, 24th March, 1931.   p/o Commissioner.

[F.—5]

MEMO. OF SERVICE.
[See Circular No. 25 of 1874.]

CHINESE MARITIME CUSTOMS.

Marine DEPARTMENT: CHINESE STAFF, River Inspectorate Staff

NAME ROMANIZED (in full).	NAME CHINESE (in full: hsing, ming and hao).
Ignatieff, Paul Ivanovitch	易 洼 羅

NATIONALITY.	YEAR, MONTH, AND DAY OF BIRTH. N.B.—Foreign and Chinese Calendars.			BIRTHPLACE.
Chinese	1876	October	30th	Toula District
	Year.	Moon.	Day.	Russia

FAMILY HOME.	TITLES.
Aigun	

Appointed to Marine Department: Chinese Staff, River Inspectorate Staff

On what Date.	To what Port.	In what Capacity.	On what Pay.	I.G.'s Despatch.
16 Sept. 1922	Aigun	Technical Adviser on River Navigation	Hk.Tls. 350 per month	No. 788 of 1922, to Aigun

CAREER IN SERVICE (CHINESE STAFF,) FROM FIRST APPOINTMENT TO DATE OF PRESENT MEMO.

PORT.	No. of I.G.'s Despatch.	IN WHAT CAPACITY.	MONTHLY PAY. Hk.Tls.	TO WHAT DATE PAID.	No. of I.G.'s Despatch.
Aigun	788 of 1922	Technical Adviser on River Navigation	350	15 - 9 - 23	788 of 1922
"		"	375	15 - 9 - 24	
"	1925	"	400	15 - 9 - 25	1925
"	1926	"	"	15 - 9 - 26	1926
"	1927	"	"	15 - 9 - 27	1927
"	1928	"	"	15 - 9 - 28	1928
"	1929	"	"	15 - 9 - 29	1929
"	1931	"	"	31 - 1 - 31	1931
"	1933	River Inspector	450	28 - 2 - 33	1933
Canton	1933	(on special duty)	450		

REMARKS.

Superannuation and Retirement Scheme Contribution.

1892-1907 Officer in the Imperial Russian Navy; left with rank of 1st Lieutenant.

1907-1920 Amur Navigation Office; left with rank of Inspector of the whole Amur Service.

1920-1922 in Harbin, Member of the Direction of the Amur Steamship and Trading Co. and in private business.

Discharge Certificate of Imperial Russian Navy & Memo of Service of Amur Navigation Office and Certificate of Marriage seen.

...

CUSTOM HOUSE

Aigun 19th September, 1931

Commissioner.

关员履历表

[见第1874号通令第23条]

中国海关

[F-3] 税课司：　　　　　　　　　　　　洋籍内班职员

姓名：(全名) Joly, Ceil Henry Bencraft	姓名：以中文书写(全名) 周骊	国籍 英国
出生日期 1892年9月17日	出生地 澳门	已婚(结婚日期)或单身 已婚,1917年12月5日

任命为税课司洋籍内班职员

就任日期	就任口岸	职位	薪俸	授权依据
1912/11/22	江海关	四等帮办后班	海关两125两/月	1912年第7222号令

海关工作经历(洋籍内班,自初任日至现任日)

注：本部分第一行的"口岸"等信息应为上面表格内的"口岸"、"授权依据"、"职位"及"薪俸"内容；凡在各口岸的晋升等人事变动,都要填写在表内；薪俸以"海关两/月"为计量单位。

口岸	授权依据	职位	月薪	发俸截止日期	人事变动授权依据
江海关	1912年第7222号令	四等帮办后班	(海关两)125	1913/9/30	总税务司署1913年电报
九江关	1913年第863号令	四等帮办后班	125	1913/10/31	总税务司署1913年第883号令
九江关	1913年第883号令	四等帮办前班	150	1915/4/30	总税务司署1915年第1047号令
北京	谕令簿	四等帮办前班	150	1915/9/30	谕令簿
北京	谕令簿	三等帮办后班	175	1916/10/31	谕令簿
浙海关	1916年第1062号令	三等帮办后班	175	1917/5/31	1917年第1096号令
蒙自关	1917年第1432号令	三等帮办后班	175	1917/5/31	1917年第1441号令
蒙自关	1917年第1441号令	三等帮办前班	200	1919/3/31	1919年第1588号令

续表

口岸	授权依据	职位	月薪	发俸截止日期	人事变动授权依据
蒙自关	1919 年第 1588 号令	二等帮办后班	250	1920/10/15	1920 年第 1716 号令
江海关休假职员待分配名单	1920 年第 1716 号令	二等帮办前班（休假一年）	250	1920/10/31	1920 年第 12222 号令
江海关休假职员待分配名单	1920 年致蒙自关第 12222 号令	二等帮办前班（休假一年）	300	1921/10/15	1921 年 10 月 3 日电报
哈尔滨关	1921 年第 2683 号令	二等帮办前班	300	1922/5/31	第 3314 号通令第 2 条
哈尔滨关	第 3314 号通令第 2 条	头等帮办后班	450	1923/10/31	1923 年第 3142 号令
厦门关	1923 年第 2864 号令	头等帮办后班	450	1925/3/23	1925 年第 3106 号令
厦门	1925 年第 3106 号令	署副税务司（头等帮办后班）	450+75	1925/3/31	1925 年第 3106 号令
厦门	1925 年第 3106 号令	署副税务司（头等帮办前班）	500+75*	1926/8/15	1926 年 8 月 13 日电报
江门关	1926 年第 1502 号令	暂行代理税务司署副税务司（头等帮办前班）	500+100	1926/10/18	1926 年第 1510 号令
厦门	1926 年第 3289 号令	署副税务司（头等帮搬前班）	500+75#	1927/3/31	1927 年第 5357 号令
厦门	1927 年第 3357 号令	署副税务司（超等帮办后班）	550+75#	1927/4/15	1926 年第 3321 号令
江海关休假职员待分配名单	1927 年致厦门第 3321 号令	超等帮办后班（休假一年）	550	1928/4/15	1928 年第 18635 号令
江汉关	1928 年第 5224 号令	超等二级帮办	550	1929/3/31	1929 年第 5439 号令

续表

口岸	授权依据	职位	月薪	发俸截止日期	人事变动授权依据
江汉关	1929 年第 5439 号令	超等一级帮办	$480+120^*$	1929/5/2	1929 年第 5472 号令
江汉关	1929 年第 5472 号令	署副税务司（超等一级帮办）	$480+120^1+50^2+25^3$	1929/6/29	1929 年第 5536 号令
江汉关	1929 年第 5536 号令	暂行代理税务司之署副税务司（超等一级帮办）	$480+120^a+100^b+40^c+100^d$	1929/8/31	1929 年第 5536 号令
江汉关	1929 年第 5536 号令	署副税务司（超等一级帮办）	$480+120+^150^2+25^3$	1930/4/14	1930 年第 5763 号令
江汉关	1930 年第 5763 号令	暂行代理税务司署副税务司（超等一级帮办）	$480+120^a+100^b+40^c+100^d$	1930/6/11	1930 年第 5763 号令
江汉关	1930 年第 5763 号令	署副税务司（超等一级帮办）	$480+120+^150^2+25^3$	1930/9/30	1930 年第 5919 号令
江汉关	1930 年第 130026 号令	署理税务司（副税务司）	$550+150^1+100^2+50^3$		
瑷珲关	1930 年第 130938 号令				

备注:
1915 年 3 月 29 日授予中文水平三等证书(见总税务司署致九江关第 1034/55760 号令)   1919 年 5 月 16 日授予中文水平二等证书(见总税务司署致蒙自关第 1594/73448 号令)   1921 年出生证明及结婚证明副本通过江海关办公室转交至总税务司署   养老(退休)储金计划参保人   1924 年 4 月 21 日授予中文水平一等证书(见总税务司署致厦门关第 2968/98347 号令)   * 代理津贴自 1925 年 3 月 24 日发放,自此日起任命为署副税务司,1926 年 8 月 15 日停职并暂时调任至江门关   # 1926 年 10 月 23 日建议发放代理津贴,自此日起管理厦门常关   % 移居国外津贴   1 移居国外津贴海关两 120 两,2 代理津贴海关两 50 两,3 特殊津贴海关两 25 两   a 移居国外津贴海关两 120 两,b 管理津贴海关两 100 两,c 运输津贴海关两 40 两,d 招待津贴海关两 100 两   1919 年 12 月 11 日收到第一阶段(每七年一次)自 1912 年 11 月 22 日至 1919 年 11 月 21 日应得的的酬劳金海关两 3000 两(见总税务司署致蒙自关第 1658/76019 号令)   1926 年 12 月 13 日收到第二阶段(每七年一次)自 1919 年 11 月 22 日至 1926 年 11 月 21 日应得的的酬劳金海关两 6000 两(见总税务司署致厦门关第 3324/114401,n.c.209 号令)

于 1930 年 9 月 14 日调职至瑷珲关 1930 年 9 月 30 日薪金由本关发放 至江海关的差旅费及里程津贴 365 银圆由本关发放至滨江关	
江汉关,1930 年 9 月 13 日	黎霭萌(E. G. Lebas) 江汉关税务司

签章:江汉关税务司

关员履历表

[见第 1874 号通令第 23 条]

中国海关

[F-3] 税课司：　　　　　　　　　　　　　洋籍外班职员

姓名：(全名) Crossland, James Alfied	姓名：以中文书写(全名) 克思澜	国籍 英国
出生日期 1900 年 2 月 15 日	出生地 伯肯黑德	已婚(结婚日期)或单身 已婚,1923 年 9 月 1 日

任命为税课司洋籍外班职员

就任日期	就任口岸	职位	薪俸	授权依据
1920/7/21	江汉关	试用钤子手	海关两 75 两 / 月	总税务司署第 2426 号通令及第 2912 号通令第 2 条

海关工作经历(洋籍外班,自初任日至现任日)

注：本部分第一行的"口岸"等信息应为上面表格内的"口岸"、"授权依据"、"职位"及"薪俸"内容；凡在各口岸的晋升等人事变动,都要填写在表内；薪俸以"海关两 / 月"为计量单位。

口岸	授权依据	职位	月薪	发俸截止日期	人事变动授权依据
江汉关	第 2426 号通令及第 2912 号通令	试用钤子手	(海关两) 75	1921/1/20	1921 年第 3484 号通令
江汉关	1921 年第 3484 号令	四等钤子手	90	1923/1/31	第 306 号特别擢升公报
江汉关	第 306 号特别擢升公报	三等钤子手	100	1924/2/29	第 320 号特别擢升公报
江汉关	第 320 号特别擢升公报	二等钤子手	115	1924/3/31	1924 年第 4140 号令
哈尔滨关	1924 年第 3220 号令	二等钤子手	115	1925/10/31	第 344 号特别擢升公报
哈尔滨关	第 344 号特别擢升公报	头等钤子手	135	1928/10/31	1928 年第 4055 号令及第 387 号特别擢升公报

口岸	授权依据	职位	月薪	发俸截止日期	人事变动授权依据
江海关	第18909/118399号令及第387号特别擢升公报	二等副验货员	155	1929/2/28	第3873号通令
江海关	第3873号通令	二等副验货员	135+20$^+$	1929/10/5	1929年第19403号令及第19785号令
江海关休假职员待分配名单	1929年第19403号令及第19785号令	二等副验货员（休假一年）§	135+20$^+$	1930/4/5	第20472/127073号令
瑷珲关	1930年第523号令	二等副验货员	135+20$^+$	1930/5/31	第4094号通令
瑷珲关	第4594号通令	二等副验货员	135+65$^+$	1930/10/31	1930年第131601号令
瑷珲关	1931年第131611号令	一等副验货员	160+65$^+$		

备注：

先前工作经历：煤车司机,三年；201 正规军火炮队炮手,三年

伦敦征募

养老(退休)储金计划参保人

自 1920 年 7 月 21 日起计算工龄

新表格(C-53)第 35 号授权依据关员证明并附有照片于 1923 年 7 月 27 日由江汉关发行

⁺ 移居国外津贴

§ 休假缩减至 1930 年 4 月 5 日 (见总税务司署致江海关第 20208/125776 号令)

"件货分类手册" 副本由江海关发行

自 1930 年 9 月 16 日起发放特殊津贴每月海关两 25.00 两,克思澜于此日接管超等外勤职员的职务),见总税务司署致瑷珲关第 554/130125 号令

1927 年 8 月 12 日收到第一阶段(每七年一次)自 1920 年 7 月 21 日至 1927 年 7 月 20 日应得的的酬劳金海关两 1620 两 (见总税务司署致哈尔滨关第 3852/113763 号令)

江海关任上休假结束后于 1930 年 3 月 31 日报到并调任至瑷珲关

1930 年 4 月 5 日薪金由本关发放

至大连关的差旅费及里程津贴 127 银圆由通过大连关发放至哈尔滨关

江海关,1930 年 4 月 7 日	李度(L. K. Little) 奉江海关税务司命令代签

关员履历表

[见第 1874 号通令第 23 条]

中国海关

[F-5] 税课司： 华籍内班职员

姓名：以罗马字书写（全名） Ch'ang Fu Yuan	姓名：以中文书写（全名：姓名和号） 常福元，字复源

国籍 中国	出生日期（年月日） 注：采用公历和农历两种历法 1901 年 10 月 13 日 光绪二十七年九月二日	出生地 北京

家庭住址 北京	称号/头衔 燕京大学文学士

任命为税课司华籍内班职员

就任日期	就任口岸	职位	薪俸	总税务司署批准文号
1925/10/31	胶州关	试用供事	海关两 45 两/月	致胶州关 1925 年第 2566 号令

海关工作经历（华籍内班，自初任日至现任日）

注：本部分第一行的"口岸"等信息应为上面表格内的"就任口岸"、"总税务司署批准文号"、"职位"及"薪俸"内容；凡在各口岸的晋升等人事变动，都要填写在表内；薪俸以"海关两/月"为计量单位。

口岸	总税务司署就任批准文号	职位	月薪	发俸截止日期	总税务司署人事变动批准文号
胶州关	1925 年 第 2566 号令	试用供事	（海关两）45	1926/10/30	1926 年 第 2687 号令
胶州关	1925 年 第 2687 号令	三等三级税务员	70	1929/2/28	第 3882 号通令第 2 条
胶州关	第 3882 号通令第 2 条	四等二级税务员	85	1929/2/28	第 395 号特别擢升公报
胶州关	第 395 号特别擢升公报	三等二级税务员	115	1930/4/30	1930 年第 3207 号令

续表

口岸	总税务司署就任批准文号	职位	月薪	发俸截止日期	总税务司署人事变动批准文号
瑷珲关	1930 年第 528 号令	三等二级税务员	115	1931/2/28	第 424 号特别擢升公报
瑷珲关	第 424 号特别擢升公报	三等一级税务员	130		

备注：

先前工作经历：任北京萃文学校高中（Tsui Wen Senior Middle School）教师

所讲方言或其他语种：普通话及英语

担保书保存于胶州关

自 1925 年 10 月 31 日起计算工龄

预计 1933 年 1 月 9 日发放酬劳金

养老（退休）储金计划参保人

上交担保金达海关两 300 两,1931 年 4 月 16 日签署明细表（F-52）

（日期）收到第阶段（每年一次）自（日期）至（日期）的酬劳金两

于 1930 年 4 月 22 日调职至瑷珲关

到的差旅费由本关发放

青岛至哈尔滨的里程津贴 55.00 银圆由本关发放

| 青岛,1930 年 4 月 21 日 | 霍李家（R. L. Warren）
胶州关税务司 |

签章：胶州关税务司

关员履历表

[见第 1874 号通令第 23 条]

中国海关

[F-5] 税课司：　　　　　　　　　　　　华籍内班职员

姓名：以罗马字书写（全名） Wang Tê-mao	姓名：以中文书写（全名：姓名和号） 王德懋,号锡勋

国籍 中国	出生日期（年月日） 注：采用公历和农历两种历法 1893 年 10 月 2 日 光绪十九年八月二十三日	出生地 河北省永平府

家庭住址 吉林	称号/头衔 无

任命为税课司华籍内班职员

就任日期	就任口岸	职位	薪俸	总税务司署批准文号
1912/1/22	哈尔滨关	试用同文供事	海关两 30 两/月	致哈尔滨关 1912 年第 803 号令

海关工作经历（华籍内班,自初任日至现任日）

注：本部分第一行的"口岸"等信息应为上面表格内的"就任口岸"、"总税务司署批准文号"、"职位"及"薪俸"内容；凡在各口岸的晋升等人事变动,都要填写在表内；薪俸以"海关两/月"为计量单位。

口岸	总税务司署就任批准文号	职位	月薪	发俸截止日期	总税务司署人事变动批准文号
哈尔滨关	1912 年第 803 号令	试用同文供事	（海关两）30	1913/1/21	1913 年第 993 号令
哈尔滨关	1913 年第 993 号令	三等同文供事副后班	40	1916/4/30	1916 年第 1501 号令
哈尔滨关	1916 年第 1501 号令	三等同文供事正后班	50	1919/6/30	第 255 号特别擢升公报
哈尔滨关	第 255 号特别擢升公报	三等同文供事副前班	60	1920/10/31	第 274 号特别擢升公报

续表

口岸	总税务司署就任批准文号	职位	月薪	发俸截止日期	总税务司署人事变动批准文号
哈尔滨关	第274号特别擢升公报	三等同文供事正前班	70	1921/9/30	1921年第2664号令
瑷珲关	1921年第1号令	三等同文供事正前班	70	1921/10/30	第289号特别擢升公报
瑷珲关	第289号特别擢升公报	二等同文供事副后班	80	1922/5/31	第3314号通令
瑷珲关	第3314号通令	二等同文供事后班	100	1925/5/31	第338号特别擢升公报
瑷珲关	第338号特别擢升公报	二等同文供事中班	115	1926/6/30	第3704号通令
瑷珲关	第3704号通令	二等二级税务员	130	1928/5/31	第380号特别擢升公报
瑷珲关	第380号特别擢升公报	二等一级税务员	150	1929/2/28	第3882号通令
瑷珲关	第3882号通令	二等一级税务员	170	1929/11/30	总税务司署1929年11月25日电报及1929年第125071号令
津海关	1929年第8670号令	二等一级税务员（额外）	170	1930/1/31	总税务司署1930年1月17日电报
瑷珲关	1930年第510号令	二等一级税务员	170	1930/5/31	第412号特别擢升公报
瑷珲关	第412号特别擢升公报	一等二级税务员	190		

备注：

在哈尔滨俄语商业学院学习七年

所讲方言或其他语种：普通话、俄语、英语及法语

养老（退休）储金计划参保人

修订后的酬劳金预计发放时间为 1931 年 3 月 31 日（见第 3704 号通令及第 47 次审计记录）

上交担保金达海关两 300 两,1926 年 1 月 14 日撤销担保书（F—52）

1923 年 5 月 14 日收到第一阶段（每十年一次）自 1912 年 1 月 22 日至 1923 年 4 月 16 日的酬劳金海关两 1200 两

1931 年 4 月 14 日收到第二阶段（每七年一次）自 1923 年 4 月 17 日至 1931 年 3 月 31 日的酬劳金海关两 2280 两（见总税务司署致瑷珲关第 589/133933 号令）

于 1930 年 1 月 18 日调职至瑷珲关 到哈尔滨关的差旅费及里程津贴 145 银圆由本关发放	
津海关,1930 年 1 月 22 日	好威乐（E.B.Howell） 津海关税务司

签章：津海关税务司

关员履历表

[见第1874号通令第23条]

中国海关

[F-4] 税课司： 华籍内班职员

姓名：以罗马字书写（全名） Chen Pei-yin	姓名：以中文书写（全名：姓、名和号） 陈培因,号虞曾

国籍 中国	出生日期（年月日） 注：采用公历和农历两种历法 1907年1月5日 光绪三十二年十一月二十一日	出生地 福州

家庭住址 北平	称号/头衔 无

任命为税课司华籍内班职员

就任日期	就任口岸	职位	薪俸	总税务司署 批准文号
1927/7/4	闽海关	华籍内班职员见习	海关两50两/月	致闽海关1927年第 3014号令

海关工作经历（华籍内班,自初任日至现任日）

注：本部分第一行的"口岸"等信息应为上面表格内的"口岸"、"总税务司署令"、"职位"及"薪俸"内容；凡在各口岸的晋升等人事变动,都要填写在表内；薪俸以"海关两/月"为计量单位。

口岸	总税务司署就 任批准文号	职位	月薪	发俸截止 日期	总税务司署人事变 动批准文号
闽海关	1927年第 3014号令	见习	（海关两）50	1928/5/31	第3806号通令
闽海关	第3806号通令	学习员	60	1928/7/3	1929年第3218号 令
闽海关	1929年第 3218号令	三等二级税务员	85	1929/2/28	第3882号通令
闽海关	第3882号通令	四等一级税务员	100	1929/2/28	第395号特别擢升 公报

口岸	总税务司署就任批准文号	职位	月薪	发俸截止日期	总税务司署人事变动批准文号
闽海关	第 395 号特别擢升公报	三等二级税务员	115*	1930/4/30	1930 年第 3357 号令
瑷珲关	1930 年第 519 号令	三等二级税务员	115	1931/4/30	第 424 号特别擢升公报
瑷珲关	第 424 号特别擢升公报	四等一级帮办	150		

备注:

养老(退休)储金计划参保人

所讲方言或其他语种:福州话、上海话、普通话、英语及法语

自 1927 年 7 月 4 日起计算工龄(见第 3733 号通令)

§ 担保书经天柱峰与太和康记签字,担保金海关两 300 两,保存在闽海关,经担保人证实出生日期真实无误。担保书已更新(见海关总税务公署第 132112 号令及瑷珲关 1931 年 1 月 15 日致总务科税务司的通函)

1931 年 7 月 22 日起担保书撤销返还(参见总税务司署第 4254 号通令)

* 收到自 1930 年 1 月 1 日起的临时津贴(占实际薪俸的 12.5%)(参见总税务司署第 4034 号通令)

_____(日期)收到第____阶段(每___年一次)自_____(日期)至_____(日期)的酬劳金海关两____两

于 1930 年 4 月 8 日调至瑷珲关
到大连关的旅费与到滨江关的里程津贴 86.00 银圆由本关发放。

闽海关,1930 年 4 月 8 日	巴闰森(P. G. S. Barentzen) 闽海关税务司

签章:闽海关税务司

保存于闽海关的担保书失效(见总税务司署致瑷珲关第 570/132112 号令);经徐翔九及吴赞臣签字确认的新担保书,其担保金海关两 300 两,保存在瑷珲关。

关员履历表

[见第 1874 号通令第 23 条]

中国海关

[F-4] 税课司： 华籍内班职员

姓名：以罗马字书写（全名） Li Yung-p'o	姓名：以中文书写（全名：姓、名和号） 李永坡，号凤梧

国籍 中国	出生日期（年月日） 注：采用公历和农历两种历法 1885 年 9 月 25 日 光绪十一年八月十七日	出生地 直隶任丘县

家庭住址 直隶任丘县	称号 / 头衔 无

任命为税课司华籍内班职员

就任日期 1922/6/22	就任口岸 瑷珲关	职位 录事	薪俸 海关两 20 两 / 月	总税务司署 批准文号 致瑷珲关 1922 年第 46 号令

海关工作经历（华籍内班，自初任日至现任日）

注：本部分第一行的"口岸"等信息应为上面表格内的"口岸"、"总税务司署批准文号"、"职位"及"薪俸"内容；凡在各口岸的晋升等人事变动，都要填写在表内；薪俸以"海关两 / 月"为计量单位。

口岸	总税务司署就任 批准文号	职位	月薪	发俸截止 日期	总税务司署人事变 动批准文号
瑷珲关	1922 年第 46 号令	录事	（海关两）20	1923/4/30	第 3429 号通令
瑷珲关	第 3429 号通令	录事	25	1925/6/21	第 3429 号通令
瑷珲关	第 3429 号通令	录事	30	1926/6/30	第 3704 号通令
瑷珲关	第 3704 号通令	录事	37	1928/6/21	第 3429 号通令及第 3704 号通令
瑷珲关	第 3429 号通令及 第 3704 号通令	录事	42	1929/2/28	第 3911 号通令

口岸	总税务司署就任批准文号	职位	月薪	发俸截止日期	总税务司署人事变动批准文号
瑷珲关	第3911号通令	录事	47	1931/2/28	1931年第577/132835号令
瑷珲关	1931年第577/132835号令	核税员	52		

备注：
保证品行端正且服从命令的担保书,与其他担保书一同保存在瑷珲关。经海关医员检查,健康状况良好。 1926年7月1日：特殊津贴自每月海关两10.00两缩减至每月海关两5.00两,根据总税务司署第3429号通令及第3704号通令所示,于下个增薪日,停止发放特殊津贴(见总税务司署第811号通函及第307/109033号令)   1931年7月15日收到第一阶段(每七年/十年一次)自1922年6月22日至1931年6月22日的酬劳金海关两624.00两(见总税务司署致瑷珲关第135701号令)

于19____调职至 到的差旅费由本关发放	
瑷珲关/大黑河,1922年6月22日	包安济(G. Boezi) 瑷珲关署理税务司

签章：瑷珲关税务司

1931年7月22日撤回担保书(见总税务司署第4254号通令)

关员履历表

[见第 1874 号通令第 23 条]

中国海关

[F-4] 税课司：　　　　　　　　　　外籍外班职员

姓名：以罗马字书写（全名）	姓名：以中文书写（全名：姓、名和号）
Sun Hung Tsao	孙鸿藻，号渐逵

国籍	出生日期（年月日） 注：采用公历和农历两种历法 1899 年 11 月 22 日 光绪二十五年十月二十日	出生地
中国		天津

家庭住址	称号/头衔
河北	无

任命为税课司华籍外班职员

就任日期	就任口岸	职位	薪俸	总税务司署批准文号
1922/7/1	江海关	华籍试用钤子手	海关两 35 两/月	第 3173 号通令

海关工作经历（华籍外班，自初任日至现任日）

注：本部分第一行的"口岸"等信息应为上面表格内的"口岸"、"总税务司署批准文号"、"职位"及"薪俸"内容；凡在各口岸的晋升等人事变动,都要填写在表内；薪俸以"海关两/月"为计量单位。

口岸	总税务司署就任批准文号	职位	月薪	发俸截止日期	总税务司署人事变动批准文号
江海关	第 3173 号通令	华籍试用钤子手	（海关两）35	1922/12/31	1923 年第 14529 号令
江海关	1923 年第 14529 号令	华籍四等钤子手后班	40	1923/2/28	1923 年第 14536 号令
津海关	1923 年第 6599 号令	华籍四等钤子手后班	40	1924/6/30	1924 年第 6985 号令
津海关	1924 年第 6985 号令	华籍四等钤子手前班	45	1926/6/30	1926 年 7539 号令及第 3701 号通令
津海关	1926 年 7539 号令及第 3701 号通令	华籍三等二级稽查员	65	1928/6/30	1928 年第 8179 号令

口岸	总税务司署就任批准文号	职位	月薪	发俸截止日期	总税务司署人事变动批准文号
津海关	1928 年第 8179 号令	华籍三等一级稽查员	75	1929/2/28	第 3874 号通令
津海关	第 3874 号通令	三等稽查员	80	1930/4/30	1930 年第 8777 号令
瑷珲关	1930 年第 523 号令	三等稽查员	80	1930/5/31	第 4094 号通令及总务科税务司第 53 号通函
瑷珲关	第 4094 号通令及总务科税务司第 53 号通函	额外三等稽查员	80	1931/5/31	1931 年第 135454 号令
瑷珲关	1931 年第 135454 号令	三等稽查员	85		

备注：
先前工作经历：任翻译达 3 年
自 1922 年 7 月 1 日起计算工龄
所讲方言：普通话
养老(退休)储金计划参保人
签署明细表(F-52),1929 年 7 月 27 日撤销担保书
修订后的酬劳金预计发放时间为：1931 年 6 月 29 日(见第 3873 号通令)
1930 年 3 月 14 日因严重渎职对其提出警告,除非重获上级信任,否则不可能得到晋升。(见总税务司署第 8750/126560 号令)
1931 年 7 月 17 日收到第一阶段自 1922 年 7 月 1 日至 1931 年 6 月 29 日的酬劳金海关两 1020.00 两(见总税务司署致瑷珲关第 135702 号令)

于 1930 年 4 月 8 日调职至瑷珲关 到滨江关的差旅费及自津海关至滨江关的里程津贴 39 银圆由本关发放	
津海关,1930 年 4 月 10 日	好威乐(E.B.Howell) 津海关税务司

签章：津海关税务司

关员履历表

[见第1874号通令第23条]

中国海关

[F-4] 税课司： 华籍内班职员

姓名：以罗马字书写（全名） Yang Ts'un-hou	姓名：以中文书写（全名：姓、名和号） 杨存厚，号博生

国籍 中国	出生日期（年月日） 注：采用公历和农历两种历法 1877年1月10日 光绪二年十一月二十八日	出生地 直隶省大兴县

家庭住址 直隶省大兴县	称号/头衔 无

任命为税课司华籍内班职员

就任日期	就任口岸	职位	薪俸	总税务司署 批准文号
1913/7/31	哈尔滨关	录事[+]	海关两25两/月	致哈尔滨关1913年第 1080号令

海关工作经历（华籍内班，自初任日至现任日）

注：本部分第一行的"口岸"等信息应为上面表格内的"口岸"、"总税务司署批准文号"、"职位"及"薪俸"内容；凡在各口岸的晋升等人事变动，都要填写在表内；薪俸以"海关两/月"为计量单位。

口岸	总税务司署就任 批准文号	职位	月薪	发俸截止 日期	总税务司署人事变 动批准文号
哈尔滨关	1913年第1080 号令	录事+	（海关两）25*	1918/12/31	税务司谕
哈尔滨关	税务司谕	录事	30	1921/9/30	1921年第2664号令
瑷珲关	1921年第1号令	录事	30	1921/12/31	第2986号通令
瑷珲关	第2986号通令	录事	35	1922/4/30	1922年第46号令
瑷珲关	1922年第46号 通令	文案	40	1923/4/30	第3429号通令

续表

口岸	总税务司署就任批准文号	职位	月薪	发俸截止日期	总税务司署人事变动批准文号
瑷珲关	第 3429 号通令	文案	55	1925/4/30	第 3429 号通令
瑷珲关	第 3429 号通令	文案	60	1926/6/30	第 3704 号通令
瑷珲关	第 3704 号通令	文案	70	1928/4/30	第 3429 号通令及第 3704 号通令
瑷珲关	第 3429 号通令及第 3704 号通令	汉文文牍员	75	1929/2/28	第 3911 号通令
瑷珲关	第 3911 号通令	汉文文牍员	90	1929/11/30	1929 年第 500 号令
瑷珲关	1929 年第 500 号令	汉文文牍员（休假）	90	1930/5/31	1929 年第 500 号令
瑷珲关	1929 年第 500 号令	汉文文牍员	90	1931/2/28	1931 年第 577/132853 号令
瑷珲关	1931 年第 577/132853 号令	汉文文牍员	100		

备注：

+ 兼职员中文教师

* 每月北京发放海关两 10.00 两,哈尔滨发放海关两 15.00 两(见总税务司署 1913 年第 1080/48234 号令)

保证品行端正且服从命令的担保书,与总税务司署第 1080/48234 号令一同保存在哈尔滨关

修订后的酬劳金预计发放时间为：1924 年 7 月 23 日

1926 年 7 月 1 日特殊津贴自每月海关两 10.00 两缩减至每月海关两 3.00 两,根据总税务司署第 3429 号通令及第 3704 号通令(总税务司署第 811 号通函)所示,于下个增薪日,停止发放特殊津贴(见总税务司署第 307/109033 号令)

1924 年 8 月 18 日收到第一阶段(每十年/十二年一次)自 1913 年 7 月 31 日至 1924 年 7 月 23 日的酬劳金海关两 660.00 两(见总税务司署致瑷珲关第 186/99873 号令)

续表

于 1921 年 9 月 30 日调职至瑷珲关	
哈尔滨关,1921 年 9 月 30 日	贾韦（R. C. L. d' Anjou） 哈尔滨关税务司

签章：哈尔滨关税务司

1929 年 12 月 1 日准予休假六个月（见总税务司署第 125140 号令）

修订后的酬劳金预计发放时间为 1932 年 12 月 7 日（见瑷珲关致总税务司署第 416 号呈）

关员履历表

[见第 1874 号通令第 23 条]

中国海关

[F-5] 税课司：　　　　　　　　　　　华籍外班职员

姓名：以罗马字书写（全名） Fan Chin Tsao	姓名：以中文书写（全名：姓名和号） 樊金藻，号丽生

国籍 中国	出生日期（年月日） 注：采用公历和农历两种历法 1900 年 5 月 25 日 光绪二十六年四月二十七日	出生地 天津

家庭住址 河北	称号 / 头衔 无

任命为税课司华籍外班职员

就任日期	就任口岸	职位	薪俸	总税务司署批准文号
1920/10/16	津海关	华籍试用钤子手	海关两 35 两 / 月	第 3065 号通令

海关工作经历（华籍外班，自初任日至现任日）

注：本部分第一行的"口岸"等信息应为上面表格内的"就任口岸"、"总税务司署批准文号"、"职位"及"薪俸"内容；凡在各口岸的晋升等人事变动,都要填写在表内；薪俸以"海关两"为计量单位。

口岸	总税务司署就任批准文号	职位	月薪	发俸截止日期	总税务司署人事变动批准文号
津海关	第 3065 号通令	华籍试用钤子手	（海关两）35	1921/4/15	1921 年第 6117 号令
津海关	1921 年第 6117 号令	华籍四等钤子手后班	40*	1922/10/15	1923 年第 6601 号令
津海关	1923 年第 6601 号令	华籍四等钤子手前班	45	1924/10/15	1924 年第 7046 号令
津海关	1924 年第 7046 号令	华籍三等钤子手后班	55	1926/6/30	第 3701 号通令

口岸	总税务司署就任批准文号	职位	月薪	发俸截止日期	总税务司署人事变动批准文号
津海关	第 3701 号通令	华籍三等钤子手后班	65	1926/10/15	1926 年第 7638 号令
津海关	1926 年第 7638 号令	华籍三等钤子手前班	75	1928/10/15	1928 年第 8260 号令
津海关	1928 年第 8260 号令	华籍二等二级稽查员	85	1929/2/28	第 3874 号通令
津海关	第 3874 号通令	华籍二等稽查员	95	1929/4/30	1929 年第 8422 号令
江海关	1929 年第 19342 号令	华籍二等稽查员	95	1930/5/31	第 4094 号通令
江海关	第 4094 号通令	华籍二等稽查员	100	1931/2/9	第 21345/132472 号令
江海关	第 21345/132472 号	华籍二等稽查员（休假两个月）	100	1931/2/28	第 423 号特别擢升公报
江海关	第 423 号特别擢升公报	一等稽查员（休假两个月）	115	1931/4/9	第 21500/133462 号令
瑷珲关	第 133500 号令	一等稽查员	115		

备注：
* 自 1920 年 10 月 16 日起计算工龄（见第 3065 号通令） 养老（退休）储金计划参保人 签署保证声明（52 英镑），于 1928 年 1 月 5 日撤回担保书
1930 年 5 月 5 日领取其第一阶段（每七／十年一次）自 1920 年 10 月 16 日至 1930 年 4 月 18 日应得的酬劳金海关两 1140.00 两（总税务司署致江海关第 20571/127765 号令）

于 19　年调职至瑷珲关 到津海关的差旅费由本关发放。	
江海关，1931 年 3 月 24 日	李度（L. K. Little） 奉江海关税务司命令代签

关员履历表

[见第 1874 号通令第 23 条]

中国海关

[F-5] 海政局：　　　　　　　　　　　　　　巡江事务局巡工科华籍职员

姓名：以罗马字书写（全名） Ignatieff, Paul, Ivanovitch	姓名：以中文书写（全名：姓、名和号） 易保罗

国籍 中国（原为俄籍） 总税务司署第 136784 号令	出生日期（年月日） 注：采用公历和农历两种历法 1876 年 10 月 30 日	出生地 俄国图拉区

家庭住址 瑷珲	称号／头衔

任命为海政局巡江事务局巡工科华籍职员

就任日期	就任口岸	职位	薪俸	总税务司署批准文号
1922/9/16	瑷珲关	黑龙江航务专门顾问	海关两 350 两／月	1922 年总税务司署致瑷珲关第 75/90949 号令

海关工作经历（华籍职员易保罗,自初任日至现任日）

注：本部分第一行的"口岸"等信息应为上面表格内的"就任口岸"、"总税务司署批准文号"、"职位"及"薪俸"内容；凡在各口岸的晋升等人事变动,都要填写在表内；薪俸以"海关两／月"为计量单位。

口岸	总税务司署就任批准文号	职位	月薪	发俸截止日期	总税务司署人事变动批准文号
瑷珲关	1922 年第 90949 号令	黑龙江航务专门顾问	（海关两）350	1923/9/15	1922 年第 90949 号令
瑷珲关	1922 年第 90949 号令	黑龙江航务专门顾问	375	1924/9/15	1922 年第 90949 号令
瑷珲关	1922 年第 90949 号令	黑龙江航务专门顾问	400	1925/9/15	1925 年第 104688 号令

口岸	总税务司署就任批准文号	职位	月薪	发俸截止日期	总税务司署人事变动批准文号
瑷珲关	1925 年第 104688 号令	黑龙江航务专门顾问	400	1926/9/15	1926 年第 109068 号令
瑷珲关	1926 年第 109068 号令	黑龙江航务专门顾问	400	1927/9/15	1927 年第 114066 号令
瑷珲关	1927 年第 114066 号令	黑龙江航务专门顾问	400	1928/9/15	1928 年第 118142 号令
瑷珲关	1928 年第 118142 号令	黑龙江航务专门顾问	400	1929/9/15	1929 年第 123634 号令
瑷珲关	1929 年第 123634 号令	黑龙江航务专门顾问	400	1931/1/31	1931 年第 134645 号令
瑷珲关	1931 年第 134645 号令	巡江事务长	400	1933/1/31	1933 年第 145726 号令
瑷珲关	1933 年第 145726 号令	巡江事务长	450	1933/2/28	1933 年第 145727 号令
粤海关	1933 年第 145727 号令	巡江事务长（特殊勤务）	450		

备注：

养老（退休）储金计划参保人

1892 年至 1907 年：沙俄皇家海军军官：退伍时担任上尉

1907 年至 1920 年：黑龙江航政部：离职时担任黑龙江整段灯塔巡灯司

1920 年至 1922 年：在哈尔滨担任黑龙江轮船贸易公司监管人员，并在私营企业工作

沙俄海军离职证明、俄阿穆尔水道局履历表和结婚证明

摘录自呈送总务科税务司的出生证明替代文件（总务科税务司 1923 年 3 月 26 日通函）

与海关签订三年合同（总税务司署第 90949 号令）

1930 年 2 月 9 日至 1930 年 3 月 31 日期间的薪俸由松花江水道委员会账户发放，同期其养老（退休）储金计划缴纳金额已由哈尔滨关征收（总税务司署第 127497 号令）

1931 年 1 月 31 日前的薪俸由江捐支付

自 1931 年 2 月 1 日起，任命为黑龙江巡江事务长，"有关黑龙江水道委员会的特殊勤务"月薪为海关两 400.00 两。

如要计算晋升、休假和酬劳金，工龄自 1931 年 2 月 1 日起计算，如要计算退休年龄，工龄自 1922 年 9 月 16 日起计算。建议每两年涨薪一次，每次涨薪海关两 50.00 两，月薪最高涨至海关两 500.00 两薪俸由海务账支付（总税务司署第 134645 号令）

南京内政部颁发的入籍证明副本呈送至总税务司署（瑷珲关第 576 号呈），在《海关职员题名录》中将国籍由俄国改为中国（总税务司署第 136784 号令）

（日期）收到第阶段（每年一次）自（日期）至（日期）的酬劳金海关两 _____ 两

| 1933 年 3 月 22 日调至粤海关 |
| 前往粤海关的旅费及里程津贴共 64.00 银圆，由本关发放 |

瑷珲关　1931 年 9 月 9 日	周骊（C. H. B. Joly） 瑷珲关署理税务司

签章：瑷珲关税务司

瑷珲关华洋职员一览表

Aigun CUSTOMS.

Return of Foreign and Chinese Staff Requirements in the Revenue Department.

(S/O CIRCULAR No. 38.)

CLASSIFICATION OF STAFF.	Staff on 1st June 1923.	Staff required.	Difference between Staff on 1st June 1923 and Staff required.		REMARKS.
			In Excess.	Short.	
I.—IN-DOOR STAFF.					
Deputy Commissioners	—	—	—	—	
Assistants, Foreign: Chief, 1st, and 2nd	—	—	—	—	
„ 3rd, 4th, Supernumerary, and Unclassed	—	—	—	—	
„ Chinese: Chief, 1st, and 2nd	—	—	—	—	
„ 3rd and 4th	1	2	—	1	
Clerks: Principal, 1st, and 2nd	3	3	—	—	
„ 3rd, Proby., Supernumerary, and Local; and Chientai	2	2	—	—	
Total: In-door Staff	6	7	—	1	
II.—OUT-DOOR STAFF.					
Tidesurveyors: Chief, A, and B	—	—	—	—	
„ Assistant	—	—	—	—	
Boat Officers	—	—	—	—	
Appraisers	1	1	—	—	
Examiners: Chief, A, and B	1	1	—	—	
„ Assistant	3	3	—	—	
Tidewaiters, Foreign: Senior, 1st, and 2nd	1	2	—	1	
„ 3rd, 4th, and Proby.; and Local Watchers	5	3	2	—	
„ Chinese: Senior, 1st, and 2nd	—	—	—	—	
„ 3rd, 4th, and Probationary	2	3	—	1	
Total: Out-door Staff	12	12	2	2	
GRAND TOTAL: I.—IN-DOOR AND II.—OUT-DOOR.	18	19	2	3	

CUSTOM HOUSE,
Aigun/Taheiho, 31st May / 1st June, 19 23.

(signature)
Acting Commissioner.

[P.—54]

AIGUN CUSTOMS.

Return of Foreign and Chinese Staff Requirements in the Revenue Department.

(S/O CIRCULAR No. 38.)

CLASSIFICATION OF STAFF.	STAFF ON 1ST JUNE, 1924.	STAFF REQUIRED.	DIFFERENCE BETWEEN STAFF ON 1ST JUNE, 1924 AND STAFF REQUIRED.		REMARKS.
			In Excess.	Short.	
I.—IN-DOOR STAFF.					
Deputy Commissioners	—	—	—	—	
Assistants, Foreign : Chief, 1st, and 2nd ...	—	—	—	—	
" 3rd, 4th, Supernumerary, and Unclassed	—	—	—	—	
Chinese : Chief, 1st, and 2nd ...	—	—	—	—	
" 3rd and 4th	1	1	—	—	
Clerks : Principal, 1st, and 2nd	3	3	—	—	
" 3rd, Proby., Supernumerary, and Local ; and Chientsi	2	2	—	—	
Total : In-door Staff	6	6	—	—	
II.—OUT-DOOR STAFF.					
Tidesurveyors : Chief, A, and B	1 *	1 *	—	—	* Acting Tidesurveyor and Harbour Master.
" Assistant	—	—	—	—	
Boat Officers	—	—	—	—	
Appraisers	—	—	—	—	
Examiners : Chief, A, and B	1	1	—	—	
" Assistant	3	3	—	—	
Tidewaiters, Foreign : Senior, 1st, and 2nd ...	—	—	—	—	
" 3rd, 4th, and Proby. ; and Local Watchers	5	5	—	—	Not including a Chief Examiner, B, acting as Tidesurveyor and Harbour Master.
Chinese : Senior, 1st, and 2nd ...	—	—	—	—	
" 3rd, 4th, and Probationary... ...	2	2	—	—	
Total : Outdoor Staff	12	12	—	—	
GRAND TOTAL : I.—IN-DOOR AND II.—OUT-DOOR ...	18	18	—	—	

Aigun/Tientsin   5th June   1924
300/425

R. J. Macquelin,
Commissioner.

AIGUN CUSTOMS.

Return of Foreign and Chinese Staff Requirements in the Revenue Department.

(S/O CIRCULAR No. 38.)

CLASSIFICATION OF STAFF.	Staff on 1st June 1925.	Staff required.	Difference between Staff on 1st June, 1925, and Staff required. In Excess.	Short.	REMARKS.
I.—IN-DOOR STAFF.					
Deputy Commissioners	-	-	-	-	
Assistants, Foreign: Chief, 1st, and 2nd	-	-	-	-	
,, 3rd, 4th, Supernumerary, and Unclassed	-	-	-	-	
,, Chinese: Chief, 1st, and 2nd	-	-	-	-	
,, 3rd and 4th	1	1	-	-	
Clerks: Principal, 1st, and 2nd	3	3	-	-	
,, 3rd, Proby., Supernumerary, and Local; and Chientsi	2	2	-	-	
Total: In-door Staff	6	6	-	-	
II.—OUT-DOOR STAFF.					
Tidesurveyors: Chief, A, and B	1 *	1 *	-	-	* Acting Tidesurveyor and Harbour Master.
,, Assistant	-	-	-	-	
Boat Officers	-	-	-	-	
Appraisers	-	-	-	-	
Examiners: Chief, A, and B	1	1	-	-	Not including 1 Chief Examiner, B, acting as Tidesurveyor and Harbour Master.
,, Assistant	3	3	-	-	
Tidewaiters, Foreign: Senior, 1st, and 2nd	2	2	-	-	
,, 3rd, 4th, and Proby.; and Local Watchers	2	2	-	-	
,, Chinese: Senior, 1st, and 2nd	-	-	-	-	
,, Proletionary	2	2	-	-	
Total: Out-door Staff	11	11	-	-	
GRAND TOTAL: I.—IN-DOOR AND II.—OUT-DOOR.	17	17	-	-	

Aigun/Thetho, 8th June, 1925.

Commissioner.

AIGUN CUSTOMS.

Return of Foreign and Chinese Staff Requirements in the Revenue Department.

(S/O CIRCULAR No. 38.)

CLASSIFICATION OF STAFF.	STAFF on 1st June 1926.	STAFF required.	DIFFERENCE BETWEEN STAFF ON 1st June 1926 AND STAFF REQUIRED. In Excess.	Short.	REMARKS.
I.—IN-DOOR STAFF.					
Deputy Commissioners ...	—	—	—	—	Note: The Aigun Staff was recently reduced on account of Trade and Frontier conditions. Should these conditions improve, it may be found necessary to increase accordingly.
Assistants, Foreign: Chief, 1st, and 2nd ...	—	—	—	—	
" 3rd, 4th, Supernumerary, and Unclassed ...	—	—	—	—	
" Chinese: Chief, 1st, and 2nd ...	—	—	—	—	
" 3rd and 4th ...	1	1	—	—	
Clerks: Principal, 1st, and 2nd ...	3	3)**	—	—	** Only 1 of these 4 Clerks has a good knowledge of the Russian language, but two are required. If Mr. Wong En Siong, 2nd Clerk B, recommended for transfer in Aigun S/O No.53 is transferred, he should be replaced by a Clerk having a good knowledge of Russian.
" 3rd, Prdy. Supernumerary and Local; and Chienhsi ...	1	1)**	—	—	
Total: In-door Staff ...	5	5	—	—	
II.—OUT-DOOR STAFF.					
(*Acting Tidesurveyor & Harbourmaster)					
*Tidesurveyors: Chief, A, and B ...	1	1 §	—	—	§ Must be non-Russian with a knowledge of the Russian language.
Assistant ...	—	—	—	—	
Boat Officers ...	—	—	—	—	
Appraisers ...	—	—	—	—	
Examiners: Chief, A, and B ...	1	1	—	—	
Assistant ...	1	1	—	—	
Tidewaiters, Foreign: Senior, 1st, and 2nd ...	2	2 §§	—	—	§§ Must be Russian or Russian speaking as at present.
" 3rd, 4th, and Prdy.; and Local Watchers ...	1	1	—	—	
Chinese: Senior, 1st, and 2nd ...	—	—	—	—	
" 3rd, 4th, and Probationary...	2	3 *	—	1	* 1 of these 3 Chinese Tidewaiters must have knowledge of Russian (Promotion of Native Watcher Yü Fu-shun recommended to fill this vacancy. He will be examined within 3 months.-Aigun S/O No.53. Aigun Despatch No.259, and I.G.Despatch No.295/107,964).
Total: Out-door Staff ...	8	9	—	1	
GRAND TOTAL: I.—IN-DOOR AND II.—OUT-DOOR.	13	14	—	1	

_J. D. S._
Commissioner.

Aigun/Tsitho 1st July 1926

CUSTOM HOUSE

[P.—54]

[F.—54]

AIGUN CUSTOMS.

Return of Foreign and Chinese Staff Requirements in the Revenue Department.

(S/O CIRCULAR No. 38.)

CLASSIFICATION OF STAFF	STAFF ON 1st July 1927.	STAFF REQUIRED.	DIFFERENCE BETWEEN STAFF ON 1st July 1927 AND STAFF REQUIRED.		REMARKS.
			In Excess.	Short.	
I.—IN-DOOR STAFF.					**Note:** The Aigun Staff has been reduced on account of Trade and Frontier conditions. Should these conditions improve, it may be found necessary to increase accordingly.
Deputy Commissioners	—	—	—	—	
Assistants, Foreign: Chief, 1st, and 2nd ...	—	—	—	—	
„ 3rd, 4th, Supernumerary, and Unclassed ...	—	—	—	—	
„ Chinese: Chief, 1st, and 2nd ...	1	1	—	—	
„ 3rd and 4th ...	1	1	—	—	
Clerks: Principal, 1st, and 2nd ...	2	1	1	—	A Russian speaking Clerk is essential for charge of the General Office.
3rd, Prely., Supernumerary, and Local; and Chienhsi ...	2	3	—	1	
Total: In-door Staff ...	**5**	**5**	**1**	**1**	
II.—OUT-DOOR STAFF.					
Tidesurveyors: Chief, A, and B (*Acting Tidesurveyor & Harbourmaster)	1	1	—	—	
„ Assistant ...	—	—	—	—	
Boat Officers	—	—	—	—	
Appraisers	—	—	—	—	
Examiners: Chief, A, and B ...	1	1	—	—	The present Assistant Examiner B (Mr. C.O.Dragge) was granted one year's leave from 10th October, 1927; he need not be replaced until the opening of navigation, 1928 (Vide Aigun despatch No.306 and I. G. despatch No.353/112,692).
„ Assistant ...	1	1	—	—	
Tidewaiters, Foreign: Senior, 1st, and 2nd ...	2	1	1	—	
„ 3rd, 4th, and Prely.; and Local Watchers	1	2	—	1	
„ Chinese: Senior, 1st, and 2nd ...	—	—	—	—	
„ 3rd, 4th, and Probationary...	2	2	—	—	Mr. Li Yuan Ching, 3rd Class (Chinese) Tidewaiter A, recommended for 4 months' leave from close of navigation (Aigun despatch No.3171. If granted, he need not be replaced until the opening of navigation, 1928.
Total: Out-door Staff ...	**8**	**8**	**2**	**2**	
GRAND TOTAL: I.—IN-DOOR AND II.—OUT-DOOR...	**13**	**13**	**2**	**2**	

CUSTOM HOUSE

Aigun/Tahoiho 2nd July, 19 27.

(signature) Acting Commissioner.

[E—54]

A I G U N CUSTOMS.

Return of Foreign and Chinese Staff Requirements in the Revenue Department.

(S.O CIRCULAR No. 38.)

CLASSIFICATION OF STAFF	STAFF ON 1st July 1928.	STAFF REQUIRED.	DIFFERENCE BETWEEN STAFF ON 1st July, 1928 AND STAFF REQUIRED. In Excess.	Short.	REMARKS.
I.—IN-DOOR STAFF.					**Note:** The Aigun staff has been reduced on account of Trade and Frontier conditions. Should these conditions improve, it may be found necessary to increase accordingly.
Deputy Commissioners ...	—	—	—	—	
Assistants, Foreign: Chief, 1st, and 2nd ...	—	—	—	—	
" : 3rd, 4th, Supernumerary, and Unclassed ...	—	—	—	—	
" Chinese: Chief, 1st, and 2nd ...	—	—	—	—	
" " 3rd and 4th ...	1	1	—	—	The appointment of one Chinese Assistant is required to replace Mr. 4th Assistant B Tiu Shou Chen granted 4 months' leave from the 1st September, 1928 (vide I. G. despatch No. 413/117,398 and Aigun despatch No.378 to I. G.).
Clerks: Principal, 1st, and 2nd ...	2	2	—	—	
" 3rd, Proby., Supernumerary, and Local; and Chienhsi ...	2	2	—	—	The present 3rd Clerk A (Mr. Liu Wen Kuei) was granted 3 months' leave from 1st October, 1928; he need not be replaced until the opening of navigation of 1929 (vide I. G. despatch No.390/116,060 and Aigun S/O No. 92 to I. G.)
Total: In-door Staff ...	5	5	—	—	
II.—OUT-DOOR STAFF.					
*Tidesurveyors: Chief, A, and B (*Acting Tidesurveyor & Acting Harbourmaster) ...	1	1	—	—	The appointment of a Russian speaking non-Russian is required as Tidesurveyor to replace Mr. G. E. Baukhum, Acting Tidesurveyor and Acting Harbourmaster, granted 6 months' Inspectorate leave from the 16th October, 1928 (vide I. G. despatch No.408/117,154). It is hoped that the new appointee will arrive at Aigun before Mr. Baukhum's departure.
Assistant ...	—	—	—	—	
Boat Officers ...	—	—	—	—	
Appraisers ...	—	—	—	—	
Examiners: Chief, A, and B ...	1	1	—	—	The present Examiner B Mr. S. E. Mikulin was granted 6 months' leave from the 16th October, 1928; he need not be replaced until the opening of navigation in 1929 (vide Aigun despatch No.367 to I. G. and I. G. despatch No.408/117,154.)
Assistant ...	1	1	—	—	
Tidewaiters, Foreign: Senior, 1st, and 2nd ...	2	2	—	—	
" 3rd, 4th, and Proby.; and Local Watchers ...	1	1	—	—	
Chinese: Senior, 1st, and 2nd ...	—	—	—	—	
" 3rd, 4th, and Probationary...	2	2	—	—	
Total: Out-door Staff ...	8	8	—	—	
GRAND TOTAL I.—IN-DOOR AND II.—OUT-DOOR...	13	13	—	—	

CUSTOM HOUSE.

Aigun 3rd July, 19 28.

[signature] Acting Commissioner.

[F.—54]

AIGUN CUSTOMS.

Return of Foreign and Chinese Staff Requirements in the Revenue Department.

(S/O CIRCULAR No. 38.)

CLASSIFICATION OF STAFF.	STAFF ON 1st July 1929	STAFF REQUIRED.	DIFFERENCE BETWEEN STAFF on 1st July 19 29 AND STAFF REQUIRED.		REMARKS.
			In Excess.	Short.	
I.—IN-DOOR STAFF.					
Deputy Commissioners	...	...	...	...	
Assistants, Foreign: Chief, 1st, and 2nd ...	...	...	...	...	
" 3rd, 4th, Supernumerary, and Unclassed	...	...	...	...	
" Chinese: Chief, 1st, and 2nd ...	1	1	...	...	
" 3rd and 4th	3	2	1	...	
Clerks: Principal, 1st, and 2nd	1	2	...	1	
3rd, Proby., Supernumerary, and Local: and Chienhsi	...	...	...	...	
Total: In-door Staff ...	5	5	1	1	
II.—OUT-DOOR STAFF.					
Acting Tidesurveyors: Chief, A, and B	1	1	...	...	
" " Assistant	...	...	...	...	
Boat Officers	...	...	...	...	
Appraisers	...	...	...	...	
Examiners: Chief, A, and B	1	1	...	...	
" Assistant	1	1	...	...	
Tidewaiters, Foreign: Senior, 1st, and 2nd ...	3	3	...	...	
" 3rd, 4th, and Proby.; and Local Watchers	...	...	...	...	
" Chinese: Senior, 1st, and 2nd ...	2	2	...	...	
" 3rd, 4th, and Probationary	...	...	...	...	
Total: Out-door Staff ...	8	8	...	...	
GRAND TOTAL: I—IN-DOOR AND II—OUT-DOOR ...	13	13	1	1	

Note: The Aigun Staff has been reduced on account of trade and frontier conditions; should they improve, it may be found necessary to increase it accordingly.

Aigun despatch No. 451 to I.G. encloses the application of Mr. Chang Yung Yung, 3rd Clerk B. for 3 months' Inspectorate leave from the 16. Oct., 1929. In S/O No. 107, it is reported that Mr. Li P'eng-tse, 2nd Clerk B. was applying for 4 months leave from 1. Aug. (Aigun despatch No. 417) but that, if necessary, his going away might be postponed until the end of the navigation season; when he need not be replaced, if the Service is short-handed until next spring. The application of Mr. Chang for leave to date from the close of navigation rather alters the situation and if it will the application of Mr. Li are both to be granted it is now recommended that the leave of Mr. Li date from the 1. Aug. (or 1. Sept. according to Circular No. 3905) as he requests, that he be replaced before his departure, and that, if necessary, Mr. Chang be not replaced until next spring. The successor of Mr. Li should be a good typist.

CUSTOM HOUSE,
Aigun, 1st July 19 29.

(signature)
Acting Commissioner.

[P.—34.]

Aigun CUSTOMS.

Return of Foreign and Chinese Staff Requirements in the Revenue Department.

(S.O CIRCULAR No. 36.)

CLASSIFICATION OF STAFF.	Staff on 1st July 1930	Staff required.	Difference between Staff on 1st July 1930 and Staff required.		REMARKS.
			In Excess.	Short.	
I.—IN-DOOR STAFF.					
Deputy Commissioners ...					
Assistants, Foreign: Chief, 1st, and 2nd ...					
" 3rd, 4th, Supernumerary, and Unclassed ...					
" Chinese: Chief, 1st, and 2nd ...					
" 3rd and 4th ...					
Clerks: Principal, 1st, and 2nd ...	2	2			
" 3rd, Proby., Supernumerary, and Local; and Chienhsi ...	3 *	3			* Excluding 1 on leave already replaced
Total: In-door Staff	5	5			
II.—OUT-DOOR STAFF.					
Tidesurveyors: Chief, A, and B ...					
Assistant ...	1	1			
Boat Officers ...		1			1 Acting boat officer.
Appraisers ...					
Examiners: Chief, A, and B ...	1	1			
Assistant ...	1	1			
Tidewaiters, Foreign: Senior, 1st, and 2nd ...					
" 3rd, 4th, and Proby.; and Local Watchers ...					
" Chinese: Senior, 1st, and 2nd ...	2	2			
" 3rd, 4th, and Probationary ...	5	5			1 Tidewaiter in charge of Aigun Substation.
Total: Out-door Staff	5	10			
GRAND TOTAL: I.—IN-DOOR AND II.—OUT-DOOR ...	10	10			

CUSTOM HOUSE,

Aigun, 1st July 1930

Acting Commissioner.

[F—54]

A I G U N   *CUSTOMS.*

Return of Foreign and Chinese Staff Requirements in the Revenue Department.

(S/O CIRCULAR No. 36.)

CLASSIFICATION OF STAFF.	STAFF ON 1ST July 1931.	STAFF REQUIRED.	DIFFERENCE BETWEEN STAFF ON 1ST July 1931 AND STAFF REQUIRED.		REMARKS.
			In Excess.	Short.	
I.—IN-DOOR STAFF.					
Deputy Commissioners					
Assistants, Foreign : Chief, 1st, and 2nd					
" 3rd, 4th, Supernumerary, and Unclassed					
" Chinese : Chief, 1st, and 2nd	1	1	—	—	
" 3rd and 4th	1	1	—	—	
Clerks : Principal, 1st, and 2nd	2	2	—	—	
" 3rd, Proby., Supernumerary, and Local; and Chienhsi	—	—	—	—	
Total : In-door Staff	4	4	—	—	
II.—OUT-DOOR STAFF.					
Tidesurveyors : Chief, A, and B					Senior Out-door Staff Officer: appointment as Acting Assistant Tidesurveyor and Acting Harbour Master recommended in Aigun S/O No.142
" Assistant					
Boat Officers					
Appraisers					
Examiners: Chief, A, and B					
" Assistant	1	1	—	—	
Tidewaiters, Foreign : Senior, 1st, and 2nd					
" 3rd, 4th, and Proby.; and Local Watchers					
" Chinese : Senior, 1st, and 2nd ...	1	1	—	—	[Including 1 in-charge of Aigun Sub-station.
" 3rd, 4th, and Probationary...	2	2	—	—	
Total : Out-door Staff ...	4	4	—	—	
GRAND TOTAL : I.—IN-DOOR AND II.—OUT-DOOR...	8	8	—	—	

CUSTOM HOUSE

A I G U N, 1st July, 1931.

(Signed) C. B. Joly
Acting Commissioner.

[F.—54]

AIGUN CUSTOMS.

Return of Foreign and Chinese Staff Requirements in the Revenue Department.

(S.O CIRCULAR No. 38.)

CLASSIFICATION OF STAFF.	Staff on 1st July 1932	Staff required.	Difference between Staff on 1st July 1932 and Staff required.		REMARKS.
			In Excess.	Short.	
I.—IN-DOOR STAFF.					
Deputy Commissioners					
Assistants, Foreign : Chief, 1st, and 2nd					
" 3rd, 4th, Supernumerary, and Unclassed					
" Chinese : Chief, 1st, and 2nd					
" 3rd and 4th					
Clerks : Principal, 1st, and 2nd	1	1	...	...	*Staff can be reduced by one during winter of 1932-1933, but successor will have to be appointed at beginning of Navigation season 1933 (vide Aigun despatch No.6321. Travel difficulties must, however, be taken into account. vide S/O No.174.
" 3rd, Proby, Supernumerary and Local; and Chienhsi	1	1	...	...	
Total : In-door Staff	3	3	...	...	
II.—OUT-DOOR STAFF.					
Tidesurveyors : Chief, A, and B					
" Assistant					
Boat Officers					
Appraisers					
Examiners : Chief, A, and B	1	1	...	...	
" Assistant					
Tidewaiters, Foreign : Senior, 1st, and 2nd					
" 3rd, 4th, and Proby; and Local Watchers	1	1*	...	...	*Third Class Tidewaiter could be spared from October 1932, but would have to be replaced at the beginning of the 1933 Navigation Season, unless the Aigun Sub-Station were closed, as recommended in Aigun S/O letter No.163. Travel difficulties must, however, be taken into account, vide Aigun S/O Letter No.174.
" Chinese : Senior, 1st, and 2nd	1	1**	...	...	§Including 1 in charge of Aigun Sub-Station.
" 3rd, 4th, and Probationary	3	3	...	...	
Total : Out-door Staff	6	6	...	...	
GRAND TOTAL. I.—IN-DOOR AND II.—OUT-DOOR.					

Aigun 1st July 1932.

Acting Commissioner.

瑷珲关

税课司所需中外职员人数一览表

（第 38 号机要通告）

[F—54]

职员类别	1923 年 6 月 1 日职员人数	所需职员人数 人数	1923 年 6 月 1 日职员人数与所需职员人数的差额 冗余	短缺	备注
一、内班职员					
副税务司	-	-			
超等、头等和二等外籍帮办	-	-	-	-	
三等、四等，另用和无等级外籍帮办	-	-	-	-	
超等、头等和二等华籍帮办	-	-	-	-	
三等和四等华籍帮办	1	2	1	-	
超等、一等和二等同文供事	3	3	-	-	
三等，试用，另用和就地供事及见习供事	2	2	-	-	
内班职员人数总计	6	7	1	-	
二、外班职员					
超等总巡、头等总巡前班及后班	-	-	-	-	
二等总巡	-	-	-	-	
三等总巡	-	-	-	-	
验估	-	-	-	-	
头等验货、二等验货前班及后班	1	1	-	-	

职员类别	1923 年 6 月 1 日职员人数	所需职员人数	1923 年 6 月 1 日职员人数与所需职员人数的差额		备注
三等验货	3	3	-	-	
超等、头等和二等外籍钤子手	1	2	1	-	
三等、四等、试用外籍钤子手及外籍就地巡役	5	3	-	2	
超等、头等和二等华籍钤子手	-	-	-	-	
三等、四等及试用华籍钤子手	2	3	1	-	
外班职员人数总计	12	12	2	2	
内班与外班职员人数总计	18	19	3	2	

1923 年 5 月 31 日 /6 月 1 日，瑷珲关 / 大黑河

签章：瑷珲关税务司

包安济（G.Boezi）

瑷珲关署理税务司

[F—54]

瑷珲关

税课司所需中外职员人数一览表

（第 38 号机要通告）

职员类别	1924 年 6 月 1 日职员人数	所需职员人数	1924 年 6 月 1 日职员人数与所需职员人数的差额		备注
			冗余	短缺	
一、内班职员					
副税务司	—	—	—	—	
超等、头等和二等外籍帮办	—	—	—	—	
三等、四等,另用和无等级外籍帮办	—	—	—	—	
超等、头等和二等华籍帮办	—	—	—	—	
三等和四等华籍帮办	1	1	—	—	
超等、一等和二等同文供事	3	3	—	—	
三等,试用,另用和就地供事及见习供事	2	2	—	—	
内班职员人数总计	6	6	—	—	
二、外班职员					
超等总巡,头等总巡前班及后班	1*	1*	—	—	*署理头等总巡兼理船厅
二等总巡	—	—	—	—	
三等总巡	—	—	—	—	

职员类别	1924年6月1日职员人数	所需职员人数	1924年6月1日职员人数与所需职员人数的差额	备注
验估	—	—	—	
头等验货、二等验货前班及后班	1	1	—	不包括一名头等验货后班，其担任头等总巡兼理船厅
三等验货	3	3	—	
超等、头等和二等外籍钤子手	—	—	—	
三等、四等，试用外籍钤子手及外籍就地巡役	5	5	—	
超等，头等和二等华籍钤子手	—	—	—	
三等，四等及试用华籍钤子手	2	2	—	
外班职员人数总计	12	12	—	
内班与外班职员人数总计	18	18	—	

1924年6月5日，瑷珲关/大黑河

签章：瑷珲关税务司

贺智兰（R. F. C. Hedgeland）
瑷珲关税务司

瑷珲关

税课司所需中外职员人数一览表

（第 38 号机要通告）

[F—54]

职员类别	1925 年 6 月 1 日职员人数	所需职员人数	1925 年 6 月 1 日职员人数与所需职员人数的差额		备注
			冗余	短缺	
一、内班职员					
副税务司	—	—	—	—	
超等、头等和二等外籍帮办	—	—	—	—	
三等、四等，另用和无等级外籍帮办	—	—	—	—	
超等、头等和二等华籍帮办	—	—	—	—	
三等和四等华籍帮办	1	1	—	—	
超等、一等和二等同文供事	3	3	—	—	
三等、试用，另用和就地供事及见习供事	2	2	—	—	
内班职员人数总计	6	6	—	—	
二、外班职员					
超等总巡、头等总巡前班及后班	1＊	1＊	—	—	＊署理头等总巡兼理船厅
二等总巡	—	—	—	—	
三等总巡	—	—	—	—	

职员类别	1925年6月1日职员人数	所需职员人数 人数	1925年6月1日职员人数与所需职员人数的差额		备注
验估	—	—	—	—	
头等验货，二等验货前班及后班	1	1	—	—	不包括一名头等验货后班，其担任头等总巡兼理船厅
三等验货	3	3	—	—	
超等，头等和二等外籍钤子手	2	2	—	—	
三等，四等，试用外籍钤子手及外籍就地巡役	2	2	—	—	
超等，头等和二等华籍钤子手	—	—	—	—	
三等，四等及试用华籍钤子手	2	2	—	—	
外班职员人数总计	11	11	—	—	
内班与外班职员人数总计	17	17	—	—	

1925年6月8日，瑷珲关／大黑河

签章：瑷珲关税务司

贺智兰（R. F. C. Hedgeland）

瑷珲关税务司

瑷珲关

税课司所需中外职员人数一览表

（第 38 号机要通告）

[F—54]

职员类别	1926 年 6 月 1 日职员人数	所需职员 人数	1926 年 6 月 1 日职员人数与所需职员人数的差额		备注
			冗余	短缺	
一、内班职员					
副税务司	—	—	—	—	注：由于边界贸易的现状，瑷珲关职员被缩减，若此状况改善，则需相应地增加职员数量
超等、头等和二等外籍帮办	—	—	—	—	
三等、四等、另用和无等级外籍帮办	—	—	—	—	
超等、头等和二等华籍帮办	—	—	—	—	
三等和四等华籍帮办	1	1	—	—	
超等、一等和二等同文供事	3	3**	—	—	**这四名职员中只有一等通俄语，但现需两名。若二等被生推荐其调职黄幼翔先生呈文供（瑷珲关第 53 号机要调职），则应由一名精通俄语的同文供事接替
三等、试用、另用和就地供事及见习供事	1	1**	—	—	
内班职员人数总计	5	5	—	—	
二、外班职员					
（*署理头等总巡兼理船厅）超等总巡，头等总巡前班及后班	1	1§	—	—	§需一名精通俄语的非苏联国籍职员

职员类别	1926年6月1日职员人数	所需职员人数	1926年6月1日职员人数与所需职员人数的差额	备注
二等总巡	-	-	-	
三等总巡	-	-	-	
验估	-	-	-	
头等验货、二等验货前班及后班	1	1	-	
三等验货	1	1	-	
超等、头等和二等外籍钤子手	2	2§§	-	§§ 目前领头是苏联国籍的职员 或讲俄语的职员
三等、四等、试用外籍钤子手及外籍就地巡役	1	1	-	
超等、头等华籍钤子手	-	-	-	
三等、四等及试用华籍钤子手	2	3+	1	+这三名华籍钤子手中须有一名精通俄语（根据瑷珲关第53号机要呈文，据瑷珲关第259号呈及总税务司署第295/107984号令推荐，擢升就地巡役于福寿填补此空缺，其将在三个月内接受考察）
外班职员人数总计	8	9	1	
内班与外班职员人数总计	13	14	1	

1926 年 7 月 1 日，瑷珲关／大黑河

签章：瑷珲关税务司

瑚斯敦（J. H. W. Houstoun）

瑷珲关税务司

[F-54]

瑷珲关

税课司所需中外职员人数一览表

（第38号机要通告）

职员类别	1927年7月1日职员人数	所需职员人数（人数）	与所需职员人数的差额（冗余）	与所需职员人数的差额（短缺）	备注
一、内班职员					
副税务司	-	-			注：由于边界贸易的现状，瑷珲关职员被缩减，若此状况改善，则需相应地增加职员数量
超等、头等和二等外籍帮办	-	-	-	-	
三等、四等、另用和无等级外籍帮办	-	-	-	-	
超等、头等和二等华籍帮办	-	-	-	-	
三等和四等华籍帮办	1	1	-	-	
超等、一等和二等同文供事	2	1	1	-	需一名讲俄语的同文供事供事管理征税汇办处
三等、试用，另用和就地供事及习供事	2	3	-	1	
内班职员人数总计	5	5	-	-	
二、外班职员					
（*署理头等总巡兼理船厅）	1	1	-	-	
*超等总巡、头等总巡前班及后班	-	-	-	-	
二等总巡	-	-	-	-	

职员类别	1927年7月1日职员人数	所需职员人数 人数	1927年7月1日职员人数与所需职员人数的差额		备注
三等总巡	－	－	－	－	
验估	－	－	－	－	
头等验货、二等验货前班及后班	1	1	－	－	准予现任三等验货后班德里格（C. O. Dreggs）先生自1927年10月10日起休假一年，直至1928年开通航运后，其职位才需被接任（参见瑷珲关第306号呈及总税务司署第353/11 2892号令）
三等验货	1	1	－	－	
超等、头等和二等外籍钤子手	2	1	1	1	
三等、四等、试用外籍钤子手及外籍就地巡役	1	2	－	－	
超等、头等和二等华籍钤子手	－	－	1	－	据瑷珲关第317号呈推荐，三等华籍钤子手李元庆先生自关闭自关航运起休假4个月，若批准其休假，则直至1928年开通航运起，其职位才需被接任
三等、四等及试用华籍钤子手	2	2	－	－	
外班职员人数总计	8	8	1	1	
内班与外班职员人数总计	13	13	2	2	

1927年7月2日，瑷珲关／大黑河

签章：瑷珲关税务司

铎博泰（R. M. Talbot）

瑷珲关署理税务司

瑷珲关

税课司所需中外职员人数一览表

（第 38 号机要通告）

[F-54]

职员类别	1928年7月1日职员人数	所需职员人数	1928年7月1日职员人数与所需职员人数的差额		备注
			冗余	短缺	
一、内班职员					
副税务司	—	—	—	—	注：由于边界贸易的现状，瑷珲关职员被缩减，若此状况改善，则需相应地增加职员数量
超等、头等和二等外籍帮办	—	—	—	—	
三等、四等、额外和无等级外籍帮办	—	—	—	—	
超等、头等和二等华籍帮办	—	—	—	—	
三等和四等华籍帮办	1	1	—	—	需任命一名华籍帮办，来接任四等级帮办屠守鑫自1928年9月1日起休假四个月时空缺的职位（参见总税务司署第413/11398号令及瑷珲关务总税务司署第378号呈）
超等、一等和二等税务员	2	2	—	—	

职员类别	1928 年 7 月 1 日职员人数	所需职员人数	1928 年 7 月 1 日职员人数与所需职员人数的差额	备注
三等、试用、额外和本口录用税务员及见习税务员	2	2	—	准予现任三等一级税务员刘文淮先生自 1928 年 10 月 1 日起休假三个月，直至 1929 年开通航运后，其职位才需被接任（参见总税务司署第 390/116060 号令及瑷珲关致总税务司署第 92 号机要呈文）
内班职员人数总计	5	5	—	—
二、外班职员		—	—	
（*署监察长兼港务长）	1	1	—	任命一名讲俄语且非苏联国籍的职员担任监察长，接任署监察长兼港务长博韩（G. E. Baukham）先生自 1928 年 10 月 16 日起休假六个月时空缺的职位（参见总税务司署第 408/117154 号令）。望此职员在博韩先生（G. E. Baukham）离岗前抵达瑷珲关
*总监察长、一等监察长及二等监察长				
副监察长	—	—	—	
监察员	—	—	—	
验估员	—	—	—	

职员类别	1928 年 7 月 1 日职员人数	所需职员人数	1928 年 7 月 1 日职员人数与所需职员人数的差额		备注
超等验货员、一等验货员及二等验货员	1	1	—		准予现任二等验货员密库林（S. E. Mikulin）先生自 1928 年 10 月 16 日起休假六个月；直至 1929 年开通航运后，其职位才需被接任（参见瑷珲关致税务总司署第 367 号呈及总税务司署第 408/11154 号令）
副验货员	1	1	—	—	
超等、一等和二等外籍稽查员	2	2	—	—	
三等、四等、试用外籍稽查员及外籍本口巡役	1	1	—	—	
超等、一等和二等华籍稽查员	—	—	—	—	
三等、四等及试用华籍稽查员	2	2	—	—	
外班职员人数总计	8	8	—	—	
内班与外班职员人数总计	13	13	—	—	

1928 年 7 月 3 日，瑷珲关 / 大黑河

签章：瑷珲关税务司

铎博泰（R. M. Talbot）

瑷珲关署理税务司

瑷珲关

税课司所需中外职员人数一览表

（第 38 号机要通告）

[F-54]

职员类别	1929 年 7 月 1 日职员人数	所需职员人数	1929 年 7 月 1 日职员人数与所需职员人数的差额		备注
			冗余	短缺	
一、内班职员					
副税务司	—	—	—	—	注：由于边界贸易的现状，瑷珲关职员被缩减，若此状况改善，则需相应地增加职员数量
超等、头等和二等外籍帮办	—	—	—	—	
三等、四等、额外和无等级外籍帮办	—	—	—	—	
超等、头等和二等华籍帮办	—	—	—	—	
三等和四等华籍帮办	1	1	—	—	
超等、一等和二等税务员	3	2	1	—	瑷珲关致海关总税务司署第 431 号呈附三等二级税务员张远扬先生自 1929 年 10 月 16 日起为期三个月的休假申请，据瑷珲关第 107 号文要呈文报告，二等二级税务员李鹏泽先生申请自 8 月 1 日起休假四个月（瑷珲关第 417 号呈），必要的话，其休假应推迟至航季季末（其职位无须接任之时），若海关职员短缺，则其申请末起航季末起的休假申请将会加剧职员短缺的现状。张先生自航季末起的休假申请及李先生的休假申请，若同时准予张先生及李先生要求，准予其自 8 月 1 日起休假，确保在其离岗前有职员接任，或 9 月 1 日起休假，确保应先生要求，则通令应所示，准予其自 8 月 1 日起（据第 3905 号通令显示，此接任者须是一名优秀的打字员，而张先生先前有职的职位，有必要都无须安排先前接任。
三等、试用、额外和本口录用税务员及见习税务员	1	2	—	1	
内班职员人数总计	5	5	1	1	
二、外班职员					
署总监察长、一等监察长及二等监察长	1	1	—	—	
副监察长	—	—	—	—	
监察员	—	—	—	—	

职员类别	1929 年 7 月 1 日职员人数	所需职员人数	1929 年 7 月 1 日职员人数与所需职员人数的差额	备注
验估员	1	1	—	
超等验货员、一等验货员及二等验货员	1	1	—	
副验货员	1	1	—	
超等、一等和二等外籍查验员	3	3	—	
三等、四等、试用外籍查验员及外籍本口巡役	1	1	—	
超等、一等和二等华籍查验员	1	1	—	
三等、四等及试用华籍查验员	2	2	—	
外班职员人数总计	8	8	—	
内班与外班职员人数总计	13	13	1	

1929 年 7 月 1 日，瑷珲关

签章：瑷珲关税务司

译博泰（R. M. Talbot）

瑷珲关署理税务司

[F—54]

瑷珲关

税课司所需中外职员人数一览表

（第38号机要通告）

职员类别	1930年7月1日职员人数	所需职员人数	1930年7月1日职员人数与所需职员人数的差额		备注
			冗余	短缺	
一、内班职员					
副税务司					
超等、头等和二等外籍帮办					
三等、四等、额外和无等级外籍帮办					
超等、头等和二等华籍帮办					
三等和四等华籍帮办					
超等、一等和二等税务员	2	2			
三等、试用、额外和本口录用税务员及见习税务员	3*	3			*不包括一名正在休假的职员，其职位已被接任
内班职员人数总计	5	5			
二、外班职员					
总监察长、一等监察长及二等监察长					
副监察长					
监察员	1	1			一名署监察员

职员类别	1930年7月1日职员人数	所需职员人数	1930年7月1日职员人数与所需职员人数的差额	备注
验估员				
超等验货员，一等验货员及二等验货员	1	1		
副验货员	1	1		
超等、一等和二等外籍稽查员				
三等、四等、试用外籍稽查员及外籍本口巡役				一名铃子手管理瑷珲关分署
超等、一等和二等华籍稽查员	2	2		
三等、四等及试用华籍稽查员	5	5		
外班职员人数总计	10	10		
内班与外班职员人数总计	10	10		

1930年7月1日，瑷珲关

签章：瑷珲关税务司

富乐嘉（H. G. Fletcher）

瑷珲关署理税务司

瑷珲关

税课司所需中外职员人数一览表

（第 38 号机要通告）

[F—54]

职员类别	1931 年 7 月 1 日职员人数	所需职员人数	1931 年 7 月 1 日职员人数与所需职员人数的差额		备注
			冗余	短缺	
一、内班职员					
副税务司					
超等、头等和二等外籍帮办					
三等、四等、额外和无等级外籍帮办					
超等、头等和二等华籍帮办					
三等和四等华籍帮办	1	1	—	—	
超等、一等和二等税务员	1	1	—	—	
三等、试用、额外和本口录用税务员及见习税务员	2	2	—	—	
内勤职员人数总计	4	4	—	—	
二、外班职员					
总监察长、一等监察长及二等监察长					
副监察长					
监察员					

职员类别	1931 年 7 月 1 日职员人数	所需职员 人数	1931 年 7 月 1 日职员人数 与所需职员人数的差额	备注
验估员				
超等验货员，一等验货员及二等验货员				
副验货员	1	1	—	超等外班职员：据瑷珲关第 142 号 机要呈文推荐，委任其为署副监察长 兼代理港务长
超等，一等和二等外籍稽查员				
三等，四等，试用外籍稽查员及外籍本口巡役				
超等，一等和二等华籍稽查员	1	1	—	其中包括一名职员管理瑷珲关分署
三等，四等及试用华籍稽查员	2	2	—	
外班职员人数总计	4	4	—	
内班与外班职员人数总计	8	8	—	

1931 年 7 月 1 日，瑷珲关

签章：瑷珲关税务司

（签字）周骊（C.B.Joly）

瑷珲关署理税务司

瑷珲关

税课司所需中外职员人数一览表

（第 38 号机要通告）

[F—54]

职员类别	1932 年 7 月 1 日职员人数	所需职员人数	1932 年 7 月 1 日职员人数与所需职员人数的差额		备注
			冗余	短缺	
一、内班职员					
副税务司					
超等、头等和二等外籍帮办					
三等、四等、额外和无等级外籍帮办					
超等、头等和二等华籍帮办					
三等和四等华籍帮办	1	1	—	—	
超等、一等和二等税务员	1	1	—	—	
三等、试用、额外和本口录用税务员及见习税务员	1	1	—	—	
内班职员人数总计	3	3*	—	—	＊在 1932 至 1933 年冬季职员人数可缩减一名，但务必安排一名接任者于 1933 年航海季始可瑷珲关第 632 号呈）。需提前将旅途的困难考虑在内（参见瑷珲海关第 174 号机要呈文）
二、外班职员					

职员类别	1932年7月1日职员人数	所需职员人数	1932年7月1日职员人数与所需职员人数的差额	备注
总监察长、一等监察长及二等监察长				
副监察长				
监察员				
验估员				
超等验货员、一等验货员及二等验货员				
副验货员	1	1	—	
超等、一等和二等外籍稽查员				
三等、四等、试用外籍稽查员及外籍本口巡役				
超等、一等和二等华籍稽查员	1	1§	—	
三等、四等及试用华籍稽查员	1	1**（§）	—	
外班职员人数总计	3	3	—	
内班与外班职员人数总计	6	6	—	

** 据瑷珲关第 163 号机要通函，自 1932 年 10 月起可缩减三等稽查员。除非瑷珲关支署另需三等稽查员于 1933 年海季始上岗接任，否则务必安排职员提前将旅途的困难季考虑在内。（参见瑷珲关第 174 号机要呈文）

§ 包括一名职员管理瑷珲关分署

1932 年 7 月 1 日，瑷珲关

签章：瑷珲关税务司

（签字）周骊（C.B.Joly）

瑷珲关署理税务司